JUNIORPLOTS 3

JUNIORPLOTS 3

A Book Talk Guide
for Use with Readers Ages 12–16

By JOHN T. GILLESPIE
with CORINNE J. NADEN

R. R. BOWKER COMPANY
New York & London, 1987

Published by R. R. Bowker Company,
a division of Reed Publishing (USA) Inc.
Copyright © 1987 by Reed Publishing USA
All rights reserved
Printed and bound in the United States of America

Library of Congress Cataloging-in-Publication Data

Gillespie, John Thomas, 1928–
    Juniorplots 3 : a book talk guide for use with readers ages 12–16 / by John
T. Gillespie with Corinne J. Naden.
      p.   cm.
    Includes indexes.
    Summary: Presents summaries of eighty fiction and nonfiction
titles for readers, ages twelve to sixteen, with suggestions to use
in motivating them to read for pleasure.
    ISBN 0-8352-2367-1
    1. Young adult literature—Stories, plots, etc. 2. Young adult
literature—Book reviews. 3. Youth—Books and reading.
[1. Literature—Stories, plots, etc. 2. Books—Reviews. 3. Books
and reading.] I. Naden, Corinne J. II. Title. III. Title:
Juniorplots three.
Z1037.A1G497 1987
028.1′62—dc19   87-27305
                                                         CIP
                                                         AC

To
Henry K. Moritz
"Let the circle be unbroken"

Contents

Preface

It seems difficult to believe that it is now over twenty years that Diana Spirt (then Lembo) and I began work on the first *Juniorplots* (Bowker, 1967). It is gratifying to note that many of the titles highlighted in that book are still in print and still enjoyed by young readers. Its continuation, *More Juniorplots* (Bowker, 1977), appeared ten years later. After another ten-year lapse, writing started on *Juniorplots 3*, the third compilation of plots and related material that will again help teachers and librarians give reading guidance by introducing deserving books to young people.

Helping youngsters select books for their reading pleasure is one of the most enjoyable responsibilities of teachers and librarians. There are many methods that can be used—for example, providing book lists—but perhaps the most potent is actually talking about the books one wishes to recommend to either an individual patron or to groups. This technique is known as booktalking. Both *Juniorplots* and *More Juniorplots* contain introductory material on the preparation and delivery of book talks. Other valuable sources include Joni Bodart's *Booktalk! 2* (Wilson, 1985), an update of *Booktalk!* (Wilson, 1980), Elinor Walker's *Book Bait* (American Library Association, 1979), and *Doors to More Mature Reading* (American Library Association, 1981). Some of the general books in teenage literature like Aileen Pace Nilsen and Kenneth L. Donelson's *Literature for Today's Young Adults* (Scott, Foresman, 1985) also contain valuable sections on the subject. It is hoped that this volume will also be of value.

The eighty plots in *Juniorplots 3* have been divided by subjects or genre popular with adolescent readers. They are (1) Teenage Life and Concerns; (2) Adventure and Mystery Stories; (3) Science Fiction and Fantasy; (4) Historical Fiction; (5) Sports Fiction; (6) Biography and True Adventure; (7) Guidance and Health; and (8) The World Around Us.

Various methods were used to choose the books to be highlighted. A basic criterion was that each had to be recommended for purchase in several standard bibliographies and reviewing sources. In addition to criteria involving quality, an important consideration was the desire to provide materials covering a variety of interests and needs at different reading levels. In spite of these concerns, some of the selections still remain personal and, therefore, arbitrary.

The individual titles are covered under five headings:

1. *Plot Summary.* Each plot briefly retells the entire story. The summary includes all important incidents and characters, while trying to retain the mood and point of view of the author.

2. *Thematic Material.* An enumeration of primary and secondary themes found in the book that will facilitate the use of the book in a variety of situations.

3. *Book Talk Material.* Techniques are given on how to introduce the book interestingly to youngsters. Passages suitable for retelling or reading aloud are indicated, and pagination is shown for these passages for the hard-cover and, when available, the paperback editions.

4. *Additional Selections.* Related books that explore similar or associated themes are annotated or listed with identifying bibliographic information. Approximately six to eight titles are given per book.

5. *About the Author.* Standard biographical dictionaries (e.g., *Something about the Author, Who's Who in America*) were consulted to locate sources of biographical information about the author. When this section does not appear, no material was found. However, the user also may wish to consult other sources, such as periodical indexes (*Reader's Guide, Education Index, Library Literature*), jacket blurbs, and material available through the publisher.

The detailed treatment of the main titles is not intended as a substitute for reading the books. Instead, it is meant to be used by teachers and librarians to refresh their memories about books they have read and to suggest new uses for these titles.

This volume is not intended as a work of literary criticism or a listing of the best books for young adults. It is a representative selection of books that have value in a variety of situations.

The author has had more helpers than can be identified by name, but special thanks should be given to Corinne Naden for her invaluable help in condensing several of the plots. She has proven to be an expert "plotter." Also many thanks to Bette Vander Werf for assistance in manuscript preparation and to Olga Weber of the R. R. Bowker Company for her many acts of encouragement.

John T. Gillespie

1

Teenage Life and Concerns

ADOLESCENTS enjoy reading about themselves—their joys, problems, and concerns. This chapter gives a cross-section of these stories—some funny, some caustic, and others that probe into the inner, secret feelings of teenagers. The gambit is wide—from minor crises involving school crushes to life-and-death decisions. Some positive in orientation, others negative, all reflecting the adolescent experience.

Blume, Judy. *Tiger Eyes*
Bradbury, 1981, $10.95; pap., Dell, $2.95

Judy Blume's phenomenally popular books for young readers now number over a dozen and span reader appeal from the primary grades, in *The One in the Middle Is the Green Kangaroo* (Bradbury, 1981, $8.95; pap., Dell, $1.95), to the senior high years with the controversial *Forever* (Bradbury, 1975, $11.95; pap., Pocket Bks., $3.50). In between are several titles that are appropriate for seventh and eighth grade readers like *Deenie* (Bradbury, 1973, $10.95; pap., Dell, $2.50) and *Then Again, Maybe I Won't* (Bradbury, 1971, $11.95; pap., Dell, $2.50; condensed in *More Juniorplots,* Bowker, 1977, pp. 179–182), but *Tiger Eyes* is her first novel written expressly for a junior high audience. It is narrated by fifteen-year-old Davey Wexler, the central character in the novel.

Plot Summary
Even on the day of the funeral, Davey, short for Davis, is in a trance-like state of disbelief concerning the death of her father. Thirty-four-year-old Adam Wexler was the manager of a 7-Eleven store in Atlantic City, a job he held to put aside enough money to pursue, one day, his first love, painting. One evening he was mortally shot during a robbery of the store. He leaves behind a young widow, Gwen, and two children,

Davey and seven-year-old Jason who, because of his youth, seems best able to cope with the family loss. Davey, like Gwen, loved gentle, compassionate Adam to the point of adoration and neither is able to comprehend or accept this senseless death. In Davey's condition of anxiety and fearfulness her health begins to crack, and even her black schoolmate Lenaya and her boyfriend Hugh are unable to reach her. At home she stays in bed for days at a time and at school she has bouts of hyperventilation and nausea. In desperation, Gwen accepts an invitation from Adam's sister Elizabeth, nicknamed Bitsy, and her husband Walter Kronick to visit them in Los Alamos where Walter is a physicist in the main laboratory. Davey dutifully packs her luggage, including a brown paper bag she has hidden in her closet, and the bread knife that she has taken to putting under her pillow at night. The Kronicks, who have been unable to have their own children, enthusiastically welcome the Wexlers plus cat Minka. Although her new hosts are extremely hospitable and their upper-middle-class home very impressive, for Davey it is not like home: Bitsy tends to be dominated by her husband who is rigid and conservative—totally the opposite of her father.

One day Davey, wanting to be by herself, explores the bottom of a canyon. Here she tries to confront her grief and calls out for her father. She is answered by an attractive young man about twenty, who is also walking the canyon. They strike up a brief conversation, he introduces himself as Wolf, and in rebuttal, Davey says her name is Tiger. Later the boy helps Davey, who's not wearing hiking boots, climb out of the canyon and away from the scampering lizards who appear to be its only inhabitants.

News reaches Gwen that the store in Atlantic City has been vandalized and now she, more shaken than before and in increasingly poor health, decides to stay on in New Mexico. This means that Jason and Davey must enroll in school even though the fall term is now underway.

In her tenth grade class, Davey meets and becomes friendly with Jane Albertson, daughter of a socially prominent family who live on prestigious Bathtub Row. Jane introduces Davey to her family and later convinces her that both should join Candy Stripers as an outside activity. As well, Davey often meets in the canyon the mysterious but solicitous Wolf. They explore their own private cave and the boy tells her that he, too, is coping with death because his own father is dying. But, as with other people, Davey is not able to discuss with him the circumstances of her father's death and her feelings regarding it.

After a brief training period, Davey begins helping out in patients' rooms as a Candy Striper. She becomes particularly fond of a terminally ill older man named Willie Ortiz who speaks with a lyrical New Mexican accent and whose bravery in the face of death both saddens and inspires her.

One day Mr. Ortiz introduces her to a visitor, his son Martin, who is none other than Wolf. The young man has taken a semester off from his studies at Cal Tech and found a job in town to be with his ailing father. Wolf tells Tiger that in the future he will be spending all his free time at the hospital because his father is failing fast.

Under the tutelage of Jane and her family, Davey is able to explore Santa Fe and becomes fascinated with native culture and crafts. But while doing so, she begins to realize that Jane has a growing drinking problem. This is noticed first on a double date pairing Davey with the attentive but unimpressive Reuben, and Jane with her boyfriend Ted when, to gain social courage, Jane becomes drunk and later violently sick.

The situation at home begins to deteriorate. Gwen sinks into a profound depression and begins visiting a counselor, Miriam Olnick, regularly. To help her reach out she begins dating a colleague of Walter's, Ned Grodzinski. Davey totally disapproves of him and nicknames him The Nerd. Davey also has frequent clashes with Walter who overly protects to the point where she feels claustrophobic. In his obsessive regard for her safety he has, for example, forbidden her to take up skiing or enroll in a driver's education course. Davey finds it ironic that Walter takes these stands when his occupation is the manufacture of nuclear armaments. Matters reach a climax when Davey brings home a so-so report card, and Walter says she is on the road to being a failure like her father and mother. Davey verbally abuses him and he slaps her across the face. Walter later apologizes but Davey is slow to forgive.

Mr. Ortiz dies and when Davey returns to the hospital she is given a note from Wolf promising to come back and see her "cuando los lagartijos corren." It is translated for her as "when the lizards run"—the Spring. Some time later she receives in the mail a small polished stone with the note, "A tiger eye for my Tiger Eyes. Wolf."

Though outwardly Davey appears to be making progress—for example, she wins the coveted role of Ado Annie and scores a great success in the school production of *Oklahoma!*—becoming reconciled to her father's death comes slowly. She takes her mother's advice and visits Miriam for counseling. Slowly she is able to recall and talk about the most terrible night of her life when, seemingly immersed in a sea of blood, she cradled her dying father's head in her lap and later saw him die on the way to the hospital. Many of her feelings she expresses in unsent letters to Wolf which are kept for his return.

One day, in a final act of acceptance, she takes the brown paper bag which contains the blood-stained clothes from the murder and her many letters to Wolf, and creates a little shrine in their cave in the canyon.

The period of grieving is over and through cartharsis comes a need to rebuild. Gwen gathers her children together and the three return to Atlantic City to begin life again.

Thematic Material

The difficulty of accepting the death of a dear one is explored in this novel, as well as complex family relationships, problems in coping with new situations, the place of fear in one's life, and the various faces of grief. These situations are explored honestly without preaching or pat solutions. There are also subtle political and social undertones concerning armaments and racial tensions, as well as a subplot involving teenage drinking.

Book Talk Material

Introducing the Wexler family and telling their story at least until they reach New Mexico should interest readers. Some specific passages are: the funeral (pp. 1–3; pp. 5–7, pap.); Davey's anxiety and the trip to Los Alamos (pp. 22–28; pp. 26–32, pap.); the first meeting with Wolf (pp. 42–51; pp. 48–57, pap.); and the second (pp. 73–75; pp. 80–82, pap.); Davey meets Jane (pp. 84–87; pp. 91–93, pap.); and Mr. Ortiz (pp. 101–103; pp. 109–111, pap.).

Additional Selections

Carly tries to forget her mother's death and her father's indifferent attitude by visiting an aunt and uncle in rural New York State in *Carly's Buck* (Clarion, 1987, $12.95) by C. S. Adler; Fergie longs for the stability and roots that his nomadic parents can't give him in James Lincoln Collier's *Outside Looking In* (Macmillan, 1987, $12.95); and Natalie must decide whether to return to her mother or stay with her father and his quintuplets in Stella Pevsner's *Sister of the Quints* (Clarion, 1987, $12.95). Two stories of adolescent friendship are Norma Fox Mazer's *A, My Name*

Is Ami (pap., Scholastic, 1986, $2.25) and *B, My Name Is Bunny* (Scholastic, 1987, $12.95; pap., $2.50). A young girl tells in journal form about her bout with mental illness in *Crazy Eights* (Harper, 1978, $11.89) by Barbara Dana. In *But in the Fall I'm Leaving* (Holiday, 1985, $12.50) by Ann Rinaldi, a young girl must reevaluate the way she regards her divorced parents. A young girl chronicles her parents' divorce in Julie Autumn List's *The Day the Loving Stopped* (pap., Fawcett, 1981, $2.25).

About the Author
Commire, Anne, ed. *Something about the Author*. Detroit: Gale Research Co., 1971. Vol. 2, pp. 31–32; updated 1983. Vol. 31, pp. 28–34.

de Montreville, Doris, and Crawford, Elizabeth D., eds. *Fourth Book of Junior Authors and Illustrators*. New York: Wilson, 1978, pp. 46–47.

Estes, Glenn E., ed. *American Writers for Children since 1960: Fiction* (*Dictionary of Literary Biography*, Vol. 52). Detroit: Gale Research Co., 1986, pp. 30–38.

Evory, Ann, ed. *Contemporary Authors* (First Revision Series). Detroit: Gale Research Co., 1978. Vols. 29–32, p. 72.

Kirkpatrick, D. L., ed. *Twentieth-Century Children's Writers* (2nd edition). New York: St. Martin's, 1983, pp. 93–95.

Metzger, Linda, ed. *Contemporary Authors* (New Revision Series). Detroit: Gale Research Co., 1984. Vol. 13, pp. 59–62.

Riley, Carolyn, ed. *Children's Literature Review*. Detroit: Gale Research Co., 1976. Vol. 2, pp. 15–19.

Who's Who in America: 1986–1987 (44th edition). Chicago: Marquis Who's Who, Inc., 1986. Vol. 1, p. 271.

Who's Who of American Women: 1987–1988 (15th edition). Chicago: Marquis Who's Who, Inc., 1986. Vol. 1, p. 78.

Brancato, Robin F.   *Come Alive at 505*
Knopf, 1980, $8.95; lib. bdg., $8.99; pap., Bantam (o.p.)

Since writing her first young adult novel in the mid-1970s, Robin Brancato has had a number of well-received books, each of which handle a difficult subject with both honesty and compassion. For example, in *Blinded by the Light* (Knopf, 1978, $7.95; lib. bdg., $7.99), a college sophomore infiltrates a religious cult, "Light of the World," to help save her brother; in *Sweet Bells Jangled Out of Tune* (Knopf, 1982, $10.95; lib. bdg., $10.99; pap., Scholastic, $2.50), the problems of aging are explored when a young girl begins to take care of her eccentric grandmother who has become a bag lady. In this novel a young man suffering from "senior panic" must make crucial decisions about his life after high school. There is some strong language in the book but it is recommended for grades seven through ten.

Plot Summary

Danny Felzer, a senior at Duncan High School, is a young man with an obsession: he has an all-encompassing ambition to be the host of his own radio show. For several years he has been preparing audiotapes in his bedroom for his own imaginary radio program, The Danny Forsythe Show (Forsythe sounds much better than Felzer), on a mythical AM radio station, WHVP at 505 on the dial. It is a combination talk and music show with a smattering of call-in audience participation, way out contests, standard DJ fare, and plenty of jokes and smart patter. His first break comes with the announcement of a talent search by his local radio station, WWTM, with the first prize being some merchandise, and, best of all, possible future employment. He is now preparing some demo tapes to accompany his entry and is confident of winning.

His mother and father, Norman and Helen Felzer, are less than enthusiastic about Danny's preoccupation and, like most middle-class suburban parents, want their son to go to college, specifically Warminster College, only a few miles from their Winfield, New Jersey, home.

Lassitude and apathy are so prevalent at Duncan High that no one is willing to run for president of the senior class. In a stroke of fanciful genius, Danny and his best friend, Marty McGowen, decide to invent a candidate named John E. Custer and be his campaign managers. To help in the scheme they recruit the school's wheeler-dealer, George Varek, and gullible Tom Rose, who is the only conspirator not told that Custer is a fabrication. To get support from the distaff side, Danny asks the aloof, highly intelligent loner, Mimi Alman, who is pretty but has a serious weight problem. She consents, and Danny is strongly attracted to her—partially because of her manner and honesty and partially because he is concerned that, at seventeen, he remains a virgin (a term he hates applying to males), and wants to change his status.

One day after school the five plotters hold their first campaign meeting. They use Tom Rose's Jeep and drive up to a steep mountainous summit called Pinnacle Park where they can be alone and undetected. It soon becomes apparent that Mimi has known George Varek in the past and is not happy to be reacquainted. After planning their strategy and preparing to leave, Varek plays a practical joke by feigning a suicide leap. The rest are not amused and Danny wonders how wise was the decision to include this rash, seemingly unprincipled young man in their prank.

That evening Danny visits Mimi to record a campaign announcement for school. He confides in her his feelings and plans for the future, and after the taping she also tells Danny about her concerns. Controlling her weight has been her major problem and lacking the willpower to diet properly, she secretly had resorted to using amphetamines two years before. At first the results had been positive and she even won a beauty contest, but after getting hooked, the pills became illegal and she had to find illicit ways to feed her habit. George Varek had been her pusher. In a final, painful confession she tells of her eventual breakdown, attempted suicide, and therapy. Unknown to both young people, Danny's tape recorder has been left on during this conversation.

Although a legitimate nominee, Melanie Arbeiter, enters the election race, most of the seniors continue to support the mysterious Custer for the presidency. The bubble bursts when Danny is unable to produce a live candidate. As punishment, the principal, Mr. Mayer, orders him to direct the school's annual "fun-raiser." This setback is counterbalanced for Danny by news that he has won the radio audition and also by his growing affection for Mimi.

One evening when the two are alone, the phone rings. It is Varek. He speaks to Mimi and reveals details of her life that were told only to Danny that evening when confidences were exchanged. She savagely accuses Danny of exploiting her and destroying a trust. In a final act of disclosure, she tells Danny that when she had no money she slept with Varek to obtain pills.

On the day of the fun-raiser and the audition, events reach a climax. With the promise of reconciliation with Mimi as bait, Varek lures Danny to the Pinnacle. There Varek reveals that after he discovered the true contents of the campaign tape he stole it and now offers to give it back for ninety dollars. Infuriated, Danny attacks him. While they fight Danny manages to get possession of the tape and escapes down the hill.

Both the fun-raising activity (a take-off on Guiness World Records) and his guest appearance on the "Strollin' with Dolan" radio show are amazing successes, as is Danny's reunion with Mimi. He is offered and accepts a part-time job at the station on weekends. The rest of his time will also be well spent because he and Mimi have decided to enter their first year at Warminster College together.

Thematic Material

This novel explores the "senior panic" that grips many students when they are forced to make career choices after high school. It also points out that an investment in further education is often the wise choice. The book also explores the tender relationship of two young people who are in different ways vulnerable and fragile. Other areas explored are the nature of trust and betrayal, drug abuse, weight problems, family relationships, friendship, and high school politics.

Book Talk Material

The first pages of the book (pp. 3–9; pp. 1–5, pap.) are an enjoyable few minutes of Danny's fantasy radio program. Danny experiences "senior panic" (pp. 24–25; pp. 16–18, pap.) and Custer is invented (pp. 30–34; pp. 22–25, pap.). In Chapter 5 (pp. 39–49; pp. 30–38, pap.), Danny approaches Mimi with the scheme; in Chapter 7 (pp. 57–74; pp. 45–58, pap.), the five plot their strategy; and in Chapter 9 (pp. 85–101; pp. 67–79, pap.), Mimi talks about her past.

Additional Selections

Eighteen-year-old Peter is trying to come to terms with his parents in *Downtown* (Morrow, 1984, $10.25; pap., Avon, $2.50) by Norma Fox Mazer. Although George's family wants him to go to college, he spends his first year after high school doing odd jobs and learning about life in Phyllis Reynolds Naylor's *The Year of the Gopher* (Atheneum, 1987, $13.95). Mike's winning lottery ticket brings unwanted complications to his life in Robin F. Brancato's *Uneasy Money* (Knopf, 1986, $11.95). Sarah gains insight into herself, family, and project partner, David, during an unusual class assignment in *First the Egg* (Dutton, 1982, $10.95; pap., Pocket Bks., $1.75) by Louise Moeri. The trauma of Jason, a seventh grader, comes hilariously alive in Jerry Spinelli's *Space Station Seventh Grade* (Little, 1982, $12.45; pap., Dell, $2.50). Jason's story continues when he is in the ninth grade in *Jason and Marcelina* (Little, 1986, $12.95). A thirteen-year-old boy tries to womanize in Ellen Conford's *Why Me?* (Little, 1985, $12.95). Henry falls for the daughter of a famous comedian in M. E. Kerr's *Him, She Loves?* (Harper, 1984, $11.89; pap., Berkley, $2.25).

About the Author

Bowden, Jane A., ed. *Contemporary Authors.* Detroit: Gale Research Co., 1978. Vols. 69–72, p. 90.

Commire, Anne, ed. *Something about the Author*. Detroit: Gale Research Co., 1981. Vol. 23, pp. 14–16.
Evory, Ann, ed. *Contemporary Authors* (New Revision Series). Detroit: Gale Research Co., 1984. Vol. 11, p. 86.
Holtze, Sally Holmes, ed. *Fifth Book of Junior Authors and Illustrators*. New York: Wilson, 1983, pp. 43–45.

Bridgers, Sue Ellen.　*Notes for Another Life*
　Knopf, 1981, $9.95; pap., Bantam, $2.25

Notes for Another Life takes place in a small southern town, the setting also used in the author's two earlier young adult novels. In *Home before Dark* (Knopf, 1976, $10.95; pap., Bantam, $2.25), the plight of a migrant worker's family and their struggle to establish a permanent home are explored. *All Together Now* (Knopf, 1979, $8.95) is the story of a summer a young girl spends with her grandparents and of her new friendships, one with an older retarded man. In this, her third novel, the author portrays the anguish and heartbreak that mental illness can bring to a family. Though written in the third person, this novel shifts points of view from one character to another so successfully that in time the reader not only understands but sympathizes with each family member. It is an introspective, somewhat slow-moving, novel that better readers in grades seven through ten will appreciate.

Plot Summary
Thirteen-year-old Wren Jackson and her sixteen-year-old brother Kevin have lived the past six years with their grandparents, Bliss and Bill Jackson. Their normal family life had been shattered when the bouts of depression and withdrawal suffered by their father, Tom, became so severe that he had to be institutionalized and their mother, Karen, moved to Atlanta to work in the area of design for a fashionable department store.

Life for the two youngsters, however, has been far from unpleasant, mainly because Bliss and Bill are caring and devoted grandparents. Wren is successfully completing eighth grade, shows a marked talent for piano playing, and has a good friend in the effervescent, boy-crazy Jolene. Kevin, on the other hand, is hardly setting records in the sophomore class, but he excels at tennis, helps his grandfather at his drugstore's soda fountain, and has a steady girlfriend, Melanie Washburn. Nevertheless, both of them, particularly Kevin, feel keenly the absence of their parents, find the visits to their father painful, and long for the day when their mother, Karen, will ask them to join her in the big city.

During the Youth Service at their local Baptist church, conducted by the young pastor Jack Kensley, Wren and Jolene sing a solo and fifteen-year-old Sam Holland delivers the sermon. Sam lives with his family on a farm on the outskirts of town, but after meeting Wren, he soon finds excuses to see her at her grandfather's drugstore. At first, Wren is embarrassed and uncertain about this attention, but gradually she learns to trust and admire this attentive, understanding young man. Sam invites her to an outing during which Wren meets his family, including his unaffected, affectionate mother, Kathryn, and father, John, who demonstrates his prowess at finding water with a divining rod.

Karen visits her family. She is a sincere, caring person who is obviously torn between being a good mother and living a life of independence and self-fulfillment. She announces that she soon will be accepting a promotion that includes living in Chicago. For her children, this means even further separation. What Karen does not tell them but later reveals to Bliss by letter is that she has also begun divorce proceedings against Tom. Bliss has the difficult task of telling this news to the youngsters. Kevin takes it particularly hard; and to compound matters, while visiting Tom in the hospital, the boy, mistakenly thinking that his father knows about the divorce, makes reference to it. Tom is visibly shaken by this revelation, and Kevin feels an additional burden of guilt and remorse.

As summer approaches and Wren begins preparations for eighth-grade graduation, news from the hospital is encouraging. Tom is responding so well to a new drug that, on an experimental basis, he is allowed to return home. At first, he appears normal and anxious to participate in family affairs, but within a short time the ominous signs of withdrawal once more reappear and the children's hopes are again destroyed. Wren, through her interest in music and her strong relationship with Sam Holland, is better able than Kevin to assimilate this bad news. Two other incidents further upset him: During a tennis match he breaks his wrist and, after a series of prolonged quarrels, he loses his girlfriend Melanie. Also, Kevin harbors the unspoken fear that he might have inherited his father's insanity.

Karen returns home for a farewell visit before moving to Chicago. To

Kevin, this is only a reminder of another rejection in his life. This plus his father's deteriorating condition leads Kevin to the breaking point. One night he takes an overdose of Seconal. Luckily, Bliss finds him in time and rushes him to the hospital. Physically, Kevin bounces back quickly, but his psychological recovery is slow. It is only through the help and understanding of their young church minister, Jack Kensley, that Kevin is able to face and articulate his fears and problems.

Gradually life reverts to its usual state. Karen is absent in Chicago; Tom returns to the hospital; Kevin, sans arm cast, resumes tennis playing and his relationship with Melanie; and Wren, now fourteen, looks forward to her first year of high school. At least for the present, the pieces have been picked up.

Thematic Material

Without melodrama or sensationalism, the author explores the nature of mental illness and its psychological effects on others. Family relationships and dependencies are strongly portrayed; particularly touching is the closeness of a brother and his younger sister. Conflicts involving family obligations versus self-realization are developed through the characters of Karen and Wren. Other topics are: adolescent friendship, problems of coping with guilt, teenage suicide, the nature of rejection, and the power of love and understanding.

Book Talk Material

Characterization is particularly strong in this novel. Perhaps an introduction to the three principal women in the book—Bliss, Karen, and Wren—might serve to interest readers. Specific passages are: the church service with Sam Holland (pp. 13–18; pp. 8–13, pap.); Karen thinks about her husband and situation (pp. 23–24; pp. 16–20, pap. [paperback version is longer and more detailed]); Wren first meets Sam (pp. 24–28; pp. 28–32, pap.); and Kevin tells his father about the divorce (pp. 107–111; pp. 87–91, pap.).

Additional Selections

A young boy finds that his father, who can no longer function mentally, is turning into a frightening, suspicious stranger in Phyllis Reynolds Naylor's *The Keeper* (Atheneum, 1986, $13.95), and fifteen-year-old Chris goes to court to fight his parents' divorce in Barbara Dana's *Necessary Parties* (Harper, 1986, $13.95). After a suicide attempt because he feels inadequate, Jake struggles to gain self-respect in Patricia Calvert's *The Hour of the Wolf* (Scribner, 1983, $11.95; pap., New Amer. Lib., $2.25). Books for teenagers about suicide include Jane Mersky Leder's *Dead Serious* (Atheneum, 1987, $12.95), Arnold Madison's *Suicide and Young People* (Clarion, 1981, $8.95; pap., $3.95), and *Teen Suicide: A Book for Friends, Family, and Classmates* (Lerner, 1986, $9.95; pap., $4.95) by Janet Kolehmainen and Sandra Handwerk. Lois Lowry portrays the friendship between Veronica and Rabble and the nervous breakdown of Veronica's mother in *Rabble Starkey* (Houghton, 1987, $12.95). Son/mother relationships are explored in Ouida Sebestyen's *IOU's* (Little, 1982, $12.45).

About the Author

Bowden, Jane A., ed. *Contemporary Authors.* Detroit: Gale Research Co., 1977. Vols. 65–68, p. 79.

Commire, Anne, ed. *Something about the Author.* Detroit: Gale Research Co., 1981. Vol. 22, p. 56.

Estes, Glenn E., ed. *American Writers for Children since 1960: Fiction (Dictionary of Literary Biography,* Vol. 52). Detroit: Gale Research Co., 1986, pp. 38–41.

Evory, Ann, ed. *Contemporary Authors* (New Revision Series). Detroit: Gale Research Co., 1984. Vol. 11, pp. 89–90.

Holtze, Sally Holmes, ed. *Fifth Book of Junior Authors and Illustrators.* New York: Wilson, 1983, pp. 47–49.

Sarkissian, Adele, ed. *Something about the Author: Autobiography Series.* Detroit: Gale Research Co., 1986. Vol. 1, pp. 39–52.

Bunting, Eve. *If I Asked You, Would You Stay?*
Harper, 1984, $10.70; pap., $2.75 (same pagination)

Eve Bunting, the Irish-born writer who now lives in California, also writes under the names of Evelyn Bolton and A. E. Bunting. She is an extremely versatile writer who is as well known for her many science books like *One More Flight* (pap., Dell, $1.25) and *The Great White Shark* (Messner, 1982, $9.92) as she is for her works of fiction. She writes fine mystery stories, some of which, like *The Ghosts of Departure Point* (Lippincott, 1982, $9.89; pap., Scholastic, $2.25), deal with the supernatural. *If I Asked You, Would You Stay?* is, on the other hand, a tender coming-of-age novel enjoyed particularly by junior high girls.

Plot Summary

At seventeen, Charles Robert O'Neill—known as Crow—has spent all his life in foster homes. But now he has a place to call his own, his "secret room"—actually, his very own three-room apartment above an old carousel on a pier overlooking the ocean. The apartment has been abandoned by beautiful Sasha, and no one knows that Crow has taken it over. He discovered it quite by accident, since the whole building is empty and even the carousel will eventually be torn down. Because Crow wants no one to know he has moved in, he slips secretly in and out, never putting on lights at night, taking showers in the public washroom near the carousel (there is no running water in his secret place), and not even telling the people he works with at Bruce's Sport Shop, where he has been lucky enough to get a summer job.

But Crow is content. No more foster homes for him (although he has to admit that Mrs. Simmons back in Illinois where he lived with young Danny, who is still there, wasn't all that bad), no more the hurt of being told to leave, no more pushing on to somewhere else. He has his secret place now.

But one night, Crow's secret place becomes a secret no longer. As he is staring out at the ocean through the darkness, he thinks he sees a head bobbing in the water. Almost without thinking, Crow races downstairs toward the water. At the end of the pier, he finds the dinghy from the bait shop and "borrows" it to speed out to the struggling swimmer. He pulls the waterlogged body into the boat, and once ashore tries hard to remember what to do to resuscitate a drowning person. About the same time Crow detects breathing movements, he also realizes that he has rescued a girl.

Crow also discovers that he has thwarted a would-be suicide. Her name is Valentine, and as Crow tells himself, she sure is a nothing-looking girl.

For the next few days, Crow allows Valentine to stay with him. He learns that she, too, is a runaway of sorts. First, she ran from a mother who didn't care and a stepfather who cared obviously too much. But what she ran to was a man named Marty, a man who had definite plans for Valentine, and all his other girls. Valentine fought him off and ran away again, but this time he is after her. In despair, she tried to drown herself.

Although Crow denies any attraction toward Valentine, he finds himself liking the young girl and enjoying her company. But when she suggests that perhaps she could stay with Crow for a time, he rebels and insists that she leave in a couple of days.

Shortly before Valentine is to leave, Crow returns from work to discover that she has prepared a celebration dinner for them. Torn between his fear of rejection once more and his sadness at seeing her go, Crow lashes out at Valentine for her carelessness in leaving the apartment entrance partway open, risking exposure of his secret place. She, in turns, chides him on his secretiveness about the mysterious Sasha whose apartment he lives in.

Their fight ends in Valentine running away.

Not wanting to admit how much she has come to mean to him, Crow desperately tries to find her. He does, but only after Marty has tracked her down first at the carousel, where, luckily for Valentine, Marty falls and is badly injured.

Valentine and Crow acknowledge their feelings for each other. She tells him that she has decided to go to Utah to live with her mother's sister and to finish school. When he says, "If I asked you, would you stay?" she tells him that she has things to finish and so does he, but thanks for asking.

In turn, Crow confesses that Sasha is actually an elderly actress who died sometime back and whose clippings he ran across in the apartment. He never knew her. Sasha's secret place had become his secret place, too.

Crow realizes that he does not want to turn away from love anymore and he sees a time, when their unfinished business is through for them both, that perhaps they will find each other once more. But for now, as he sends Valentine off to Utah, he thinks that a trip back to Illinois is in order, to Mrs. Simmons and to Danny. Perhaps they need him.

Thematic Material

This is a warm, gentle, out-of-the-ordinary love story of two young people so hurt by being rebuffed or mishandled that they are afraid to reach out, to need, for fear of being hurt again. Crow's sensitivity and goodness are nicely detailed, and his growing awareness of his true feelings is well portrayed.

Book Talk Material

To introduce the character of Crow, use pp. 4–10. Other interesting passages are: Crow reacts to Valentine's poetry (pp. 20–21); Crow's and

Valentine's first "intimate" conversation (pp. 25–27); they walk the beach (pp. 57–63); Crow and Valentine talk under the sleeping bag (pp. 75–84).

Additional Selections

Elsie Edwards, the heroine of Barthe De Clements's earlier novels, tries to get her life in order in *Seventeen and In-Between* (Viking, 1984, $11.95). Alix finds she can be like other kids through her friendship with Nick in Hila Colman's *Nobody Told Me What I Need to Know* (Morrow, 1984, $10.25). In Colman's *Suddenly* (Morrow, 1987, $11.75), Emily feels oppressive guilt when the car in which she is riding accidentally kills a seven-year-old boy. For a younger audience, Irene Bennett Brown's *I Loved You, Logan McGee!* (Atheneum, 1987, $11.95) explores the hurt and hate that result when thirteen-year-old Calla loses her boyfriend. Fourteen-year-old Melanie forms a beautiful friendship with a boy she later realizes is a popstar in Ann M. Martin's *Just a Summer Romance* (Holiday, 1987, $12.95). In *Finding David Dolores* (Harper, 1986, $11.50), by Margaret Willey, a thirteen-year-old experiences the intensity of her first crush; and Vicky falls in love for the first time in Paula Fox's *A Place Apart* (Farrar, 1980, $10.95; pap., New Amer. Lib., $2.25). A girl's desperate attempts to snare the boy of her dreams are recounted in Paul Zindel's *The Girl Who Wanted a Boy* (Harper, 1981, $11.89; pap., Bantam, $2.50).

About the Author

Commire, Anne, ed. *Something about the Author*. Detroit: Gale Research Co., 1980. Vol. 18, pp. 38–39 (under Anne Evelyn Bunting).

Evory, Ann, ed. *Contemporary Authors* (New Revision Series). Detroit: Gale Research Co., 1982. Vol. 5, p. 85.

———. *Contemporary Authors* (New Revision Series). Detroit: Gale Research Co., 1987. Vol. 19, pp. 97–99.

Holtze, Sally Holmes, ed. *Fifth Book of Junior Authors and Illustrators*. New York: Wilson, 1983, pp. 60–61.

Kinsman, Clare D., ed. *Contemporary Authors*. Detroit: Gale Research Co., 1975. Vols. 53–56, pp. 75–76.

Kirkpatrick, D. L., ed. *Twentieth-Century Children's Writers* (2nd edition). New York: St. Martin's, 1983, pp. 136–137.

Who's Who of American Women: 1987–1988 (15th edition). Chicago: Marquis Who's Who, Inc., 1986. Vol. 1, p. 388.

Childress, Alice. *Rainbow Jordan*
Coward, 1981, $9.95; pap., Avon, $2.50

In her first novel for young adults, *A Hero Ain't Nothin' but a Sandwich* (Coward, 1973, $8.95; pap. Avon, $2.50; condensed in *More Juniorplots*, Bowker, 1977, pp. 54–57), Alice Childress introduces us to a thirteen-year-old black boy, Benjie Johnson, his friends and family, and his many encounters with drugs. Rainbow Jordan is in some respects his female counterpart, but her chief problem, apart from finding a home for herself, is how far to go in sexual matters. Like *Hero,* it is written from the points of view of several characters, often in the strong street language of Harlem. This technique gives a multifaceted layering effect to the novel that adds an extra dimension of depth. The novel is read by students in grades seven through ten.

Plot Summary
There are three narrators in this novel: The first one is Kathie Jordan. Kathie was only fifteen when she had her child, Rainbow. The father, Leroy, also only a teenager, married her, but neither was ready for marriage and, after a few months together, they parted. Kathie then moved in with her only other close relative, a great-aunt, but when Rainbow was four the great-aunt died. Since then, in a haphazard fashion, Kathie has been taking care of Rainbow herself. Kathie is very attractive and supplements what income she gets from Social Service and from Leroy, now in Detroit, by being a go-go dancer in clubs. She loves the fast lane and has had many boyfriends. Although basically well-meaning, she resents the confines and restrictions that caring for Rainbow has placed on her life and frequently lashes out verbally and physically against her daughter. These scenes always lead to brief periods of remorse and guilt where extravagant gifts are given to Rainbow to assuage her conscience. She frequently stays out late at night or is away for a few days on a gig. These separations often have caused problems. When only five, Rainbow was left alone the night their apartment building caught fire. As a result, Kathie faced child neglect charges. On other occasions, her daughter has temporarily been taken from her by the authorities and placed in the home of Josephine Lamont until Kathie has been able to regain custody. She's now twenty-nine and has taken up with a brutish alcoholic named Burke who is so insanely jealous of her

that she lives in constant fear. She has gone out of town with Burke for a club date but finds that it has been rescheduled. Without any money, she is now trapped with a drunken Burke in a motel room and unable to get back to New York and Rainbow.

The second narrator is Rainbow Jordan. Rainbow is now fourteen and, in spite of the terrible buffetings life has given her, she is still a remarkably open and trusting girl. She is conscientious in all she does including her school work, and tries hard to please everyone, particularly her mother. She is understanding of others to the point of even making excuses for her mother's blatant neglect. However, she is basically lonely and in need of love but wrongly blames herself for her problems to the point of self-deprecation. At school, Rainie (she hates the name Rainbow and tells everyone her real name is Lorrain) often is in trouble because of her outspoken honesty, but she has a few friends. Her boyfriend is the good-looking Eljay who is becoming tired of their petting-only sessions and is now demanding that Rainbow go all the way. His best friends are Buster and Beryl, who are intimate together. Beryl also tries to talk Rainbow into sleeping with Eljay but Rainbow cares enough for herself to say no; besides, Beryl is gradually showing that she is basically unwholesome—she shoplifts, accepts money from an older man, Don, for his quick feel, and is now pregnant by Buster. At the novel's beginning, once more Kathie has taken off with the hateful Burke, leaving Rainbow alone awaiting another stay with Miss Josie.

The third narrator is Josephine Lamont. Miss Josie, a black woman who claims to be only fifty, is termed by the welfare authorities an "interim guardian." She and her husband, Hal, an accountant, have tried unsuccessfully to have children and now, partly as a pastime and partly for money, she does some dressmaking and supplies short-term care for youngsters who will soon be returned to their families or be placed in foster-care facilities. Rainbow has stayed with her before but is her only "repeater." Josephine possesses good instincts and middle-class values but her pursuit and worship of the decorous life has led her to pretentions bordering on the phoney. For example, she always has dinner by candlelight and calls her husband's customers "clients." She dotes on Hal and tends to his every need, but it is essentially a joyless marriage and Hal's eyes are beginning to rove. Now the social worker Mayola has called her to tell her Rainbow will be coming once again.

Rainbow leaves her mother's apartment neat and clean and once more accompanies Mayola to her temporary home with Miss Josie whom she

likes, even though inwardly she finds her affectations essentially dishonest. Mr. Lamont is absent when she arrives—visiting a cousin in Atlanta is
Josie's hasty explanation. Rainbow hopes her mother will return soon,
particularly because Kathie has promised faithfully to be present for the
much postponed mandatory parent-teacher conference scheduled in the
next few days. Within a short time Rainbow meets two of Josie's acquaintances. The first is Mrs. Anderson, for whom Josie sews. She is a wealthy
black suburban matron who, in Josephine's eyes, has reached Nirvana:
the upper middle-class. Rainbow is not as impressed. The other is Miss
Rachel, an elderly white Quaker woman who lives her faith every day
and talks to Rainbow about poetry and the important values in life. She
also explains the concept of centering down, that is, of thinking about a
problem until a solution arrives.

After school one day, knowing Josie is out, Rainbow invites her friends
to see her "aunt's" elegant apartment (she tells no one that Josie is her
guardian). Things soon get out of hand. Buster begins smoking grass
and during a fight between him and Eljay, a precious wine goblet is
broken. Josie arrives and becomes hysterical and, in a trauma of self-pity,
announces she is through being exploited by other people, including her
husband. Rainbow soothes her and peace is restored.

Eljay continues to pressure Rainbow for sex but, in a frank discussion
of birth control with her, gives no assurance that precautions will be
taken. Soon he begins dating a fast girl at school, Janine, and Rainbow
realizes she will lose him if she doesn't give in. After arranging a rendezvous with Eljay, she takes the key to her mother's apartment from Josie's
home, enters, puts special sheets on the bed, showers, dresses in her
mother's caftan, and waits for Eljay. He arrives with Janine in tow and
very obviously shows that he is no longer interested in Rainbow, who
now feels anger and humiliation. After they go, an agitated Josie, who
has missed her key, arrives and receives a disarmingly honest explanation of the situation. She sends Rainbow home while she shops. On the
stoop of the Lamont's apartment house, Rainbow meets Miss Christopher, the neighborhood gossip who tells her that Hal has always been a
womanizer and has left town with a much younger woman. Now inside
the apartment, Rainbow notices that Josie has been sorting out old photos and letters and she sees that the age on her passport is fifty-seven, not
fifty as claimed. Josie arrives and forces Rainbow to read aloud a letter
from Hal asking for a divorce. The two talk openly and sometimes
heatedly about their respective problems. Both need more honesty in

their lives: Josie must lower her defenses and face a bleak future, and Rainbow must realize that her mother really doesn't love her as much as she believes.

The next day is conference day and still no Kathie. Josie volunteers to go and pretend to be an aunt. "No," says Rainbow, "Let's do it right. I'm tellin' them you my friend who take care of me cause my mother is away." Both are beginning the process of centering down.

Thematic Material

This is basically the story of a young girl's search for love and security but it is also an exploration of the nature and need for honesty and truth in one's life. Other subjects dealt with are betrayal by loved ones; the possible levels of forgiving and forgetting; difficult sexual decisions faced by adolescents; various methods people use to protect themselves from reality; and the problem of loneliness in people's lives. Though far from being a moral tract, this novel explores the sad consequences of unwanted pregnancies.

Book Talk Material

An introduction to the three principal characters and the plot up to the point of Rainbow's return to Miss Josie's should interest readers. Rainbow's and Kathie's passages are in street jargon and might be hard to reproduce intact, but some specific passages of interest are: Rainbow talks about her relations with her mother in two passages (pp. 9–12; pp. 8–11, pap.; and pp. 30–32; pp. 27–30, pap.); the fire (pp. 34–38; pp. 31–34, pap); Rainbow describes Miss Josephine (pp. 53–54; pp. 47–48, pap.); and disturbing episodes with Beryl (pp. 58–64; pp. 52–57, pap.).

Additional Selections

A black ghetto family is destroyed when its talented oldest son turns to drugs in *Teacup Full of Roses* (Viking, 1972, $10.95; pap., Penguin, $3.95) by Sharon Bell Mathis. When a black girl wins a reciting contest over a white boy, threats begin in Ouida Sebestyen's novel set in 1910, *Words by Heart* (Little, 1979, $12.45; pap., Bantam, $2.50). Its sequel is *On Fire* (Atlantic, 1985, $13.95). *Marked by Fire* (pap., Avon, 1982, $2.25) by Joyce Carol Thomas tells about the childhood and adolescence of a black girl who was raped at age ten. This is followed by *Bright Shadow* (pap., Avon, 1983, $2.50). Kelly has to cope with her physically abusive father in Linda Woolverton's *Running before the Wind* (Houghton, 1987, $12.95). Louis

Lamb befriends DeWitt Clauson, the black kid next door, in Gary W. Bargar's *Life Is Not Fair* (Houghton, 1984, $11.95). Girls face problems involving their sexuality in such novels as Deborah Hautzig's *Hey, Dollface* (Greenwillow, 1978, $11.88) and Norma Fox Mazer's *Up in Seth's Room* (Delacorte, 1979, $13.95; pap., Dell, $2.50).

About the Author

Commire, Anne, ed. *Something about the Author*. Detroit: Gale Research Co., 1975. Vol. 7, pp. 46–47.

Evory, Ann, ed. *Contemporary Authors* (New Revision Series). Detroit: Gale Research Co., 1981. Vol. 3, pp. 122–124.

Holtze, Sally Holmes, ed. *Fifth Book of Junior Authors and Illustrators*. New York: Wilson, 1983, pp. 65–67.

Kinsman, Clare D., ed. *Contemporary Authors*. Detroit: Gale Research Co., 1974. Vols. 45–48, p. 93.

Who's Who of American Women: 1987–1988 (15th edition). Chicago: Marquis Who's Who, Inc., 1986. Vol. 1, p. 493.

Conford, Ellen.   *We Interrupt This Semester for an Important Bulletin*
  Little, 1979, $12.45; pap., Scholastic, $2.95

Readers were first introduced to vivacious Carrie Wasserman in the author's earlier *Dear Lovey Hart, I Am Desperate* (Little, 1975, $12.45; pap., Scholastic, $2.25) when, as a freshman at Lincoln High School where her father is head guidance counselor, she takes a position on the school newspaper, the *Lincoln Log,* and immediately falls in love with its good-looking editor, Chip. Complications arise when Carrie, now the writer of an advice to the lovelorn column, gives advice that produces disasterous but often hilarious results. Furthermore, Carrie is convinced that Chip is out to snag her best friend, Claudia. Eventually these misunderstandings are eliminated and all ends well. This lighthearted novel and its sequel are enjoyed by girls in grades six through nine.

Plot Summary

It is the beginning of a new school year and our narrator, Caroline (Carrie) Wasserman, now a sophomore, is once again working on the school newspaper, the *Lincoln Log,* under the leadership of its handsome editor and her steady boyfriend, Chip Custer. The old staff, including

Bob Teal, Jessie Krause, and Cindy Wren, are back, along with some new faces like freshman Peter Kaplan and the faculty advisor, attractive Mr. Thatcher, who in a great display of trust and magnaminity, allows the students free reign concerning the paper's contents.

Carrie's position is Features Editor, and although she complains bitterly about this to her friends Claudia and Terry, she proceeds on her first article, an interview with the new biology teacher, Mr. Sacks. Carrie is not familiar with interviewing techniques, and the result is a dull, flatly written piece that Chip reluctantly rejects. She tries again using as a subject dreamy Mr. Thatcher. Here she indulges in gushing subjectivity and once again the piece is unsuitable. Chip or no Chip, she is about to throw in her journalistic sponge when two events occur that make her stay on. First Chip, who is fired by thoughts of investigative reporting á la Watergate, is convinced that there is graft and corruption involved in the management of the school cafeteria, particularly after an employee informant known only as "Cottage Cheese" begins telling Chip about bribery and contract rigging within the operation. Secondly, Prudie Tuckerman, a Southern cupcake, complete with batting eyelids and a generous supply of "you-alls," volunteers for work on the *Log* and, with her fabulous good looks, zeros in on an easy moving target, Chip.

Carrie must do something fast or lose both her man and her status on the newspaper. She concocts a wild scheme to further Chip's investigation and also win him back by bugging the office of the cafeteria's manager, Mr. Fell. After getting some technical advice from friend Terry's on/off steady, Steve, and borrowing a tape recorder from another friend, Claudia, she and helper Pete plant the tape recorder in Mr. Fell's office when he is out to lunch. After narrowly escaping detection she realizes what a foolhardy escapade this was, particularly in light of her father's position in the school. However, it is too late to turn back. She retrieves the tape which contains a telephone conversation in which Mr. Fell states he wants to substitute hogs for beef to further profits. The newspaper staff interpret this as a sure sign of cupidity and begin work on the feature article whose headline will be "Lunch Program Riddled with Corruption."

Meanwhile Prudie, the Dixie belle, continues her path of conquest by inviting the entire staff of the *Log* to a swanky dinner party at her family's mansion. The group is suitably awed by their surroundings but unfortunately, Carrie underestimates the potency of Brandy Alexanders and becomes very tipsy. At dinner she is so loud and boisterous that she embarrasses everyone, including Chip. Luckily she gets home before becoming sick.

The next morning, hung over and miserable, she is comforted by her family, including her young sister, Jen, but consolation is hard to find because Carrie is convinced that Chip no longer wants to date her.

Even more serious problems, however, lie in store. When the first issue of the paper appears, the staff is summoned to the office of Mr. Bauer, the principal, where Mr. Fell is also present. Both are enraged at the story, which turns out to be completely false. Mr. Fell plays the commodities market, thus the hogs and beef conversation, and "Cottage Cheese" is a disgruntled employee on termination notice who lied about the corruption to cause trouble. Chip and Carrie are stunned. Apologies, retractions, and general atonements are demanded and justifiably given by the chastised staff. During this period of penance, Prudie is conspicuously absent from the *Log*'s office. Like the proverbial rat and sinking ship, she decides to leave the staff to pursue other interests, i.e., Terry's boyfriend, football player, Steve.

Carrie and Chip are together again and are confident that in the future the *Lincoln Log* will be the best darn newspaper around.

Thematic Material

This is basically a light-as-air frothy comedy served up by a master of this genre. It contains believable characters, suspense, and extremely humorous dialogue. As well, it explores boy-girl relationships, a close family situation, and friendships. Most important is the theme involving responsible journalism and the limits of investigative reporting.

Book Talk Material

Some interesting incidents are: the interview with Mr. Sacks (pp. 14–18; pp. 13–17, pap.); the story about Mr. Thatcher (pp. 33–39; pp. 33–40, pap.); enter Prudie (pp. 49–53; pp. 50–54, pap.) and "Cottage Cheese" (pp. 55–58; pp. 56–59, pap.); planting the tape recorder (pp. 64–73; pp. 66–77, pap.); and the dinner at Prudie's (pp. 103–125; pp. 107–130, pap.).

Additional Selections

In Christi Killien's *All of the Above* (Houghton, 1984, $12.95), MacBeth Langley is looking for love and finds it in dreamy Blake Honeycutt whom she later discovers is using her to help his father. Jenny and her baseball playing boyfriend exchange bodies for three days in Susan Smith's *Changing Places* (pap., Scholastic, 1986, $2.50), and Skeeter McGee's lie to a pen pal is exposed in Christi Killien's humorous *Putting On an Act* (Houghton, 1986, $12.95). Marcy Lewis is the engaging heroine of Paula Danziger's *The Cat Ate My Gymsuit* (Delacorte, 1974, $12.95; pap., Dell, $2.50) and *There's a Bat in Bunk Five* (Delacorte, 1980, $13.95; pap., Dell, $2.50). Overweight Enid Tennebaum has a crush on the school's intellectual but is afraid a blond cheerleader will win him in Jane Breskin Zalben's *Here's Looking at You, Kid* (Farrar, 1984, $10.95). In Lois Lowry's *Anastasia, Ask Your Analyst* (Houghton, 1984, $9.95; pap., Dell, $2.50), it's Anastasia versus Freud and science projects in this riotous continuation of a successful series. The daughter of a New York psychoanalyst tells her very funny story in Winifred Rosen's *Cruisin' for a Bruisin* (pap., Dell, 1977, $1.95).

About the Author

Commire, Anne, ed. *Something about the Author*. Detroit: Gale Research Co., 1974. Vol. 6, pp. 48–49.

Evory, Ann, ed. *Contemporary Authors* (First Revision Series). Detroit: Gale Research Co., 1978, Vols. 33–36, pp. 203–204.

Holtze, Sally Holmes, ed. *Fifth Book of Junior Authors and Illustrators*. New York: Wilson, 1983, pp. 82–83.

Metzger, Linda, ed. *Contemporary Authors* (New Revision Series). Detroit: Gale Research Co., 1984. Vol. 13, p. 117.

Senick, Gerard J., ed. *Children's Literature Review*. Detroit: Gale Research Co., 1986. Vol. 10, pp. 87–100.

Cormier, Robert. *The Bumblebee Flies Anyway*
Pantheon, 1983, $10.95; pap., Dell, $2.75 (same pagination)

In his novels, Mr. Cormier explores the behavioral limitations placed on humans by various societal systems and conventions and the futility often involved when one challenges those systems. For example, in his first novel for young adults, *The Chocolate War* (Pantheon, 1974, $11.95; pap., Dell, $2.95; condensed in *More Juniorplots*, Bowker, 1977, pp. 28–32), the author pits a young idealistic boy against the entire power structure of his school when he refuses to participate in a chocolate sale. His humiliating and painful defeat makes a mockery of the quotation he has answered affirmatively, "Do I Dare Disturb the Universe?" In *The Bumblebee Flies Anyway* the young protagonist futilely questions the ultimate limitation on human existence, death. This bleak and disturbing theme is relieved somewhat in the novel by the character of Cassie, her tender relationship with Barney, the book's hero, and her redemption through faith. The novel offers a challenging but rewarding experience for readers in grades seven through ten.

Plot Summary

Sixteen-year-old Barney Snow has been in the Complex only a few weeks but he knows he is different from the rest of the patients. The Complex is an experimental clinic where the terminally ill have voluntarily been confined to participate in a series of medical procedures using experimental drugs, nicknamed—by Barney—merchandise. Barney believes he is not really sick but merely there to help with some special projects involving drugs and memory. Therefore, he is different from the other young but doomed patients in Section 12, all of whom are the care of Dr. Edward Lakendorp (also known by Barney as the Handyman) and Nurse Bascam. Some of these patients are Billy the Kidney, a lonesome foster child whose disease has confined him to a wheelchair; Allie Roon, a pathetic youngster who has lost motor control and is now a bundle of twitches and stammers; and the enigmatic, exquisitely handsome Alberto Muzzofoner, called Mazzo, a cynical young man about twenty who is disliked by all for his continuously insulting and deprecating remarks. Mazzo has chosen to come to the Complex hoping that the experiments will hasten his death.

One day while exploring a junkyard neighboring the Complex, Barney spots a scarlet MG seemingly in perfect condition. However, the sight of the car triggers a strange nightmarish memory: He is in a car, hurtling out of control on a slanted street when a girl steps into its path. The incident ends in a cacophony of screams and a howling car horn. In spite of this horrifying mental association, Barney later decides to explore the car further and finds to his amazement that it is a fake—merely a plywood model without an engine that, according to a label on it, was a project of the local high school's woodworking class.

Through the influence of his wealthy mother whom he actively loaths and will not allow to visit, Mazzo is given an outside telephone. In order to secure privileges for Billy the Kidney to use the telephone so he can have some outside contacts, Barney agrees to act as a buffer between Mazzo and his twin sister, Cassie, when she visits him to affect a reconciliation. Barney is immediately attracted to this beautiful, gentle girl, who is even able to bring out the human, less abrasive side of Mazzo's character. Mazzo, however, proclaims that he wants no visitors, not even Cassie, during this, his last, stay in the hospital. Later Cassie secretly visits Barney and begs him, for her sake, to make friends with and stay close to Mazzo; she in turn will visit Barney regularly to get an update on her brother's health. Barney is torn between wanting to be with Cassie, with whom he is now infatuated, and his natural instinct to avoid Mazzo and his biting tongue. However, Cassie prevails and, reluctantly, Barney begins visiting Mazzo daily.

In the meantime, Barney continues to be the subject of more memory-illuminating experiments. On one occasion he is so fearful that he will lose all sense of identity while in the drug-induced coma that he conceals, under a Band-Aid, a piece of paper containing his name and age. But a few days after each experiment his short-term memory returns and along with it recurring remembrances of that horrible car accident.

Slowly Barney is able to break down the wall of hostility and resentment Mazzo has built around himself. He tells Barney stories of his past, why he blames his mother and her divorce proceedings for the death of his father, and how he longs once again to get behind the wheel of a sports car the way he often did when he was well. In moments of despair, he even begs Barney to remove his life-support system so he can die in peace. Most of this Barney conveys to Cassie who, in turn, also confides in the young boy many of her inner fears and concerns. She is a devout Catholic who spends much of her time in retreats and she is now seriously contemplating becoming a nun. In spite of the circumstances of their meetings, there is great joy in the relationship for Barney. But Cassie does not reveal to him that she has a nervous system sympathetic to her brother's, so that when he feels pain, she does also. Knowing this, she is continually tormented by the question of what will happen to her when Mazzo dies.

Barney rashly promises Mazzo a last ride in a sports car and to fulfill this he devises a scheme to dismantle the fake MG, smuggle the parts into the attic of the hospital, and reassemble them there. When Cassie learns about the model car, she names it the Bumblebee because in the same way that a bee flies in defiance of the laws of science, so will Barney's model car perform like a real one.

While moving parts to the attic via the service elevator, Barney takes a detour to explore rooms on a different floor in the clinic. In one room he finds the car from his nightmare and in front of it a screen. By pressing buttons, images on the screen re-create the ghastly car accident. Dr. Lakendorp, the Handyman, finds him in the room and is forced to give him an explanation. This intense traumatic incident has been used continually to enable Barney to blot out the truth from the past that he has refused to accept: Barney, who was orphaned as a child and has no family, is really not unlike the others in the Complex. He, too, is suffering from an incurable disease. Mazzo's health begins to decline rapidly and soon Barney notices on his own skin the first ugly blotches that mean the end is near. The Handyman tells Barney that he is no longer part of an experiment, and in a day or two he will be transferred to a regular hospital. He has one last meeting with Cassie that ends with her giving him a gentle kiss for remembrance. Barney knows he must put his plan into action. That night he creeps into Mazzo's room. The boy is dying and consents to having his support system removed. Barney, with Billy's help, takes Mazzo to the attic where they move the Bumblebee through the skylight onto the roof. As Mazzo dies, Barney pushes the car free and it soars triumphantly from the roof into the night.

At her home, Cassie feels within her the dying pains of her brother. She prays fervently to remain alive and through her fierce affirmation of life, she vanquishes the power of death. At the hospital Barney is back in his bed, slowly sinking into a final coma, but still he remembers the Bumblebee and its flight to glory.

Thematic Material

Although this is a novel about death and dying, it is also paean to the beauty of life and to lasting values like friendship, love, and caring for one another. The deaths in the end are coupled with dignity and triumph and teach us lessons on both how to live as well as how to die. This is an inspiring book, one that on the surface is depressing but on further contemplation is one of great warmth, insight, and inspiration.

Book Talk Material

This is a challenging book—one that requires the reader's full attention to understand the setting and basic situation. If too much is told in a book talk the excitement of piecing these clues together might be spoiled. Therefore, perhaps a brief introduction to the patients in Section 12 might suffice. Some specific incidents are: Barney sees the model car and has his first memory trauma (pp. 14–15); Billy explains why he wants to use Mazzo's phone (pp. 18–20); the Handyman tells Barney about his new drugs (pp. 44–52); Barney and the Band-Aid (pp. 63–67); Barney meets Cassie (pp. 68–74).

Additional Selections

The first sorrows of youth are explored in ten stories collected by Charlotte Zolotow in *Early Sorrow* (Harper, 1986, $12.95). After her parents' divorce, Carole welcomes the friendship of self-confident Marty until her friend suggests that the logical solution to their problems is suicide, in Winifred Morris's *Dancer in the Mirror* (Atheneum, 1987, $13.95). Two youngsters undergoing psychiatric care help each other in the healing process in Mildred Ames's *The Silver Link, the Silken Tie* (Scribner, 1984, $12.95; pap., Scholastic, $2.25). Roger Baxter gradually loses touch with reality as he descends into insanity in Kin Platt's *The Boy Who Could Make Himself Disappear* (pap., Dell, 1971, $2.75; condensed in *More Juniorplots*, Bowker, 1977, pp. 124–127). A rich, spoiled boy takes to the woods after he becomes involved in an accident in a stolen car in Joan Phipson's *Hit and Run* (Atheneum, 1985, $9.95). The illness and death of a young girl from cancer is told in Alden R. Carter's *Sheila's Dying* (Putnam, 1987, $13.95), and a nineteen-year-old freshman tries to overcome the grief of her brother's death in Meg Wolitzer's *Sleepwalking* (Random, 1982, $12.50; pap., Avon, $2.25). A seventeen-year-old girl lives alone, raising rabbits for a living, while trying to sort out the half-remembered incidents from her past in Lynn Hall's *The Solitary* (Scribner, 1986, $11.95).

About the Author

Commire, Anne, ed. *Something about the Author*. Detroit: Gale Research Co., 1976. Vol. 10, p. 28; updated 1986. Vol. 45, pp. 58–65.
Estes, Glenn E., ed. *American Writers for Children since 1960: Fiction (Dictionary of Literary Biography*, Vol. 52). Detroit: Gale Research Co., 1986, pp. 107–114.
Evory, Ann, ed. *Contemporary Authors* (New Revision Series). Detroit: Gale Research Co., 1982. Vol. 5, pp. 130–132.
Holtze, Sally Holmes, ed. *Fifth Book of Junior Authors and Illustrators*. New York: Wilson, 1983, pp. 86–87.
Kirkpatrick, D. L., ed. *Twentieth-Century Children's Writers* (2nd edition). New York: St. Martin's, 1983, p. 203.

Senick, Gerard J., ed. *Children's Literature Review*. Detroit: Gale Research Co., 1987. Vol. 12, pp. 144–155.
Who's Who in America: 1986–1987 (44th edition). Chicago: Marquis Who's Who, Inc., 1986. Vol. 1, p. 581.

Crawford, Charles P.   *Letter Perfect*
Dutton, 1977, $9.95; pap., Pocket Bks., $1.95 (same pagination)

Charles P. Crawford's two earlier books for young adults published by Dutton were *Three Legged Race*, about three teenagers confined to a hospital, and *Bad Fall*, a novel that, like *Letter Perfect*, explores the levels of friendship. Both, unfortunately, are out of print. All three are taut, psychological novels that pose ethical problems while telling suspenseful stories. The credibility of *Letter Perfect* is enhanced by having the story narrated by Chad, a basically fine young person who becomes involved in seemingly harmless pranks that escalate in gravity until he loses control of his involvement. This has been a popular novel for many years with junior high school readers.

Plot Summary
If a teacher popularity poll were conducted at Chad Winston's high school in the small town of Louella, Pennsylvania, his first-year English teacher, Mr. Patterson, would most certainly score lowest. Not only is he despotic in temperament, but he also generously uses sarcasm and belittling remarks to keep the class in order. He is, however, consistent in his behavior, knows his subject, and seems to apply his rigorous high standards of excellence both to his own performance as well as that of his classes.

Chad is a conscientious, somewhat above average student who usually manages to avoid running afoul of Mr. Patterson; but one day, during a test, his friend, B. J. Masterson, attempts to compare answers and is caught. Mr. Patterson, with accompanying withering remarks, punishes them both by giving each one-half of their combined average scores as a final grade.

B. J., who is disinterested in school and inclined to be rebellious, is particularly incensed at the judgment, as is his and Chad's friend, the aptly nicknamed Toad. The three have been chums for years. Even Mr.

Patterson has noticed this and, with his usual finesse, has called them the Three Stooges.

B. J. suggests that for the next day each should plan a "perfect crime," an act of defiance against the establishment. In a spirit of fun and adventure, all three agree. The next day Chad removes some shelf supports in the school library, causing an unsuspecting patron to produce a cascade of books, and Toad manages to put his sister's bra over the eyes of the stuffed warthog outside the science room. But it is B. J. who produces the chef d'oeuvre—he puts rancid cat food and sour milk in the hot air blower of Mr. Patterson's room, causing such a stench that the class has to be evacuated, ironically at the beginning of their discussion of *Paradise Lost.*

Flushed with victory, B. J. assigns test number 2; each must treat the others to something free. That night, a Friday, Chad manages to sneak all three into the local movie house, and B. J. gets them tipsy (and Toad sick) on a bottle of Gallo Hearty Burgundy wine that he has stolen, but Toad's plan to get free hamburgers in the local diner by placing a cockroach in one misfires and a partial payment is demanded.

Now B. J. is really warming up to the game. His third test is that each must follow someone unseen and bring back proof of the hunt.

After school on Monday, Chad accidentally passes Mr. Patterson on the street and, remembering the assignment, begins the pursuit. He follows him to a neighboring town via a local suburban train and eventually to an apartment building where Chad, as his proof, takes from a hallway table a letter addressed to Mr. James Patterson.

The next day each reports. Toad had followed the school's femme fatale, Roxanne Spiese, to a tryst at her boyfriend's home. Proof: a number pulled from the house sign. B. J. had trailed an old lady into a supermarket and discovered that she is an ace shoplifter. Proof: her cash register receipt.

Chad produced his proof. It is a letter from a naval officer with whom Mr. Patterson had attended basic training. Reference is also made to Patterson's honorable discharge after a nervous breakdown caused by inhumane persecution by a sadistic officer.

B. J. realizes that with this letter they have the perfect instrument for both blackmail and revenge. He persuades Toad and a reluctant Chad to place a letter addressed to Patterson in his school mailbox threatening to inform the school board of his past unless sixty dollars is paid in a plain envelope to be dropped from the commuter train at a specified spot.

The next day in class Mr. Patterson shows signs of nervous distraction. That evening, however, instead of an envelope with money, the boys collect only a note that reads, "To Whom It May Concern: Go screw yourself. J. P."

The situation now becomes a challenge for B. J. Without consulting Chad, but with Toad's help, a second letter is written demanding $120 or the letter will be sent to newspapers. In class, B. J. openly goads Patterson until he loses his customary composure. Later, under B. J.'s direction, Chad feigns an accident in the cafeteria and spills spaghetti over Patterson, who becomes so agitated that he grabs Chad and shoves him against a wall. B. J. is convinced he is cracking up, but Chad is only feeling guilt and anxiety at the growing seriousness of the situation.

That evening, when Patterson again does not respond with money, the three follow him home, and B. J. spray-paints the word PSYCHO on his apartment window. Inside, Patterson sees it and throws a chair at the window. Chad is cut by the flying glass, but all three escape undetected.

Chad begs B. J. to drop the scheme, but B. J. is determined to continue until Patterson either cracks or pays up. Chad's distress and pangs of bad conscience increase. Later that evening he adds hypocrisy to his faults when his parents, knowing him to be honest and fair, consult him on how to deal with a younger sister who has been caught cheating.

The next day Chad retrieves the original letter from B. J.'s locker and, without revealing the names of the other plotters, returns it to Mr. Patterson with apologies for his actions. B. J. and Toad are furious and, as revenge, plant some marijuana joints by Chad's locker where they can be seen by Mr. Boughman, the assistant principal. Mr. Patterson intervenes, claiming the cigarettes are his.

The following day the class has a new English teacher. Mr. Patterson has resigned and left town. Weeks afterward Chad learns that he is teaching in a private school in New Hampshire. The boy writes to him giving both his thanks and his regrets concerning the whole sordid venture. The reply from Mr. Patterson is one expressing reconciliation and appreciation at Chad's thoughtfulness. Later that year, Chad learns that B. J. and Toad are planning another blackmail scheme against a different teacher. This time Chad has the satisfaction of preventing its execution by threatening to expose his former friends.

Thematic Material

Parallels between the classic text *Paradise Lost* and the novel's happenings are often made. For example, both explore the nature and disguises of temptation—injured egos, personal power, revenge—and both deal with the loss of innocence. The conflict of conscience versus loyalty to friends is explored, as is the fine division between practical jokes and criminal action. Moral responsibility, courage, and the importance of friendship are other important themes. The ease with which one can become involved in harmless pranks and the difficulty of extricating oneself from these schemes when they go out of control are also dealt with, as is the final situation when Chad, the perpetrator, becomes the victim.

Book Talk Material

An explanation of the significance of the title and the concept of a perfect crime should interest readers. Some important passages are: Chad and B. J. are caught cheating (pp. 1–6); the first prank: the library (pp. 17–19), the warthog (pp. 19–21), the stench (pp. 23–29); Toad flunks the second test (pp. 37–42); the third test: trailing Mr. Patterson (pp. 54–59), Toad and Roxanne (pp. 63–66), and B. J.'s shoplifter (67–69); and the contents of the letter to Mr. Patterson (pp. 73–74).

Additional Selections

In a fit of anger, a teenager causes the death of a younger boy and tries to hide it in Michael French's *Pursuit* (Delacorte, 1982, $9.95; pap., Dell, $2.50). Hoping for popularity, Corey joins a group called the Eight, whose activities get out of control in *Fridays* (pap., Archway, 1981, $1.95) by Patricia Lee Gauch. The power of choice becomes important when a daredevil friend is drowned in Marion Dane Bauer's *On My Honor* (Clarion, 1985, $11.95). Martin Muller and Bill Pronzini have edited a collection of stories with children as heroes and villians in *Child's Ploy* (Macmillan, 1984, $14.95). The story of two girls' friendship from kindergarten through high school is told in Marilyn Sachs's *Class Pictures* (Dutton, 1980, $10.95; pap., Avon, $2.50). Two other novels with school settings are Lynn Hall's *The Giver* (Scribner, 1985, $11.95) and Julia First's *The Absolute, Ultimate End* (Watts, 1985, $10.90). In *Dunker* (Lodestar, 1982, $9.95; pap., Bantam, $2.25) by Ronald Kidd, sixteen-year-old Bobby Rothman learns the importance of self-respect. Rilla runs from an accident and spends a *Haunted Summer* (Lothrop, 1967, $10.25; pap., Pocket Bks., $1.95) in this novel by Hope Dahle Jordan.

About the Author

Commire, Anne, ed. *Something about the Author*. Detroit: Gale Research Co., 1982. Vol. 28, pp. 67–68.

Kinsman, Clare D., ed. *Contemporary Authors*. Detroit: Gale Research Co., 1974. Vols. 45–48, p. 109.

Cresswell, Helen. *Bagthorpes Abroad*
Macmillan, 1984, $10.95
Cresswell, Helen. *Bagthorpes Haunted*
Macmillan, 1985, lib. bdg., $11.95

It was in 1977 that Helen Cresswell unleashed on an unsuspecting America the zany antics of the outlandish English family the Bagthorpes in the first installment of their nonsensical misadventures, *Ordinary Jack* (Macmillan, 1977, $9.95). Since then, young readers have been reeling with the hilarity that each new installment brings. In these, the fifth and sixth parts of the Bagthorpe saga, the family takes a vacation trip to Wales to hunt ghosts—and Wales will never be the same again.

The family consists of Mr. Bagthorpe, a television scriptwriter, whose feelings of importance and righteousness are shared by no one, and his wife, a jill of several trades, including writing a monthly "Agony Aunt" advice column under the pen name of Stella Bright. Mrs. Bagthorpe believes in Positive Thinking and always making the best of a bad situation. In her household this is practically a full-time job. They have four children, William, Jack, Tess, and the youngest, Rosie. All but Jack are geniuses and budding eccentrics. Jack is average, normal, and well adjusted—and, therefore, considered the oddball in the family. There is also Grandma Bagthorpe, who makes Lucrezia Borgia look like a rank amateur at stirring up trouble, and Grandpa, who seems to be the happiest member of the family. Perhaps this is because he has a severe hearing problem. Their cook and general factotum is Mrs. Fosdyke, known to the children as Fozzy, who is able to tolerate the general pandemonium at the Bagthorpes only by having, in the evening, at the Fiddler's Arms a few pints of Guinness for her nerves. Completing the household are

Jack's mongrel dog Zero and Thomas the Second, Grandma's spoiled cat.

The Bagthorpes are frequently joined by rich Uncle Russell Parker and his ditzy wife, Aunt Celia, who is given to answering questions with half-remembered fragments of poetry. This couple, fortunately, has only one child, a hell-raising, totally uncontrollable five-year-old named Daisy, whose pet goat, Billy Goat Gruff, is the most unfinicky eater of all time.

In these books there are sometimes English expressions that might elude American readers. For example, reference is made to Mastermind, a once-popular British TV show, and to meth, short for methyl alcohol, the fuel used in camp stoves. But these are few and will not spoil the fun that readers in grades six through eight have been enjoying in these books.

Plot Summary

It is the end of the school year, and the Bagthorpe children are outdoors with a camp stove engaged in the term-end ritual of steaming open the envelopes that contain their report cards and forging complimentary remarks from their teachers. For Jack, these changes involve his academic progress, but for the others, it is a question of softening the comments that reveal that in conduct and behavior they are regarded as the school's scourges.

At lunch that day, the Bagthorpes are joined by Uncle Parker and his family and their goat. Mr. Bagthorpe announces that to prevent an incipient nervous breakdown, he will take the family on a seven-week holiday. They mistakenly think they are going to the Continent, but "abroad" turns out to be Wales, where Mr. Bagthorpe has rented, via an advertisement, a house complete with ghosts. This apparent act of generosity actually hides the fact that his latest script on ghosts has been returned for lack of authenticity and he must do some research. The discussion of their plans is interrupted by Billy Goat Gruff, which, after being fed Mr. Bagthorpe's best Scotch by Daisy, goes on a drunken spree, destroying and eating everything in sight.

In a few days, preparations are complete, and in a hired minibus (the Bagthorpes don't travel light) plus their car, they set off. Ty Cilion Duom, the Welsh name of their summer home, turns out to live up to its name in English, House of Black Corners. It is a squalid hovel whose furnishings are several cuts below those of Her Majesty's prisons. Mrs. Fosdyke is so appalled at the kitchen that she sinks into a comalike trance.

The next day they are visited by the Parkers and the goat. In an uncontested victory of one-upsmanship, Uncle Parker has booked rooms down the road at a converted castle that is now a five-star hotel, and he generously, but not without a hint of condescension, invites the Bagthorpes to dinner that evening. When Mr. Bagthorpe discovers the goat munching on his tape recorder, he attacks it with Mrs. Fosdyke's umbrella, and in the ensuing chase, he charges the housekeeper, whose shock is so great that she becomes her normal, complaining self.

That evening, Grandpa, who had gone fishing, can't be found, so the family leaves for dinner without him. From the terrace of the hotel they can see the dilapidated roof of their shanty. Mr. Bagthorpe feigns indifference and plays with his food, but the rest enjoy the first full meal they have had in two days. Over coffee, they hear a police siren and see a flashing blue light at home. They rush home and find that two policemen have brought Grandpa home after he has been found wandering dazedly in town and soaking wet from a fall in the stream. The Bagthorpes are embarrassed at their seeming negligence and invite the policemen in for a séance and a cup of tea. When a hazy blue light is seen through the windows and a mysterious crashing sound is heard, it appears that a spirit is going to visit them. It is only Daisy, who, while playing cop in the unguarded police car, has turned on all the switches and released the hand brake so the car has rolled downhill and collided with her father's. She has also inadvertently made a radio call to headquarters and soon another squad car appears. These policemen are also invited in, and in a few moments, another crash—Daisy has done it again! When a third police car arrives, the scene becomes complete chaos. Thus endeth the Bagthorpe's first full day in Wales.

In *Bagthorpes Haunted*, their stay reaches a sudden and hectic end through several more misadventures. Billy Goat Gruff wanders into town and frightens the residents, including the police magistrate's wife. Meantime, the family conducts another séance that produces sounds of heavy breathing. This proves to be only Mrs. Fosdyke sleeping off the few pints she had at a local pub. Mr. Bagthorpe, however, is determined to see a ghost and stays up most of the night, but nary an apparition appears. The next day the family attends an auction. Mr. Bagthorpe's secret bidding signal to the auctioneer is a yawn. He is so tired by the previous night's activities that in his drowsiness he acquires a vanload of unwanted furniture. Finally, Mr. Bagthorpe realizes that the house is uninhabited, but he has vowed not to leave Wales without seeing a ghost. Therefore, to save face, he hires a group of locals to "haunt" Ty Cilion Duom, not knowing that Uncle Parker has done the same thing so that Daisy could have her wish of ghost sighting. The mix-up that develops causes both families to leave happily the next morning to spend the rest of the summer safely (?) and quietly (?) at home.

Thematic Material

These novels are to be read for pure fun and enjoyment. On the surface they have a great deal in common with the best television situation comedies, but they also contain a penetrating family portrait, sly wit, and deft social comments.

Readers will enjoy the all-to-common dilemma of prospective tenants who rent sight unseen and will also empathize particularly with Jack and Grandpa, two refugees clinging to reality in a sea of chaos.

Book Talk Material

A description of the Bagthorpe family would be enough to interest readers. Some passages in *Bagthorpes Abroad* that could be used are: doctoring the report cards (pp. 1–9); Mr. Bagthorpe tells about renting the house (pp. 26–30); Billy Goat Gruff gets drunk (pp. 34–36); the trip to Wales (pp. 50–55); Mr. Bagthorpe attacks the goat (pp. 101–106); and Grandpa's adventure (pp. 131–135).

Additional Selections

The American counterpart of the Bagthorpes are in many ways the zany, mixed-up Skinners, who also decide to go on a holiday in Stephanie S. Tolan's *The Great Skinner Getaway* (Four Winds, 1987, $11.95). Others in this series are *The Great Skinner Strike* (Four Winds, 1983, $8.95; pap., New Amer. Lib., $2.25) and *The Great Skinner Enterprise* (Four Winds, 1986, $11.95). Two other series that Bagthorpe lovers should enjoy are the McGurk mysteries (e.g., *The Case of the Muttering Mummy*, Macmillan, 1986, $10.95) and the Ghost Squad adventures (e.g., *The Ghost Squad and the Halloween Conspiracy*, Dutton, 1985, $10.95; pap., Tor, $1.95). Both series are by E. W. Hildick. A delightful family that lives on the edges of society is created by Betsy Byars in *The Not-Just-*

Anybody Family (Delacorte, 1986, $13.85). Also use Byars's *The Night Swimmers* (Delacorte, 1980, $11.95; pap., Dell, $2.25). Henry's big mouth always gets him into trouble in Bruce Clement's *I Tell a Lie Every So Often* (pap., Farrar, 1974, $3.45). Two other humorous novels are *The Cybil War* by Betsy Byars (Viking, 1981, $10.50; pap., Scholastic, $1.95), in which two boys vie for the attention of the same girl; and Barbara Robinson's *The Best Christmas Pageant Ever* (Harper, 1972, $9.89; pap., Avon, $2.50), in which a gang of rotten kids decide to take part in a Christmas pageant.

About the Author

Commire, Anne, ed. *Something about the Author.* Detroit: Gale Research Co., 1971. Vol. 1, pp. 70–71.

de Montreville, Doris, and Crawford, Elizabeth D., eds. *Fourth Book of Junior Authors and Illustrators.* New York: Wilson, 1978, pp. 105–106.

Ethridge, James M. *Contemporary Authors* (First Revision). Detroit: Gale Research Co., 1967. Vols. 17–18, p. 116.

Evory, Ann, ed. *Contemporary Authors* (New Revision Series). Detroit: Gale Research Co., 1983. Vol. 8, pp. 129–131.

Kirkpatrick, D. L., ed. *Twentieth-Century Children's Writers* (2nd edition). New York: St. Martin's, 1983, pp. 204–205.

Dragonwagon, Crescent, and Zindel, Paul.   *To Take a Dare*
Harper, 1982, $11.25; lib. bdg., $10.89; pap., Bantam, $2.75

Paul Zindel's name is synonymous with the modern young adult novel. Ever since the appearance of his groundbreaking story of two unhappy teenagers and their friendship for a lonely old man, *The Pigman* (Harper, 1968, $13.70; pap., Bantam, $2.95), his books have found an eager reading public with teenagers everywhere. Crescent Dragonwagon is more frequently associated with literature for a younger group. This, however, is an excellent collaborative effort. The novel is suitable for both junior and senior high school students.

Plot Summary

Chrissie Perretti is a thirteen-year-old caught in an eighteen-year-old's body. Although somewhat startled herself by the rapid changes in her development, she is pleased to discover the sudden interest that the boys at school show in her. And even though their attentions frighten her a little, she soon realizes that "flirting" can be fun and that, for whatever reason, it's great to be popular. Gradually, Chrissie begins to change from a mousy preteen in cardigan sweaters and loafers to a "swinger" in tight jeans and even tighter T-shirts.

The change in Chrissie goes largely unnoticed by her mother, an obese, spaced-out woman who spends her days avoiding anything she doesn't want to see or hear, so much so that she gives her daughter a white, frilly "communion" dress for her birthday. Chrissie's father notices the change in her, however. A beaten man for whom life is a continual disappointment, his reaction to his daughter's development is to call her a slut and scream at her to behave.

In the months that follow her thirteenth birthday, it is all too easy for Chrissie to seek solace from the young men around her who are all too eager to give it. Inexperienced but sexually active, she develops and is treated for a case of gonorrhea, a fact that her father discovers.

Because she can find no happiness in either her personal or family life, Chrissie leaves home shortly before her fourteenth birthday. Once out of Benton, Illinois, she feels that perhaps she will stay on the road forever. And during the next few months as she wanders around the country, she tries to come to terms with the two people she has become—the tough, punk queen who is a survivor and the scared high school dropout who is an avid reader.

Eventually working her way to southern California, Chrissie meets her first real friend, Lissa, who looks as though her hair is plugged into an electric socket. Together they decide to hitch a ride to New Orleans.

But for Chrissie (who becomes Chrysta as a symbol of her new life) the journey ends in Excelsior Springs, Arkansas, a little tourist town of about 1,200 people and a motto that says, "Where the Misfit Fits." At first sight, Chrysta feels that she has come home. Although she cannot convince Lissa to stay with her, Chrysta settles down in the tiny town, where she first begins to experience what the word *home* really can mean. And it is in Excelsior Springs that three people come to symbolize the word for her.

There is kind Nettie, a wisp of a gray-haired lady who shows her the ropes in the kitchen of the General Palace Hotel where Chrysta finds a job.

There is gentle, wise Luke, dishwasher, stock boy, and song singer, who works summers at the hotel while he pursues his schooling and who, according to Nettie, actually manages the kitchen operation.

And then there is Dare, the scrawny, tough-acting kid with the perfect angel face, the homeless, parentless waif whom Chrysta takes to her heart.

The months pass, and life becomes wonderfully monotonous for Chrysta as she settles into the routine of learning the business of cooking for a hotel kitchen. Except for the occasional pains in her stomach, which she shrugs off as cramps, she decides that life might not be so bad after all.

But her stomach pains are not cramps, and one night they become so bad that Chrysta can no longer ignore them. Later, she wakes up from an operation to be told that her bout with gonorrhea at the age of thirteen left an infection in her ovaries, and she will never bear children.

Saddened, Chrysta begins her recovery buoyed by the fact that Lissa returns from New Orleans to take care of her and that her new "family" of friends takes up a collection to help her pay her hospital bills.

After her recovery, Chrysta is offered a job promotion that will eventually make her manager of the hotel kitchen. She moves into a small house of her very own, and with both body and mind on the mend and an increasing friendship with Luke, she begins to feel that perhaps she has found the true Chrysta Perretti at last. Perhaps it is now her time to be happy.

But Chrysta has not figured on the pull of affection she feels for the homeless Dare, who more and more has taken to hanging around the hotel kitchen, where she is sometimes able to see that he has food to eat. And then the idea comes to her—she can take Dare into her house and give him the home he needs!

So Chrysta, now nearing sixteen years old, takes in young Dare. But what seems the perfect home atmosphere to her soon begins to sour. The first problem occurs over the subject of dope. Chrysta tells Dare that she will have none of it in the house. The boy must also be in by ten and attend school regularly. Somewhat reluctantly, he agrees.

As time passes, Chrysta is afraid to admit that something is wrong. Nettie and Luke try to warn her that Dare has been kicked around much of his young life and that perhaps even her best intentions cannot turn him into the model "child" she is looking for. And when she confronts Dare once too often, a terrible scene follows in which the boy loses control of his temper and runs off . . . just as Chrysta did.

In her anguish, Chrysta turns again to gentle, understanding Luke, and the two young people gradually fall in love, speaking of a future together when Luke completes school and Chrysta becomes established in her new job. For a time, even Dare, who eventually returns to Chrysta's small house, seems happy for them. Then one day Chrysta learns from Dare's teacher that he has beaten up a seven-year-old child in a fury. When she confronts him with the story, he runs off again.

At this point, Luke tries to tell Chrysta that she has done all she possibly can for Dare, that he is beyond her ability to cope with, that perhaps he is beyond anyone's ability to cope with. But Chrysta is still determined not to let go.

Dare returns once again, and as his thirteenth birthday nears, Chrysta receives a phone call from his father, whom she had barely known existed. The man says he will be visiting his son on his birthday. The boy waits all day for the father who never comes. When Chrysta tries to comfort him, he lashes out—throwing a radio, plants, burning matches, and finally a knife. Dare leaves her home for the last time.

In the months that follow, Chrysta, secure now in her love for Luke and in her future, tries to understand her attachment for Dare. Perhaps he had become the child she knew she would never have. Whatever the reason, Chrysta realizes that at least she tries. She knows herself now as a trier, a doer, a fighter. And she knows she has grown. So much so that perhaps it is now time to place that long-overdue call back to Benton, Illinois.

Thematic Material

Chrysta is portrayed as a sensitive, defiant young girl who makes some bitter mistakes by reacting too quickly without thinking through the consequences. Some of the difficulties faced by young people making their own way "on the road" are vividly drawn. Some of the reasons for "casual sex" are well explored in this novel, as are such subjects for teenagers as the growing pains of adolescence, the inability to communicate with family members, and coping with the responsibilities of a job and a home.

Book Talk Material

Chrysta's adventures on the road would be a good way to introduce this book. Some good examples are: Chrysta's first months out (pp. 45–51; pp. 46–49, pap.); Chrysta meets Lissa (pp. 56–65; pp. 52–61, pap.); and Chrysta meets Dare (pp. 69–73; pp. 64–68, pap.). For a discussion of Chrysta's awareness of how she is changing, see pp. 18–20; pp. 16–20, pap.

Additional Selections

Pat gets more than bargained for when she decides to hitchhike home in Isabelle Holland's *Hitchhike* (Lippincott, 1977, $12.70; pap., Dell, $2.25). Fifteen-year-old Laurie learns valuable lessons in Caryl Hansen's *I Think I'm Having a Baby* (pap., Avon, 1982, $1.95). After her parents' divorce, Robin becomes involved with her mother's boarder and her problems in Pam Conrad's *Holding Me Here* (Harper, 1986, $11.89; pap., Bantam, $2.95). Abby confesses to her boyfriend Chip that she is being sexually abused by her father in Hadley Irwin's *Abby, My Love* (Macmillan, 1985, $11.95; pap., New Amer. Lib., $2.50). Fourteen-year-old Stephanie runs away from home and is soon caught up in the world of prostitution in Fran Arrick's *Steffie Can't Come Out to Play* (pap., Dell, 1979, $2.50). A girl's fling with the most popular boy in school has serious consequences in *In Love and In Trouble* (pap., Pocket Bks., 1981, $2.25) by Laurel Trivelpiece. A talented performing arts student is torn between two men in Marilyn Levy's *Life Is Not a Dress Rehearsal* (pap., Fawcett, 1984, $2.25). A girl copes with an unplanned pregnancy in John Neufeld's *Sharelle* (New Amer. Lib., 1983, $12.95; pap., $2.50).

About the Author (Dragonwagon, Crescent)
Bowden, Jane A., ed. *Contemporary Authors*. Detroit: Gale Research Co., 1977. Vols. 65–68, p. 178.
Commire, Anne, ed. *Something about the Author*. Detroit: Gale Research Co., 1977. Vol. 11, p. 81; updated 1985. Vol. 41, pp. 75–83.
Metzger, Linda, ed. *Contemporary Authors* (New Revision Series). Detroit: Gale Research Co., 1984. Vol. 12, pp. 143–144.

About the Author (Zindel, Paul)
Commire, Anne, ed. *Something about the Author*. Detroit: Gale Research Co., 1979. Vol. 16, pp. 283–290.
Estes, Glenn E., ed. *American Writers for Children since 1960: Fiction* (*Dictionary of Literary Biography*, Vol. 52). Detroit: Gale Research Co., 1986, pp. 405–410.
Holtze, Sally Holmes, ed. *Fifth Book of Junior Authors and Illustrators*. New York: Wilson, 1983, pp. 343–344.
Kirkpatrick, D. L., ed. *Twentieth-Century Children's Writers* (2nd edition). New York: St. Martin's, 1983, pp. 853–854.
Locher, Frances C., ed. *Contemporary Authors*. Detroit: Gale Research Co., 1978. Vols. 73–76, p. 659.

Senick, Gerard J., ed. *Children's Literature Review*. Detroit: Gale Research Co., 1978. Vol. 3, pp. 244–254.

Who's Who in America: 1986–1987 (44th edition). Chicago: Marquis Who's Who, Inc., 1986. Vol. 2, p. 3073.

Eyerly, Jeannette. *Someone to Love Me*
Lippincott, 1987, $11.89

For many years Jeannette Eyerly has been regarded as one of the foremost writers of "problem" novels for young adults that explore various social themes, as, in this case, premarital pregnancy. She writes with compassion and understanding in a simple, straightforward style. Some of her titles include *Radigan Cares* (Lippincott, 1970, $11.89; pap., Pocket Bks., $1.50), in which a boy's attraction to a girl leads to his involvement in political reform; *If I Love You Wednesday* (Lippincott, 1980, $12.25; pap., Archway, $1.95), about a boy who falls in love with his teacher; and *See Dave Run* (Lippincott, 1978, $12.95; pap., Pocket Bks., $2.25), in which a runaway's life ends in suicide. These novels are standard fare for junior high school students.

Plot Summary

Lance Carter is considered one of the prize catches of the senior class. He is popular and handsome and has curly blond hair and a fine "bod." He is also very attached to Stephanie Towne, another senior of the "in" crowd, who, in Lance's eyes, has only one fault: She won't have sex with him. Therefore, to satisfy this part of his nature, he looks around for suitable prey and finds it in a naive, somewhat mousy, fifteen-year-old sophomore.

Her name is Patrice Latta. She lives alone with her divorced mother, a receptionist in a law firm. Her father is Patrick Shannon, a Hollywood bit player who left his family when Patrice was in first grade to seek his fortune in movies. She has not seen her father in five years when he spent a few hours with her between planes. Her mother has had a series of boyfriends. The current one is Mr. Boesrup, an elder version of a yuppie and not inspiring in Patrice's eyes. There are few signs of affection and understanding in the Latta household, and Patrice feels left out of her mother's inner life and longs for something beyond the latchkey life she has lived all these years.

One day in January, when Patrice is walking home from school with her best, indeed, only true, friend, Lauren Spivak, Lance begins his campaign. He drives up to the two girls and offers Patrice a seemingly harmless ride home. She is flattered beyond belief and accepts. The next day the invitation is repeated, but this time the ride home involves stopping in Sherwood Park and a deep kiss that both shocks and excites Patrice. This after-school ritual continues and soon Patrice is hopelessly infatuated with this Greek God who ignores her in school but shows increased signs of affection during their now regular after-school meetings. Lance knows that Patrice's mother does not get home until early evening, and so his final move is made one afternoon when outside her home he asks to use the telephone. He also tours the house and in Patrice's bedroom begins to caress her. This leads to the inevitable "If you love me, you will," and because she loves him, she does. This is the first of many such assignations.

As weeks pass, Patrice blossoms with the love she believes is being reciprocated, but she also notices some disturbing physical changes, like bouts of nausea, particularly in the mornings, and undue feelings of fatigue. Her friend, Lauren, questions Patrice about her condition and Patrice blurts out the truth. Together they go to a Women's Health Center where Patrice has a urine pregnancy test. The results are positive, but the girl, who is so pitifully uninformed about sex that she is even careless about charting her menstrual periods, is only half-willing to accept the truth. She hopes that a mistake has been made.

Two nights later she entertains Lance at home while her mother is attending a concert with Mr. Boesrup. She makes elaborate preparations, but Lance only wants sex.

As days pass, Patrice notices further bodily changes and she tells Lance of her condition. He upbraids her for not taking proper precautions and cruelly suggests that the baby might be someone else's. He also tells her that at school's end (in another month) he will be leaving for a summer job in Colorado. Her condition becomes so noticeable that finally Patrice's mother confronts her with what is now an apparent truth. Patrice now admits that she is pregnant. Her mother's reaction is a selfish one. She worries only that Mr. Boesrup will find out and, therefore, she demands that there be an abortion. Not knowing what this involves, Patrice takes books out of the library and is so horrified at the graphic descriptions of these procedures that when her mother again approaches the subject, she becomes hysterical. Neighbors, including Mrs. Fawcett from next door, are aroused and intercede. Mrs. Latta is forced to change her mind.

At the public clinic where her mother takes her, Patrice undergoes a humiliating physical examination at the hands of the unsympathetic Dr. Doolittle, who tells them the baby is due in late November. The next night, with Lauren, she attends the high school commencement exercises and through tear-filled eyes sees Lance and Stephanie graduate.

She spends a lethargic and cheerless summer and is only prevented from becoming a total vegetable by the frequent visits of friend Lauren. Her mother breaks up with Mr. Boesrup, and Lance sends her $100 and a note telling her she should have an abortion. Later that summer his engagement to Stephanie is announced.

In the fall she enters an alternative high school where she attends half-day classes with other pregnant single girls and unwed mothers who bring their children to its day-care center. They are a dispirited group and the atmosphere is depressing. Patrice's friendship with a fellow student, Georgianna Jones, a girl with Raggedy Ann red hair, and a baby shower organized by Mrs. Fawcett shed a little light in her otherwise bleak life.

One day Patrice is rummaging through some family documents. On her mother's marriage certificate she discovers that her parents were married only five months before her birth. That night, mother and daughter talk and Mrs. Latta confesses that as a young, inexperienced girl she, too, had confused sex with love.

In late November, as predicted, her baby—a fine, healthy boy—is born. In the hospital Patrice is visited by Mr. Boesrup. He now realizes that her mother broke off their friendship because she was too ashamed of her daughter's condition to tell him the truth. He asks Patrice to intercede on his behalf, which she happily does.

When the day comes to name her baby, Patrice realizes that to call him Lance, as she had planned, would be wrong. That part of her life is dead. Instead, gazing at the baby she loves, she names him Chance.

Thematic Material

This is a heart-wrenching tale of a trusting and innocent girl who, in her need for love, succumbs to the urgings of a calculating young man. Without undue preaching, the author paints such a dismal picture of the seamy, distasteful side of unmarried pregnancy that it decidedly becomes a cautionary tale. Details of abortion procedures and clinical routines contrast shockingly with the girl's abysmal lack of information on these subjects and make an important if unstated plea for greater attention to sex education. Mother and daughter relations are interestingly explored, as are themes involving friendship and family life.

Book Talk Material

Describing Patrice's situation and the advances made by Lance should be used to introduce this book. There are only a few specific passages suitable for presentation to a group, but two could be Lance's first move (pp. 3–5) and mother-daughter relations (pp. 14–17).

Additional Selections

Anna discovers she is pregnant after her boyfriend leaves her in Mildred Lee's *Sycamore Year* (Lothrop, 1974, $11.88; pap., New Amer. Lib., $2.50); and in Richard Peck's *Don't Look and It Won't Hurt* (pap., Avon, 1979, $2.50), a fifteen-year-old girl discovers her older sister is pregnant. Two teenagers are forced into a marriage for which they are ill-prepared in *Mr. and Mrs. Bo Jo Jones* (Putnam, 1967, $9.95; pap., New Amer. Lib., $2.25; condensed in *More Juniorplots*, Bowker, 1977, pp. 157–160) by Ann Head. An unwed father wants to keep his baby in Jeannette Eyerly's *He's My Baby, Now* (pap., Pocket Bks., 1985, $2.25); and a sought-after boyfriend tells Trudy, *You Would If You Loved Me* (pap., Avon, 1982, $2.50) in a novel by Nora Stirling. Rape is the subject of Gloria D. Miklowitz's *Did You Hear What Happened to Andrea?* (Delacorte, 1979, $7.95; pap., Dell, $2.25). *The Abortion Controversy* (Messner, 1987, $9.79; pap., $4.95) by Carol Emmens explores the pros and cons of this issue. After losing a leg in a car accident, Izzy reevaluates her life and friendship in Cynthia Voigt's *Izzy, Willy-Nilly* (Atheneum, 1986, $14.95).

About the Author

Commire, Anne, ed. *Something about the Author*. Detroit: Gale Research Co., 1973. Vol. 4, p. 80.

Evory, Ann, ed. *Contemporary Authors* (New Revision Series). Detroit: Gale Research Co., 1981. Vol. 4, p. 227.

Holtze, Sally Holmes, ed. *Fifth Book of Junior Authors and Illustrators*. New York: Wilson, 1983, pp. 109–111.

Metzger, Linda, ed. *Contemporary Authors* (New Revision Series). Detroit: Gale Research Co., 1987. Vol. 19, pp. 181–182.

Who's Who in America: 1986–1987 (44th edition). Chicago: Marquis Who's Who, Inc., 1986. Vol. 1, p. 842.

Fleischman, Paul. *Rear-View Mirrors*
Harper, 1986, lib. bdg., $10.89

Paul Fleischman is the son of the distinguished writer of juveniles, Sid Fleischman. Where his father has concentrated on the tall tale exploits of his hero, the wily McBroom, Paul has specialized in award-winning mysteries. Two of his popular titles are *Graven Images: Three Stories* (Harper, 1982, $10.89) and *Path of the Pale Horse* (Harper, 1985, $10.89). Unlike these, *Rear-View Mirrors* deals with delicate father-daughter relationships and is popular with junior high readers.

Plot Summary

For Olivia Tate, the short period between high school graduation and a month spent at a "dig" in Maine is a time to earn a different sort of diploma, a rite of passage as it were. Its quest has brought her back to the small New Hampshire town of North Hooton, and to the image of a father she barely knew and has now lost. Back to the white clapboard house that will be hers when she is twenty-one—if she wants it—and the old barn that houses the green ten-speed Raleigh, now hers as well.

Just a year before, Olivia could not even remember ever having seen Hannibal Tate, whom her mother had divorced when Olivia was eight months old. Since that time she and her mother have lived in the intellectual atmosphere of Berkeley, California, where her mother teaches sociology. Not once in all those years of growing up had her father called or written or, as far as Olivia knows, ever inquired about the health and well-being of his only child.

And then suddenly one day at the end of her junior year, there was the cryptic note from New Hampshire, with a bus ticket as an invitation.

Curiosity brought Olivia to New Hampshire that summer and her first remembered meeting with the strange man who was Hannibal Tate, a huge—so that's where I got my height, she had thought upon meeting—slightly flabby writer of mystery stories, a gibing, irreverent debunker of fatherly ways, and, as Olivia quickly realizes, a man desperately sick, sick with the fear of his own death.

Indeed, Olivia soon learns that her father's fear is behind the reason for her unexpected visit. Certain that he has heart trouble—which he claims runs in the family—and sure of his own speedy demise, he has suggested that his only child spend a month with him, sort of, as Olivia realizes, a recruitment to see if she is a worthwhile recipient of his house and his worldly possessions.

From the start, father and daughter play a game of verbal one-upmanship, sparring with words, as slowly, ever so slowly, they come to know, to respect, although perhaps never to say they love each other. And Olivia also begins to learn of another way of life—of living with ever-present mosquitoes and worshiping the Boston Red Sox, of discovering the beauty of butterflies, garden mulch, and Bluebird ale.

But almost as quickly as it has begun, it ends. For some time after her return from that first trip, her father is killed by lightning, not the death he had envisaged, but his death nonetheless.

And now Olivia is back. Ready for college in the fall, she is to spend the month of July at a dig in rural Maine. But first she must return to her father's house to fulfill a journey she feels she must undertake. Each year her father would get out the old dust-covered bike from the barn and travel what Olivia discovers to be a seventy-mile loop around Lake Kiskadee. There was one important stipulation, however, to the journey as her father explained it; it must be completed in one day, and by sunset.

As Olivia sets off on her own rite of passage, she recalls the month she had spent with the strange man who was her father. Along the way, she comes to feel a kinship with the New England countryside he so loved, and she renews a friendship with Owen, the young man whom she had accused her father of trying to fix her up with the year before.

At journey's end, Olivia has reached a new kind of graduation. Perhaps she is not the sort of daughter her father would have chosen; perhaps he was not the sort of father she would have wished for. But she is not a copy of either of her parents, she realizes. She is simply her own person. Last summer her father had said at her departure, "I think you've got the inside track," meaning as position of his heir. As Olivia locks up the clapboard house and heads off to Maine and her future, she feels that somehow she has received Hannibal Tate's blessing.

Thematic Material

Shyly and with good humor, this book details the often painful process of coming to know and to love a parent who does not fit the conventional mode. It is also the story of a young girl's maturing, of coming to feel a sense of her own worth as an individual. The characters of the clipped New Englander and the outwardly self-assured but vulnerable young girl are understated but touching in their realism.

Book Talk Material

A brief description of the meeting of father and daughter can be used to initiate a discussion of the sometimes painful growth of intimate family relationships. Passages that can be used in a book talk on the growth of understanding and respect between people are: the unemotional first meeting between Olivia and her father (pp. 14–19); her father's discussion of her mother (pp. 48–50); and their first hint of an affectionate interchange when her father explains his imaginary "French baseball league" and Olivia responds (pp. 83–86).

Additional Selections

A thirteen-year-old girl comes to terms with her new step-family in Susan Terris's *No Scarlet Ribbons* (Farrar, 1981, $10.95; pap., Avon, $2.25), and at summer camp, three girls try to rid themselves of their rich, shabby image in Pat Lee Gauch's *Night Talks* (Putnam, 1983, $10.95; pap., Pocket Bks., $2.25). Darcie searches for her father and the paternal love she never had while also being charmed by the enigmatic Roman in *What I Did for Roman* (Harper, 1987, $12.89) by Pam Conrad. Twelve-year-old Isaac's relations with his father worsen after the death of his older brother in Janni Howker's novel set in early twentieth-century England, *Isaac Campion* (Greenwillow, 1987, $10.25). A girl tries to exclude a returning mother from her life in Patricia Calvert's *Yesterday's Daughter* (Scribner, 1986, $11.95). A lesbian relationship between two teenagers causes small town prejudices to emerge in Sandra Scoppettone's *Happy Endings Are All Alike* (Harper, 1978, $11.89; pap., Dell, $1.75), and Melanie discovers that her boyfriend is gay in *Happily Ever After* (pap., Scholastic, 1986, $2.25) by Hila Colman. Two young people are devastated by their parents' plan to separate in Barbara Dana's *Necessary Parties* (Harper, 1986, $13.89).

About the Author

Commire, Anne, ed. *Something about the Author.* Detroit: Gale Research Co., 1983. Vol. 32, p. 71; updated 1985. Vol. 39, pp. 72–73.

Holtze, Sally Holmes, ed. *Fifth Book of Junior Authors and Illustrators.* New York: Wilson, 1983, pp. 114–116.
May, Hal, ed. *Contemporary Authors.* Detroit: Gale Research Co., 1985. Vol. 113, p. 158.

Kerr, M. E.   *Gentlehands*
Harper, 1978, $11.89; pap., Bantam, $2.50

During the course of many of her young adult novels, M. E. Kerr often has her protagonists facing two major problems simultaneously. For example, in *Is That You, Miss Blue?* (Harper, 1976, $11.89; pap., Dell, $1.75; condensed in *More Juniorplots*, Bowker, 1977, pp. 35–37), Flanders must adapt to life in a new prep school while coping with ambivalent feelings toward her separated parents. In a later novel for more mature readers, *Night Kites* (Harper, 1986, $11.22), Erick alienates his friends when he beds down with his best pal's girlfriend while he also makes drastic personal adjustments to the news that his beloved elder brother has AIDS. Similarly, in *Gentlehands,* an average sixteen-year-old boy, Buddy Boyle, faces conflicts with his parents over his infatuation with an older teenager, wealthy Skye Pennington and, at the same time, adjusts to growing suspicions about his grandfather's unsavory past. This novel is read and enjoyed by both boys and girls in grades seven through nine.

Plot Summary

Buddy lives with his mother and father, who is a sergeant on the local police force, and five-year-old brother, Streaker, in the fashionable summer resort town of Seaville, New York, close to Montauk Point, at the tip of Long Island. His sixteenth summer begins most promisingly. He has a job waiting tables at the Sweet Mouth Soda Shoppe run by a pot-smoking ex-actor named Kick Richards and, through this job, has met and become enchanted by Skye, attractive, sophisticated daughter of the man who heads Penn Industries and owns the Pennington summer mansion, Beauregard, complete with a huge swimming pool and servants including Peacock, the butler. Buddy's parents, particularly his father, are less than enthusiastic about this attachment and believe that Buddy's reaching for friends outside his class will only cause problems.

Sensing his parents' hostilities and inwardly ashamed of his middle-class roots, Buddy takes Skye to meet and, he hopes, be impressed by his grandfather, Frank Trenker, who lives some twelve miles away at Montauk Point. Mr. Trenker is still something of an unknown quantity to Buddy. He was born in Germany and was forced to marry Buddy's maternal grandmother because of pregnancy. After her daughter's birth, Buddy's grandmother migrated to America and subsequently was granted a divorce. Many years later, some time after World War II, Mr. Trenker also came to America and settled nearby but, because of the indifference he showed toward both his wife and daughter, has been almost totally ignored by the Boyles. Mr. Trenker is a most cultivated and cultured man who loves opera, knows wine, and displays a style and wisdom toward life and living that both Buddy and, as expected, Skye find captivating.

Buddy lies to his parents about working overtime in order to spend an afternoon with Skye and her snobby friends around the Pennington pool. Here he meets a houseguest, Nick DeLucca, an investigative reporter who, like Buddy, seems out of place in this waspy, upper-class environment. Mr. Boyle discovers the truth and when his son returns home, he punches him twice in the face and grounds him for two weeks. But when Buddy is invited by Skye to attend a picnic at Beauregard he again accepts. After Skye and her friends tell some anti-Semitic jokes around the bonfire, Mr. DeLucca reveals that he is a Jew and recites a poem called "Gentlehands," written by his cousin during her last days in Auschwitz. Ashamed and embarrassed, Skye asks to leave the party and persuades Buddy to take her to visit his grandfather. During this evening of good music and conversation, Buddy pretends to be an experienced wine drinker but instead drinks too much and passes out. The next morning Mr. Trenker loans him his jeep to get to work and Buddy, feeling the rift with his parents to be irreparable, moves in with his grandfather, whom he now not only respects but loves.

Mr. Trenker is able to affect a partial reconciliation when he invites his daughter to have dinner with him and Buddy. The dinner is interrupted by Trenker's dog Mignon, who has discovered a raccoon caught in a neighbor's steel trap. As he does with all animals and birds, Mr. Trenker shows tenderness toward this wounded animal.

One day, Buddy sees DeLucca spying on his grandfather's house and later, while they were both under the influence of marijuana that Buddy has found at the soda shop, Skye reveals that the reporter is on the trail of the sadistic SS concentration camp guard nicknamed Gentlehands, who played opera recordings while his victims went to their deaths. DeLucca believes him to be in the area.

Later that evening, Mr. Trenker plays on the phonograph for Buddy and Skye an aria from his favorite opera *Tosca*, "O Dolci Mani," translation, "O gentle hands." Buddy is convinced that it is only a coincidence, but evidence mounts against Mr. Trenker and soon the local paper prints a news item headlined "Montauk Man Accused of Being Nazi." Fearful of being involved in the scandal, Mr. Boyle orders his son to come back home. Buddy continues to believe it is all a mistake even when Skye's brother, Og, shows him DeLucca's folder of evidence. When he once more visits his grandfather, Buddy finds that Mr. Trenker is being harrassed by threatening calls and they discover in the car the body of his dog Mignon, whose throat has been slit. Mr. Trenker tells Buddy that it is too dangerous for him to visit again. He asks Buddy to phone the Stanton Stamp Shop in New York City run by his friend, Werner, to tell him that "the package from Trenker is on its way." With tears rolling down his cheeks, Buddy bids farewell to his grandfather.

When the story hits the New York papers with further evidence and photographs that also implicate a certain Dr. Werner Renner, even Buddy must accept the truth. When he learns that his grandfather has left Montauk he realizes that the "package" was actually Trenker. He tells the authorities about the stamp shop. Renner is caught but his grandfather escapes.

By the end of the summer, the Penningtons are getting ready to leave Seaville; Skye to enter college at Bryn Mawr. Buddy knows that the gap that separates them will only widen and he probably will not see her again. It has been for Buddy a summer of losses but also a summer in which he gained maturity and memories.

Thematic Material

During this novel, Buddy grows toward emotional adulthood through the painful lessons of one summer. The novel explores such topics as the difficulty inherent in facing truth; family loyalties; coping with disillusionment; the differences between true and superficial values; and the necessity to uphold important values even though loved ones might be adversely affected. The necessity of facing consequences for one's decisions is treated when Buddy makes some unwise choices, as well as when he makes the final, fateful decision to reveal his grandfather's whereabouts. Class differences and the difficulties these can produce are well handled, as is the material related to the Holocaust and anti-Semitism.

Book Talk Material

Without revealing too much about Mr. Trenker, the book talk could introduce Buddy, his home town, and his two new friends of the summer and discuss how both relationships are causing him problems. Specific passages: Skye and Buddy visit his grandfather for the first time (pp. 20–30; pp. 18–23, pap.); Buddy describes the Penningtons to his parents but his lying is found out by his father (pp. 52–58; pp. 39–43, pap.); the picnic, anti-Semitism, and the introduction to "Gentlehands" (pp. 71–76; pp. 53–56, pap.); and Mrs. Boyle visits her father (pp. 106–110; pp. 78–81, pap.).

Additional Selections

Different backgrounds are explored in Todd Strasser's *Workin' for Peanuts* (Delacorte, 1983, $13.95; pap., Dell, $2.50), in which Melissa's father owns the company for which her boyfriend works. When cruelty, drinking, and sex become the chief pursuits of the "in" crowd, Robin decides to drop out in Norma Howe's *In with the Out Crowd* (Houghton, 1986, $12.95). A teenage boy begins to understand himself while adjusting to his grandfather's Alzheimer's disease in Norma Klein's *Going Backwards* (Scholastic, 1987, $12.95). Similar subjects are explored in Richard Graber's *Doc* (Harper, 1986, $13.95). An adolescent German girl discovers her aunt was once a member of the Hitler Youth movement in *The Visit* (Viking, 1982, $10.95) by T. Degens, and a young girl faces growing up in a Nazi concentration camp in Sara Zyskind's *Stolen Years* (Lerner, 1981, $11.95; pap., New Amer. Lib., $3.50). A glimpse of what life was like in Nazi Europe is dramatically given in the true story by Aranka Siegal, *Upon the Head of the Goat: A Childhood in Hungary, 1939–1944* (Farrar, 1981, $10.95; pap., New Amer. Lib., $2.25) and its sequel, *Grace in the Wilderness: After the Liberation 1945–1948* (Farrar, 1985, $11.95). The story of Nazi war criminals is told in Richard B. Lyttle's *Nazi Hunting* (Watts, 1982, $8.90).

About the Author

Commire, Anne, ed. *Something about the Author.* Detroit: Gale Research Co., 1980. Vol. 20, pp. 124–126 (under Marijane Meaker).

de Montreville, Doris, and Crawford, Elizabeth D., eds. *Fourth Book of Junior Authors and Illustrators.* New York: Wilson, 1978, pp. 210–212.

Kirkpatrick, D. L., ed. *Twentieth-Century Children's Writers* (2nd edition). New York: St. Martin's, 1983, pp. 428–429.

May, Hal, ed. *Contemporary Authors.* Detroit: Gale Research Co., 1983. Vol. 107, pp. 332–336 (under Marijane Meaker).

Sarkissian, Adele, ed. *Something about the Author: Autobiography Series.* Detroit: Gale Research Co., 1986. Vol. 1, pp. 141–154.

Who's Who in America: 1986–1987 (44th edition). Chicago: Marquis Who's Who, Inc., 1986. Vol. 2, p. 1902 (under Marijane Meaker).

Klass, Sheila Solomon. *The Bennington Stitch*

Scribner, 1985, $12.95; pap., Bantam, $2.50 (same pagination)

In each of her novels for young adults, Sheila Solomon Klass writes about adolescents and their problems with rare sensitivity and feeling. In *To See My Mother Dance* (Scribner, 1981, $10.95; pap., Fawcett, $1.95), a young girl trying to adjust to life with a new stepmother fantasizes about her real mother, a dancer who abandoned her years ago. The problems of coping with a father's remarriage are also dealt with in *Alive and Starting Over* (Scribner, 1983, $10.95; pap., Fawcett, $1.95). *The Bennington Stitch* is narrated by the central character, Amy, and takes place from January through June of a typical school year in Eastfield, a small town in Connecticut close to New York City. Klass's novels are enjoyed by readers in grades seven through nine.

Plot Summary

Amy Hamilton and Rob Barton, best friends since nursery school, are both suffering from acute cases of parental great expectations. When Amy was born, by a complicated caesarian section, her mother announced in the delivery room that her daughter's name was Amelia Bloomer Hamilton and that she would attend Bennington College. This caused the attending physician, Rob's father, Dr. Barton, almost to drop a stitch during the postoperative procedures. Dr. Barton, in turn, has decreed that, because his older son Pete left home four years ago to play professional baseball, the mantle of the Barton family medical tradition has, therefore, fallen on Rob, who must become a doctor. Neither is happy with the parental choices.

Amy, whose father died in a motorcycle accident fifteen years ago when she was two, is disturbed about disappointing her mother, an English teacher at Amy's high school and a closet novelist who years before had been denied the quality education she desired. Nevertheless, Amy feels for several reasons that college is not for her. She has a severe psychological block toward examinations that has caused her great academic problems at school, but more importantly her interests are totally unlike her mother's and tend toward sewing and cooking rather than the liberal arts. Rob's situation is less complicated. He is an excellent student in all subjects but his true talents lie in art, where his teachers believe he has extraordinary gifts.

It is now mid-January of their senior year and events are reaching a climax because, as their popular college counselor and demented movie buff Mr. O (short for O'Brian) tells them, senior SAT scores will arrive shortly and college application deadlines are approaching. When the scores do arrive, they are as expected—Rob's are brilliant, Amy's below average. The parents continue their pressure to the point, in Rob's case, where his father refuses to pay tuition for anything other than a pre-med program. They commiserate with one another but are at a loss for a solution.

Suave, sophisticated, and single Uncle George, a success in New York publishing, visits for a weekend at the bidding of his sister, Doris, Amy's mother. Her immediate problem is lack of funding for the school's literary magazine, *Pen & Ink*, and she asks him to find an inexpensive publisher in New York. Amy is very fond of Uncle George, who shows great understanding and sympathy for her problem. He advises a long talk with Mr. O, a man whom he thinks his sister should have married years ago.

While walking in town, Amy takes her uncle to a bakeshop owned by Jessie, the attractive mother of her school friend Jan. Jessie is separated from her husband, a would-be sociology professor. George and Jessie become immediate friends.

Amy meets with Mr. O and convinces him that a noncollege plan would be best for her; but when he meets with Doris, he has no more success convincing her than Rob has had with his father. An armed standoff sets in for the winter months.

Uncle George returns with good news about a publisher whose printing fees for the *Pen & Ink* will be only $200. How to raise that amount is the subject of a meeting of interested students at Jessie's Colonial Cookery. It is suggested that the students bake specialty breads in the school on Sunday for George to take to New York to sell to a gourmet food store he patronizes. Doris gets the permission of the principal, Mr. Rooter, and George begins a series of weekend commutes until the money is collected. This also allows him to visit Jessie frequently, a situation Jan finds upsetting because she hopes for a parental reconciliation.

Spring comes and with it Senior Project time when each student spends six weeks in an apprentice-type situation exploring a work area of interest. Though his father objects, Rob chooses art therapy at the State Psychiatric Hospital. Amy is intrigued by a placement notice sent in by an elderly quilter advertising for a helper. She applies. Doris is not thrilled at the idea, but Mr. O convinces her when he admits that the quilter is really his feisty and softhearted spinster Aunt Edna who lives alone in West Hartford some miles away. He also explains that in accepting this opportunity, Amy will be learning a valuable and fast-disappearing art form.

Amy spends an idyllic, productive six weeks with this wonderfully wise old lady. Amy even creates a unique stitch using wooden beads. In honor of her mother's ordeal years ago, she calls it the Bennington Stitch. When it is time to go, she promises Aunt Edna that she will ask permission from her mother to return in the summer as a full-time apprentice.

Doris, now realizing that she must consent to her daughter's happiness, agrees reluctantly. Mr. O visits with news that Bennington is offering an off-campus master's program in creative writing. Amy's mother applies and is accepted. There will be a Bennington graduate in the family after all. Uncle George does not fare quite as well. Much to Jan's delight, Jessie and her husband reconcile, so George is again seeking a fiancé.

Graduation takes place. Rob has decided to enter the arts program in a state university and, through help from his brother and part-time jobs, go it alone. Amy is eagerly looking forward to the summer, particularly now that her mother and Mr. O have announced wedding plans. She muses that in her case happy endings are the best of all.

Thematic Material

Clashes between parents and children concerning career plans are not uncommon, and this novel deals with this subject honestly, with candor and sometimes humor. Two solutions—one amicable and the other not—are presented, but the novel is also a plea to let young people with proper self-knowledge become independent and determine their own futures. Both Amy and Rob are likable, forthright young adults with a loving relationship and the inner strength to question their parents' unwise decisions. The adult romances form interesting subplots.

Book Talk Material

A brief discussion of situations when questioning parental authority is advisable or of the danger in preplanning children's lives could be used to introduce this novel. Some interesting passages: Amy's birth and a discussion of her name (pp. 8–11); the SAT scores arrive (pp. 21–25); mother and the SATs (pp. 30–33); Rob and his family situation (pp. 50–53); and Amy discusses her future with Mr. O (pp. 45–60).

Additional Selections

In Sheila Greenwald's *Blissful Joy and the SAT's* (Little, 1982, $12.95; pap., Dell, $2.50), Bliss scores high on grades and popularity but not on the SAT's. Usually debonair tour guide Palmer Swain is so smitten by Liana that he is overcome by hiccups in Peter Silsbee's *Love among the Hiccups* (Bradbury, 1987, $12.95). The complexities of mother-daughter relationships are explored in Lynn Hall's *Letting Go* (Scribner, 1987, $11.95). Sandy Fishman is saddled with a Jewish mother who only wants her daughter to get thin and get married in Merrill Joan Gerber's delightful *Also Known As Sadzia! The Belly Dancer* (Harper, 1987, $12.89). Another mother-daughter conflict is explored in Isabelle Holland's *Toby the Splendid* (Walker, 1987, $12.95). Three generations of mother-daughter relationships are chronicled in Peter Burchard's *Sea Change* (Farrar, 1984, $10.95), and Tansey's life seems over when she discovers that her mother has abandoned her in Stephanie S. Tolan's *The Liberation of Tansey Warner* (pap., Dell, 1982, $1.95). In Barbara Corcoran's *You Put Up with Me, I'll Put Up with You* (Atheneum, 1987, $12.95), a seventh grader and her mother move in with two other families to open a cooperative business.

About the Author

Commire, Anne, ed. *Something about the Author*. Detroit: Gale Research Co., 1986. Vol. 45, pp. 119–120.

Evory, Ann, ed. *Contemporary Authors* (First Revision Series). Detroit: Gale Research Co., 1979. Vols. 37–40, pp. 299–300.

Kinsman, Clare D., ed. *Contemporary Authors*. Detroit: Gale Research Co., 1973. Vols. 37–40, pp. 273–274.

Metzger, Linda, ed. *Contemporary Authors* (New Revision Series). Detroit: Gale Research Co., 1984. Vol. 13, pp. 295–296.

Landis, J. D. *Daddy's Girl*
Morrow, 1984, $10.25; pap., Pocket Bks., $2.50

J. D. (John David) Landis is also known for his novel about two girls who are rivals in the world of ballet, *The Sisters Impossible* (Knopf, 1979, $6.99; pap., Bantam, $2.25). In *Daddy's Girl*, a novel about marital infidelity, this otherwise grim theme is lightened by a hilarious subplot involving the Simonize family. Although the story is told with tact and discretion, because the author is trying to depict teenagers and their conversation somewhat accurately, the language sometimes gets a bit raunchy. This book is enjoyed in grades seven through nine.

Plot Summary

Until that fateful Monday, life seemed ideal for thirteen-year-old Jennie Marcowitz. She is an excellent student, particularly in French, at Ms. Richter's Feminist Day School in the upper West Side of Manhattan. In addition to the conventional subjects and Women's Studies, students are taught at Ms. Richter's that all men are beasts and not to be trusted. The few boys that attend the school, including her brilliant but totally lunatic best friend, Howie Simonize, must either endure the humiliation of using the Women's Room when nature calls or endure the agonies of abstinence. Jennie's other friends are rich Rita Fleugleman, who is so adroit at shoplifting that her nickname is Rita Bandita, and the girl who has circulated the unproven claim to have balled every boy of worth in school, dirty-mouthed Kathleen McDuffie, Jr.

Tom and Helen Marcowitz, Jennie's parents, are in their early forties and still as in love as on their wedding day, but now they share this love with their only daughter whom Tom calls Daddy's girl. Her adored father is a successful importer of French wines and her mother is a prominent psychologist, whose first book on the family has just been published.

But back to that Monday. Jennie is walking home after a late tennis practice, when on the street she sees her father passionately kissing a young blond. She is stunned by the sight and rushes home. She shows visible disquiet with her mother and is fearful of seeing her father. However, he does not arrive home, claiming a dinner engagement with a wine dealer from Bordeaux. Jennie fears the worst and suspects an assignation; but later that night she hears from her room where she has been crying her father's return with the gentleman wine dealer in tow. Perhaps her fears are groundless.

The next afternoon Jennie skips school and phones her father's office to check on his whereabouts. To disguise her voice, she pretends to be a Frenchwoman, Mademoiselle Baiser. The trick works better than expected. Her father thinks the call is from a girl he affectionately calls Susan and says he will meet her shortly.

Jennie waits for her father to leave his office building and follows him by cab to an upper Manhattan address. He enters a small apartment building. On the address plate Jennie sees the name Susan Lacoutre. She telephones Miss Lacoutre and without identifying herself asks for Tom Marcowitz. When he comes to the phone, she hangs up.

Too miserable to go home, Jennie visits friend Howie, who is in the living room, fully clothed, paddling in a prefab swimming pool, a gift from shoplifting Rita Bandita. Later, in his room, Jennie, in her confusion and bewilderment, demands that Howie seduce her but the scene ends in a fit of giggles and a confession from Howie that he has a new girlfriend.

That evening Jennie can no longer avoid a confrontation with her father. As the two clean up after dinner, she asks him to give up Susan Lacoutre. At first, he denies the affair, but then with tears in his eyes, admits the truth. He asks Jennie not to tell her mother about Susan but to meet him for lunch the next day.

Once more she sneaks out of school but not before applying makeup in the Women's Room much to the embarrassment of Shelden Farber, who is using the facilities (Shelden later transfers to an all-boys school).

With feelings of both excitement and dread, Jennie goes to Le Cygne, a very fashionable restaurant, where she meets Susan and her father. Susan is a poised and attractive twenty-two-year-old graduate student at Columbia. While Tom peruses the menu and orders lunch, Susan tells of their first meeting a year ago when she unsuccessfully applied for a position in his firm and of their love for one another that has culminated in a proposal of marriage from Tom that she has refused. Wretched beyond belief both for herself and her mother, Jennie returns home.

The next day at school, she is summoned to Ms. Richter's office, called the Ovary because of its shape, to explain her absences. The principal, surrounded by her feminist doll collection, misunderstands Jennie's explanation and thinks Tom is making sexual advances toward his daughter. The mix-up is resolved but Jennie does not receive the hoped-for advice to help answer her own problem.

Again she leaves school early, this time to talk to her mother in her office. When Jennie bursts into uncontrollable sobbing, her mother realizes that her daughter now knows what she has known for many months. They talk openly about her father's infidelity. Her mother says loving someone is never easy and often it demands extraordinary acceptance and understanding.

In time, wounds are healed. Susan gives up Tom, and Jennie, who has transferred to another school, regains Howie. Although love reenters her family circle, Jennie knows she will never be Daddy's girl again.

Thematic Material

This is a touching, often anguished, account of a youngster's discovery and adjustment to a parent's sexual infidelity. Coping with disillusionment when an adored one's flaws are uncovered is also an important theme. The power of love and compassion to help overcome problems is well portrayed, as are the difficulties that even the happiest marriages can face. The sexual awakening of teenagers and the absurdities of overzealous feminists are important subthemes. Jennie is an appealing character in both her vulnerability and her ingenuity, and Howie Simonize and his family are so zany that they must be read about to be believed.

Book Talk Material

Introducing Jennie and her encounter with her father and his girlfriend on the street should interest readers. Some passages are: seeing the kiss (pp.12–14; pp. 12–14, pap.); phoning her father's office (pp. 60–64; pp. 57–61, pap.); and calling Susan's apartment (pp. 86–91; pp. 82–86, pap.). Some humorous passages are: Ms. Richter's school (pp. 2–4; pp. 2–8, pap.); the cab ride following her father (pp. 69–77; pp. 65–73, pap.); meeting Howie (pp. 99–105; pp. 93–99, pap.); and the would-be seduction (pp. 106–116; pp. 100–109, pap.).

Additional Selections

J. D. Landis's *Joey and the Girls* (Bantam, 1984, $2.95), for mature readers, explores the life of an offbeat hero who has everything, but whose life is coming apart. Carrie is jealous about her father's growing attachment to his secretary and tries to make him pay more attention to her in Nancy J. Hopper's *Carrie's Games* (Dutton, 1987, $11.95). In *Family Secrets* by Norma Klein (Fawcett, 1987, $2.95), Leslie discovers that her mother is having an affair with the father of her best friend. A daughter and father face conflicts when a new family moves onto their citrus farm in Vera and Bill Cleaver's *Hazel Rye* (Lippincott, 1983, $11.89; pap., Harper, $2.95). From her boyfriend Brian, Stephanie learns about men in general and fathers in particular in Mary Ann Gray's *The Truth about Fathers* (Bradbury, 1982, $9.95). Rebecca Walker's father is accused of embezzling in Susan Shreve's *The Masquerade* (pap., Dell, 1981, $2.25). In Janet Taylor Lisle's *Sirens and Spies* (Bradbury, 1985, $12.95; pap., Berkley, $2.50), a girl discovers her idol has feet of clay. In the humorously told *Maggie, Too* (Harcourt, 1985, $11.95) by Joan Lowery Nixon, a twelve-year-old girl gradually gets to know her very busy father.

About the Author

Who's Who in America: 1986–1987 (44th edition). Chicago: Marquis Who's Who, Inc., 1986. Vol. 2, p. 1615.

Lasky, Kathryn. *Pageant*
Four Winds, 1986, $12.95

Kathryn Lasky's output of books for young adults covers a wide range of places and times. For example, in *Night Journey* (Viking, 1986, $12.95; pap., Penguin, $4.95), the action alternates between present and past as a thirteen-year-old girl keeps her great-grandmother company and listens to the story of the family's escape from czarist Russia. On the other hand, the subject of *Beyond the Divide* (Macmillan, 1983, $11.95; pap., Dell, $2.95) is the grueling trek into the American West of 1850 by a young Amish girl and her father. *Pageant* takes place during the turbulent 1960s in the United States. These novels are intended for a junior high school audience.

Plot Summary

It is 1960, and thirteen-year-old Sarah Benjamin's life alternates from boredom to disaster to excitement. A self-proclaimed assimilated Jew in stuffy and overwhelmingly Christian Stuart Hall, Indianapolis's exclusive girls' school, Sarah has strong opinions about almost everything. She thinks black stable-boy statues on the lawns of her well-to-do neighborhood are racist; she thinks Stuart Hall has too many stupid rules about everything in the world; and she thinks that John F. Kennedy is going to win the next presidential election.

November finds Sarah as a shepherd in the annual school pageant, a role she thinks is impossibly boring and more than a little ridiculous. But election day finds her on top of the world at the news of Kennedy's election, an excitement she can share only with her older sister Marla, a senior at Stuart Hall, and with another friend. Together the girls make up the only Democratic supporters in the entire WASP enclave.

With Kennedy now president, Sarah enters her sophomore year filled with his dream of a New Frontier, which she hopes will extend into her own life. But November once again finds her as a shepherd in the annual pageant. And even though she is still secure in the loving warmth of her parents, Sarah's world slowly begins to turn sour. Marla has gone off to college in the East; Sarah's best friend has become more interested in a boy than in sharing things with her; and Aunt Hattie, who manages a strange assortment of performing artists (including the eccentric and aging Serge Vronsky) and is usually in New York or roaming about the globe, more or less becomes an unwanted permanent fixture in Marla's old room.

In November of her junior year, once again Sarah Benjamin is a bored shepherd. And more and more she rebels in small ways against the strict conservatism of the school.

Added to the stultifying atmosphere of Stuart Hall, Sarah begins to run up against the all too real world. A classmate becomes pregnant and must leave school; Marla is too busy with school and career and a romantic interest to "be there" for Sarah as she once was; and her first real date turns into a nasty experience with a preppy bigot. And perhaps worst of all for Sarah, she cannot understand how family and friends seem to regard sex as some kind of joke she does not share.

The pains of growing up reach a climax in 1963, when, once again in her shepherd's role, Sarah decides to make a brief, little-thought-out escape from the atmosphere that is choking her. In a strange turn of fate, she picks November 21 to run off—the day John F. Kennedy is assassinated. The death of her idol and the consequences of her own hasty actions forever change the course of life for Sarah Benjamin.

Covering her tracks so that she will not be missed by the school or by her parents for some time, and with little actual thought of where she will go, Sarah sets off in her car and finds herself on the highway headed for New York City. Armed with Cokes and candy bars and still wearing, for a time, her shepherd's cloak from the pageant, Sarah finally decides that she is heading for the comfort and counsel of her sister Marla.

Although she is inexperienced as a driver, Sarah reaches the New Jersey Turnpike without mishap, and it is there that she learns of the death of the president she so admires. Devastated by the news and with tears blinding her vision, Sarah reaches her sister's New York apartment only to discover that Marla has acquired a roommate—his name is Pinchas Rozans.

Sarah realizes she cannot stay with her sister under these conditions, and Aunt Hattie, as usual, is out of town. Then she remembers Serge Vronsky, and it is to Serge that Sarah pours out her heartaches and frustrations—the president's death, Marla's leaving, Aunt Hattie's intrusion in her life, and the choking conservatism of her school.

After her parents are notified of her whereabouts and while Sarah awaits their arrival, she makes an important decision about her future. She cannot go back to Indianapolis; her happiness is elsewhere. With her parents' reluctant approval, Sarah decides to remain in New York City with Aunt Hattie and finish high school there. And before she starts college, a stint in the Peace Corps looms in her future. Sarah Benjamin, former shepherd, has come home.

Thematic Material

With much wit and compassion, Kathryn Lasky tells the story of a young girl's coming of age. Sarah and her family are warm, human characters who can bring a smile or a tear to the reader. The story also reflects some of the idealism and enthusiasm generated by the New Frontier, especially in its early days.

Book Talk Material

How Sarah feels about Kennedy's election (see pp. 29–32), one of Sarah's "slight" rebellions against the school (see pp. 40–48), and Sarah's description of herself as an assimilated Jew (see pp. 85–87) are fine introductions to this likable character. Young readers would also enjoy the conversations from year to year of Sarah and the "other shepherds" on stage (see pp. 2–5, 40–43, 122–124, 170–173).

Additional Selections

In a humorous "with-it" novel, a sixteen-year-old girl tires of her wonderful family and decides to go off on her own in Susan Shreve's *The Revolution of Mary Leary* (Knopf, 1982, $9.95; pap., Avon, $2.25). Sixteen-year-old Kate runs away from home to find her sister in Elissa Haden Guest's *Over the Moon* (Morrow, 1986, $11.75). Susan's plans for a quiet senior year change when her sister, a rock musician, returns home in Caroline B. Cooney's *Don't Blame the Music* (Putnam, 1986, $13.95). Meg's life changes completely when her mother becomes president in Ellen Emerson White's *The President's Daughter* (pap., Avon, 1984, $2.95). Two stories that deal with runaways are Gertrude Samuel's *Run, Shelley, Run* (Crowell, 1974, $12.70; pap., New Amer. Lib., $2.50), about how a girl flees her training school; and Marilyn Harris's *The Runaway's Diary* (pap., Pocket Bks., 1983, $2.25), the story of a fifteen-year-old girl who escapes an unhappy home life. Lacey and her unwed mother return to their hometown and complications begin in Doris Smith's *Return to Bitter Creek* (Viking, 1986, $11.95). *The Incredible Sixties* by Jules Archer (Harcourt, 1986, $15.95) tells the fascinating story of "the stormy years that changed America."

About the Author
Bowden, Jane A., ed. *Contemporary Authors*. Detroit: Gale Research Co., 1978. Vols. 69–72, p. 374.

Commire, Anne, ed. *Something about the Author*. Detroit: Gale Research Co., 1978. Vol. 13, pp. 124–125.

Evory, Ann, ed. *Contemporary Authors* (New Revision Series). Detroit: Gale Research Co., 1984. Vol. 11, p. 320.

Senick, Gerard J., ed. *Children's Literature Review*. Detroit: Gale Research Co., 1986. Vol. 11, pp. 112–122.

L'Engle, Madeleine. *A Ring of Endless Light*
Farrar, 1980, $11.95; pap., Dell, $2.95

Readers were first introduced to the Austin family and the narrator, daughter Vicky, in *Meet the Austins* (pap., Dell, $2.50; condensed in *Introducing Books*, Bowker, 1970, pp. 14–17). In this novel, Dr. and Mrs. Austin, who are living in the small New England town of Thornhill with their family of four—sons John and Rob, daughters Vicky and Suzy—find that their warm, loving family relationship becomes strained when they are required to care for a troubled orphan girl, Maggy Hamilton. This book is followed by *The Moon by Night* (Farrar, 1963, $11.95; pap., Dell, $2.75), the account of the Austins' adventures in a cross-country camping trip during which they meet the fabulously wealthy Mr. and Mrs. Gray and their spoiled, impulsive son Zachary to whom fourteen-year-old Vicky is extremely attracted. In *The Young Unicorns* (Farrar, 1968, $12.95; pap., Dell, $2.95), the Austins are in New York City, where Dr. Austin is spending a year on a research project. Here they confront evil and danger when they encounter a street gang who are out to kill a former member and his blind student. *The Arm of the Starfish* (Farrar, 1965, $11.95; pap., Dell, $2.95), an unrelated adventure novel, has teenage Adam Eddington as its hero. Adam, Zachary, and, of course, the Austins all play important roles in *A Ring of Endless Light*, the most mystical, somber, and introspective novel in the series. It is recommended for perceptive readers in grades seven through ten.

Plot Summary

The Austins are spending the summer following their New York City stay and before their return to Thornhill, where Dr. Austin will return to private practice, at the New England island home of widowed Grandfather Eaton, the wise and humane retired pastor and patriarch of the clan. Vicky, again the narrator, is now almost sixteen, her brother John has completed his first year at college, and Suzy and Rob are thirteen and seven, respectively. It should be an idyllic summer: Dr. Austin is using the time to write his research reports, John has an interesting job at the local Marine Biology Station, and Mother and the rest of the family can relax in the sun and surf. But a heavy cloud hangs over the family. The real reason for being on the island is that Grandfather is dying of leukemia and has only a few months to live. Grandfather has an extraordinary serene and stoic attitude toward his condition and tries to explain to Vicky that death, in essence, is an affirmation of life, but she cannot accept its inevitability and the loss that it will bring.

After only one week on the island the Austins experience an unexpected loss. Commander Rodney, the well-liked chief of the Marine Biology Station, suffers a fatal heart attack after rescuing a young man from drowning. The family is further disturbed when they learn that the young man is bad-penny Zachary Gray, who has come East to seek out Vicky. In a conversation with her, he explains that the incident was actually a foiled suicide attempt, and that he needs her love and her positive attitudes to give him back the will to live.

Soon two other young men also begin to play important roles in Vicky's life. One is Leo Rodney, the dead commander's son. At first, Vicky regards him as "a slob," but his genuine feelings for her and his difficult adjustment to his father's death bring her to understand and sympathize with him and to regard him (though he wishes more) as a dear friend. The other is Adam Eddington, an eighteen-year-old attractive college student who, like John, has a summer job at the station. He is engaged in a project with Dr. Jed Nutteley on communicating with bottle-nosed dolphins. One day he takes Vicky to see the subjects of his research, the three dolphins Una, Nini, and the pregnant Ynid, who are kept in captivity, but the great thrill of the day for Vicky happens when, after swimming out into the bay with Adam, she meets Basil, a free dolphin who comes regularly at Adam's call to play with him.

The summer suddenly becomes a juggling act for Vicky: fancy dinners and expensive parties on the mainland with Zachary; homey conversations and sharing lemonades with Leo; and also becoming involved with Adam and his dolphin research. Her best times, however, are the mornings when she reads to her grandfather and has lengthy conversations with this wise and wonderful man. Vicky writes poetry and her grandfather often recites verses to her like the Henry Vaughan poem that begins

> I saw Eternity the other night
> Like a great ring of pure and endless light.

Her attraction for Adam increases and she becomes more involved in his work. One day Basil brings a female dolphin to play and Vicky names her Norberta. Soon they are joined by a third, Norberta's young pup, Njord, god of the sea. Adam senses that Vicky, in her naive purity, is miraculously able to communicate nonverbally with the dolphins. They obey her commands and allow her privileges (denied anyone else) like riding on their backs. This amazing gift is tested many times, and soon Vicky is receiving thought sensations and dream pictures from the dolphins that convey entirely different concepts of life and time.

The excitement of these discoveries is blunted by a series of tragic events. Ynid's baby dies, Jed Nutteley is struck by a motorcycle and lies unconscious between life and death in the mainland hospital, and Grandfather's condition is steadily deteriorating, so that he often hemorrhages and frequently requires transfusions. On one trip to the mainland with Leo to collect blood for her grandfather, Vicky meets in the hospital's emergency room a pathetic young mother, Grace, and her ailing daughter, Binnie, who suffers from a congenital heart condition that also must be treated by blood transfusions. Vicky feels that except for Adam and his dolphins she is surrounded with death and dying.

Zachary continues to entertain Vicky in his manic, cavalier manner. Typically, he is now taking flying lessons. One day he, Vicky—whom he calls Vicky-O—and his flight instructor, Joe, go for a ride in the Piper Cub. Zachary takes over the controls and, in a show of reckless bravura, narrowly misses colliding with a passing jet. Back on the ground, Vicky, still in shock from this incident, tries to get back to the island and finds that during her absence Grandfather has had another seizure and is in the hospital. She makes her way to the emergency room and, while awaiting news, Grace arrives with a very sick Binnie. She gives the child to Vicky to hold while she seeks help; during Grace's absence, Binnie has convulsions and dies in Vicky's arms. Suddenly the forces of darkness envelop the young girl. She becomes numbed by the accumulated grief and sorrow around her; and even though she learns that Grandfather has weathered his attack and Jed is improving, Vicky, for several days, appears to wander in a daze, unable to comprehend or accept the crushing events she has experienced. Slowly, through the tender support and advice from both Grandfather and Adam and the life-giving gentleness of the dolphins, she is able to accept the present and once again face the future.

Thematic Material

This is one of the most profound and disturbing of Madeleine L'Engle's novels. On one level it is a novel about dying and various ways of adjusting to death, but more importantly, it explores the meaning of faith and the dimensions of human existence. As Grandfather states, "When one tries to avoid death, it's impossible to avoid life." The theme of oneness in nature is explored in the episodes involving animal ESP and nonverbal communication. Wholesome family situations are well depicted, as are various aspects of love and friendship and the necessity of developing and maintaining moral standards to sustain a constructive life.

Book Talk Material

Showing the covers of either the hardcover or the paperback edition plus an explanation of the dolphin experiments should produce interest. Specific early passages of importance are: Vicky comforts Leo (pp. 31–33; pp. 35–37, pap.); Zachary talks about his life and suicide attempt (pp. 47–53; pp. 52–58, pap.); Zachary and Grandfather discuss cryonics (pp. 42–45; pp. 47–50, pap.); Vicky talks about Zachary and life's problems with Grandfather (pp. 56–64; pp. 61–69, pap.); and Vicky meets the dolphins (pp. 86–106; pp. 91–111, pap.).

Additional Selections

Rachel must take care of her ornery, difficult grandfather, Izzy, in *After the Rain* (Morrow, 1987, $11.75) by Aimee Duvall. Some anthologies of poetry that readers like Vicky might enjoy are *Going Over to Your Place* (Bradbury, 1987, $12.95), *Strings: A Gathering of Family Poems* (Bradbury, 1984, $11.95), and *Postcard Poems* (Bradbury, 1979, $9.95), all edited by Paul B. Janeczko. A young girl becomes attached to a beautiful chestnut stallion and his handsome owner during a summer in New Hampshire in Joanne Hoppe's *Pretty Penny Farm* (Morrow, 1987, $11.75). A *Summer to Die* (Houghton, 1977, $10.95; pap., Bantam, $2.75) by Lois Lowry tells of thirteen-year-old Meg and her coping with her sister's illness and death. The fishbowl existence of growing up as minister's children is told in Suzanne Newton's *I Will Call It Georgie's Blues* (Viking, 1983, $12.95; pap., Dell, $2.75) and Madeleine L'Engle's novel *A House Like a Lotus* (Farrar, 1984, $13.95; pap., Dell, $3.50) tells about the discovery by a young girl that the kindly woman who befriended her is a lesbian. *Skindeep* (Harper, 1986, $13.95) by Toeckey Jones reveals the tragedy that is present-day South Africa in a love story about a white girl and a black man.

About the Author

Block, Ann, and Riley, Carolyn, eds. *Children's Literature Review*. Detroit: Gale Research Co., 1976. Vol. 2, pp. 129–134.

Commire, Anne, ed. *Something about the Author*. Detroit: Gale Research Co., 1971. Vol. 1, pp. 141–142; updated 1982. Vol. 27, pp. 131–140.

Estes, Glenn E., ed. *American Writers for Children since 1960: Fiction* (*Dictionary of Literary Biography*, Vol. 52). Detroit: Gale Research Co., 1986, pp. 241–249.

Ethedge, James M. *Contemporary Authors* (First Revision). Detroit: Gale Research Co., 1967. Vols. 1–4, pp. 582–583.

Evory, Ann, ed. *Contemporary Authors* (New Revision Series). Detroit: Gale Research Co., 1981. Vol. 3, pp. 331–332.

Fuller, Muriel, ed. *More Junior Authors*. New York: Wilson, 1963, pp. 137–138.

Kirkpatrick, D. L., ed. *Twentieth-Century Children's Writers* (2nd edition). New York: St. Martin's, 1983, pp. 467–469.

Who's Who in America: 1986–1987 (44th edition). Chicago: Marquis Who's Who, Inc., 1986. Vol. 2, p. 1666.

Who's Who of American Women: 1987–1988 (15th edition). Chicago: Marquis Who's Who, Inc., 1986, p. 476.

Levitin, Sonia.   *The Return*
Atheneum, 1987, lib. bdg., $12.95

Sonia Levitin has been closely associated with the most devastating event in Jewish history. She was born in 1934 of Jewish parents who were forced to leave Germany when she was three. In *The Return* she writes of another traumatic experience in the history of her people. Not all of her books deal with such weighty subjects. In *The Mark of Conte* (Macmillan, 1976, $8.95; pap., $1.95), for example, a high school student named Conte Mark gets two programs from the computer (the other for Mark Conte) and decides to be two students. These novels are enjoyed by junior high school students.

Plot Summary

Desta is Ethiopian—black, African, poor, little educated, and parentless. She is also what other Ethiopians derisively call Falasha—a stranger—because Desta and her people are Ethiopian Jews. Treated as outcasts, they are often caught between the warring factions of their tormented land, blamed for the drought and famine that afflict their country, regarded as undesirable because they are Jews.

Despite her stark life, however, Desta loves her beautiful homeland, as she loves the traditions of her faith, as she loves the kindness of her aunt and uncle who have provided a home for her, as she loves her older brother, Joas, and her little sister, Almaz. Although she is skilled at pottery making, Desta would like to return to school, but she cannot. Not sure of her own age, she awaits the day when her elders will decide that it is time for her to marry the quiet, unsmiling Dan who visits from another village. Desta does not know if she really wants to marry Dan, but she does know that she has no choice in the matter.

The Ethiopian Jews of Desta's village and the countryside live in great hardship and constant fear of persecution from their revolutionary government and from their fellow countrymen. Joas talks of escape and he longs to run from this life. He tells Desta that he is thinking of making the long trek to the Sudan, from where he has heard it is possible to escape to freedom in the land of the Jews, Israel. Joas begs Desta and Almaz to go with him. At first, Desta is incredulous and terrified. But, like her brother, she becomes caught up in the dream of Israel. And one day, when soldiers are spotted heading toward the village for what the inhabitants fear will mean a time of plunder—and worse—the three young people, with the hurried blessings of their aunt and uncle, flee from their home and head toward the Sudan and the unknown.

What follows is a harsh story of courage and fear and faith and determination. Wrenched from the only life she has ever known, as bleak and as hard as it was, Desta faces a terrifying journey across an alien land in a world she knows nothing about. But at least she has stalwart Joas to guide her and Almaz. Then, to her horror and despair, Joas is killed. Desta and Almaz bury their brave brother. Now Desta has only one thing to guide her and Almaz to the Sudan and then to the Promised Land— her unwavering faith in the promise of her religion.

For the rest of her journey, Desta faces dangers and deprivations that would make many adults run in terror. Not only is Desta without the guidance of her brother, but now she has the responsibility for her young sister's safety. With but a brief thought to returning to the relative security of her aunt and uncle's village, Desta makes the decision to pursue their dream of Israel.

At one point, she attempts to trade the blue beads of her mother that she carries with her for some food. But the villagers recognize her as a Falasha and drive her and Almaz away. When Desta meets some travelers who are not Falasha but as hungry as they are, she persuades the man to go to the village and trade her beads for food for them all.

From other travelers, Desta learns that they must head for a Red Cross station, and it is on that road that she runs into a familiar face, Dan's cousin, Melake. Eventually, they join up with Dan and others of his village.

The long arduous trip to the refugee camp in the Sudan is even more harrowing for Desta than the beginning of the journey. They are hounded and shot at, starved, sore, and bleeding. And always she must care for young Almaz. Yet when they reach the refugee camp, more horror awaits, for famine has touched the thousands and thousands who are there.

Although Desta loses track of the time spent in the wretchedness of the refugee camp, at last she hears that a rescue operation is in progress to remove Jews from the camp at night and fly them to Israel.

Frightened and unsure of whom to trust, Desta and Almaz become two of the lucky Ethiopian Jews to be spirited away from the camps into the safety of Israel, where if a land of milk and honey does not await them, at least there is freedom and help, and hope.

The Return is the story of one young girl's courage and faith, of her modern-day exodus to Israel, and of her decision not to marry Dan, to whom she has been promised. This tale of personal bravery and courage is based on the secret airlifting, called Operation Moses, of Ethiopian Jews to Israel in 1984–1985.

Thematic Material

Sonia Levitin tells this story of Operation Moses and the Ethiopian Jews with stark realism. She presents a grim picture of life for a people who live in constant hardship and fear of persecution, who cling to their age-old beliefs as a beacon of light in a uncompromising world. The discerning young reader, however, will find much to admire in this story of one young girl's bravery and refusal to give in to despair.

Book Talk Material

The character of this young Ethiopian girl comes through vividly, and her curiosity and awakening mind, plus her love of small pleasures, will make an interesting introduction to the people of this little known or understood land. Specific passages are: Desta wonders about Jews in America (pp. 28–29); Desta and Joas discuss leaving for the Sudan (pp. 32–36); Desta and her aunt talk about marriage (pp. 40–41); Desta goes to the marketplace (pp. 49–54); and she makes a decision (pp. 54–57).

Additional Selections

A Chinese boy migrates to America in Laurence Yep's historical novel, *Mountain Light* (Harper, 1985, $11.89). This is a sequel to the novel *The Serpent's Children* (Harper, 1984, $12.95) about the Taiping Rebellion and battles against the Manchus. David Kherdian tells about his mother's childhood in Turkey when she was persecuted as a member of the Christian Armenian minority and eventually deported in *The Road from Home* (Greenwillow, 1979, $13) and in *Finding Home* (Greenwillow, 1981, $11.75) his mother arrives in America as a mail-order bride. A young Vietnamese boy tells about his family's journey to Australia in Jack Bennett's *The Voyage of the Lucky Dragon* (Prentice-Hall, 1982, $9.95). A fictionalized account of a group of Jews coming to the United States in 1904 is given in *Voyage* (Atheneum, 1983, $12.95) by Adele Geras. In novelized format, Jamake Highwater tells of the life of Charles Eastman, an American Indian doctor and writer who is alienated between two cultures in *Eyes of Darkness* (Lothrop, 1985, $13). A young girl makes a courageous escape from China during the Cultural Revolution in *Eighth Moon* (pap., Avon, 1983, $2.95) by Sansan; and in *So Far from the Bamboo Grove* (Lothrop, 1986, $10.25), by Yoko Kawashima Watkins, a Japanese girl escapes from Korea during World War II.

About the Author

Commire, Anne, ed. *Something about the Author*. Detroit: Gale Research Co., 1973. Vol. 4, pp. 144–145.

Evory, Ann, ed. *Contemporary Authors* (First Revision Series). Detroit: Gale Research Co., 1978. Vols. 29–32, p. 395.

Holtze, Sally Holmes, ed. *Fifth Book of Junior Authors and Illustrators*. New York: Wilson, 1983, pp. 191–193.

Kinsman, Clare D., ed. *Contemporary Authors*. Detroit: Gale Research Co., 1972. Vols. 29–32, p. 361.

Metzger, Linda, ed. *Contemporary Authors* (New Revision Series). Detroit: Gale Research Co., 1985. Vol. 14, p. 290.

Sarkissian, Adele, ed. *Something about the Author: Autobiography Series*. Detroit: Gale Research Co., 1986. Vol. 2, pp. 111–126.

Lipsyte, Robert. *The Summerboy*
Harper, 1982, $11.25; pap., Bantam, $2.25 (same pagination)

In *The Contender* (Harper, 1967, $11.89; pap., Bantam, $2.50; condensed in *More Juniorplots*, Bowker, 1977, pp. 66–69), Lipsyte's first young adult novel, he tells the story of Alfred Brooks, a black youth growing up in Harlem, and his encounters with boxing, drugs, and delinquency. Ten years later, readers were introduced to Bobby Marks, a fourteen-year-old boy who conquers a severe weight problem in *One Fat Summer* (Harper, 1977, $11.89; pap., Bantam, $2.50). In the first sequel, *Summer Rules* (Harper, 1981, $11.89), Bob, now sixteen, is a camp counselor, who, in his usual droll, cordial, wisecracking way, confronts many anxieties, including those associated with first love. In *The Summerboy*, it is now 1957. Bob is eighteen and has returned home from his freshman year at college. Though some of the references in the novel to contemporary hit songs, movies, and sports heroes might be missed by today's young readers, this often wildly funny and sometimes very serious first-person novel is enjoyed by readers in grades seven through ten.

Plot Summary
When Bobby Marks, fresh from the triumph of his first year of college, returns to his upper-middle-class New Jersey home, he notices a sign outside Lenape Laundry advertising for a truck helper and immediately imagines himself in a clean white uniform riding through neighborhoods dispensing goodwill, machismo, and clean sheets like a Sir Galahad of the starched shirt department. He is interviewed for the job by a young man who dispenses so many literary allusions that he appears to be more at home in the halls of academe than with caldrons of steaming laundry. Bob learns that the man is the owner of the laundry, Roger Sinclair, an English doctoral student who gave up his studies when his wife inherited the family business. His disinterest in the laundry is matched only by his greed for the fast buck. He hires Bob partly in hope that the boy will report to him any malcontents and agitators in his work force.

Bob's reception the first day at work is as chilly as Byrd's Antarctica. His coworkers regard him not only as Sinclair's stoolie but also as a dilettante summer replacement whom they nickname "The Summerboy." Bob realizes that all these accusations are partly correct, but he puts on a brave front before Bump Ennis, the truck foreman, and drivers Jim, Red, superhippie Ace, and immediate enemy gorillalike Cliff.

On Bob's first assignment to take a truck to a garage, its worn brakes fail (an example of Sinclair's penny-pinching) and the truck crashes. Bob is unharmed but banished to the folding room where he works in sweatshop conditions folding sheets with a dauntless septuagenarian named Lolly. His only compensations are proximity to a beautiful but aloof and embittered blond named Diane Cooke and the dreams of conquest she provokes.

Joanie Miller, Bob's long-standing platonic girlfriend, invites him to a party at her lakeside home. Here, while trying to impress two young French girls named Marie and Mignon, Bob dives off the dock. In midair Bob remembers that Mr. Miller has just had a truckload of gravel dumped around the dock—and emerges from the water with a face like chopped beef. Luckily, a local doctor named Bushkin, who has developed a shady reputation for questionable medical practices, is able to pick out most of the sand and stones from the wounds.

Back at work, people believe Bob's been in a fight. Soon rumors circulate that he beat up four toughs, and, because there are no marks on his hands, he is touted as a black belt karate expert. Basking in this fabricated glory, Bob is once more assigned to the trucks, but, unfortunately, King Kong's reincarnation, ol' Cliff, decides to challenge Bob to a test fight. Happily, Joanie appears; she intervenes and saves Bob from a fight worse than death.

Joanie frequently asks Bob to cover up with excuses for her absences from home. She confesses to Bob that she is having a relationship with an older man. Bob, who is living alone because his parents are in Manhattan awaiting his father's hernia operation, finds it easy to make these excuses but is concerned about Joanie's future. He inadvertently finds out who the man is when one day on his route he sees on a tennis court Joanie kissing none other than the laundry lothario, Roger Sinclair.

On a Fourth of July picnic Bob talks to Diane and her father, nicknamed Cookie. Mr. Cooke, a former laundry employee, is now confined to a wheelchair because of an accident caused, once again, by Sinclair's negligence and disregard for his employees' safety. Bob now realizes the cause of Diane's bitterness as well as her attacks against him, whom she still regards as Sinclair's stooge.

One evening a pale and distraught Joanie visits Bob. She is pregnant and needs his help to arrange an abortion. Dr. Bushkin is contacted and the operation is performed at his upper Manhattan office. Bob brings a weak and tearful Joanie home.

Lolly is hospitalized for burns caused by a defective pressure valve exploding, again because of Sinclair's neglect. When Diane tries to take up a petition against Sinclair, she gets so little support that Bob, now also enraged, meets with Sinclair alone in his office and confronts him with both the news of Joanie's abortion and demands for a safer workplace. After gathering the workers together, Bob exhorts them to unite for better working conditions. Sinclair accepts the demands on the condition that Bob quit the laundry. He agrees, and with the sounds of the negotiations in the distance, Robert Marks, like one of his movie heroes, walks alone but proud into the sunset.

Thematic Material

In spite of his nonchalant, self-deprecating bravado, when put to the test, Bob displays courage, integrity, and inner resources not otherwise apparent. In spite of the many laugh-aloud situations in the book, serious themes are developed: the value of friendship, barriers caused by economic and social differences, abortion, the dangers of adolescent infatuations, and labor-management relations.

Book Talk Material

Page 1 describes Bob's dreams of glory concerning the job. Other amusing passages include: his interview with Roger Sinclair (pp. 3–6); his accident with the truck (pp. 17–20); sheet folding with Lolly (pp. 29–34); an encounter with Diane (pp. 42–44); diving off the Millers' dock (pp. 45–49); and Cliff and Bob square off (pp. 73–77).

Additional Selections

In Constance Greene's wildly funny *The Love Letters of J. Timothy Owen* (Harper, 1986, $11.25), Tim sends cribbed love letters to the object of his desire and gets unexpected results, and in Dallen Malmgren's hilarious *The Whole Nine Yards* (Delacorte, 1986, $14.95), a boy spends his high school years chasing girls but is unprepared when he catches one. *The Adrian Mole Diaries* (Grove, 1986, $14.95) by Sue Townsend are humorous entries on teenage living. In Suzanne Newton's *M. V. Sexton Speaking* (Viking, 1981, $9.95; pap., Fawcett, $2.25), Martha's life changes when she takes a summer job in a bakery. Annie and three other teenage girls become summer interns for *Image* magazine in New York City in Susan

Beth Pfeffer's *Fantasy Summer* (Putnam, 1984, $12.95), and Annie's story is continued in *Getting Even* (Putnam, 1986, $13.95). Jenny wins the date of a lifetime with a super rock star in Mary Anderson's *Do You Call That a Dream Date?* (Delacorte, 1987, $14.95). Michael French's *Soldier Boy* (Putnam, 1986, $13.95) is the story of four young people on the verge of entering the adult world.

About the Author
Commire, Anne, ed. *Something about the Author*. Detroit: Gale Research Co., 1973. Vol. 5, p. 114.
Ethridge, James M. *Contemporary Authors* (First Revision). Detroit: Gale Research Co., 1968. Vols. 19–20, p. 214.
Evory, Ann, ed. *Contemporary Authors* (New Revision Series). Detroit: Gale Research Co., 1983. Vol. 8, pp. 329–330.
Holtze, Sally Holmes, ed. *Fifth Book of Junior Authors and Illustrators*. New York: Wilson, 1983, pp. 196–198.
Kinsman, Clare D., ed. *Contemporary Authors* (First Revision Series). Detroit: Gale Research Co., 1976. Vols. 17–20, p. 449.

Mazer, Harry. *When the Telephone Rang*
Scholastic, 1985, $11.95; pap., $2.50 (same pagination)

Harry Mazer has written a number of excellent novels for young adults. Several of them, like *Snow Bound* (pap., Dell, $2.25) and *The Island Keeper* (Delacorte, 1981, $13.95; pap., Dell, $2.50), are exciting survival stories; others deal with concerns facing young people as they move from adolescence into adulthood. Some examples are *The Dollar Man* (Delacorte, 1974, o.p.), the sequel *I Love You, Stupid!* (Crowell, 1981, $11.89; pap., Avon, $2.50), and *When the Telephone Rang*. This latter novel covers a five-month traumatic period from January through June in the history of the Keller family and is set in a reclaimed residential area of a big city—though not identified it appears from references to be Brooklyn Heights. The novel is popular with young readers in grades six through nine.

Plot Summary
It is the end of January and sixteen-year-old Billy Keller and his twelve-year-old sister Lori are awaiting their parents' return from a week-long vacation–work junket to Bermuda. Billy has checked to make

sure that the family car, an ancient Mercedes, is okay and he and his sister have tried to tidy up the apartment. The other member of their family is Kevin, who, at twenty-one, is completing his undergraduate work in a Boston college before entering medical school. The Kellers moved only four months ago from a small town to the Big City where they have bought a refurbished brownstone and rented out the two other apartments, one to a young couple, Steve and Holly, and the other to the more elderly Mr. and Mrs. Stein. An unfinished rooftop apartment is being worked on by Billy and his dad.

Only hours before their parents are scheduled to arrive, the phone rings. It is the airline; their parents were killed when their plane exploded over the Caribbean. The youngsters are extremely disturbed but not without hope that a mistake has been made. They notify Kevin, who returns home. Even though the news becomes final, the reality and magnitude of the calamity seem impossible to accept. Soon their mother's brother, Uncle Paul, and his wife, Aunt Joan, arrive from Flint, Michigan, with Grandma Betty. They begin organizing the family's affairs and arrange a modest memorial service in the apartment during which Billy drinks some whiskey to calm his nerves and feels he disgraces himself when he gets quite tipsy.

The relatives make some decisions about the future. Kevin will return to school, Lori will live with Grandma, and Billy will return with Aunt and Uncle to their home. Billy is particularly upset at breaking up the family. He speaks privately with Kevin, who Billy has always regarded as his rescuer, and asks him to prevent the separation. Kevin agrees. He will move from Boston, find a job, and enroll part-time in school. This way, with some occasional financial help from relatives when necessary, they should be able to manage.

When everyone leaves, the three young people are still so dazed and disoriented by events and in need of a grieving period that they are almost immobilized for a few days, but soon Lori and Billy return to school and Kevin begins job hunting. Adjustments are difficult, and each of them, particularly Billy, feels guilty when even for a moment the parents are forgotten. Friends provide some solace. Billy has L. J. Braun, a fat kid who seems to understand his grief. He also develops a crush on Margaret Geri, an older girl who works at the Catholic Youth Organization, a club for after-school activities. Lori, in turn, has girlfriends Sam and Maryanne. The latter Billy does not like. She is a brusque, tough girl who seems to be gaining too much control over Lori. Kevin finds a job as an ambulance paramedic, but when he has free weekends spends them in Boston with his girlfriend Kathy.

Taking care of the house is more work than expected. Garbage and dirt accumulate, dishes go unwashed, and soiled clothes stay where they are dropped. As well, quarrels about responsibilities and obligations cause increasing stress and turmoil. One day, while Kevin is working, they are visited by a social worker, Milo Miller from Children's Services. He sees the condition of the house, and Billy is fearful of the report he will submit.

Kevin wants to dispose of his parents' possessions so he can sleep in their bedroom instead of the living room. He also makes ominous sounds about selling the Mercedes, but Billy wants to cling to everything that his parents owned. One day, nevertheless, Billy returns from school and finds that Kevin has disposed of the bedroom's contents. He feels a sense of betrayal.

While the boys are increasingly involved in their own problems, Lori becomes more distant and more attached to her friend Maryanne, who showers her with affection and gifts. She feels particularly ignored when Billy forgets her birthday.

Because of his absences on trips to Boston, Kevin loses his job and, to fill in time, tries to complete the rooftop apartment with Billy's help. Billy works on the plumbing. When he thinks he has it satisfactorily completed, the water is turned on and in no time the Steins' apartment is flooded from water dripping through the ceiling. The repairs force them into debt, and so, without consulting Billy, Kevin sells the Mercedes. When Billy finds out, he physically attacks his brother. In the fight, Billy is badly beaten.

In a local department store, Billy sees Maryanne with Lori and watches with horror as Maryanne shoplifts several articles. When confronted with the crime, they both deny it, but in Lori's room Billy finds a box filled with stolen jewelry and cosmetics. He leaves it open on her bed.

When Lori returns home and sees the open box, she becomes so disturbed that she runs to the roof and seems ready to jump when Billy grabs her and pulls her to safety. They talk and she tells how in her misery and loneliness she had turned to the only person she felt offered her the affection and attention she needed. Very courageously, she admits the thefts to Kevin and they make plans to return the stolen goods secretly.

Even though Kevin gets a job as a taxi driver that helps the situation financially, Billy is now convinced that the experiment has failed and that recent events have spelled the end of the Keller family. This is reinforced when Grandma Betty returns for a visit and Lori responds so totally to her attention that Billy thinks perhaps she should be living permanently with her grandmother.

When Grandma Betty leaves, Billy suggests that perhaps the family should split as the relatives originally wanted. Both Kevin and Lori so vehemently disagree that Billy becomes once again optimistic about his family's future. The worst times are over; things are bound to get better.

Thematic Material

This is a moving story not only about the adjustment to the death of loved ones but also about the grieving period and its often conflicting emotions of anguish, guilt, loneliness, and self-pity. It also tells of the conflicts that can result within a family when each is trying to work out his or her own private pain and disorientation. The nature of friendship is explored, as are feelings of first love. But above all it is a reaffirmation of the strength of family ties and the power of love and caring.

Book Talk Material

An explanation of the significance of the title should interest prospective readers. Some passages are: when the phone rang (pp. 8–12); the memorial service (pp. 33–37); the relatives' solution about the children's future (pp. 42–45); Billy talks to Kevin about it (pp. 47–51); Milo Miller visits (pp. 73–78); finishing the upstairs apartment (pp. 122–125); and the brothers fight over selling the car (pp. 129–132).

Additional Selections

When his father dies and his older brother becomes his guardian, sixteen-year-old Don Rennie goes on a backpacking trip to sort himself out in Thomas Baird's *Walk Out a Brother* (Harper, 1983, $12.89). Orphaned at sixteen, Spence is being raised by five older sisters and his grandparents in Norma Klein's *Give and Take* (Viking, 1985, $14.95). A girl comes to terms with her grandmother's dying and her own awakening womanhood in Katharine Joy Bacon's *Shadow and Light* (Macmillan, 1987, $12.95), a sequel to *Pip and Emma* (Macmillan, 1986, $11.95). Jodi's stepbrother Scott is a shoplifter and she is blamed for shoplifting in C. S. Adler's *In Our House Scott Is My Brother* (Macmillan, 1980, $9.95). In Marc Talbert's *Dead Birds Singing* (Little, 1986, $12.95), Matt must live with his best friend's family after his mother's death. In Richard Peck's *Close Enough to Touch* (Delacorte, 1981, $13.95; pap., Dell, $2.50), Matt feels alienated from everyone after his girlfriend dies. A seventeen-year-old girl mourns the death of her father while sorting out her own life in Hila Colman's *Sometimes I Don't Love My Mother* (Morrow, 1977, $11.88; pap., Scholastic, $1.95). At seventeen, Freddie Flores, a Mexican-American, is orphaned, angry, and wealthy in T. Ernesto Bethancourt's *The Me Inside of Me* (Lerner, 1985, $10.95). The problem of handling grief is well covered in Elizabeth Richter's *Losing Someone You Love: When a Brother or Sister Dies* (Putnam, 1986, $11.95).

About the Author

Commire, Anne, ed. *Something about the Author*. Detroit: Gale Research Co., 1983. Vol. 31, pp. 126–131.

Holtze, Sally Holmes, ed. *Fifth Book of Junior Authors and Illustrators*. New York: Wilson, 1983, pp. 203–204.

Locher, Frances C., ed. *Contemporary Authors*. Detroit: Gale Research Co., 1981. Vols. 97–100, pp. 355–356.

Miklowitz, Gloria D.   *The War between the Classes*
Delacorte, 1985, $13.95; pap., Dell, $2.75 (same pagination)

In the short time that Gloria D. Miklowitz has been writing young adult novels, she has produced a number of well-received popular books. Each deals with contemporary teens and their concerns. In *The Love Bombers* (Delacorte, 1980, $11.95; pap., Dell, $1.95), she writes about a girl who must save her brother from a religious cult, and in *Close to the Edge* (Delacorte, 1983, $13.95; pap., Dell, $2.25), a popular pretty girl tries to bring meaning to her life partly through a rediscovery of her Jewish heritage. *The War between the Classes* is the story of a girl torn between two cultures, and, like these other novels, is enjoyed mainly by junior high girls.

Plot Summary

Amy Sumoto shifts easily and for the most part complacently between her two worlds—the world of her middle-class, traditionalist Japanese parents (who address her by her given name of Emiko) and the world of her American high school and friends of differing socioeconomic backgrounds and cultures. In fact, she considers herself most fortunate, especially because Adam Tarcher, of the golden hair, blue eyes, and socially prominent family, has singled her out to be his girl.

If Amy could change anything about her life, she would wish that her parents would accept Adam and see him for the wonderful, kind person he truly is. But they, especially her father, wish only that she date boys of Japanese ancestry, and although they do not prevent her from seeing Adam, Amy is well aware of their disapproval. She understands, too, that part of their concern stems from the fact that Amy's older brother, Hideo, left home to marry Sue, an American girl. For a year her parents had not seen Hideo, and only now are they tentatively reestablishing some kind of communication.

Amy is also well aware that Adam's mother, a wealthy society matron, heartily disapproves of her son's attachment to a girl of Oriental ancestry.

But life is too full of school and friends and dances and being in love with Adam to be caught up in the prejudices and bigotry of adults. Or so Amy thinks until she and Adam and her classmates become involved in the "color game."

The class has agreed to take part in a four-week social experiment, which, as the teacher, Mr. Otero, explains, "will change your world." The students are divided into four color groups and must wear colored armbands to designate blue, the upper class; dark green, the middle class; light green, the lower middle class; and orange, the lowest of the low. Oranges can speak to the upper classes only when spoken to; all lower classes must bow upon meeting upper-class members and are subject to their whims and authority. Beyond the color rules, all males must defer to females. The students' activities are to be monitored by G4, the police force. Too many demerits can mean demotion to a lower class; but certain behaviors, such as spying on others or squealing on someone else's infractions of the rules, can mean promotion to a higher level.

What starts out as a fun game quickly turns into an eye-opening experience for Amy and her friends. Although each student supposedly is able to choose what color he or she will become, it is obvious that the game has been rigged—Adam, for instance, is an orange, as are most of his upper-class friends, whereas the middle class and poorer students are either blues or dark greens. Amy is somewhat delighted, despite herself, to find herself a blue.

In the days that follow, Amy begins to question both her own values and prejudices and those of her fellow students. At first embarrassed by the bows of those wearing lower-class bands, Amy begins to enjoy the feeling of confidence that her blue band gives her. And when she is forced to speak her own mind as a blue, she realizes how meek and submissive she has always been, how she has always tried hard to please friends and family at the expense of stating her own opinions or feelings. And suddenly Amy finds herself looking at Adam in a new way, too. Why does she always defer to his feelings or preferences? Why does she type his papers, for instance, when he is perfectly capable of doing so and she has work of her own to do?

As the color game goes on, Amy rebels more and more against the unfairness and bigotry of judging people by, in this case, the color of their armbands. Somewhat to her own surprise, she becomes the ring-leader of a plan to fight back. She enlists the aid of another student and together they set up posters around the school urging all colors to unite and stop the harassment of the lower classes. But, also to her surprise, she learns that many of her friends, especially those from the lower social classes who are now tasting the power of snobbery, are not at all pleased with her attempts to homogenize the student body.

For her part in the attempt to end the color game, Amy is demoted to orange. But her first flight into leadership has left her with a taste for more, and, now part of Adam's group, she spearheads another try at neutralizing the color game. This time they devise bands of all four colors for the students to wear to show their solidarity. However, just before the rally is planned, the armbands are stolen.

But Amy cannot be stopped now. With help from an upper-class friend, the group organizes the students into all wearing bands of red ribbons to show their togetherness.

At the end of the four-week experiment, Amy feels she has learned a good deal about her family, about her friends, about Adam, and most of all about herself. And she realizes that none of them will ever look at each other in quite the same way again.

Thematic Material

The effects and workings of social prejudices are told vividly and clearly in this novel. The ease with which young people sometimes accept the biases of adults is pointed out simply but with lasting force. The author also presents a compassionate picture of adults from another culture trying to maintain their ties in a sometimes alien land.

Book Talk Material

Although the main theme of this novel is the workings of prejudice through the color game, interesting discussions might focus on the difficulties that sometimes arise in communication between adults raised in one culture and under one system and their children who grow up in an altogether different world; see Amy and her father discuss Adam (pp. 13–14); Adam and Amy talk about parents (pp. 15–18); Amy and her family visit her brother (pp. 18–23). Also see the workings of prejudice in: Amy and Adam's sister show the differences in their upbringings (pp. 62–63) and Amy learns a lesson in prejudice from the experiment (pp. 73–75).

Additional Selections

In *Kim/Kimi* (McElderry, 1987, $12.95), Hadley Irwin writes about a Japanese American girl torn between two cultures and her search for information about her late father's family who were incarcerated during World War II. An interracial family (black/white) is depicted in the wise and gently humorous novel *I Only Made Up the Roses* (Greenwillow, 1987, $10.25) by Barbara Ann Porte. Jill, a senior in high school, falls in love with her radical Iranian classmate, Shaheen, in Kate Gilmore's *Remembrance of the Sun* (Houghton, 1986, $12.95). Elisabet McHugh's young Korean orphan, Karen, is featured in several novels, including *Karen and Vicki* (Greenwillow, 1984, $10.25). A course in marriage economics brings unforeseen results in Gloria Miklowitz's *The Day the Senior Class Got Married* (Delacorte, 1983, $12.95; pap., Dell, $2.50). A girl suspects that her parents are trying to break up her relationship with Rajee, her Indian boyfriend, in Stella Pevsner's *Lindsay, Lindsay, Fly Away Home* (Houghton, 1983, $10.95; pap., Pocket Bks., $2.25). The special benefits and problems of children in interracial families are explored in the nonfiction *The Rainbow Effect* (Watts, 1987, $11.90) by Kathlyn Gay. A true story of Japanese American internment in World War II is told in Jeanne and James D. Houston's *Farewell to Manzanar* (pap., Bantam, 1974, $2.50).

About the Author

Commire, Anne, ed. *Something about the Author*. Detroit: Gale Research Co., 1973. Vol. 4, pp. 154–156.

Evory, Ann, ed. *Contemporary Authors* (New Revision Series). Detroit: Gale Research Co., 1983. Vol. 10, p. 331.

Nasso, Christine, ed. *Contemporary Authors* (First Revision Series). Detroit: Gale Research Co., 1977. Vols. 25–28, p. 490.
Riley, Carolyn, ed. *Contemporary Authors*. Detroit: Gale Research Co., 1971. Vols. 25–28, p. 510.

Oneal, Zibby. *In Summer Light*
Viking, 1985, $11.95; pap., Bantam, $2.95

In Summer Light is Zibby Oneal's third book for young adults. It was preceded by *The Language of Goldfish* (Viking, 1980, $13.95; pap., Fawcett, $1.95), a moving first-person novel about a thirteen-year-old girl who is suffering a mental breakdown but who receives help from an understanding psychiatrist after a suicide attempt, and by *A Formal Feeling* (Viking, 1982, $11.50; pap., Fawcett, $1.95), in which a young girl adjusts to her mother's death and father's remarriage. In the year of their publication each was named one of the "Best Books for Young Adults" by the American Library Association. *In Summer Light* takes place during a single summer on a Nantucket/Martha's Vineyard–like island in Massachusetts. It is read mainly by girls in grades seven through ten.

Plot Summary

Seventeen-year-old Kate had hoped to spend the summer before her senior year in boarding school working in a summer resort on Long Island with roommate Leah. Unfortunately, mononucleosis intervened and instead she is recovering her strength with her parents and seven-year-old sister, Amanda, at their island home off the coast of Massachusetts. Kate's father is the renowned artist Marcus Brewer, who is acknowledged by all, even grudgingly by Kate, to be one of the world's greatest living painters. Kate's attitude toward her father has undergone many changes. As a child she worshiped him and would sit for hours in his studio with her paintbox watching him paint. But now his indifference toward her, because of his towering ego and total devotion to his art, has alienated her from him to the point where she has set aside the development of her own very promising artistic talents to major in English. Kate's mother, on the other hand, accepts this situation and even ended her own modest career in art to care for her husband after their marriage. Ironically, Marcus is so preoccupied with his work that he is unaware of these conflicts. Kate compares her father to Prospero, the subject of a summer literature paper she is writing on *The Tempest*. Everyone regards Prospero as a benevolent magician, who, because of his genius, is forgiven any transgression, but for Kate he is only a selfish tyrant.

Their thrice-weekly cleaning lady, Mrs. Hilmer, often brings her pesky daughter Frances, age ten, with her to the Brewers. One day Mrs. Hilmer comments on a picture over the mantelpiece that Marcus painted of Kate when she was only ten, and asks if Mr. Brewer would paint her daughter. Kate replies that her father is not a portrait painter, and recalls inwardly that this painting symbolizes her conflicts. She had always wanted to regard it as a portrait painted by a caring father, but he refers to it as only an interesting study in light and has named it "The Studio—Morning."

Two occurrences help enliven Kate's otherwise uneventful summer. The first is the arrival of a twenty-five-year-old graduate student from California, Ian Jackson, who is to work for six weeks on the preparation of a catalog of Brewer's paintings for a retrospective exhibition in Berkeley. Because he is staying in the back room of her father's studio, Kate sees him often. During Ian's off hours she takes him first to the pond on their property and then to the ocean beach. He tells her how he grew up in the shadow of a brilliant, scientifically inclined older brother and of his adoration of him and the problems this involved. Kate makes silent comparisons to her own situation. She feels at ease and increasingly attracted to this open, knowledgeable young man.

Several days later, Leah visits for a weekend. She is a high-spirited unsophisticated young girl who is thrilled to meet Kate's father. Marcus basks in her obvious admiration, and Kate notices that he extends himself and his cordiality more than usual. This arouses further resentment in Kate, who confides to Leah that she really abandoned painting to spite her father after he showed indifference bordering on the insulting toward her work.

After Leah leaves, Kate looks forward even more to her few meetings with Ian. On one of their walks she tells him how as a child she used to paint the large rocks on the beach with red clay from the cliffs. Ian invites her to go rock painting again. As she daubs layers of clay into universal geometric shapes, she again feels the joy of creating and the sense of release and exhilaration it brings.

Ian perceives her problems and confusion and, after seeing one of her old paintings, gently suggests that she return to her art. Kate responds to his encouragement and praise. She buys a set of watercolors and even attempts a portrait of Mrs. Hilmer's obnoxious Frances.

As Ian's remaining days on the island grow fewer, Kate realizes that she has fallen in love with him. When he tells her he must go to Boston for a few days, Kate asks him to take her with him. Ian replies it wouldn't be right and leaves. On his return he tries to explain that the difference in their ages and the trust her father has placed in him make a close relationship impossible at this time, but he takes her gently in his arms and, stroking her hair, tells her how beautiful she is.

After Ian's departure for California, Kate begins to paint seriously. As well, she talks about art once more with her father, who responds with an unusual openness and willingness to listen.

At summer's end, Kate leaves the island to return to school. From the ferry she sees the houses, the beaches, rocks, and red clay cliffs gradually recede. Soon the island is only a vague shape in the distance.

Thematic Material

This is a coming-of-age novel that is rich in atmosphere and ideas. The difficulties of living with family when one is constantly being overshadowed and suffocated by a more dominant member are well explored, as are the complicated expectations a girl feels toward her father. The awakening of Kate's artistic talent is realistically portrayed, as is the progress of a first love and its inevitable end through parting. The ambience of a resort island in summer is described well, but of greater importance is the way in which the author has captured on every page the essence of painting—color, light, shape—so that the reader becomes aware of the meaning of art and the process of creation.

Book Talk Material

Discussing the problems of being the daughter of a famous person could serve as a suitable introduction before talking specifically about Kate. Some important passages: Ian enters Kate's life (pp. 8–16; pp. 6–14, pap.); Kate and Ian talk about their families (pp. 40–45; pp. 40–45, pap.); Kate tells Leah about her father (pp. 65–68; pp. 66–69, pap.); and rock painting (pp. 89–93; pp. 90–94, pap.).

Additional Selections

A fifteen-year-old girl gets to know her alcoholic father during a summer vacation in Nova Scotia in Paula Fox's *The Moonlight Man* (Macmillan, 1986, $12.95), and one of Jamie's major problems (the other is his girlfriend) is trying to communicate with his father in C. S. Adler's *Roadside Valentine* (Macmillan, 1983, $9.95; pap., Berkley, $2.50). Rob, sinking into drugs, is sent to the family farm in North Carolina and falls in love with Ellery, a beautiful, unhappy girl, in Sue Ellen Bridgers's *Permanent Connections* (Harper, 1987, $12.89), and Penny must discover her own identity when her adored older sister goes to college in Marilyn Sachs's *Baby Sister* (Dutton, 1986, $12.95). A young teenager is growing up trying to forget that he is *The Son of Someone Famous* (Harper, 1974, $11.89; pap., New Amer. Lib., $2.50) by M. E. Kerr. After Nina moves in with her boyfriend, problems begin in Norma Fox Mazer's *Someone to Love* (Delacorte, 1983, $13.95), and in Bonnie and Paul Zindel's *A Star for the Latecomer* (Harper, 1980, $12.89; pap., Bantam, $2.25), a girl must decide between a dancing career or her boyfriend. Maureen Daly has written a gentle love story in *Acts of Love* (Scholastic, $12.95).

About the Author

Commire, Anne, ed. *Something about the Author*. Detroit: Gale Research Co., 1983.
Vol. 30, pp. 166–167 (under Elizabeth Oneal).
Locher, Frances C., ed. *Contemporary Authors*. Detroit: Gale Research Co., 1982.
Vol. 106, pp. 381–382 (under Elizabeth Oneal).

Paterson, Katherine.   *Jacob Have I Loved*
Crowell, 1980, $11.89; pap., Avon $2.50

Katherine Paterson is one of the very few authors to have been awarded the Newbery Medal twice. She received it first in 1978 for *Bridge to Terabithia* (Crowell, 1977, $11.70; pap., Avon, $2.95), a tender story for younger readers of a friendship interrupted by death, and in 1981 for *Jacob Have I Loved*. The title is from a Bible verse (Romans 9:13) in which the Lord says, "Jacob have I loved, but Esau have I hated." In the novel this verse is whispered to the heroine Louise by her spiteful grandmother and refers to the family situation, where, like Esau and his brother Jacob, the narrator Louise appears to have lost her birthright to her sister Caroline.

Except for a brief opening prologue and a few closing pages, the story takes place on small windswept Rass Island in Chesapeake Bay and covers the teenage years of twin sisters during World War II and immediately after. It is enjoyed mainly by girls in grades seven and up.

Plot Summary

Louise Bradshaw, nicknamed by her sister Wheeze, is a study in contrasts to Caroline, her younger, by a few minutes, twin sister. Caroline is blond, poised, pretty, and vivacious. She is always the center of attention and very aware of it. Furthermore, she has so much talent musically that her parents have sacrificed financially, first, to get her piano lessons and, later, when her singing ability developed, to send her across the bay weekly for voice lessons in Salisbury.

Louise is the opposite. She is more thoughtful, withdrawn, and in looks, quite plain and ordinary by comparison. She tends to think of others before herself and, as a result, is often shunted into the background and ignored in spite of the efforts of her loving mother and father. She is an ugly duckling who is becoming increasingly aware of this status and miserable about it.

The girls' father, Truitt, is a sturdy, hardworking waterman who, in his boat the *Portia Sue,* combs the bay for crabs and oysters. Their mother, Susan, first came to Rass as a young, idealistic schoolteacher and, after marriage, remained to raise her family. The other member of the family is their cantankerous, Bible-thumping Methodist grandmother, who, though only in her sixties, is becoming more meanmouthed and difficult. As well, she openly shows favoritism toward Caroline.

Louise helps supplement the family income by crabbing in her skiff with her friend McCall Purnell, better known as Call. He is one year older than she and, although somewhat unimaginative and plodding, is her best friend.

When Pearl Harbor comes, Louise suggests to her teacher, Mr. Rice, that out of feelings of sacrifice the school should forgo its annual concert. She is overruled and made to feel foolish. At the concert, of course, Caroline is once again the star.

There is great excitement in the island community when one day a distinguished-looking elderly man of about seventy arrives and moves into the deserted Wallace place close to the shore. It is Hiram Wallace, who more than forty years before had left his island home after suffering endless humiliation and contempt from the residents as a result of an act of cowardice during a violent summer storm. At first, Louise imagines that he might be a counterspy, but when through curiosity she and Call visit him one day, she realizes that he is a wise and friendly man who, without family, has come back to Rass to live out his remaining years. She calls him Captain Wallace and all three become close friends and helpmates. Later, much to Louise's dismay, Caroline also joins the circle.

In her search for individuality, Louise answers an advertisement and submits a poem to Lyrics Unlimited in the hope of untold riches. It proves to be a scam, and the girl is once more frustrated and belittled.

A neighbor and former acquaintance of the Captain, Auntie Trudy Braxton, suffers a stroke and is taken off the island, leaving sixteen wild cats to be disposed of. Caroline has the brilliant idea of feeding them paregoric to temporarily pacify them and peddling them door to door. The plan works through a combination of her charm, sweet talk, and some beatific-looking cats.

A hurricane hits the island in 1942, doing great damage and destroying the Captain's house. When he receives the news, in a comforting gesture, Louise puts her arms around the Captain and is alarmed at the feelings of love she experiences. Grandmother notices how Louise feels about the man and, in her half-senile way, openly accuses the girl of an improper attachment.

After a short stay with the Bradshaws, the Captain moves into Auntie Braxton's vacant home on a temporary basis. When the old lady becomes well enough to return from hospital, helpful Caroline alarms Louise by suggesting a marriage of convenience between the Captain and the spinster. Both parties agree and once more Louise loses.

As the war progresses, Call turns from a pudgy adolescent into an attractive young man, a phenomenon not unnoticed by Caroline. He quits school to help Mr. Bradshaw on his boat and later leaves the island to join the Navy.

When Trudy Braxton dies, the Captain gives part of her bequest to the Bradshaws to enable Caroline to study voice up north. Louise suffers pangs of resentment she cannot hide.

While still only in her midteens and the war half over, Louise drops out of school to help her father full time on his boat while studying at odd hours under her mother's tutelege at home. The work is sometimes unbearably harsh but is partly compensated for by working closely with her adored father and sharing his empathy with the sea, a quality that is revealed by his singing to the oysters. At war's end Call is demobilized and returns home via New York, where he spends some time with Caroline, who is studying at Juilliard. He tells Louise and her family that he and Caroline are engaged and plan to marry soon. Louise valiantly stifles the renewed animosity she feels toward her sister.

Mr. and Mrs. Bradshaw attend the wedding at Christmas 1946 while Louise stays home and prepares a holiday dinner for her crochety grandmother and the Captain.

As she sinks deeper into a life of bitterness and acrimony, Louise finally realizes she must help herself. With her parents' encouragement, she decides to enter college on the mainland. A climax in her life occurs when, after asking her mother if she will miss her as much as she does Caroline, the reply is, "More."

In a brief epilogue, Louise describes her days of self-fulfillment and independence. She becomes a nurse-midwife in a small Appalachian community and meets Joseph, a widower with three small children and the almost unpronounceable last name of Wojtkiewicz. She marries him because he seems like the kind of man who would also sing to oysters.

She names her first child Truitt, and, after the death of her grandmother and father, returns once more to Rass Island to bring her mother back to live with her. Another cycle in life has been completed.

Thematic Material

This story tells of the crushing effects of growing up in the shadow of a beautiful, talented sibling, and how a person's fine qualities if they are neither showy nor superficial can remain unknown and unappreciated in the process. It also tells of a girl's struggle to conquer feelings of inferiority, resentment, and guilt in order to find a life of fulfillment, confidence, and self-reliance. The strength of family ties is well portrayed, as is the author's brilliant re-creation of the hardships and joys of life in a tiny fishing village and of the perennial struggle of humanity against the sea. A youngster's first awakening to love is an interesting subtheme. The use of a World War II setting effectively coincides with Louise's internal war.

Book Talk Material

The concept of the origins and effects of sibling rivalry could lead into an introduction to Louise and Caroline. Some passages of note are: background information about the twins (pp. 14–21; pp. 20–25, pap.);

Mr. Rice and the Christmas pageant (pp. 25–30; pp. 28–32, pap.); Call and Louise visit the Captain for the first time (pp. 54–62; pp. 51–57, pap.); a reply from Lyrics Unlimited (pp. 81–82; pp. 72–73, pap.); getting rid of the cats (pp. 92–99; pp. 81–86, pap.); and the storm hits (pp. 103–109; pp. 89–94, pap.).

Additional Selections

A Taste of Daylight (Atheneum, 1984, $12.95) is the last of Crystal Thrasher's five-volume series about a rural midwestern family and how they survived the Depression. When three generations of women live together they embark on the joyous but often sad voyage of self-discovery in Hadley Irwin's *What about Grandma?* (Atheneum 1982, $9.95; pap., New Amer. Lib., $2.50). Contemporary whaling life, Eskimo culture, and the young teenager coming of age are all themes explored in Jean Craighead George's *Water Sky* (Harper, 1986, $11.89). On an isolated sheep station in New Zealand, a young girl questions her future in Deborah Savage's *A Rumour of Otters* (Houghton, 1986, $12.95), and Peter joins a traveling preacher under whose spell he has fallen in *A Fine White Dust* (Macmillan, 1986, $13.95) by Cynthia Rylant. Farrell lives a lonely if luxurious life until Ted begins paying attention in Jean Ferris's *Amen, Moses Gardenia* (Farrar, 1983, $10.95). Penny is growing up in the shadow of a spoiled but idolized older sister in Marilyn Sachs's *Older Sister* (Dutton, 1986, $12.95). A boy must compete with his sister for a place in ballet in Rumer Godden's *Thursday's Children* (Viking, 1984, $14.95; pap., Dell, $2.95).

About the Author

Commire, Anne, ed. *Something about the Author*. Detroit: Gale Research Co., 1978. Vol. 13, pp. 176–177.

Estes, Glenn E., ed. *American Writers for Children since 1960: Fiction* (*Dictionary of Literary Biography*, Vol. 52). Detroit: Gale Research Co., 1986, pp. 296–314.

Harte, Barbara, ed. *Contemporary Authors*. Detroit: Gale Research Co., 1970. Vols. 23–24, p. 322.

Holtze, Sally Holmes, ed. *Fifth Book of Junior Authors and Illustrators*. New York: Wilson, 1983, pp. 236–238.

Kirkpatrick, D. L., ed. *Twentieth-Century Children's Writers* (2nd edition). New York: St. Martin's, 1983, pp. 603–604.

Nasso, Christine, ed. *Contemporary Authors* (First Revision Series). Detroit: Gale Research Co., 1977. Vols. 21–24, p. 662.

Senick, Gerard J., ed. *Children's Literature Review*. Detroit: Gale Research Co., 1984. Vol. 7, pp. 224–243.

Who's Who in America: 1986–1987 (44th edition). Chicago: Marquis Who's Who, Inc., 1986. Vol. 2, p. 2160.

Peck, Richard. *Remembering the Good Times*
Delacorte, 1985, $13.95; pap., Dell, $2.95 (same pagination)

In Richard Peck's fine earlier book, *Father Figure* (Viking, 1978, $11.50; pap., New Amer. Lib., $2.50), a son and his estranged father are brought together by the suicide of the mother. In this novel the opposite takes place: A suicide changes the warm intimacy shared by three close friends. Although this story reaches heights of poignancy unusual even for this talented writer, it is also filled with excitement and humor, the latter often caustic, indeed sometimes bordering on the cynical. To Peck's gallery of memorable character creations, like Blossom Culp of several earlier books, such as *The Ghost Belonged to Me* (Viking, 1975, $13.94; pap., Dell, $2.50; condensed in *More Juniorplots*, Bowker, 1977, pp. 140–143), we must add from this novel, Polly Prior, an ancient, crotchety eccentric with a sharp tongue but an understanding heart. The novel is suitable for both boys and girls in the seventh through tenth grades.

Plot Summary

The story focuses on the friendship shared by three young people. The triumvirate consists of the narrator, Buck Mendenhall, a perceptive, outgoing, average youngster who is making an adjustment to his parents' divorce; Kate Lucas, a spunky, often outspoken girl who is living with her working mother and invalid great-grandmother, Polly Prior; and Trav Kirby, a highly intelligent, sensitive youngster who is a perfectionist and also a compulsive worrier.

The action takes place in a once rural area called Slocum Township that is now developing a suburban subculture caused by the influx of a professional upper-middle-class group working in a new IBM plant. The Kirbys belong to such a group but Kate is from the original farm stock and Buck's father is a construction worker newly arrived in the area.

Buck first meets Kate during the summer following the sixth grade when he is exploring a rundown orchard owned by Kate's great-grand-mother. Kate invites Buck to witness a foal being born on a neighboring horse farm and Buck in turn shows Kate his summer home: his father's trailer that is hooked up behind a service station owned by Mr. Mendenhall's friend, Scotty MacDonald, and his wife, Irene.

Two years later, at the beginning of the eighth grade, Buck's mother remarries and he moves permanently to Slocum Township to share the trailer with his father, whom he adores. At school he finds himself in the same class with the attractive, hoydenish Kate, and with a newcomer in town, Trav Kirby. When the eighth-grade bully, gorillalike Skeeter Calhoun, runs rampant during a homeroom period and cannot be controlled by their inexperienced first-year teacher Ms. Sherrie Slater, it is Trav who calms him by gently placing his hands over Skeeter's. This act of courage impresses both Kate and Buck who immediately become friends with this gentle but often anxiety-ridden youngster. The three begin hanging out every day after school at Kate's farmhouse home where they talk over mutual problems, walk in the orchard, and play an assortment of card games with Polly Prior, the blunt, plain-spoken elder of the family.

The Kirbys have a housewarming party at their elegant new home and Buck's father uncomfortably escorts Kate's mother, who has a reputation for being loud and somewhat vulgar. It is evident that neither fits into this strata of society but the graciousness of the hosts prevents the disaster which both Kate and Buck feared. During the party Trav shows his friends his room and they are amazed to find it full of memorabilia from his childhood, including a stuffed Paddington bear. The collection seems to be a pathetic attempt to retain the security of an earlier period and to forestall the changes that adolescence will bring.

Skeeter again causes trouble. He steals Buck's father's hard hat and begins wearing it defiantly to school. For Buck, retrieving the hat becomes a matter of family honor. He confronts Skeeter and, in the ensuing fight, Buck is knocked unconscious. Skeeter is frightened off when Kate and Trav arrive and, in his haste, leaves behind the hat. Buck, though badly beaten, still feels a sense of triumph.

Buck spends the summer between eighth and ninth grades with his mother. On his return he mistakenly thinks that Kate and Trav have become so close that they no longer want his friendship. Hurt and jealous, he terminates their after-school meetings by joining the freshman football team and taking up with a flashy, wisecracking cheerleader named Rusty Hazenfield. Kate and Trav reassure Buck of their genuine concern and friendship and manage to rescue him from both football and Rusty.

Their freshman year is a welter of confused class schedules and less-than-inspiring teachers. Trav is particularly disturbed by the confusion and lack of challenge. By accident, the three learn that their English teacher, the ineffective Ms. Slater, has been receiving obscene notes from Skeeter. Kate realizes that he must be stopped and secretly plans revenge.

The three decide to attend a costume party at school dressed in outfits retrieved by Polly from her storehouse of old clothes dating back to World War I. During the festivities, Kate puts her plan into action by luring Skeeter down a dark road where he is attacked and beaten by Ms. Slater's husband. Trav is horrified at this violence and once again internalizes the event.

During the Spring semester, Kate gains the coveted leading role of Laura in the school's production of *The Glass Menagerie,* but on opening night a tragedy occurs: Trav is arrested for shoplifting some toys from a local store. This seemingly senseless act is actually a cry for help, but it goes unheeded. Hastily he is sent away by his parents to spend the summer on a farm in Iowa.

During his absence, two important events occur. First Polly sells the orchard to developers in order to ensure funds for Kate's future education, and then, not long afterward, Scotty's station is robbed and he is shot dead.

When Trav returns he appears rested but his calm disappears quickly when he learns of the summer's events. One day he gives his friends two of his prized possessions: Buck receives his calculator and Kate, the stuffed Paddington bear. They are puzzled by his behavior. They later discover it is actually Trav's last will and testament. Two days later he commits suicide by hanging himself from a tree in the orchard.

Everyone is stunned by his death. Buck and Kate are so numbed by their loss that they are unable to grieve. At a public meeting to discuss the suicide, speakers try to place the blame on various agencies. Signs of acrimony are emerging when Polly Prior speaks up from her wheelchair. First she makes a plea to stop bickering and trying to find a scapegoat, and then she talks simply but movingly about the mild, loving Trav and what a void has been left by his death. Her gentle words release the pent-up emotions felt by Buck and Kate and they weep openly.

In time, the friends' sorrow abates and life goes on, but in moments of reflection they speak fondly of Trav and spend moments remembering the good times.

Thematic Material

The two major themes depicted in this novel are the nature of friendship and the causes and effects of suicide. Other themes involve adjustments to the death of a friend; differences in family relationships—particularly the contrast between Trav's distance from his parents and the closeness of Buck and his father—the difficulty of understanding another's feelings and emotions; the necessity of adjusting to change; and ways of handling a bully. Difficulties of coping with new school situations are also dealt with, as is the problem of surmounting social barriers caused by wealth and position. Generational differences and how to overcome them are well depicted in the scenes with the youngsters and Polly.

Book Talk Material

This book could be introduced by describing the three protagonists, the nature of their friendship, and hinting at its future. Specific passages for retelling are: Buck takes Kate to the trailer (pp. 5–8); Buck meets Polly Prior (pp. 9–12); Trav calms Skeeter (pp. 21–23); the party at the Kirbys (pp. 42–46); Buck and Kate talk about parents (pp. 46–48); and Skeeter and the hard hat (pp. 54–63).

Additional Selections

A model student and star athlete hangs himself in Fran Arrick's *Tunnel Vision* (Bradbury, 1980, $10.95; pap., Dell, $2.75) and everyone asks, "Why?" In Bettie Cannon's *A Bellsong for Sarah Raines* (Scribner, 1987, $12.95), Sarah and her mother leave Detroit for a new life after her father's death by suicide. Fourteen-year-old Kelly must cope with her mother's mental illness and suicide attempt in *The Shell Lady's Daughter* by C. S. Adler (Coward, 1983, $10.95; pap., Fawcett, $1.95). The adjustments made by Lynn and her friends after David kills his parents and commits suicide are told in Susan Beth Pfeffer's *About David* (Delacorte, 1980, $11.95; pap., Dell, $2.50). Some nonfiction books on the subject of suicide are John Chiles's *Teenage Depression and Suicide* (Chelsea, 1986, $15.95) (part of the Encyclopedia of Psychoactive Drugs series); *Death and Dying*, edited by David L. Bender (Greenhaven, 1987, $12.95) (part of Opposing Viewpoints series), with articles on how to prevent suicide, deal with grief, and euthanasia. Also use Francine Klagsbrun's *Too Young to Die: Youth and Suicide* (Houghton, 1976, $10.95; pap., Pocket Bks., $3.50) and John Langone's *Dead End: A Book about Suicide* (Little, 1986, $12.95).

About the Author

Commire, Anne, ed. *Something about the Author.* Detroit: Gale Research Co., 1980. Vol. 18, pp. 242–244.

Holtze, Sally Holmes, ed. *Fifth Book of Junior Authors and Illustrators.* New York: Wilson, 1983, pp. 238–240.

Kirkpatrick, D. L., ed. *Twentieth-Century Children's Writers* (2nd edition). New York: St. Martin's, 1983, pp. 610–611.

Locher, Frances C., ed. *Contemporary Authors.* Detroit: Gale Research Co., 1980. Vols. 85–88, pp. 458–459.

Metzger, Linda, ed. *Contemporary Authors* (New Revision Series). Detroit: Gale Research Co., 1987. Vol. 19, pp. 366–370.

Sarkissian, Adele, ed. *Something about the Author: Autobiography Series.* Detroit: Gale Research Co., 1987. Vol. 2, pp. 175–186.

Who's Who in America: 1986–1987 (44th edition). Chicago: Marquis Who's Who, Inc., 1986. Vol. 2, p. 2176.

Petersen, P. J.   *Would You Settle for Improbable?*
Delacorte, 1981, o.p.; pap., Dell, $2.50 (same pagination)

This is Petersen's first book for young adults. It has been followed in quick succession by a number of other fine novels, including a sequel, *Here's to the Sophomores* (Delacorte, 1984, $14.95), in which Michael Parker and his friends of the previous book enter high school and Warren Cavandish becomes the center of a controversy. Both novels are set in a northern California town, Hendley, and are narrated by Michael. Because of their humor, authentic school atmosphere, and fast-moving plots, they are greatly enjoyed by youngsters in the junior high school grades. *Would You Settle for Improbable?* takes place in the last three months of a school year, from April through June.

Plot Summary

Michael Parker considers himself an average, normal ninth grader attending an average, normal school. His best friends at Marshall Martin Junior High, Harry Beech and Warren Cavandish, would certainly be less magnanimous about the school rating, particularly Harry, who considers it a third-rate prison with the principal, a martinet named Mr. Bellows, its warden. Harry is a flip, carefree TV addict who has been living with his father in a trailer since his parents' divorce. Warren is the opposite: fat, brilliant, and supercilious to the point of sometimes being obnoxious.

In an otherwise drab school day, the three friends enjoy their last-period English class with Ms. Karnisian, a practice teacher. She is a giant of a woman, nicknamed King Kong Karnisian, who makes her students work hard, particularly in notebook writing assignments, but is also a fair, honest, and stimulating teacher.

One Friday Ms. Karnisian asks the three buddies to stay after class. She explains that at her evening job at the county juvenile detention home she has gotten to know a bright but thoroughly incorrigible fifteen-year-old boy, Arnold Norberry. She describes him as a liar, thief, and cheat but with the potential and perhaps the desire to turn his life around. He will be released this weekend and be entering their school on Monday. She asks the boys to meet Arnold on Saturday at a bowling alley to act as a welcoming party. They agree, but Warren says the situation sounds impossible. Ms. Karnisian replies, "Would you settle for improbable?"

Arnold arrives an hour late and lives up to his reputation. He is tough, insulting, and smug. He even looks the part, with long hair, low-slung pants, and a shirt open to his navel. At school he continues to alienate people by borrowing articles and not returning them, trying to steal Mike's calculator, and showing no gratitude even toward Warren after he intervened to prevent Arnold from being creamed by the school bully Link Kauffman.

In order that an exciting film being shown by Ms. Karnisian is not interrupted by the endless messages and threats from Mr. Bellows on the intercom, Warren secretly snips the wire to its loudspeaker. When the principal tries to contact the room and receives no reply, he appears, discovers the vandalism, and demands the name of the culprit. No one confesses, though several know his identity. Mr. Bellows begins grilling each class member one by one, when suddenly Arnold admits his guilt, giving a farfetched explanation that his knife slipped when he was adjusting the volume switch. Mr. Bellows falls for the line and lets Arnold off with a warning. Arnold shrugs off the thanks of his classmates, but he has become the class hero, and everyone, including attractive Jennifer Kirkpatrick, applauds his action.

One day Mike bikes over to Arnold's slum neighborhood. Their conversation on the stoop of the dilapidated tenement building in which Arnold lives is interrupted by a sleezy, obviously drunk woman with pink hair. It is Arnold's mother. She abuses him physically until he takes her inside. Mike realizes how barren Arnold's life is and, by comparison, how fortunate he is in his comfortable middle-class home.

Everyone in the class is abuzz with talk of graduation and the dance that will follow. Suddenly Arnold is also caught up in the excitement and asks if he too will graduate. Ms. Karnisian investigates and finds that all he lacks is a passing grade in a state-required test on the Constitution that the others had taken in the eighth grade. It now becomes a class project, particularly for Warren, Jennifer, Harry, and Mike, to tutor Arnold in American government. Everyone's hopes are high, but on the day of the test, Arnold, in typical fashion, doesn't appear. Not deterred, his friends find out when another class is taking the test, and when Arnold finally does arrive, force him into the classroom. As expected, he passes with 82 percent and the class has an Arnold Passed Party to celebrate.

Arnold borrows a bike from Mike and the two visit Jennifer. They meet her father, an overbearing snob who cares more for his vintage Thunderbird automobile than for people. Mr. Kirkpatrick is decidely not impressed with Arnold.

Although Mike has not yet summoned up the courage to ask classmate Margaret Olsen to the graduation dance, Arnold gets an affirmative answer from Jennifer.

Arnold's mother is jailed for drunk and disorderly conduct and the boy moves to Mike's house temporarily. He tells Mike that he would like to move on and talks about driving up to Canada and starting over. Also, to Mike's horror, he gives a demonstration on how easy it is to steal a car.

With the help of another teacher, Miss Kellaher, the class plans a party for Ms. Karnisian and collects twenty-one dollars to buy her a set of Jane Austen novels from a local bookstore. The day that the class finds out the set has already been sold is also the day that a tearful Jennifer tells Arnold that her parents will not allow her to attend the dance with him. In a rare show of unselfishness, Arnold volunteers to take the money and buy a substitute present.

The next day at the party Arnold is again a no-show. Jennifer confides to Mike that the previous evening someone had broken into their garage and completely trashed her father's T-Bird. After the party, Ms. Karnisian tells Harry, Warren, and Mike that late last night Arnold was arrested in a neighboring city traveling the wrong way on a one-way street in a stolen car.

A few days later, from the juvenile detention home, Arnold writes a letter of apology to the class, claiming that he stole the car to buy the gift books in a neighboring city. Mike expects he is not the only one who doesn't believe this explanation.

Later, at graduation, while listening to dull speeches, Mike wonders if Arnold's lot in life will always be to travel the wrong way on a one-way street; but for himself tonight is the graduation dance and he is going to it with Margaret.

Thematic Material

Mike is a most likable, idealistic boy who learns one of life's most bitter lessons: the acceptance of conditions that can't be changed. The realization of life's limitations and injustices and that some are irrevocable is difficult, particularly for youngsters. An authentic classroom atmosphere is created in this novel, along with humor, snappy dialogue, and memorable characterizations. The causes and effects of juvenile delinquency are well explored, as are such subjects as friendship, different family lifestyles, adolescent growing pains, rejection, and coping with shattered hopes.

Book Talk Material

Two interesting ways to introduce this book would be either to explain its title or read some of the many entries in the students' notebooks (pp. 1–2 and pp. 45–46 are good examples). Other passages of interest: Ms. Karnisian asks for the boys' help (pp. 13–17); at the bowling alley (pp. 27–35); the incident with Link Kauffman (pp. 41–44); Arnold gives a lesson in ethics (pp. 49–54); Arnold tries to steal Mike's calculator (pp. 58–61); and Mr. Bellows's inquisition about the snipped wires (pp. 73–81).

Additional Selections

In Frances A. Miller's *Aren't You the One Who . . . ?* (pap., Fawcett, 1985, $2.25), a teenager tries to escape from a scandal in his past. Norman, a teacher, and several school chums campaign to save their school in Ivy Ruckman's *What's an Average Kid Like Me Doing Way Up Here* (Delacorte, 1983, $11.89; pap., Dell, $2.50). Mel Glenn conveys the emotions of teen life in his well-illustrated book of poems, *Class Dismissed: High School Poems* (Houghton, 1982, $11.95) and *Class Dismissed II: More High School Poems* (Clarion, 1986, $12.95). Katie falls in love with her new classmate Thad Marshall, a.k.a. Brick in the soap "Lonely Days, Restless Nights," in *You Never Can Tell* (Little, 1984, $12.95) by Ellen Conford, and Enid spends a fascinating summer in Boston in Lois Lowry's *Taking Care of Terrific* (Houghton, 1983, $9.95; pap., Dell, $2.50). Charlie moves to Northern California and tries to shake off his good-guy image in P. J. Petersen's *Goodbye to Good Ol' Charlie* (Delacorte, 1987, $14.95). A ninth-grade student falls in love with her English teacher in June Foley's *It's No Crush, I'm in Love* (Delacorte, 1982, $12.95; pap., Dell, $2.50). Nina finds that her mathematics teacher is her father's new wife in Stella Pevsner's *A Smart Kid Like You* (Houghton, 1975, $10.95; pap., Scholastic, $1.95).

About the Author

Commire, Anne, ed. *Something about the Author*. Detroit: Gale Research Co., 1986. Vol. 43, p. 186.

May, Hal, ed. *Contemporary Authors*. Detroit: Gale Research Co., 1985. Vol. 112, p. 395.

Sebestyen, Ouida. *Far from Home*
Little, 1980, $12.95; pap., Dell, $2.95

In Ouida Sebestyen's first novel for young adults, *Words by Heart* (Little, 1979, $12.45; pap., Bantam, $2.50), she explored the theme of racial prejudice through the experiences of the only black family living in a small southwestern town in 1910. This, her second book, is set in a northern Texas town in 1929 and investigates various aspects of love, its dimensions and delimitations—as revealed by seven characters living together for a short time in a run-down boarding house. The novel is suitable for readers in grades seven through nine.

Plot Summary

Salty Yeager is thirteen, homeless and, except for his great-grandmother, Mam, also without a family because only a few weeks ago his mother died. She was Dovey Yeager, a mute domestic servant who had worked for many years at a boarding house called The Buckley Arms. Without her income there is no food on the table and now Salty's home on the outskirts of the town of Wickwire has been sold and he and Mam are being evicted. His only shred of hope lies in a note his mother left him which reads, "Go to Tom Buckley. He take you in. Love him." Reluctantly the boy walks into town and presents himself at the boarding house run by Tom and Babe Buckley. Tom is far from enthusiastic about having two nonpaying guests move in but Babe—partly through compassion and partly because both she and Tom, who still suffers the effects of being gassed during World War I, could use a helper—prevails and Mam, Salty, plus his pet Embden gander, Tollybosky, relocate: Mam to an upstairs bedroom, Salty to a tiny room in the basement where his mother had slept, and Tolly to the garage. Tom insists that this is only a temporary arrangement because he will shortly be selling the house.

Salty meets the two other residents of the boarding house, Babe's nephew, the wise-cracking, n'er-do-well, Hardy McCaslin, and his wife, Rose Ann. Hardy is a good-natured failure who calls himself "the family sponge." He is currently unemployed, nursing a broken arm from an accident on the last of his jobs. During the first evening in The Buckley Arms, Salty has a long talk with Hardy during which Hardy reveals that in spite of his many precautions, Rose Ann has deliberately become pregnant. Hardy has just learned the news and is baffled, frightened, and somewhat resentful.

While out on an errand for Babe, Salty accidently meets a very pregnant girl who is looking for a cheap hotel room. She has no money and is half-starved, so Salty, feeling sympathy for her, brings another stray to the boarding house. Her name is Jo Miller, the young wife of a prohibition bootlegger named Kell Miller. Although she loves Kell, Jo has learned that he has allowed an innocent man to be convicted of the crimes for which he himself was guilty. Horrified, she has fled from him with only a few dollars in her purse. Again Babe's generosity prevails and Jo is given a room. She is a gentle, understanding girl and almost immediately a bond of friendship and compassion grows between her and Salty.

In the next few days things appear to be going well at The Buckley Arms. Tom has taken a job at the ice house, Salty is working well at his chores, and Babe is trying to adjust to Mam's set ways, including chewing tobacco and using old tin cans as spittoons. Even Hardy gets some work at a local bakery.

However, Salty is undergoing an inner conflict. He has never known who his father was but always longed to learn his identity. His mother, without the power of speech, never communicated this information to him, but some kids, like Idaler Eversole, who lives across the street from the boarding house, claim he is a "bastid." In the few days he has been in the house, pieces of evidence and remembrances surface that unmistakably point to Tom Buckley as his father. First there was his mother's note ending, "Love him," then Mam's allusions to Tom's close feelings for Dovey and the news that he had been secretly paying the rent on their former home, plus the fact that less than a year prior to going to war and to Salty's birth, Tom and Babe had a period of estrangement but Dovey continued to live in the house. Tom also knows things about Salty's past that others don't; for example, that his name actually is Saul T. Lastly, there is the ambivalent behavior that Tom displays toward Salty—one moment caring and paternal, the next hostile and dismissive as though Salty was the representation of some inner guilt. Salty confers with Hardy who agrees with his suspicion but maintains that Tom's silence on the subject is not a sign of lack of love for Salty, but rather because he does not wish to hurt Babe.

That night Jo visits Salty in his room for a talk, but before she can return upstairs labor pains begin, and she delivers her own baby on Salty's bed. The next morning amid great bustle and fanfare, Jo and her baby boy, whom she names Micah, are triumphantly transported upstairs. Rose Ann, however, feels very differently about her pregnancy. She believes Hardy does not want the child whom he flippantly refers to as "the bean." They quarrel and Rose Ann, trying to sort out her emotions, leaves to visit her sister.

Under Tom's urging Jo decides that she must return to her husband to give him another chance. So on the morning of the Fourth of July, six days after Micah's birth, she borrows train fare from Tom, leaving her wedding ring as collateral. She and Salty say a tearful farewell at the station, but this is only the first of several emotional upheavals that will happen this day to Salty.

When he returns home from the station, he finds that Tolly, his gander, has been given to a farmer because of a provoked attack on the Eversole children. Furthermore, Babe and Mam have fought so violently that Babe wants her to leave. Feeling both anger and betrayal, Salty tells the Buckleys that he has as much right as anyone to live in their home. Before he can tell Babe the truth, Tom orders him out of the house. Salty attacks his father but Hardy separates them and drags Salty outdoors and forces him to join the Independence Day festivities. During the parade Tom catches up with Hardy and delivers the horrifying news that Rose Ann has had an abortion and is in the hospital. Hardy is sickened at the news and, realizing that he is partly to blame, decides he must see her. While waiting at the station with Hardy and Salty, Tom talks about his love and guilt concerning Dovey and why he had to reject Salty after his return from the war for Babe's sake.

On returning home, Tom and Salty find that Mam has wandered off alone. After frantic searching, they find her back on her old property. She has suffered a stroke and is disoriented.

On the way back to The Buckley Arms, Tom and Salty talk about the future. Tom says that he will not sell the boarding house and that there will always be room there for Salty and Mam. Salty is also given assurance that he will be able to visit Tolly, but he is afraid that the bird will still feel unloved. Tom says, "Then he'll have to go on loving you on faith. Like people do when they can't tell each other." "Like us," Salty says. "Yes," Tom replies.

Thematic Material

Toward the end of the book Tom asks the question, "Why do we have rules for loving?" This book explores life's rules for loving in several different relationships. It is also the story of one boy's search for identity and his birthright. Family relationships are well developed as are the concepts of responsibility toward others, facing the consequences of one's actions, and the nature of trust and friendship. Details of small town life in 1929 are carefully interwoven into the plot to create an authentic picture of American life sixty years ago.

Book Talk Material

Paraphrasing Chapter 1 in which Salty first visits The Buckley Arms with his mother's note should intrigue readers. Other passages: Salty meets Tom and Babe and is accepted (pp. 12–17; pp. 17–23, pap.); some first adjustments (pp. 34–36; pp. 43–45, pap.); Salty encounters Jo (pp. 48–51; pp. 58–61, pap.); and Jo tells her story (pp. 62–65; pp. 73–76, pap.).

Additional Selections

After her grandmother dies, an eighteen-year-old girl tries to solve the mystery of her past in Irene Bennett Brown's *Answer Me, Answer Me* (Atheneum, 1985, $13.95). A shy ninth grader, Barry Wilson, learns about life in visits to elderly people in Pat Derby's *Visiting Miss Pierce*

(Farrar, 1986, $11.95). A girl must move from her beloved hometown to the city in Suzanne Newton's *A Place Between* (Viking, 1986, $11.95). Seventeen years after a kidnapping case, the victim reappears to claim her inheritance—or is she an imposter?—in E. L. Konigsburg's *Father's Arcane Daughter* (Atheneum, 1976, $11.95; pap., Aladdin, $1.95). Thirteen-year-old Bernie decides to live with his grandfather when his mother remarries, in Hilma Wolitzer's *Wish You Were Here* (Farrar, 1984, $10.95). When tragedy strikes her family, a teenage girl begins to question her life in Phyllis Reynolds Naylor's *A String of Chances* (Macmillan, 1982, $11.95; pap., Fawcett, $2.25). A sixteen-year-old learns that she is considered "illegitimate" in Patricia Calvert's *Yesterday's Daughter* (Scribner, 1986, $11.95). A family is disintegrating and its effects are felt directly by a teenage girl in Marilyn Levy's *Summer Snow* (pap., Fawcett, 1986, $2.50).

About the Author

Commire, Anne, ed. *Something about the Author.* Detroit: Gale Research Co., 1985. Vol. 39, pp. 187–189.

Holtze, Sally Holmes, ed. *Fifth Book of Junior Authors and Illustrators.* New York: Wilson, 1983, pp. 279–280.

May, Hal, ed. *Contemporary Authors.* Detroit: Gale Research Co., 1983. Vol. 107, p. 466.

Strasser, Todd.   *Friends till the End*
   Delacorte, 1981, o.p.; pap., Dell, $2.50 (same pagination)

In 1979, Todd Strasser's first novel, *Angel Dust Blues* (Coward, 1979, $9.95; pap., Dell, $1.75), appeared and was an immediate success. It is the story of Alex Lazar, a high school senior who is arrested for drug dealing. Strasser's other young adult novels deal with equally timely themes. For example, *Rock 'n Roll Nights* (Delacorte, 1982, o.p.; pap., Dell, $2.50) tells how seventeen-year-old Gary Spector and his band try to break into the New York City rock scene. Its sequels are *Turn It Up!* (Delacorte, 1984, $14.95; pap., Dell, $2.50) and *Wildlife* (Delacorte, 1987, $14.95). All of Strasser's novels are suited for readers in grades seven through ten. *Friends till the End* is narrated by its central character, David Gilbert.

Plot Summary

David Gilbert's life could be described as comfortable and complacent. He is entering his senior year at the high school in Cooper's Neck, an affluent New York suburb on Long Island's so-called Gold Coast. His parents, though not as wealthy as many of their neighbors, nevertheless manage very well. Mr. Gilbert is a successful local real estate broker and Dave's mother teaches second grade. Dave has an attractive steady girlfriend, self-sufficient, talented Rena Steuben, whose overriding passion (even Dave comes second) is photography. Her divorced mother is frequently absent, which allows the young people many enviable nights alone.

Dave is the goalee on the school's much-trophied soccer team. It appears that Dave, along with his best friend and team captain, Chuck Lowell, and the other star of the team, Billy Lee, are all assured of sports scholarships and perhaps a future in the big leagues. The prospect of this future now troubles Dave. Although he loves the game, he really does not want to make it his life as his father hopes he will. Instead he would like to forget the scholarship and enter a good pre-med program with the hope eventually of becoming a doctor.

During the first week of school Dave meets at the bus stop Howie Jamison, another senior whose family has just moved up from Florida. He is an ingenuous, open young man, anxious to make friends, and totally without the sophisticated gloss of Dave's other acquaintances. However, he is not at the bus stop during the second week of school and Dave learns he is in the hospital sick with leukemia.

Because of his mother's humanitarian urgings, Dave reluctantly visits Howie and is impressed with his straightforward upbeat attitude in spite of the gravity of his situation. He also meets Mrs. Jamison, who is pathetically clinging to any shred of hope she can find and irrationally blames their move from Florida for precipitating Howie's illness. Dave visits Howie again and slowly a friendship begins.

Rena's snooty friend Sara Parker invites a few of the high school elite, including Dave and Chuck, her new boyfriend, to a very elegant dinner at her home. During dinner, Dave becomes so exasperated at their superficial talk of death and dying that he tells them about Howie, his illness and aloneness, and upbraids them for their indifference to this situation.

Howie returns home during a brief period of remission, and Dave visits him. After a dinner with somewhat strained conversation with Mr. and Mrs. Jamison, the two boys go out for a walk. They talk and Howie openly wonders if his illness is punishment for some unknown sins he has committed. Later he attends a soccer game to cheer on Dave and his teammates.

Dave's close relationship with Rena begins to disintegrate. She is influenced by Sara, who dislikes Dave. As well, Rena is decidedly unsympathetic with Dave's attention to Howie and to his plan to give up sports for medicine. A breakup occurs.

Overriding his mother's protests, a bald (from chemotherapy) Howie insists on accepting Dave's invitation to attend a soccer victory party at Chuck's. There, Dave meets Katie, who has a sympathetic ear for his problems, and loses track of time. At 2 A.M. he brings a completely exhausted and somewhat tipsy Howie home. Mrs. Jamison is furious and almost forbids Dave to see her son again. Later, at school, Howie meets Rena who reverses her distant attitude. However, within a short time, his condition worsens and he is sent back to the hospital.

Ironically, the more victories won by Dave's team and the closer they get to the state championship, the weaker Howie becomes and the less hopeful his situation. During one of Dave's visits, Howie talks about dying and then, at first sobbing with self-pity and later defiant in anger, questions the fairness of life.

Rena organizes an emergency blood drive to help Howie, and Dave gets many of his teammates, including a reluctant Chuck, to give platelets. However, the evasive answers they receive from Howie's doctor about the possibility of a cure make them realize that the boy is doomed. The ordeal of helping Howie brings Rena and Dave back together, and, the night before the state championship game at Ithaca, the two make love at Rena's home.

When the team returns victorious, chiefly because of a brilliant save by Dave, they learn that the Jamisons have moved back to Florida and Howie has been transferred to a hospital there.

As Christmas approaches, Dave's life begins to stabilize again. Both his family and friends are reconciled to his future plans and he and Rena are as close as before. Mr. Jamison returns for a few days to clear out the house and he tells Dave that Howie is in very bad condition. Later, Dave writes his friend several times but receives no answer.

Thematic Material

Dave and his friends are introduced for the first time to death and dying, and this experience makes them, including Howie, question the justice of life and to examine and reevaluate their standards and values.

As the paperback blurb states, "Some things are more important than sports and parties." Howie's courage and love of life radiate throughout the book. Dave's coming of age and achieving independence by making difficult career choices in defiance of others are important added themes, as are his first strong first love experience and the meaning of loyalty and friendship. For the sports-minded there are also many exciting scenes of fast soccer action.

Book Talk Material

The descriptions of Dave, Cooper's Neck, and Howie's situation should interest readers. Some passages of importance are: Rena and Dave first meet (pp. 17–19); Dave and Howie's first talk at the hospital (pp. 31–32); Dave's second visit with Howie (pp. 41–45); the dinner party at Sara's (pp. 56–64); Dave and Howie go for a walk (pp. 74–78); and Dave talks to his father about Howie's health (pp. 80–81).

Additional Selections

A mother describes her son's gallant but losing battle with leukemia in Doris Lund's *Eric* (Harper, 1974, $16.45; pap., Dell, $2.95; condensed in *More Juniorplots*, Bowker, 1977, pp. 118–121). In Monica Hughes's novel *Hunter in the Dark* (Atheneum, 1983, $11.95; pap., Avon, $2.50), a young boy trailing a white-tail buck recalls his bout with leukemia the year before. In Alice Bach's *Waiting for Johnny Miracle* (Harper, 1980, $12.89), a high school senior must enter the hospital, have chemotherapy, and an operation to treat her cancer. An eleven-year-old girl discovers she has diabetes and learns to live with it in Willo Davis Roberts's *Sugar Isn't Everything* (Atheneum, 1987, $12.95). A photography-loving girl falls for a grocery clerk in June Foley's *Falling in Love Is No Snap* (Delacorte, 1986, $14.95), and Tyler and Mitzi share more than their love of photography in Barbara Wersba's *Crazy Vanilla* (Harper, 1986, $11.95). In the true story by Richard E. Peck, *Something for Joey* (pap., Bantam, 1978, $2.75), a star football player takes care of his younger brother who has leukemia. Theresa Nelson's *The Twenty-Five Cent Miracle* (Bradbury, 1986, $11.95) tells the story of the anguish experienced by a widowed father and his daughter coping with death.

About the Author

Commire, Anne, ed. *Something about the Author*. Detroit: Gale Research Co., 1985. Vol. 41, p. 217; updated 1986. Vol. 45, pp. 197–200.

May, Hal, ed. *Contemporary Authors*. Detroit: Gale Research Co., 1986. Vol. 17, p. 419.

Tchudi, Stephen.   *The Burg-O-Rama Man*
Delacorte, 1983, o.p.; pap., Dell, $2.50 (same pagination)

This, Tchudi's first young adult novel, is a thought-provoking revelation of the phoniness and distortion often associated with both the advertising and fast-food industries and of the seaminess that underlies much of the surface glamor and glory. Facing these ugly truths for the first time is the young narrator of the story, Karen Wexler, whose experiences in the novel are both disillusioning and enlightening. This is a popular book in grades seven through nine.

Plot Summary

The 995 students of Crawford High School in Crawford City, Ohio, receive some startling and exciting news during a special assembly period. The principal introduces Robert Lesenly from the Burg-O-Rama fast-food chain, who tells the students that their school has been selected for the shooting of a series of "slice of life" commercials advertising the chain's burger products. Background shooting will start immediately, but eventually five people will be chosen to be highlighted in these spots and each will receive actors' rates plus residuals totaling about $20,000. In addition, the school will be awarded grants for its education program. The signal indicating that a particular individual has been selected will be Mr. Lesenly's invitation to lunch.

The school is abuzz with the news, and Mr. Lesenly soon becomes known simply as the Burg-O-Rama man, and his cameraman, Kenneth Deitrick, is nicknamed Big Fella after a special kind of hamburger Burg-O-Rama sells. Within a short while their presence in the school becomes commonplace.

The five most influential seniors, known as the Power Mongers, also show a keen interest in these proceedings. The first member of the group is Karen Wexler, editor and chief writer of the school newspaper, the *Tiger Eye*. She is a serious, hardworking girl with integrity and a strong sense of justice. Her best friend is Jane Heath, a very popular girl active in club activities. Jane has a long-standing crush on another member of the group, Tom Garver, captain of the football team, but he has eyes only for Kelly Flynn, the vain, spoiled captain of the cheerleaders. The fifth member is George Foley, president of the senior class. Each thinks that at least one of the successful candidates should come from this group; Kelly openly hopes it will be she.

At basketball state championship time, the hopes of Crawford High rest on Jeff Leuders, a six-foot-nine-inch court star. Jeff confesses to Karen that the responsibility and pressure placed on him to win weigh heavily and cause him much anxiety. On the night of the big game in Cincinnati the opposition places a wrestler type, nicknamed Bruiser, opposite Jeff. Bruiser muscles him so much that Jeff is unable to play properly. It seems like a losing game, but by relying on his teammates to make the shots he can't, Jeff is able to bring in a victory. During this moment of celebration, the Burg-O-Rama man approaches Jeff and invites him to lunch. Number one has been chosen.

Mr. Walton is considered to be the best teacher at Crawford High. His science classes are stimulating and rewarding and he is known for his honesty and high principles. With his small salary and a wife and two children to support, he is having financial problems and is now studying law part time. With regrets he plans to leave teaching for this more lucrative profession. One day he questions the class to which Karen and her friends belong about the ethical nature of a school, in effect, endorsing a fast-food chain. From this comes a discussion on nutrition and the assignment of student reports. The report given by Russel Moffett, which coincidently is being filmed by the Big Fella in the presence of the Burg-O-Rama man, is a particularly powerful indictment of the industry, giving details on the ingredients and processes that produce onion rings, hot dogs, and hamburgers. At the end of the discussion, the Burg-O-Rama man steps forward and invites Mr. Walton to lunch. To everyone's amazement he accepts.

Karen is particularly shocked and disillusioned at what she considers Mr. Walton's selling out. "What price law school?" she thinks. Obviously enough to sidestep principles.

One Saturday while riding her bike through the Italian section of town, Karen stops at Costello's Market. Behind the counter is an acquaintance from school, Mary Costello, an excellent A student with a sweet disposition, who has to spend all her spare time helping her father in his business. For Karen, the store is a revelation—a bit of Italy—full of pastas, cheeses, salami, and the exotic odor of espresso coffee. As Karen and Mary talk, Karen is drawn toward this quiet, hardworking girl. She accepts an invitation to attend an Italian festival at St. Anthony's Church the next week. Even there Karen notices that, apart from the Costello booth, the goods and atmosphere are synthetic and phony; for example, the "Kiss Me I'm Italian" T-shirts are made in Taiwan.

Mr. Costello suffers a sudden heart attack and dies. Mary feels she must leave school to manage the store and help support her mother and grandmother. While waiting with Karen outside the administration office for an appointment, she is approached by the Burg-O-Rama man, who informs her that she is the next winner. She has been chosen because she is, in many ways, a model student. With the money from the commercial she will be able to hire help for the store and remain in school.

Rehearsals for the spring musical begin. The production is *Cabaret* and the leading role of the MC is being filled by an excellent dancer and actor, Donnie Hamilton. Karen is a stagehand and chief curtain raiser, and Kelly a dancer and a member of the chorus. All the girls are secretly in love with their talented leading man, but both Tom and George claim Donnie is gay and nickname him Twinkle Toes. Karen invites them to a rehearsal to prove how manly and strong a dancer must be. Donnie performs brilliantly at the rehearsal, but Tom becomes so agitated at the intimate way he holds Kelly during dance numbers that he reverses himself, becomes insanely jealous, and challenges Donnie to a fight. The young dancer manages to extricate himself just as the Burg-O-Rama man appears and invites him to lunch.

One month has passed since the Burg-O-Rama man appeared and one more person must be chosen. To get an inside view on the selection of candidates, Karen invites him to be interviewed for the *Tiger Eye*. They have a frank, honest discussion that ends with him asking her to lunch. Moments later she realizes that she has been chosen as winner number five. She pauses to weigh the consequences of acceptance. Somehow she cannot allow herself to be bought by an enterprise for which she has little respect. She declines but tells no one about the incident. Kelly is overjoyed to be chosen in her stead. While Kelly basks in the celebrity spotlight, Karen at least has the satisfaction of being her own person.

Thematic Material

Like many people, Karen has difficulty in sorting out what is honest and true in life from what is artificial and false and also in realizing and confronting the ulterior motives of those who try to confuse the two. The often phony and sometimes insidious nature of advertising is brought out in this novel, as is the difficulty of maintaining principles when expedient compromises will bring immediate rewards. The capriciousness of fate, the rivalry that results from competition, and the varying reactions to securing instant fame and money are important additional themes, as are those of the vagaries of friendship and first love.

Book Talk Material

Explaining who the Burg-O-Rama man is and the reasons for his presence in the school should interest readers. Some important passages: the Burg-O-Rama man talks about the project (pp. 3–7); the Power Mongers talk over the situation (pp. 10–14); the script for the first general commercial (pp. 22–24); Karen interviews Jeff Leuders (pp. 30–38); the basketball game (pp. 49–59); Jeff's commercial (pp. 60–62); and Russ Moffett's report on fast food (pp. 78–90).

Additional Selections

In a later novel by Tchudi, David Morgan fights the local government and big business to save a swamp in *The Green Machine and the Frog Crusade* (Delacorte, 1987, $14.95). In a humorous novel by Gordon Korman, *Son of Interflux* (Scholastic, 1986, $12.95), a group of students in a fluke real estate deal challenge the power of a giant manufacturing company. By the same author is *Don't Care High* (pap., Scholastic, 1986, $2.50). Owen, fourteen, stages a sit-in to fight the establishment in Avi's *A Place Called Ugly* (Pantheon, 1981, $8.99; pap., Scholastic, $1.95), and Harry exposes the pollution caused by a local factory in *When the Stars Begin to Fall* by James Lincoln Collier (Delacorte, 1986, $14.95). Some wild and funny kids declare open hostilities on some teachers in Stanley Kiesel's *The War between the Pitiful Teachers and the Splendid Kids* (Dutton, 1980, $10.95; pap., Avon, $2.50). It's sequel is *Malinky Leads the War for Kindness* (Lodestar, 1984, $12.95). Two eighth-grade students are in love with the same teacher in Tina Sunshine's *An X-Rated Romance* (pap., Avon, 1982, $2.25). The male lead in a ballet production tells his story in the witty novel by Jean Ure, *What If They Saw Me Now?* (Delacorte, 1984, $13.95; pap., Dell, $2.50). Its sequel is *You Win Some, You Lose Some* (Delacorte, 1986, $14.95).

Voigt, Cynthia. *Homecoming*
Atheneum, 1981, $13.95; pap., Fawcett, $2.25

Homecoming is the story of a harrowing but finally rewarding odyssey of the four abandoned Tillerman children in search of a home. Its sequel is *Dicey's Song* (Atheneum, 1982, $10.95; pap., Fawcett, $2.50), the Newbery Medal winner of 1983. Dicey's Song begins "And they lived happily ever after. Not the Tillermans" and chronicles the adjustment of the children to life with Gran. In particular, Dicey has trouble letting go of some of the maternal responsibilities she has assumed while also getting along at school and making new friends. A minor character in this novel, Jefferson Greene, becomes the central character of a spin-off novel, *A Solitary Blue* (Atheneum, 1983, $10.95; pap., Fawcett, $2.50), which tells of a boy's reaction to his parents' divorce and his relations with his father "the Professor" and Melody, his mother, who cares more about serving various social causes than helping her unhappy son. These novels are popular with readers from grades six through nine.

Plot Summary

Thirteen-year-old Dicey Tillerman notices that her mother is acting increasingly vague and distant as though suddenly the troubles and hardships of caring for her brood of four fatherless children have suddenly overpowered her reason. As well as Dicey there are precocious ten-year-old James; Maybeth, age nine, a sweet, silent child whom some believe is retarded; and Sammy, a boisterous, somewhat stubborn boy of six. Only Dicey vaguely remembers a father who left several years ago. Since then the family has eked out an existence in a small house on the dunes in Provincetown, Massachusetts. Their only known living relative is Great-Aunt Cilla, who lives in Bridgeport, Connecticut, and sends them a Christmas card each year.

One night Mamma packs up her family in their beat-up jalopy and announces that they are going to visit Aunt Cilla. The following morning, scarcely having made it into Connecticut, she parks at a shopping mall and leaves them, supposedly to return shortly. By nightfall she hasn't come back, and Dicey realizes that her mother, in her deranged state, has abandoned them. With insufficient money to take the bus to Bridgeport but fearful of remaining and facing separation by the authorities, Dicey gathers together the family and the next morning the four gallantly set off to walk to their aunt's home where they also hope their mother has gone.

Their journey, lasting more than two weeks, is a saga of courage, tenacity, and devotion one to another. Their methods of survival vary. They sleep in parks, graveyards, abandoned buildings; they fish and clam in streams and ocean bays; and they earn money in a variety of ways like carrying grocery bags in shopping centers. Everyday, though getting more and more desperate and discouraged, they walk a little closer to their goal.

In one state park they meet an older pair of runaways, Louis and Edie, who give them some help, but it is at the college common in New Haven when, without money or physical strength and almost ready to give up, they meet a real savior, a young summer session student, Windy, who feeds them and takes them to his dorm room shared by friend Stewart. The next day Stewart drives them the rest of the way and deposits them on Aunt Cilla's doorstep.

Here further disappointment awaits them. Aunt Cilla died several months before and the only inhabitant of the house is her timid, mousy daughter, Eunice. Though well intentioned and sincere, Eunice, who is deeply religious and plans to enter a convent shortly, is ill-prepared to cope with these new responsibilities. She gets help from her counselor, Father Joseph, who begins placing the children in local summer camps and care centers. Dicey realizes that these are only stopgap solutions and that come school in the fall they will probably again face separation and foster homes.

The children discover that their mother is in a mental institution in Massachusetts but that they have a maternal grandmother, Mrs. Abigail Tillerman, who has a reputation for orneriness and eccentricity and who lives in Crisfield, a town on the tip of the Eastern Shore of Maryland. Dicey's financial situation has improved from working for Mr. Platernis, the local grocer, and from the sale of her mother's car in Connecticut, and she decides to investigate Crisfield as her last chance of keeping the family together permanently. Again the Tillermans hit the road.

In order to escape detection, they travel by bus only to Annapolis and there they once more begin their nomadic existence. Two teenage boys, Jerry and Tom, ferry them across Chesapeake Bay, but on the other shore they run afoul of a cruel farmer, Mr. Rudyard, who tries to kidnap them. They are aided in their escape by the owner of a small traveling circus, a black man named Will Hawkins, and his assistant, the dog trainer Claire. The children stay with the circus more than a week while it travels south. On one of his free days, Will takes them to Crisfield.

Abigail Tillerman lives up to her reputation. She is a bad-tempered recluse who wants no part of her grandchildren. Years before she had disowned her daughter for not marrying her boyfriend, Francis Verricker, the children's father, and since Abigail's husband died and her son was killed in Vietnam she has lived alone in what had once been an attractive farmhouse with well-kept acreage. Now all is in a state of ruin and decay, and through loneliness and disappointment, she has become the village oddity.

Fortunately Abigail allows the children to stay on a day-to-day basis, and gradually she begins to mellow and show concern for their future. In time she concedes that the only major barrier to their staying is a financial one. When it is shown that through social security and reworking the farm this could be overcome, she is happy to change her mind. The Tillermans have found a home at last.

Thematic Material

This is not only a moving story of courage and resourcefulness but also a testimony to the strength of family ties and devotion. The loving, nurturing relationship among the children is excellently presented, and Dicey, in her quiet, unassuming way, exemplifies true heroism by assuming responsibility and facing almost impossible obstacles. The importance of a real home in a child's life is stressed; and through her suspenseful narrative the author shows that exciting survival stories do not require a desert island or a remote wilderness.

Book Talk Material

An introduction to Dicey, her sister and brothers, and the situation they confront when deserted should interest readers. Specific passages are: Dicey faces the situation (pp. 9–12; pp. 13–16, pap.); James and Sammy fish and James has an accident (pp. 49–53; pp. 53–57, pap.); Sammy bargains for food (pp. 72–73; pp. 76–78, pap.); carrying bags at the shopping center (pp. 76–80; pp. 81–84, pap.); and the children meet Windy (pp. 89–97; pp. 94–100, pap.).

Additional Selections

Five teenage brothers flee an abusive father in Joyce Sweeney's *Center Line* (Delacorte, 1984, $14.95). In pioneer Nebraska, young Louisa sees the young wife of Dr. Berryman slowly sink into madness and death in Pam Conrad's *Prairie Songs* (Harper, 1985, $10.89). An eleven-year-old girl and four brothers and sisters are placed in the care of a cruel grandmother in Robbie Branscum's *The Girl* (Harper, 1986, $11.50), and in P. J. Petersen's *Going for the Big One* (Delacorte, 1986, $14.95), three teenagers, deserted by their stepmother, must journey alone to find their father. When their father dies, three youngsters, led by Mary Coll, must keep their family together in Vera and Bill Cleaver's *Where the Lilies Bloom* (Lippincott, 1969, $12.25; pap., New Amer. Lib., $1.95; condensed in *More Juniorplots*, Bowker, 1977, pp. 128–131), followed by *Trial Valley* (Lippincott, 1977, $12.25). A sixteen-year-old girl gradually comes to terms with her feelings during an island summer in Ruth Wallace-Brodeur's *Steps in Time* (Macmillan, 1986, $10.95). Kate and her family aren't certain if an arrogant slum girl is really her sister in Vivien Alcock's *The Cuckoo Sister* (Delacorte, 1986, $14.95). Fourteen-year-old Jay Barry Lee and his dog spend an unusual summer with 29 monkeys that have escaped from a circus in Wilson Rawls's *Summer of the Monkeys* (Doubleday, 1977, $12.95; pap., Dell, $2.75).

About the Author
Commire, Anne, ed. *Something about the Author*. Detroit: Gale Research Co., 1983. Vol. 33, p. 226.
Holtze, Sally Holmes, ed. *Fifth Book of Junior Authors and Illustrators*. New York: Wilson, 1983, pp. 320–321.
Locher, Frances C., ed. *Contemporary Authors*. Detroit: Gale Research Co., 1982. Vol. 106, p. 508.
Metzger, Linda, ed. *Contemporary Authors* (New Revision Series). Detroit: Gale Research Co., 1986. Vol. 18, p. 468.
Who's Who in America: 1986–1987 (44th edition). Chicago: Marquis Who's Who, Inc., 1986. Vol. 2, p. 2867.

Wilkinson, Brenda. *Ludell and Willie*
Harper, 1977, $11.89; pap., Bantam, $2.25

Ludell Wilson is a sensitive, poor black girl growing up in Waycross, a small Georgia town. She was first introduced in her title novel, *Ludell* (Harper, 1975, $11.89; pap., Bantam, $2.25), that covers three years of her life (in the mid-1950s) from grades five through seven, and her first meetings with her faithful boyfriend Willie. This sequel deals with the senior year in high school of these two engaging teenagers and the many problems that the year brings. It ends with a parting when Ludell leaves for New York City with her mother. Her experiences there form the basis of a further sequel, *Ludell's New York Time* (Harper, 1980, $10.89). These novels are written in black dialect, which might prove initially difficult for readers, but after a few pages most will adjust and enjoy this authentic touch. All of these titles are suitable for readers in grades seven through nine.

Plot Summary

Ludell is growing up under the repressive, very strict supervision of her elderly grandmother, Mrs. Wilson, whom she calls Mama. Mrs. Wilson has seen the life of her only child, Dessa, blighted by an unwanted premarital pregnancy and she is determined that her granddaughter will be spared a similar fate. Dessa is now living in New York City and, although she is not as attentive as she might be, she does send occasional checks to help support her mother and daughter. Mama makes a meager living cleaning for white folks, sometimes derisively called crackers, as does Ludell on Saturdays for the Seaman family at fifty cents an hour. Ludell resents having to peform these menial chores and the condescending, sometimes heartless, behavior of Mrs. Seaman. But this Saturday she is in luck—the Seamans are away—so after completing her work she luxuriates in her first tub bath and even leaves early.

Next door to the Wilsons lives the light of Ludell's life: good looking, ever-attentive Willie Johnson. Many years before, Mr. Johnson had left the family to find work and hasn't been heard from since. Mrs. Johnson does housework to support her five children: Willie, at seventeen, the oldest living at home, Ruthie Mae, Buddie Boy, Hawk, and the youngest, ten-year-old Cathy. She is assigned the job of taking care of a five-year-old nephew, Alvin, who is also living with them. Even though all the children take odd jobs and work in the tobacco fields in the summer, the Johnsons are usually destitute and frequently have the water and electricity cut off. Willie has thought of joining the army to help the family, but has been dissuaded by Ludell, who not only wants him to finish high school, but also could not bear to part with him. They plan to marry immediately after graduation.

The only time Ludell and Willie are alone is in the evening when they are allowed a moment or two on the Wilson's porch to say goodnight. One evening the usual intervention from Mama does not occur. Worried, the two hasten inside and find her unconscious on the kitchen floor. She has suffered a minor stroke and as a result is no longer able to go out to work.

At the youngster's still segregated high school there is great excitement. An unknown arsonist (actually a progressive young preacher) has set fire to and destroyed the school's shamefully antiquated science lab in an effort to force construction of a new one. Also, the football team, under the leadership of Captain Willie, is chalking up a string of victories. In a rare burst of magnanimity, Mama gives Ludell permission to go to both the big game against Carver High and the dance afterward. Willie again produces a victory and, while awaiting his appearance at the dance, Ludell talks to Bobbie Jean, the troubled, pathetic daughter of their Bible-thumping pastor, the Reverend Copeland. She has come to the dance without permission. Later her father appears, looking for her, and when she gets home she is beaten so badly she misses school for a week. For Ludell and Willie, however, the dance is a complete joy and an evening they will never forget.

When Bobbie Jean returns to school, she violently attacks a fellow student who makes fun of her crush on an English teacher. After a few days at home, she once more comes back to school, now so completely tranquilized that she is scarcely more than a vegetable.

Willie's team goes on to be state champions, but unfortunately Ludell can't attend these out-of-town games like the beautiful but dumb cheerleader Lilly Hargrove who, during the bus trip to one game, makes an unrequited pass at Willie. Ludell feigns sickness to skip church and greet her conquering hero. They are seen by a neighbor, kindly Miss Lizzie who fortunately doesn't tell Mama, but does warn Ludell of the perils of sex.

Mama's health continues to deteriorate. Her increased forgetfulness causes a terrible scene when she forbids Ludell permission to attend a basketball game for which she had already twice given her consent. She also often wanders away from home. Once she was found in the cemetery talking to her husband's grave. A group of friendly neighbors led by Miss Lizzie help look after her, but she is soon completely bedridden and increasingly becomes Ludell's responsibility. In desperation, Ludell calls her mother, Dessa, for help; she arrives from New York just hours after Mama dies.

Dessa announces that after the funeral she and Ludell will return to New York together. The girl protests vehemently but to no avail. She must say goodbye not only to Mama forever, but now also to Willie. She prays for a miracle but none comes, and the two say painful goodbyes. Ludell leaves but she and Willie know that the strength of their love will reunite them soon.

Thematic Material

This is essentially a tender love story of two innocents continually separated by forces they can't control. It also gives a picture of families that, though shackled by poverty, face their problems with dignity and courage. The novel explores in a matter-of-fact way the injustice of segregation and the problems of growing up under these conditions. The author also brilliantly introduces small town life and concerns in the South during the early 1960s and the various social levels that existed in the black community.

Book Talk Material

There are several fine passages that could be used: Ludell is off to the Seamans (pp. 1–7; pp. 1–5, pap.); her day at the Seamans (pp. 13–18; pp. 10–13, pap.); Ludell and Willie talk about problems (pp. 18–30; pp. 14–22, pap.); they go to church with Mama (pp. 34–40; pp. 25–29, pap.); the big game (pp. 74–78; pp. 56–58, pap.); and Ludell meets up with Bobbie Jean (pp. 80–83; pp. 60–62, pap.).

Additional Selections

Two collections of short stories deal with the black experience in America. The first is Kristin Hunter's *Guests in the Promised Land* (pap., Avon, 1976, $1.50), and the second, Julius Lester's *Long Journey Home* (Dial, 1972, $7.95). In *Breadsticks and Blessing Places* (Macmillan, 1985, $11.95) by Candy Dawson Boyd, a young black girl comes to terms with the death of her best friend. A friendly, black ex-soldier helps some refugee nuns in William E. Barrett's *Lilies of the Field* (Doubleday, 1962, $8.95; pap., Warner, $2.50; condensed in *Juniorplots*, Bowker, 1967, pp. 35–37). A white boy whose best friends are a black boy and his sister begins to suspect his father of Klan activities in William H. Hooks's *Circle of Fire* (Atheneum, 1982, $12.95). In Nicholasa Mohr's *Nilda* (Harper, 1973, $11.89), a young Puerto Rican girl comes of age in New York City's El Barrio. Other fiction by Mohr include *Going Home* (Dial, 1986, $11.89) and *In Nueva York* (Dial, 1977, $7.95).

About the Author

Bowden, Jane A., ed., *Contemporary Authors*. Detroit: Gale Research Co., 1978. Vols. 69–72, pp. 607–608.

Commire, Anne, ed. *Something about the Author*. Detroit: Gale Research Co., 1978. Vol. 14, pp. 250–252.

Holtze, Sally Holmes, ed. *Fifth Book of Junior Authors and Illustrators*. New York: 1983, pp. 324–325.

2

Adventure and Mystery Stories

It has been said that everyone loves a mystery and teenagers are no exception. In this tiny sampling there are novels of high adventure, stories that involve the supernatural, and mysteries that probe our social problems.

Bennett, Jay. *The Skeleton Man*
Watts, 1986, $10.95

One of Jay Bennett's first novels for young adults was *Deathman, Do Not Follow Me* (pap., Scholastic, 1986, $2.50). It tells of a boy who has discovered an art fake being stalked by a gang of killers. Since that time, Bennett has continued a steady flow of quality mysteries for teenage readers. They all have certain qualities in common: short, fast-moving, suspenseful plots with logical denouements. *The Skeleton Man* is no exception. It is read and enjoyed by both junior and senior high school students.

Plot Summary

With $30,000 in a safe deposit box in the bank, the future seems secure at last for eighteen-year-old Ray Bond. "For your college education," his Uncle Ed said, and then added, "And nobody is to know of this. Nobody." They shook hands on that promise. The next day his uncle was found dead on the sidewalk outside the hotel where he lived. The suicide note to Ray included the message—remember your word.

Ray has not seen his own father since he was two years old, and he grew up under his mother's care, the two of them scrimping by, living a shabby existence in a shabby house, his mother working long hours, Ray

118

working whenever he could after school. But his father's brother has been good to him. Ray hasn't seen him much, but he has given him the college money out of the blue so that Ray can realize his dream of becoming a lawyer. Now Uncle Ed is gone.

Not long after his uncle's death, Ray finds himself slowly drawn into a frightening tangle of mysterious happenings that begin to terrify him. First there is a phone call and a meeting with the man who calls himself Alfred Dawson. He informs Ray that his uncle was a gambler, that the supposedly secret money he gave to his nephew is not secret and wasn't his to give anyway. Dawson warns Ray that he had better give it back. But Ray, remaining true to his promise to his uncle, does not even admit that he has the money.

Sometime later, Ray receives a call from Alice Cobb, a woman who says she knew his uncle. She begs him to meet her in another city where she is staying and she warns him that he must be careful not to be followed. On the bus trip to his meeting, Ray finds himself drawn into a conversation with a stranger who seems very interested in talking to the young man.

Alice Cobb tells Ray of his uncle's gambling sickness; it was true. She tells him also of the man's love for his nephew and of why Edward Bond called himself the "skeleton man." Because, Alice tells him, there was nothing left of him anymore; his obsession with gambling had stripped him of everything, down to his very bones.

But the most frightening thing that Ray learns from this strange woman is that his uncle did not commit suicide. Alice Cobb tells him that Edward Bond was murdered, murdered for the money he could not pay back. Ray believes her.

Now the web grows tighter. Albert Dawson turns up again, demanding the return of the money. At one point, Ray does go to his safe deposit box with the intention of giving in and returning the money, but at the last moment he decides to remain true to his promise.

As Ray more and more begins to feel the terror of being pursued, he withdraws more and more into himself. Afraid of involving his girlfriend Laurie, whom he loves, and aware that his uncle's enemies might harm her, he shuts her out more and more until the lack of communication between them both surprises and then alienates her. And his fear and silence are driving a wider rift between him and his mother. But Ray feels that to talk is to betray his promise.

Then there is more terror. Once again Alice Cobb calls Ray to come to her, but this time he discovers that she, too, has been killed.

Ray at last realizes that Albert Dawson will stop at nothing, so he removes the money from his safe deposit box and agrees to meet Dawson to turn it over. Instead, Dawson orders Ray into his car and drives off to the beach and the deserted Kent Inn. Ray is aware that he, too, is to be killed so that he cannot talk, but there is little he can do.

Inside the inn, Dawson admits that he has been sent to retrieve the money and to get rid of Ray. But as he takes out his gun, Dawson himself is killed. Ray's life has been saved by the man he met while traveling on the bus to meet Alice Cobb. Pete Wilson is a treasury agent who has been trailing Dawson.

Wilson tells Ray that perhaps they will never know for certain if his uncle committed suicide or was murdered. But the agent does think that after a time the confiscated money will be returned to Ray.

The young man's reunion with Laurie ends his nightmarish ordeal.

Thematic Material

The Skeleton Man is a taut, understated novel of suspense and intrigue. Beyond the main themes of murder and mystery, this is a sad story of the despair that a sick obsession such as gambling can bring to people's lives. It is also the story of how some people live out their days in bitterness and with little hope, as does Ray's mother.

Book Talk Material

Several passages can be used to discuss the difficulties people often have in trying to talk to each other or trying to draw closer. Examples are: Ray's mother talks about his father, about his uncle's death, and about life (pp. 5–17, 19–25, 52–54, 104–106); Ray lies to Laurie about what is troubling him (pp. 57–59); Alice Cobb talks about Ray's uncle (pp. 89–101).

Additional Selections

Nine U.S. marines disappear and the search is on in Otto R. Salassi's *And Nobody Knew They Were There* (Greenwillow, 1984, $9.50). In Jay Bennett's *The Death Ticket* (Avon, 1985, $2.50), Gil's winning lottery ticket unfortunately brings more than money. Julian Thompson's *A Band of Angels* (Scholastic, 1986, $12.95) tells of five teenagers who are camping out but are also the targets for death by government agents. Adam Farmer tries to reconstruct his past while held in a prisonlike hospital in Robert Cormier's *I Am the Cheese* (Pantheon, 1977, $11.95; pap., Dell,

$2.75). Ely uncovers a skeleton and a town's unsavory past is revealed in Harry W. Paige's *The Summer War* (Warne, 1983, $9.95). Two novels by Carol Beach York are particularly exciting. In the first, *Remember Me when I'm Dead* (Lodestar, 1980, $8.95; pap., Bantam, $1.75), disturbing things begin to occur after Sara's mother has been dead for one year, and in the second, *The Secret* (pap., Scholastic, 1984, $1.95), plans to get even with a rival end in tragedy. The adult novels by Mary Higgins Clark such as *A Stranger Is Watching* (pap., Dell, 1979, $3.95) and *Where Are the Children?* (pap., Dell, $3.95) could also be used.

About the Author

Bowden, Jane A., ed. *Contemporary Authors.* Detroit: Gale Research Co., 1978. Vols. 69–72, p. 62.

Commire, Anne, ed. *Something about the Author.* Detroit: Gale Research Co., 1982. Vol. 29, p. 32; updated 1985. Vol. 41, pp. 36–37.

Evory, Ann, ed. *Contemporary Authors* (New Revision Series). Detroit: Gale Research Co., 1984. Vol. 11, pp. 52–53.

Bethancourt, T. Ernesto.   *Doris Fein: Legacy of Terror*
Holiday, 1984, $10.95

Doris Fein first appeared as the sidekick of Larry Smith in *Dr. Doom, Super Star* (Holiday, 1978, o.p.) in which the two of them save the life of a glamorous rock star threatened by murder. The novel also introduces the tough, colorful newspaperman Harry Grubb. The first adventure starring our feisty heroine was *Doris Fein: Superspy* (Holiday, 1980, $10.95), and since its success several sequels have appeared. This is number seven and, like the others, some old characters reappear. Former familiarity with them is unnecessary, although one should know that the name Petunia refers to Doris's ever-hungry alter ego. These short, easily read mysteries are enjoyed particularly by reluctant readers in grades seven and up.

Plot Summary

Ms. Doris Fein, nineteen, a university student in Southern California and part-time security agent for the federal government's IGA (Information Gathering Agency), has inherited a newspaper, the *Santa Amelia Register,* plus $15 million from the crusty, hardheaded newspaper owner and reporter Harry Grubb with whom she had shared many previous adventures. Harry died supposedly without family, but now a man in Chicago, Ashford Miller, has surfaced, claiming to be Grubb's lost son. Doris and her lawyer, straitlaced, humorless Brian Donnelly, are now flying to the Windy City to investigate.

When ensconced at the Drake, the two travel by limousine to the ghetto area of South Side Chicago to Miller's address. They stop in front of a two-story house, one of the few remaining buildings on the block, with a sign outside saying Uhuru House. It is a local rehabilitation and recreational center mainly for kids in trouble. The two are greeted by Ash Miller, its owner, and are surprised to see he is black.

In a dignified, straightforward manner, Ash explains that his mother was Luene Miller, a Josephine Baker–like entertainer. A star attraction at the Chicago Onyx Club in the late 1920s, she had become the moll of the owner, a white racketeer named Jimmie Le Castro, who had given her the then-elegant town house as a present. When he was rubbed out by the mob, she had an affair with a young crime reporter for the *Tribune* named Harry Grubb. Then, fearing further mob activity, she fled to Paris, where she discovered she was pregnant. By mail, Harry acknowledged his relationship with Luene and, as proof, Ash produces a birth certificate naming Harry as his father.

Ash finishes his story by saying that when war was imminent, his mother, now the toast of café society, sent him to New York where he was raised by his grandmother. Ash drifted gradually into drugs and low life, but after rehabilitation and receiving a small legacy and the building through his mother's will, he began devoting his life to helping others.

Doris is impressed by this friendly, obviously honest man. After dinner together, they return to Uhuru (Swahili for "freedom") House and find that in their absence it has been consumed by fire. In this act of arson, Ash loses both his home and the evidence of his birthright! Doris arranges for accommodations for him at the Drake, but when they arrive at the hotel they are accosted by two pistol-carrying thugs who force them into a car and drive off. Their heads are covered with a blanket and after a long drive they are dragged into a darkened house. Ash is taken in to meet the boss. After some time he comes back, having had at gunpoint to sell what was left of Uhuru House for a small figure. With threats of certain death if either talks to the authorities, they are driven away.

Back at the hotel, Ash wants to leave Chicago immediately and start life again in California, but Doris, who reveals that she is a secret agent, asks him to grant her twenty-four hours to crack the case. He agrees.

Doris calls Speedy Ginsberg, a West Coast IGA connection, for clearance to work in the Chicago area and to make immediate arrangements for Bruno, formerly labeled a psychopathic killer, but now a computer expert and her devoted servant, to fly from California to Chicago.

Bruno arrives the next morning, and together they go first to the IGA office in Chicago, which uses a dental clinic as a front, and then to the Illinois Records office to conduct data searches on a computer concerning property ownership around Uhuru House. Doris has the uneasy sensation that she and her friends are being followed. From the searches it is discovered that properties in the area have been systematically bought up by the Casia Development Corporation under the leadership of Dominic Le Castro, younger brother of Luene's former protector. Doris forwards this information to the FBI. She is also intent on proving Ash's legitimate parentage, and through further searching, she uncovers the name of Joel Katz, a stand-up comedian whose father, Oscar, was a close friend of Harry Grubb when he lived in Chicago.

She meets Joel, an irrepressible comic, who takes her to visit his father in a nursing home, but the old man's brain is cloudy and he is incoherent. Later, at the hotel, Doris receives a call telling her that Mr. Katz is now lucid and is asking for her. She returns to the home and there the old man tells her that Ash's real father was Jimmie Le Castro, who had married Luene before his death. To give the baby protection from further mob violence, Harry had later claimed parentage.

Before she can deliver this news to Ash, she is again kidnapped and taken once more to the darkened house. Ash is dragged in and the two are confronted by the big gang boss, Dominic Le Castro. He tells them that Ash's property is part of a parcel that the government intends to purchase for redevelopment and that the sale will net him great profits. Unfortunately, because of Doris's meddling, embarrassing inquiries had already started at Le Castro's office by the FBI. Now he must kill both of them to silence them forever. Faced with certain death, Doris plays her trump card and tells Le Castro that in killing Ash he is taking his own nephew's life. With this revelation, the racketeer relents somewhat and makes the two promise to leave Chicago immediately and remain quiet about these matters. It is a promise that does not have to be kept, however, because at that moment FBI agents, also following Doris, enter and arrest the criminals. With assurances to Ash that she will give him enough money to open another halfway house in California, Doris closes another case tidily.

Thematic Material

This is simply a fast-reading, razzle-dazzle entertainment filled with suspense and danger that is nevertheless several notches above Nancy Drew & Co. Doris is a feisty, intrepid character, and her stories are told with humor and up-to-date jargon and references. This novel gives interesting insights into past and present mob activities in Chicago and, through Ash's story, supplies glimpses of the effects of racial discrimination.

Book Talk Material

Introducing Doris Fein and the meaning behind the title should interest readers. The prologue (pp. 3–4) sets the stage for the rest of the story. Other passages are: Ash tells his story (pp. 25–30) and the first kidnapping (pp. 45–50).

Additional Selections

During her summer job at a boarding house, fifteen-year-old Cicely discovers clues to an unsolved murder mystery in Marguerite Murray's *Odin's Eye* (Atheneum, 1987, $12.95). For slightly younger readers, Lisa Eisenberg's *Mystery at Snowshoe Mountain Lodge* (Dial, 1987, $13.95) is the story of two amateur sleuths who investigate strange happenings at a ski resort. In Joan Lowery Nixon's *The Other Side of Dark* (Delacorte, 1986, $14.95), a girl awakes from a four-year coma and must identify her mother's murderer. A ghost tries to find eternal rest by ensnaring a family into a strange plot in Eve Bunting's *Ghost behind Me* (pap., Archway, 1984, $2.25). Sixteen-year-old Billie solves the mystery of who is terrorizing a group of retired people in Susan Dodson's *Shadows across the Sand* (Lothrop, 1983, $11.25; pap., Fawcett, $2.25). Kerry happens on a drug drop in a deserted mansion and is kidnapped in Janet Allais Stegeman's *Last Seen on Hopper's Lane* (Dial, 1982, $11.95; pap., Scholastic, $2.25). A young sponge diver finds she is in deadly danger at the hands of drug smugglers in *Alexandra* (Houghton, 1984, $12.95; pap., Fawcett, $2.25) by Scott O'Dell. Also use O'Dell's *The Spanish Smile* (Houghton, 1982, $12.95; pap., Fawcett, $2.25) and its continuation, *The Castle in the Sea* (Houghton, 1983, $12.95; pap., Fawcett, $2.25).

About the Author

Commire, Anne, ed. *Something about the Author*. Detroit: Gale Research Co., 1977.
    Vol. 11, pp. 27–28.

Holtze, Sally Holmes, ed. *Fifth Book of Junior Authors and Illustrators*. New York: Wilson, 1983, pp. 31–32.
Senick, Gerard J., ed. *Children's Literature Review*. Detroit: Gale Research Co., 1978. Vol. 3, pp. 18–20.

Duncan, Lois. *Locked in Time*
Little, 1985, $12.95; pap., Dell, $2.95 (same pagination)

Lois Duncan's name is associated with fast-moving, suspenseful mystery novels for teens. Some, like this novel and *Stranger with My Face* (Little, 1981, $14.45; pap., Dell, $2.75), involve elements of the supernatural and the occult. Others, such as *Killing Mr. Griffin* (Little, 1978, $13.45; pap., Dell, $2.75), are more firmly based in realism. All are popular with young readers from grades six through ten.

Plot Summary
One would think that a seventeen-year-old girl would eagerly anticipate spending a summer away from her New England boarding school and staying at a Tara-like southern mansion in Louisiana, but Nore, short for Eleanor, Robbins is not. It is less than a year since her wonderful mother was killed in a car accident, and her father, the successful novelist Charles "Chuck" Robbins, has already remarried and moved to his new wife's estate, Shadow Grove. Nore dreads meeting her new stepmother, Lisette Bergé, and her family from a previous marriage, seventeen-year-old Gabe and his sister Josie who is thirteen.

On arriving at Shadow Grove, a sprawling antebellum manor house some forty miles from the nearest town, Merveille, Nore's uneasiness is somewhat assuaged by the beauty of the surroundings and the reception by her father and stepfamily, particularly movie-star handsome Gabe. That evening, however, in a dream, her mother appears before her in an apparition and begs her to leave Shadow Grove because she and her father are in extreme danger.

Nore tries to shake off this nightmare, but she notices that, despite the somewhat forced conviviality, there is an odd, almost eerie, component within the Bergé family, as though time has stood still for them. Josie, for example, makes a reference to being in Hartford, Connecticut, and witnessing an event that Nore secretly knows took place some forty years ago, and Gabe talks about more escapades and happenings in his life than he could possibly have experienced in only seventeen years. There is also mention of a brother, Louis, younger than Gabe, who died some years earlier after being thrown from a horse. Again, the exact year of his death seems unclear. As well, there is Lisette's very apparent need to isolate Shadow Grove from outsiders. There is no telephone, although she claims to be on a waiting list, and there are no full-time servants, just a Cajun girl, Celina, who cleans one day a week. This isolation is broken for a few days when workmen arrive to repair the roof. One of them, the company owner's nephew, is Harvard-bound Dave Parlance, a nice young man who Josie finds very attractive but in his short time there shows much more interest in Nore.

One evening the young people request permission to go into town to a disco, Teen Dance Machine, but Lisette is adamant in her refusal. Later, Nore overhears an argument between Lisette and Josie in which the mother tries to justify her actions by stating mysteriously that Nore is a grave threat to the family and she and Gabe must be kept separated. Reference is also made to a strange pact that had been agreed to many years before.

Undaunted by his mother's attitude, Gabe gives Lisette and Chuck an after-dinner anisette laced with a sleeping potion and the three leave for the disco. There, Nore meets Dave and invites him to visit her at Shadow Grove. On the way home, Gabe suddenly becomes despondent, and as though he has lost the will to live, drives so recklessly that only the siren of a police car brings him to his senses. Before stopping, he confesses to not having a driver's license. Nore changes places with him and accepts the speeding ticket.

As the weeks slip by, life becomes rather humdrum for Nore. Several people suggest that at least she take dips in the pool, but she doesn't know how to swim. One day Dave visits them, and when Lisette learns of this she becomes visiby agitated. The next day Gabe asks Nore to accompany him fishing. At an isolated part of the river, he stops the motor and quite unexpectedly asks Nore to run away with him. When she refuses, Gabe begins talking about his former girlfriend Felicité with whom he claims to have lived as man and wife for eight years. Once more Nore confronts the seeming timelessness of this family's experiences. When she attempts to change the subject and stands in the boat to collect the lunch basket, Gabe revs the motor. She falls overboard and he speeds away. Luckily, she finds a floating log and half-alive makes it to shore convinced she has been the victim of a murder attempt.

Chuck dismisses his daughter's story as an exaggeration caused by concussion and suggests she rest. That evening, Nore searches Gabe's room and finds an old faded family photograph from the late 1890s. It is the Bergé family with father and son Louis. Nore gasps because the other three look exactly as they do at present. Somehow time has stopped for them and locked them in place.

She needs more proof and decides she must do further sleuthing in town. Unfortunately, Lisette insists that Josie accompany her, but a short distance from home Nore orders Josie out of the car. With Dave's help, she locates Charlie Lacouture, an old man who was once the gardener at Shadow Grove. He tells Nore and Dave that every few years the family would leave the house and a new generation appear with the same family composition—mother, one daughter, and two sons but with a different husband. After a few years each of these husbands would die a mysterious, violent death. Nore is now convinced that she and her father have been trapped by an ageless black widow and her brood.

That night, Nore, who has been ordered to her room for leaving Josie behind, steals Lisette's key ring to explore the old slave quarters cabin that Lisette uses as a storeroom. There she confirms her suspicions through photographs, letters, death certificates, and an eighteen-year journal kept by Lisette Bergé covering the years 1878 to 1895. In it, Lisette tells of her first marriage, her home life, the births of her three children—Gabe, Louis, and Josie—and of her increased, at times pathological, fear of growing old and losing her looks. Later, she finds that her husband is having an affair with a Cajun witch woman. When Lisette confronts her, a bargain is struck; in exchange for continuing the affair, the witch woman will administer to Lisette and her children a secret potion that will suspend them in time at their present ages. Thus, to keep the family together and prosperous, Lisette has engaged in a series of marriages, and when their secret is threatened, resorts to murder. Obviously, Louis had tired of being trapped in eternal adolescence and had become increasingly reckless and, in effect, committed suicide. Nore now recognizes the same feelings of helplessness and desperation in Gabe's erratic behavior.

The next morning Nore confronts her father and Lisette with her findings. Again he won't believe her, and before she can convince him, he is called away on a business trip. Nore, knowing that Dave has promised to check on her safety that evening, flees the house and hides until he arrives. Unfortunately, both are captured by a gun-wielding Lisette, who forces them into the slaves' cabin. She then douses it with gasoline and sets it on fire. They are saved by Josie, whose love for her half-sister is greater than feelings for her own safety. She says that Gabe and her mother have driven into town, supposedly to alert the fire department. They do not return. Gabe's death wish is fulfilled by the automobile crash he hadn't the courage to effect some weeks before. Only Josie is left, but Nore vows that she and her children and children's children will take care of this waif who is locked in time.

Thematic Material

The author combines the elements of a cliff-hanging page turner with the intriguing subject of eternal life. The theme of when clinging to life becomes less important than the content of that life is well handled, as is the subject of the limits of family devotion. Nore displays the elements of a true heroine—courage, resourcefulness, tenacity, and loyalty. Her feelings of attraction to Gabe and later to Dave are well portrayed.

Book Talk Material

The question "Would you like forever to be your present age?" should stimulate discussion and supply an introduction to the book, as would a brief description of Shadow Grove and its inhabitants. Some special passages of interest are: Nore is visited by her mother (pp. 19–22); Josie makes her first slip (pp. 30–33); Nore overhears the disco argument (pp. 60–62); and the ride back home (pp. 80–84).

Additional Selections

When Jean Wainwrite begins sorting out a family's documents, she realizes her life is in danger in Cynthia Voigt's *The Callender Papers* (Macmillan, 1983, $11.95; pap., Fawcett, $2.25). A family outing to Camp Allegro produces mysterious threats in Barbara Corcoran's *Mystery on Ice* (Atheneum, 1985, $10.95). Fantasy and realism blend in Nancy Willard's *Things Invisible to See* (Knopf, 1985, $14.95; pap., Bantam, $3.50), about an evil twin who makes a pact with the devil to harm his brother. In Barbara Michaels's *Be Buried in the Rain* (Atheneum, 1985, $13.95), sinister family secrets are revealed when two skeletons are found by two young people. An evil presence is trying to control Kelly in *Blink of the Mind* (pap., Dell, 1982, $1.95) by Dorothy Brenner Francis. Kate goes to sleep in the 1980s but awakens in the 1850s in Jean Marzollo's *Halfway down Paddy Lane* (Dial, 1981, $9.95; pap., Scholastic, $2.25). Julie is haunted by images that could only have occurred in a past life in Carol Beach York's *On That Dark Night* (pap., Bantam, $2.50). Could the relentless blizzard that buried a New England town be caused by a hermit? The answer is in Nancy Garden's *Fours Crossing* (Farrar, 1981, $10.95; pap., Scholastic, $1.95).

About the Author

Commire, Anne, ed. *Something about the Author*. Detroit: Gale Research Co., 1971. Vol. 1, p. 13; updated 1984. Vol. 36, pp. 67–72.

Evory, Ann, ed. *Contemporary Authors* (New Revision Series). Detroit: Gale Research Co., 1980. Vol. 2, p. 189.

Holtze, Sally Holmes, ed. *Fifth Book of Junior Authors and Illustrators*. New York: Wilson, 1983, pp. 106–107.

Kirkpatrick, D. L., ed. *Twentieth-Century Children's Writers* (2nd edition). New York: St. Martin's, 1981, pp. 252–254.

Sarkissian, Adele, ed. *Something about the Author: Autobiography Series*. Detroit: Gale Research Co., 1986. Vol. 2, pp. 67–79.

Guy, Rosa. *The Disappearance*
Delacorte, 1979, $13.95; pap., Dell, $2.50 (same pagination)

Rosa Guy first came into prominence with a trilogy of books about young black people growing up in an urban situation. In *The Friends* (Holt, 1973, $7.95; pap., Bantam, $2.25), a young girl from the West Indies named Phyllisia is befriended by Edith Jackson, a good-hearted but slovenly girl. The second is an adult novel, *Ruby* (o.p.), and the third, *Edith Jackson* (Viking, 1978, $11.50), tells how Edith, now a seventeen-year-old foster child in Peekskill, New York, must make important decisions when she finds out she is pregnant. The hero of *The Disappearance*, Imamu, is back in Harlem in its sequel, *New Guys around the Block* (Delacorte, 1983, $14.95), making new friends, facing new problems, and on the trail of a phantom burglar. These novels are intended for both junior and senior high school audiences.

Plot Summary

Imamu Jones—black, intelligent, tall for his age, and looks older than his sixteen years. Whenever he is uncertain or fearful, whenever the world closes in on him too much, he chews on toothpicks to keep up his defenses. And Imamu needs defenses in his world, in the streets of

Harlem where more often than not he must search out his wine-sotted mother and take her back to their trashy apartment to sleep it off. But even so, when Imamu gets a chance to leave this environment, he is reluctant to go, as though he is deserting this woman who cared for him with love and tenderness for so many years, until his father died and his mother's world, and his, fell apart.

But after being acquitted of a murder in a grocery store, which a friend of Imamu's committed, he is offered the chance of a foster home in Brooklyn, and so he reluctantly, but with hope, joins the Aimsleys and a way of life that is totally foreign to him.

There is Ann Aimsley, the gray-haired, gentle lady who attended his trial each day and, after his acquittal, offered him her home and her love. There is Peter, her husband, hardworking, king in his castle, and not so willing to take in a tough kid from the streets of Harlem. There is seventeen-year-old Gail, who is attracted to Imamu and belligerent because of it; there is the baby, called Perk, a mischievous eight year old whom the others dote on. And there is also Dora Belle, Ann's best friend and Peter's former girlfriend, a long time ago—Dora Belle of the sexy dresses and constant stories of her way with men.

In this family and their immaculate brownstone in Brooklyn, Imamu is a misfit, resented by Gail, doubted by Peter, pestered by Perk, oogled by Dora Belle, but always loved and befriended by Ann.

And then one day, Perk does not return home from school. When the hours become days and the missing child is not found, Ann, in her terror and grief for what she fears has happened, turns against Imamu. She becomes hysterical when his cut hand and a bloody towel (the boy had broken one of her crystal glasses and hid it) seem to indicate that he is perhaps the culprit.

Imamu is taken to the police station where he is worked over. But it is Gail alone of the family who realizes how unfair their accusations are. When he is released, she and Imamu try to conduct their own search of the neighborhood for the missing child. Imamu, with his street smarts and knowledge beyond his years of the ways of the world, convinces Gail that her sister must be nearby, dead or alive, and that they can find her.

Eventually, Imamu's detective work around the neighborhood leads him to the house of Dora Belle, where he walks in on her unexpectedly. The vain Dora Belle is sitting naked in front of her dressing table drying her hair. Imamu admires her attractive body until, with horror, he realizes that she is completely bald! Dora Belle lunges at him in fury, but the boy escapes.

Sometime later all the pieces fall into place for Imamu and he returns to Dora Belle's house, where he and the Aimsley family discover the grim truth in the too-clean basement—the body of young Perk.

Over the anguished cries of Ann Aimsley, Dora Belle sobs out the story. Perk had accidentally walked in on her, almost as Imamu had, and discovered that Dora Belle, unknown to anyone in the family, suffered from an illness that had caused the loss of her hair. "I grab she to shake she," Dora Belle cries to Ann. "She fall and hit she head on me bureau. . . . But I ain't mean it, Ann, Peter."

The Aimsley family are reunited in their sadness, and Ann asks Imamu's forgiveness and urges him to stay with them. But the young boy from Harlem has learned something new about himself from his experience. He tells the Aimsleys that he has decided to go back to his filthy Harlem apartment, to clean it up, and to help clean up his mother's life; to help in whatever way he can to bring her back to the land of the living, to make a life for them both.

"But what if she doesn't want you?" Gail asks him.

"She does," Imamu replies, "she just doesn't know it."

Thematic Material

Although this is a grimly realistic story of the harshness of inner-city life, it is also a story of hope, of dignity, and of love. It brings out the strength of a family building their own world of pride and closeness. Most of all, it is the story of the goodness of character that wins out over the sometimes ugliness of ghetto life in one young boy.

Book Talk Material

Contrasts between Imamu's life in a Harlem tenement and the Aimsleys' brownstone in Brooklyn may introduce a discussion of the difficulties that young people may face in moving from one environment to another and the ways in which they are influenced by such surroundings; see Imamu in Harlem (pp. 2–4); his mother returns home drunk (pp. 6–9); Gail thinks about her parents (pp. 14–15); Imamu meets the Aimsleys (pp. 23–29); and Imamu returns to his old neighborhood (pp. 54–59).

Additional Selections

Stuff recalls growing up with friends on 116th Street in New York City in *Fast Sam, Cool Clyde and Stuff* (Viking, 1975, $12.95) by Walter Dean Myers, who also wrote *Mojo and the Russians* (Viking, 1977, $12.95). A promising young black writer and student commits suicide and his best friend tries to find reasons in Eve Bunting's *Face at the Edge of the World* (Clarion, 1985, $12.95). In Mildred Pitts Walter's *Trouble's Child* (Lothrup, 1985, $10.25), a fourteen-year-old black girl growing up in the Louisiana bayou contemplates her future. A white family faces problems in adopting a black child in John Neufeld's *Edgar Allan* (Phillips, $12.95; pap., New Amer. Lib., $1.95; condensed in *Introducing Books*, Bowker, 1970, pp. 17–20). A withdrawn white boy is befriended by some black classmates in Emily Cheney Neville's *Garden of Broken Glass* (pap., Dell, 1986, $1.75). The adolescence of Mina, a strong, intelligent black girl, is told in Cynthia Voigt's *Come a Stranger* (Atheneum, 1986, $14.95). A girl from North Carolina is raised in the black slums of New York City in Ellease Southerland's harrowing but inspiring *Let the Lion Eat Straw* (Scribner, 1979, $7.95; pap., New Amer. Lib., $3.50).

About the Author

Commire, Anne, ed. *Something about the Author*. Detroit: Gale Research Co., 1978. Vol. 14, p. 77.

Ethridge, James M. *Contemporary Authors*. Detroit: Gale Research Co., 1967. Vols. 17–18, p. 194.

Holtze, Sally Holmes, ed. *Fifth Book of Junior Authors and Illustrators*. New York: Wilson, 1983, pp. 140–141.

Kirkpatrick, D. L., ed. *Twentieth-Century Children's Writers* (2nd edition). New York: St. Martin's, 1983, pp. 344–345.

Metzger, Linda, ed. *Contemporary Authors* (New Revision Series). Detroit: Gale Research Co., 1985. Vol. 14, pp. 210–211.

Mahy, Margaret.   *The Changeover: A Supernatural Romance*
Atheneum, 1984, $12.95; pap., Scholastic, $2.25.

Margaret Mahy, a writer from New Zealand, has had the unusual distinction of winning the Carnegie Medal, the British equivalent of the Newbery Medal, twice. In 1984 she was awarded the medal for the present novel and in 1982, her earlier novel, *The Haunting* (Atheneum, 1982, $10.95; pap., Scholastic, $1.95), was the winner. It tells of an eight-year-old boy who is terrified at premonitions of his imminent death, and his encounters with Uncle Cole, who is a wizard. Both of these novels are suitable for readers in grades seven through ten. For a slightly older audience, a later novel, *The Tricksters* (Atheneum, 1987, $11.95), also deals with the occult. It tells how a group of holidayers, including a seventeen-year-old girl, fall under the spell of three sinister young men. Like her other novels, *The Changeover* takes place in present-day New Zealand, but with the descriptions of suburban sprawl and shopping malls, the setting often seems like contemporary America.

Plot Summary

It is morning in the Chant household. Kate is trying to get her three-year-old son Jacko, short for Jonathan, ready to drop off at his babysitter, Mrs. Fangboner, while herself dressing for a workday as manager of a bookstore in the Gardendale Shopping Complex. The other member of the family is fourteen-year-old Laura. Laura is distracted from her preparation for a school day in the fourth form of Gardendale Secondary School by strange inner feelings that in the past have foretold trouble—like the day three years ago when she experienced these same sensations immediately before her father's leaving home to live with Julia, then his girlfriend, now his wife. Laura calls these feelings warnings, and though Kate tries to reassure her daughter, the girl is seriously unnerved by this experience.

At the gate of her school, Laura exchanges meaningful glances with the perfect, eighteen-year-old Sorry, real name Sorensen Carlisle. He is a strange young man—witty, sophisticated, articulate beyond his years, and often otherworldly in his behavior. He lives in a large isolated mansion with his reclusive mother, Miryan, and grandmother, Winter. Sorry has piercing silvery eyes, and Laura, with her sixth sense, is convinced that regardless of his sex he is a witch. Though they rarely speak, she finds him attractive, partly because of his aloof mysterious ways and partly because she shares his secret.

After school, Laura retrieves Jacko and they visit their mother's shop and other haunts in the shopping complex. They notice a new curio shop, and upon entering are confronted by the owner Carmody Braque and the strange cloying aroma of stale peppermint. He is a cadaverous-looking man whose skin is so tight on his skull that he appears mummified. As a supposed gesture of kindness, he stamps Jacko's hand with a rubber stamp depicting Braque's face. The young boy recoils as though touched by fire and, in spite of frantic rubbing, is unable to remove it. Laura and Jacko hurry from the store.

That evening Jacko falls ill. He begins to show signs of aging, has convulsionlike fits as though possessed, and emits at times the sickening stench of stale peppermint. By next morning, the stamp mark has disappeared. Laura believes it has been absorbed into his blood. Kate nurses him using conventional methods, but as his condition grows worse, Laura inwardly knows that more unconventional methods are needed.

Kate meets and is attracted to a friendly, personable customer at her shop. He is Chris Holly, a Canadian librarian on an exchange assignment. He is very likable; but Laura, who is jealously fond of her mother, resents this attachment, particularly with Jacko becoming more ill each day.

When Laura notices that, by comparison, Carmody Braque is growing healthier and more robust, she decides her only recourse is to visit Sorry Carlisle at his home, Janua Caeli (the Door of Heaven). The ladies of the household are most solicitous toward the girl and her problem, but Sorry, who mistakenly thought that the purpose of Laura's visit is a possible seduction, is disappointed and unsupportive. The next morning, however, he visits Laura and explains that Braque is a lemure, or wicked spirit of the dead, who must continually absorb the life force of others to keep himself alive. He invites her to visit his home that evening to discuss solutions.

Jacko is taken to the hospital, and because Kate wishes to remain at his bedside, arrangements are made for Laura to spend the night at the Carlisles. The two ladies again are most welcoming, and while Sorry is in his study they recount some family history. Each had fully expected that Miryan's illegitimate child would be a girl and that under the magic powers of three they could act as an occult trio. Disappointed when a boy was born, they placed him in a foster home at age one month, but when Sorry miraculously reappeared through telepathic powers just three years ago they rejoiced knowing that, male or not, he was every inch a witch.

Later in their conference the three Carlisles tell Laura that to save Jacko a witch must place her mark of possession on Carmody Braque and intervene in the process that is killing her brother. Because Braque knows the Carlisles, the women suggest that Laura undergo a supernatural process known as a changeover in order to become a witch and use her own stamp on an unsuspecting Braque. Sorry, however, who is now more than casually attracted to Laura, warns her that the process is irreversible and that life can be difficult for an abnormal being. She must decide soon.

Early the next morning, Laura arrives home with Sorry on his motorbike, and sees Chris clad only in her mother's raincoat, taking in the morning milk. She is shocked and horrified at her mother's actions, but after a long mother-daughter talk realizes that Kate is also in need of consolation and escape.

Because the doctors now state that Jacko's death is imminent, Laura consents to the changeover and that evening returns to the Carlisle home. A complex series of rites and rituals begins. After drinking a glass of mulled wine in which a drop of her own blood has been mixed, Laura begins a wonderful and terrible voyage through time and space during which she sees fantastic images, meets people from her past, and observes figures who inhabit the world of the supernatural, folklore, and fairy tales. She retreats in time and undergoes a rebirth experience, emerging as a witch with her own stamp.

The next day, in the company of Sorry, she visits Braque; and after the lemure refuses to free her brother from his spell, she places her stamp on his hand. He begins sniveling for mercy but almost instantly begins losing his powers.

Jacko's recovery is quick, and during it Laura has a reconciliation with her father, Stephen, who has come to visit his sick son.

Carmody Braque, now completely under Laura's mental powers, visits her at school and begs her to allow him to remain on this earth, but in an act of great courage to save others like her brother, she banishes him to the grave.

Chris and Kate decide to marry. Sorry, who is graduating from high school, registers for a four-year wildlife training program. He asks Laura to wait for him and she consents. After all, they have a great deal in common.

Thematic Material

The novel, subtitled "a supernatural romance," deals in part with the growing attachment between Laura and Sorry and the difficult choices on how far physically this should be consummated. It is also a first-rate adventure horror story à la Stephen King with totally believable characters and situations. Jacko's recovery is a triumph of love over evil. Laura's family situation is well handled, including her jealousy in sharing her mother's love, resentment toward her divorced father, and ambivalence in accepting Chris into the household.

Book Talk Material

The concept of witchcraft and the idea that witches need not be malevolent beings could introduce readers to the Carlisles. Some important passages: Laura experiences the warning (pp. 3–5; pp. 4–6, pap.); the visit to Carmody Braque (pp. 19–24; pp. 23–29, pap.); Jacko's illness (pp. 35–37; pp. 43–46, pap.); Laura's first visit with the Carlisles (pp. 59–73; pp. 73–90, pap.); Jacko gets worse (pp. 74–77; pp. 91–95, pap.); Sorry tells about lemures (pp. 82–83; pp. 101–112, pap.); and the changeover (pp. 135–155; pp. 166–190, pap.).

Additional Selections

In Eileen Dunlop's *Clementina* (Holiday, 1987, $12.95) set in present-day Scotland, youngsters seem helpless to prevent the repetition of conditions that caused a death over 200 years before. The slums of Victorian London complete with opium dens and a search for a mysterious ruby are elements in Philip Pullman's *The Ruby in the Smoke* (Knopf, 1987, $11.99). A beautiful girl who is actually a witch demands her lover's life in Louise Lawrence's *The Earth Witch* (Harper, 1981, $10.89; pap., Ace, $2.95). In Gillian Cross's *The Dark behind the Curtain* (Oxford, 1984, $12.95), a school student assumes the identity of the murderer in the class play. Also use Cross's *On the Edge* (Holiday, 1985, $10.95). In Eve Bunting's *The Cloverdale Switch* (Lippincott, 1978, $10.89), whose paperback title is *Strange Things Happen in the Woods* (pap., Pocket Bks., $1.95), the inhabitants of a town are being replaced by aliens from the planet Paca. A hoax involving a dead composer's works precipitates supernatural occurrences in William Sleator's *Fingers* (Atheneum, 1983, $12.95; pap., Bantam, $2.50). Two girls find that a mysterious disease that is plaguing the children of their town is also destroying their souls in Otto Coontz's *The Night Walkers* (Houghton, 1982, $9.95; pap., Pocket Bks., $2.25).

About the Author

Bowden, Jane A., ed. *Contemporary Authors*. Detroit: Gale Research Co., 1978.
   Vols. 69–72, pp. 391–392.
Commire, Anne, ed. *Something about the Author*. Detroit: Gale Research Co., 1978.
   Vol. 14, pp. 129–131.

de Montreville, Doris, and Crawford, Elizabeth D., eds. *Fourth Book of Junior Authors and Illustrators*. New York: Wilson, 1978, pp. 248–250.

Kirkpatrick, D. L., ed. *Twentieth-Century Children's Writers* (2nd edition). New York: St. Martin's, 1983, pp. 504–506.

Metzger, Linda, ed. *Contemporary Authors* (New Revision Series). Detroit: Gale Research Co., 1984. Vol. 13, p. 342.

Senick, Gerard J., ed. *Children's Literature Review*. Detroit: Gale Research Co., 1984. Vol. 7, pp. 176–188.

Murphy, Barbara Beasley, and Wolkoff, Judie. *Ace Hits Rock Bottom*

Delacorte, 1985, $15.95; pap., Dell, $2.75 (same pagination)

Both of these writers are well known separately as authors of books for young people. The former has written such young adult novels as *No Place to Run* (Bradbury, 1977, $8.95; pap., Pocket Bks., $1.95) in which a newcomer to New York City falls in with the wrong crowd and the latter, *Happily Ever After . . . Almost* (Bradbury, 1982, $10.95; pap., Dell, $2.50) about the numerous complications when the parents of two girls each remarries.

Ace was first introduced in his first-person account, *Ace Hits the Big Time* (Delacorte, 1981, $13.95; pap., Dell, $2.75) when Horace "Ace" Hobart and his family move to the big city from the suburbs where, in a comedy of errors, he has to contend with such urban problems as a gang known as the Falcons. His eyepatch (to cover a disgusting looking sty), however, makes him an instant hero and he becomes the star of a low-budget movie. The Ace books are enjoyed by junior high students.

Plot Summary

Horace "Ace" Hobart and his mother have a difference of opinion. Ace "Hot Property" Hobart thinks he's a movie star. And it is true that he does have a movie to his credit. *Bound and Gagged,* in which Ace and his gang, known as the Falcons, were featured a few months back to great acclaim, would lead to a future, so Ace thought, of stardom. With that in mind, Ace purchased a water bed, a stereo, Atari set, no-fog clock, a chiming telephone, and umpteen Claude Clerc shirts. The bills are still unpaid.

Which is where his mother's difference of opinion comes in. Mrs.

Hobart does not consider Ace a movie star, nor does she think he is going to be one in the future. As far as his Manhattan-dwelling family is concerned (including his telephone repairman father and sarcastic younger sister Nora), Ace and his buddies just happened to be in the right place at the right time when the movie company was looking for some "types."

While Ace has plans of movie contracts, his mother has plans for getting him a summer job before school starts again in the fall.

Just as Ace is about to knuckle under to his mother's irrefutable logic that someone—and it won't be her—has to pay his bills, he gets a call from Jerry Cone, the agent who got the Falcons a part in the movie. Cone tells Ace that he and the other fellows have a job at The Wartzburg on the Grand Concourse in the Bronx, and they'd better get there right away.

On the way to round up his gang members, Ace stops off to tell his girlfriend, Raven Galvez, of the great news. Raven is less than enthusiastic. "You guys are so gullible," she tells him. The movie was a fluke; go get a job, in other words!

Undaunted, Ace rounds up the Falcons: Freddy, who can bench press 300 pounds; J.D., who has forsaken his Afro and gone conservative since his movie career; Slick, who fancies himself the next Rudolf Nureyev; and George, the smart one who bought a computer to program the best odds for horse races. So far, it hasn't worked.

Despite Ace's enthusiasm, the other Falcons are not happy about going into the Bronx even to further their movie careers. The Bronx is the turf of the Piranhas, and the Piranhas are way too tough for the Falcons. However, when Ace points out that all of them are in hock forever without this job, they reluctantly pile on the subway.

Once at The Wartzburg, the Falcons discover to their dismay that instead of a movie to be made, there are dishes to be washed, meals to be served, and lawns to be cut. The Wartzburg is a home for retired theater professionals, and each summer they offer jobs to young people with some "theater background." Because the boys know they will all be disowned by their parents if they come home without a job, they "accept" the offer.

The menial, unglamorous work is bad enough, but now the Falcons are faced with crossing the Piranhas' turf every day. Ace decides to solve this problem by traveling "incognito." Accompanied by J.D., who sports a false handlebar mustache, Ace wraps himself up in a sari (a gift to his mother) and they ride "as a couple" through the dangerous Piranha turf.

But despite their dislike of the work, Ace and his pals come to enjoy their time spent at The Wartzburg, where, even if they are not furthering their acting careers, they are soaking up theater lore and tradition by talking to Pearl Orient and to Sir Cecil Bancroft, to Miss Otterbridge, and to the other delightfully and sometimes zany characters who reside at The Wartzburg.

However, the residents of the home, as well as Ace and his friends, are disturbed at the increasing number of fires in the neighborhood—an arsonist on the loose. So Ace is especially pleased when he thinks he has come upon the name of the leader of the arsonist gang, in a tip from—of all people—Piranha Stab Evans! Stab informs Ace that the head of the racket is a man with the sweet-sounding name of Bob Garsen. He also tells Ace that Garsen's capture means ten thousand dollars to the one who turns him in. Evans convinces Ace that it would be too risky for the Piranhas to turn in someone so near their own turf.

Ace dutifully turns in Garsen, only to discover that the man is the police commissioner of New York City. Ace Hobart has been had!

But lucky for Ace, the next few days are too busy for him to worry about looking foolish. The Dramafest is coming up at The Wartzburg, an annual event in which everybody contributes. This year, the residents are staging four plays, and for one of them, Ace has been selected to play Cyrano de Bergerac!

Ace works dutifully at his lines over the next weeks, under the tutelage of Sir Cecil. But to his dismay, he discovers something new about himself. Ace "Hot Property" Hobart is no longer thrilled about acting! It just isn't there for him anymore, he tells Raven. Her reply? "You may just have felt scared standing on that stage, Ace. Did you think of that?"

Ace denies ever feeling scared about anything (except maybe the Piranhas), and he begins to think that just maybe his mother might be right; he may have to get a real job after all.

But the night of the Dramafest proves Raven to be the wiser. Not only does Ace lose his stage fright and regain his thrill of acting, but he does so well he is awarded the Guild's Young Actors Scholarship Award. He will receive acting lessons every Saturday at The Neighborhood Playhouse. Ace Hobart, actor, is on his way! And as icing on the cake, Ace has earned enough money during the summer to pay his bills (which makes his mother very happy) and he takes Raven for the romantic evening of his dreams to dinner at the Tavern-on-the Green in Central Park.

It's all thumbs up for Ace Hobart. Well, almost . . . when six of the dreaded Piranhas visit Ace's home (where he can't believe his sister Nora is entertaining them when he walks in!), Ace laughingly hears their story about this time fingering the *real* arsonist of the Bronx. And how come the Piranhas don't turn the arsonist in for the reward, Ace asks with a sneer? Because they're sworn to a loyalty oath, say the Piranhas. They can't squeal on a family member.

Ha, says Ace, and escorts them out the door. Not long after, sister Nora is able to buy herself a water bed just like Ace's. Seems the Piranhas were telling the truth this time. Stab Evan's stepfather was involved, and Little Nora gets the reward!

Thematic Material

The authors have written a lighthearted, fast-paced romp through the streets of New York City with bumbling Ace Hobart and his good-natured members of the Falcon gang. In addition to the themes of adolescent fantasies of stardom and romance, the compassion and understanding that can grow between the very young and the very old are nicely developed. The novel also warmly portrays the concerns of a middle-class black family struggling to get along in the city.

Book Talk Material

Because this book centers on the life of teenagers in a large metropolitan city, some of the scenes on the subways and streets might be of interest to the readers; see, Ace meets the Falcon members at the health club (pp. 9–13); the Falcons meet the Piranhas (pp. 33–36); Ace and J.D. "dress up" for the ride through Piranha turf (pp. 53–58); and the fire (pp. 72–74).

Additional Selections

The school klutz and prize wimp meets a girl with clairvoyant powers and solves a local mystery in Frank Bonham's *Premonitions* (Holt, 1984, $11.95). Members of a tough school gang intent on revenge follow Danny Sullivan to Alcatraz in Eve Bunting's *Someone Is Hiding on Alcatraz Island* (Houghton, 1984, $10.95). Young Ben Pollock discovers a criminal hiding in the camp on an archaeological dig in Georgess McHargue's *The Turquoise Toad Mystery* (Delacorte, 1982, $11.95; pap., Dell, $2.25).

There are many collections of mystery stories under the Alfred Hitchcock banner that could be used; for example, *Alfred Hitchcock's Witch's Brew* (Random, 1977, $6.99; pap., $2.50). Sixteen-year-old Laura believes she is bound for stardom in Mary Anderson's *The Rise and Fall of a Teenage Wacko* (pap., Bantam, 1982, $2.25). Three youngsters try to secretly transport an elephant to a safari park one hundred miles away in Vivien Alcock's *Travelers by Night* (Delacorte, 1985, $14.95). A high school junior tries to save the life of her favorite rock star in Jeanne Betancourt's *The Edge* (pap., Scholastic, 1985, $2.25). Steve Forrester and pet bulldog Sinbad solve four mysteries in *The Ghost of Hellsfire Street* (Delacorte, 1980, $12.95) by Kin Platt.

About the Author (Murphy, Barbara Beasley)
Commire, Anne, ed. *Something about the Author.* Detroit: Gale Research Co., 1973. Vol. 5, p. 137.
Evory, Ann, ed. *Contemporary Authors* (First Revision Series). Detroit: Gale Research Co., 1979. Vols. 41–44, pp. 495–496.
Kinsman, Clare D., ed. *Contemporary Authors.* Detroit: Gale Research Co., 1974. Vols. 41–44, p. 442.

About the Author (Wolkoff, Judie)
Commire, Anne, ed. *Something about the Author.* Detroit: Gale Research Co., 1985. Vol. 37, p. 226.
May, Hal, ed. *Contemporary Authors.* Detroit: Gale Research Co., 1985. Vol. 115, p. 480.

Nixon, Joan Lowery. *The Séance*
Harcourt, 1982, $12.95; pap., Dell, $2.50

This author's reputation has been built on a significant number of suspenseful mysteries aimed at a variety of reading levels from the primary grades up. In her Edgar Allan Poe Award novel for young adults, *The Kidnapping of Christina Lattimore* (Harcourt, 1979, $8.95; pap., Dell, $2.25), a young heroine must prove that she is not an accomplice in her own kidnapping. For the same audience there are several additional books, including *The Séance, The Specter* (Delacorte, 1982, $12.95; pap., $2.50), and *The Stalker* (Delacorte, 1985, $14.95; pap., Dell, $2.50). They are extremely popular with young readers, particularly girls, in grades seven through ten.

Plot Summary

The life of seventeen-year-old Lauren, the narrator of this novel, has changed considerably since Sara Martin moved in four months ago via a foster care agency to live with Lauren and her generous Aunt Mel McIvary in their small East Texas town. Lauren, a senior in high school and an orphan who has lived with her aunt since age four, has her own problems involving insecurity and questions about her future after high school. Now she finds that her status in the household is threatened by this beautiful, boy-crazy young girl who seems able to charm everyone. Lauren also knows that Sara, though also only seventeen, is a shameless flirt. Lauren has seen her work on the sheriff's deputy, Jep Jackson, on the school's baseball hero, attractive Carley Hughes, and on their cross-the-fence neighbor, Fant Lester, even though his wife has been kind to Sara. Lauren also knows that at night Sara sneaks out of the house for a rendezvous with a man or men unknown.

Against Lauren's better judgment, Sara persuades a shy, mousy Cajun girl at school, Roberta Campion, who supposedly has psychic powers, to hold a séance for some of the girls on Friday evening. Reluctantly, Lauren agrees to attend, and she, her best friend, Allie Krump, Sara, plus Luemma, Dana, and Maddie, use the pretext of going to a party and assemble at Roberta's house.

The lights are turned out and a single candle lit. In this eerie atmosphere Roberta begins speaking in strange tongues and telling the girls secrets about themselves. Suddenly, Sara begins shrieking uncontrollably and falls forward on the candle. For several minutes in the total darkness there is complete confusion. When the lights are turned on, Sara is missing, even though both the front and back doors are bolted!

They call Sheriff Ashe Norvell, who questions them vigorously while maintaining that one of them must have helped Sara leave the locked house. Finally, he sends them home.

Saturday morning the town is abuzz with gossip about the disappearance when news arrives that a hunter has found Sara's body in a dense forest area out of town called the Thicket. She has drowned in a swamp.

The townspeople are stunned. A few believe that it was an accident, others suspect murder, and still others think that it was the work of evil spirits unleashed at the séance. One of the latter is Ila Hughes, Carley's grandmother with whom he lives. Ila is a superstitious, fearful lady who believes in the supernatural. Nevertheless, after Sunday church service, she shows great sympathy toward Lauren and invites the girl to her home for a visit.

Mrs. Doris Martin, Sara's mother, arrives from Houston for the funeral. She is a tough, somewhat wild, unsavory woman whose life has been difficult and who had been forced to give up Sara when she was unable to control the girl's wild ways after her father died. After the funeral, she leaves but, meantime, Sheriff Norvell, convinced that Sara left the séance for an assignation, questions the girls, particularly Lauren, about Sara's many boyfriends. He is still convinced that one of the girls is Sara's accomplice.

Lauren visits Ila Hughes, but instead of receiving comfort she is only amazed at the woman's belief in demons and outerworld spirits.

The sheriff tries to re-create the séance to get clues, and all but Roberta show up. Instead of obtaining information, though, the sheriff seems only to add to the girls' nervousness and growing fear. These feelings reach the point of hysteria when two days later Roberta's body is also found in the Thicket. Now everyone knows it is murder.

Norvell continues to pound at Lauren for information. She reviews mentally Sara's boyfriends, but, because she doesn't wish to implicate them, remains silent. When the sheriff takes her to the scene of the crime, Lauren's resolve breaks and she confesses that although she was not told his identity, she did know that Sara was planning to run away with a man that night and it was she who helped her escape from the locked house. Obviously the killer had thought Roberta was the accomplice and had silenced her by murder. Would Lauren be next?

Several nights later, while Aunt Mel is helping neighbor Feenie Lester, Carley Hughes visits Lauren and tells her that he was the person with whom Sara intended to leave town but unfortunately he was late. Sara had already left the meeting place when he arrived. Lauren is attracted to this boy and together they decide to do some sleuthing.

After he leaves, Lauren hears padded footsteps slowly approach. Obviously her conversation with Carley had been overheard by the murderer. Lauren panics and, turning out the lights, tries to flee into the backyard but is caught from behind by a strong arm around her neck. She struggles out of this grip, but at gunpoint her assailant orders her to a car parked in the driveway. It's Mrs. Hughes, Carley's grandmother, who confesses that she committed the murders to prevent her grandson from being bewitched and losing both his soul and bright future to the devilwoman Sara.

She forces Lauren into the driver's seat of her car. Frantically the girl thinks of a method of escape. She has no alternative but to drive headlong into the side of a brick building. Later, recovering in the hospital, she learns that Mrs. Hughes is undergoing psychiatric tests, but, best of all, Aunt Mel has been making plans for her entrance into college next year.

Thematic Material

This is basically an edge-of-the-seat thriller that successfully creates an atmosphere of growing danger and terror. The story of Aunt Mel and Lauren's relationship shows how adversity can bring people together. Small-town pettiness and gossip are also well portrayed.

Book Talk Material

Discussing the subject of séances should serve as a brief introduction to the book. Some useful passages are: Sara and Lauren quarrel (pp. 11–16; pp. 16–22, pap.); the séance (pp. 24–30; pp 32–39, pap.); Sheriff Norvell investigates (pp. 31–37; pp. 40–47, pap.); and Lauren reviews Sara's boyfriends and learns of her death (pp. 44–46; pp. 55–58, pap.).

Additional Selections

Sid and her friend Joel investigate ghostly apparitions that are haunting their community theater in Pamela F. Service's *When the Night Wind Howls* (Atheneum, 1987, $12.95). A seventeen-year-old babysitter is terrorized by a phone call in Beverly Hastings's *Watcher in the Dark* (Berkley, 1986, $2.50). Lee thinks his grandmother is being duped by a spiritualist in Kathleen Kigore's *The Ghost Maker* (Houghton, 1984, $11.95; pap., Avon, $2.50). Susan's friend dies supposedly of a drug overdose but perhaps it was murder. The answer is told in Ellen Emerson White's *Friends for Life* (pap., Avon, 1983, $2.50). In its sequel, *Life without Friends* (Scholastic, 1987, $12.95), a girl suffers ostracism because of her innocent role in the murder. A young girl—either a psychic healer or a fraud—is held by her stepfather and a teenage boy tries to rescue her in Peter Dickinson's *Healer* (Delacorte, 1985, $14.95). Two young girls' adventures in New York include a kidnapping in Joyce Cool's *The Kidnapping of Courtney Van Allan and What's Her Name* (Knopf, 1981, $8.95; pap., Bantam, $2.25). Also use Lois Duncan's mysteries including *Stranger with*

My Face (Little, 1981, $14.45; pap., Dell, $2.57) and *The Third Eye* (Little, 1984, $14.45; pap., Dell, $2.75).

About the Author

Commire, Anne, ed. *Something about the Author.* Detroit: Gale Research Co., 1976. Vol. 8, pp. 143–144; updated 1986. Vol. 44, pp. 131–139.

Ethridge, James M. *Contemporary Authors* (First Revision). Detroit: Gale Research Co., 1965. Vols. 11–12, p. 297.

Evory, Ann, ed. *Contemporary Authors* (New Revision Series). Detroit: Gale Research Co., 1982. Vol. 7, pp. 363–364.

Holtze, Sally Holmes, ed. *Fifth Book of Junior Authors and Illustrators.* New York: Wilson, 1983, p. 230.

Kinsman, Clare D., ed. *Contemporary Authors* (First Revision Series). Detroit: Gale Research Co., 1974. Vols. 9–12, pp. 678–679.

Pinkwater, Daniel.   *The Snarkout Boys and the Avocado of Death*
Lothrop, 1982, $11.25; pap., New Amer. Lib., $2.25

Daniel Manus Pinkwater has made his reputation with young adult readers through his way-out, tongue-in-cheek science fiction novels, like his earlier *Alan Mendelsohn, the Boy from Mars* (Dutton, 1979, $11.95). In the sequel to the *Avocado of Death, The Snarkout Boys and the Baconburg Horror* (Lothrop, 1984, $11.75; pap., New Amer. Lib., $2.50), in which a werewolf prowls the streets of Baconburg, the readers are reacquainted with such characters as the detective Osgood Sigerson and the fiendish Wallace Nussbaum. All three books are enjoyed by upper elementary and junior high students.

Plot Summary

Winston Bongo and the narrator, Walt Galt, became acquainted at the abysmal Genghis Khan High School through personal appearance appraisals: Each thinks the other looks retarded and, therefore, requires attention and kindness. Winston proudly claims to be the inventor and sole practitioner of Snarking Out, a habit he has of surreptitiously leaving his parents' apartment about 1 A.M., catching a bus to Snark Street, and thence to the Snark All Night Movie Theater where such mismatched double bills as *Frankenstein* and Disney's *Song of the South* are shown every night. Walt, who also loves high adventure and old movies, is introduced to the sport and together they enter a life of

Snarking. One night, at a particularly heady Laurel and Hardy festival, they walk home via Blueberry Park, Baconburg's answer to London's Hyde Park Corner, and hear a hipster labor leader speaking jive lick. Fortunately, a kindly black man who is accompanied by a performing chicken translates admirably.

When Winston Bongo contracts German measles, Walt realizes his time has come—he is ready for his first solo Snark. It must be something special, however, something that will make Winston proud of him. He decides to give his maiden speech at Blueberry Park, and that night he regales the crowd about the terrible teachers and appalling conditions at G. K. High.

At its conclusion, he is approached by a punky girl his age with spiky green and blond hair. She is Bentley Saunders Harrison Mathews, aka Rat Face, and a co-high school sufferer from neighboring George Armstrong Custer High. In a moment of uninhibited confidence sharing, she also confesses to be a hard core Snarker with a penchant for old James Dean movies. True to her word, several nights later after Winston's recovery, the boys meet her at a double bill of *Rebel without a Cause* and *Attack of the Mayan Mummy*. She introduces them to her uncle, Flipping Hades Terwilliger, who has been Snarking for seventeen years—an all-time record that towers over poor Winston's comparatively paltry canon. Uncle Flipping is a self-confessed mad scientist who is noted for his frequent disappearances as well as experiments with avocado plants.

Rat and her uncle invite the boys home for breakfast, where they meet the rest of the family, each kookier than the next: Rat's wealthy father, Saunders Harrison Mathews II; her mother; Minna, Terwilliger's wife; and the blond, blue-eyed, fair-complexioned Chinese butler, Heinz. In the middle of breakfast, Uncle Terwilliger disappears.

Shortly afterward, Heinz also disappears, and now Rat decides to search for her uncle in his favorite hangouts with the help of Winston and Walt. At the Hasty Tasty Cafe across from the Snark Theater, the boys spot two men in grotesque Holmes and Watson disguises. Rat later identifies them as the greatest living detective Osgood Sigerson and his companion Dr. Ormond Sacker. The presence of this august pair in town means that they must be on the trail of the archfiend and master criminal Wallace Nussbaum. Rat is fearful of the fate of her missing uncle and his avocado experiments.

Their search continues at another of Terwilliger's haunts, Lower North Aufzoo Street, in the heart of Baconburg's inner city. Here the glitterati go slumming and debutantes rub elbows with underworld denizens. On a deserted part of the street, the trio meets the chicken-owning black man, who identifies himself as Captain Shep Nesterman, and his pet chicken, Dharmati. After taking them to a fantastic night spot named Beanbender's Beer Garden, Shep and Chicken thrill them with their fiery floor show performance (he dances, she sings) and later introduce them to Osgood Sigerson and his bodyguard, a star wrestler and uncle to Winston, Mighty Gorilla. Later, Doctor Sacker arrives with news that the villainous Wallace Nussbaum and his co-conspirator, a once-respectable but now brainwashed orangutan, are holding Uncle Terwilliger captive at the uncle's secret laboratory in a storage warehouse. The group arrives moments too late: The miscreants and their captive have escaped, leaving behind Terwilliger's recent project, a gigantic avocado called the Alligatron whose emanating energy was intended by Rat Face's uncle to drive out aliens from outer space that have gained control of the minds of real estate brokers in this country. Nussbaum had been working to deter the avocado's work.

By following the trail of the poorly disguised orangutan, the gang stumbles on Nussbaum's lair, where a grisly sight meets their eyes: The scoundrel has been torturing Terwilliger by forcing him to watch old German movies. The evildoers are captured, but unfortunately not before a second orangutan has been dispatched to destroy the Alligatron and seal the fate of all licensed realtors. Nussbaum's clever disguise is removed, revealing that he is actually Heinz. As usual, the butler did it.

Thematic Material

This is a genial spoof that not only pokes fun at the conventions of science fiction but also at our educational system (see pp. 46–49; pp. 41–45, pap.), dietary habits, rock music, social conventions, and taste in movies. In short, it is another delightful excursion into the wacky, erratic, highly imaginative world of Daniel Pinkwater.

Book Talk Material

Some humorous short passages to read or retell are: meeting Winston Bongo (pp. 7–10; pp. 1–4, pap.); "Snarking Out" (pp. 11–12; pp. 4–6, pap.); Walt's family (pp. 14–16; pp. 8–11, pap.); Blueberry Park's hipster (pp. 23–25; pp. 17–19, pap.); Walt's speech there (pp. 36–43; pp. 30–38, pap.); and Rat's family (pp. 63–68; pp. 58–63, pap.).

Additional Selections

Lester and Wally determine the identity of a local murderer in Scott Corbett's *Witch Hunt* (Little, 1985, $13.95). Two unlikely teenagers solve a musical puzzle in the humorous *Sizzle and Splat* (Lodestar, 1983, $10.95; pap., Dell, $2.50) by Ronald Kidd. Johnny Dixon and Professor Childermass appear in many of John Bellairs's scary mysteries including *The Curse of the Blue Figurine* (Dial, 1983, $11.89; pap., Bantam, $2.50). Teenage sleuths are featured in Milton Dank and Gloria Dank's Galaxy Gang series which began with *The Computer Caper* (Delacorte, 1983, $12.95; pap., Dell, $2.25) and has included such titles as *A UFO Has Landed* (Delacorte, 1983, $13.95; pap., Dell, $2.25) and *Treasure Code* (Delacorte, 1985, $11.95). Brian unraveled the mystery of people who have gone into suspended animation in Frank Bonham's *The Missing Persons League* (pap., Scholastic, 1983, $2.25). A young girl cloned from a famous scientist finds she is scheduled for extermination in Mildred Ames's *Anna to the Infinite Power* (Macmillan, 1981, $11.95; pap., Scholastic, $2.25). Leon Garfield mixes mayhem, English history, and high adventure in such mysteries as *Footsteps* (Delacorte, 1982, $12.95) and *The Sound of Coaches* (pap., Penguin, 1985, $2.95; condensed in *More Juniorplots*, Bowker, 1977, pp. 86–88).

About the Author

Commire, Anne, ed. *Something about the Author*. Detroit: Gale Research Co., 1976. Vol. 8, pp. 156–157; updated 1987. Vol. 46, pp. 178–191.

Evory, Ann, ed. *Contemporary Authors* (First Revision Series). Detroit: Gale Research Co., 1978. Vols. 29–32, p. 529.

Holtze, Sally Holmes, ed. *Fifth Book of Junior Authors and Illustrators*. New York: Wilson, 1983, pp. 246–247.

Kinsman, Clare D., ed. *Contemporary Authors*. Detroit: Gale Research Co., 1972. Vols. 29–32, p. 478.

Metzger, Linda, ed. *Contemporary Authors* (New Revision Series). Detroit: Gale Research Co., 1984. Vol. 12, pp. 371–372.

Sarkissian, Adele, ed. *Something about the Author: Autobiography Series*. Detroit: Gale Research Co., 1987. Vol. 3, pp. 221–226.

Senick, Gerard J., ed. *Children's Literature Review*. Detroit: Gale Research Co., 1982. Vol. 4, pp. 161–171.

Who's Who in America: 1986–1987 (44th edition). Chicago: Marquis Who's Who, Inc., 1986. Vol. 2, p. 2220.

St. George, Judith. *Haunted*
Putnam, 1980, $9.95; pap., Bantam, $2.50 (same pagination)

Judith St. George divides her creative time between mysteries and historical writing. As an example of the latter we have *The Brooklyn Bridge* (Putnam, 1982, $11.95). Some of her mysteries, like *Haunted*, rely on supernatural elements; others give logical explanations in their denouements. *Do You See What I See?* (Putnam, 1982, $9.95), for example, tells how a seventeen-year-old boy's suspicions about a neighbor's mysterious activities are confirmed and a murderer is caught. These novels are enjoyed by junior high youngsters.

Plot Summary
Alex Phillips looks forward to his first summer away from home since he was ten years old. Here at Wye Mills, Pennsylvania, he thinks he might be free from all the hassles his parents are giving him about his grades, his two automobile accidents, and the fact that he quit his after-school job. But by the end of the summer, which he is to spend in the company of Cousin Bruce, who at nineteen is three years older, Alex is sure he can show his father just how grown up and responsible he is.

However, when Alex and his father arrive at Red Roof Farm, where Bruce and he are to "house sit" for the summer, Alex feels anything but confident. Massive and hideous, the grounds overgrown and untended, the farm proves to be far more isolated than Alex, or even his father, could have imagined. And although Alex had known of the murder-suicide that occurred there a short time before, when Baron Friedrich Von Durst shot his wife, Wilma, and then killed himself, it is quite another thing actually to look into the room where the horror had taken place.

Cousin Bruce is due at the farm in a few hours, but Alex's father is reluctant to leave the boy alone there even for a short time. However, Alex's hearty assurances (hiding some deep misgivings) send the father off on his business trip, after he first makes sure that all three of the vehicles in the barn will start, in case Alex needs anything.

Once his father is gone, Alex begins to feel more and more uneasy as he waits for Bruce. At one point, as he is outside looking up at the huge old house, he thinks he sees someone watching from the upstairs window! Just as Alex decides that the house is freaking him out, the phone rings. To his consternation, he learns that Cousin Bruce not only missed his flight but will not be arriving until the end of the week.

Unable to reach either his father or his mother until the next day, Alex realizes he cannot bring himself to stay alone in this isolated, eerie farmhouse. But when he goes into the barn to drive one of the three vehicles into the town, not one of them will start!

Trying not to panic but far too afraid to spend the night in the farmhouse, Alex discovers an old cottage on the grounds and reluctantly spends a fitful night there.

The next morning things look a little better in the sunlight, and when Alex discovers that the Jeep suddenly will now start, he decides that he might stay and wait for Cousin Bruce after all.

But before Bruce arrives, other strange things happen. Looking through old photograph albums, Alex begins to realize that the Von Dursts—known as the baron and baroness—were Nazis during World War II. Then a huge German shepherd appears on the grounds, and Alex realizes that this is the dog that belonged to the Von Dursts. It was said that they had had a dog named Klaus, who ran away shortly after the murder-suicide. Alex tries to be friendly, but the dog attacks and nearly kills him. After that, the animal seems to undergo strange periods of friendliness and savagery.

By the time Alex has decided once again to leave Red Roof Farm, Cousin Bruce arrives. A happy-go-lucky young man, Bruce laughs off the mysterious happenings and prods Alex into staying to house sit as they had agreed to do.

Although Alex does agree to stay and even begins to enjoy himself a bit with the added company of two girls, Sherrie and Joanna, who he meets in town, slowly he begins to change his opinion of Bruce, whom Alex had always regarded as someone to look up to. Now he begins to wonder if perhaps his Cousin Bruce isn't just a bit irresponsible.

But that thought is shoved aside by the eerie things that continue to happen at the farm. Alex becomes convinced that the Von Dursts hid some terrible secret in this old house. Why did the baron kill his wife and then take his own life?

One day, while Sherrie and Joanna are visiting from town, the dog Klaus once again tries to attack Alex. He escapes with his life by leaping to the hood of Sherrie's VW, where the dog almost manages to reach him in a fit of fury. Finally, Alex is able to drive the dog off into the woods, where Bruce pursues him with a rifle.

After this attack, Alex believes that Klaus will answer to one master only—the baron, dead or alive—although Alex does not understand how this could be so.

Bruce is unable to find Klaus in the woods, but the next day the boys locate the animal—his stomach has been ripped open and he is near death. They bandage the dog and care for him until it seems as though he will survive.

Not long afterward, Alex comes upon some German letters left in the baron's desk and when he discovers that Joanna has been studying German, he asks her to translate them for him. In this way, Alex learns that the baron's wife, some time before the murder-suicide, had discovered that she had been adopted in Germany and that her real mother, a Jew, had died in a concentration camp! The estate, which was to be left to the Nazi party on the deaths of the Von Dursts, actually belonged to the baroness. Unbeknownst to her husband, she changed her will. The baron must have found out and killed her, probably because the Nazi had learned that his wife was part Jewish.

With some clever detective work, Alex locates the baroness's new will in the cottage where he spent his first night at Red Roof Farm. He rescues the will just before the cottage burns.

Alex was right. The baroness had willed that all her money be given over to two American organizations instead of the Nazi party. And she had died for it.

Although Alex is not sure he understands all of the strange happenings of the summer, he knows that with the burning of the cottage and the uncovering of the mystery, the dog Klaus is now in some way free of the terrible grip of the baron—just as Alex had wanted to be free to be his own person. Klaus belongs with him, Alex decides, and plans to take the dog with him when he returns home in the fall. But for now, there is still some summer fun ahead.

Thematic Material

The author has woven World War II and Nazi party history into this modern setting to produce an exciting, suspenseful novel. This is also the story of a young man coming to grips with his own fears, of shouldering responsibility in the face of at times almost paralyzing fear.

Book Talk Material

Some of the most frightening episodes in the book deal with Alex's confrontation with the German shepherd. Alex's handling of these situations might lead to discussions of overcoming fear (see pp. 51–54; 55–60; 91–95). Readers will also enjoy some of Alex's detective work (see pp. 44–48, 66–68, 71–75).

Additional Selections

Vesper Holly is the fearless hero of Lloyd Alexander's rapid-fire adventure stories, *The Illyrian Adventure* (Dutton, 1986, $12.95; pap., Dell, $2.50) and *The El Dorado Adventure* (Dutton, 1987, $12.95). Ancestral ghosts finally rest when a family secret is revealed in Jan O'Donnell Klaveness's *The Griffin Legacy* (Macmillan, 1983, $10.95). Skyjacking incidents provide the basis of two adventure stories set in the wilderness area in Minnesota: Thomas J. Dygard's *Wilderness Peril* (Morrow, 1985, $10.25) and James Nichols's *Boundary Waters* (Holiday, 1986, $12.95). Andy has nightmares after his brother's death that lead to several supernatural encounters in Eleanor Cameron's *Beyond Silence* (Dutton, 1980, $10.25; pap., Dell, $2.75). Cindy spends a summer at Rockcove Hall and discovers a poltergeist in Norma Johnston's *The Watcher in the Mist* (pap., Bantam, 1986, $2.95). A fourteen-year-old Eskimo boy embarks on a 1,400-mile journey across the fields in Gary Paulsen's *Dogsong* (Bradbury, 1985, $11.95); and in Roderic Jefferies's *Trapped* (pap., Harper, 1972, $2.95) two teenage boys disappear when a blizzard strikes.

About the Author

Bowden, Jane A., ed. *Contemporary Authors*. Detroit: Gale Research Co., 1978. Vols. 69–72, p. 509.

Commire, Anne, ed. *Something about the Author*. Detroit: Gale Research Co., 1978. Vol. 13, pp. 187–188.

Metzger, Linda, ed. *Contemporary Authors* (New Revision Series). Detroit: Gale Research Co., 1985. Vol. 14, pp. 420–421.

Thompson, Julian F.   *The Grounding of Group 6*
Avon, 1983, pap., $2.50

Julian F. Thompson worked exclusively with teenagers before devoting his full-time efforts to writing. In the 1970s he even helped a group found their own high school. When it first appeared in 1983, *The Grounding of Group 6* was a trailblazer in at least two ways. First its subject was shocking and second it was one of the first quality novels for young adults to appear first in paperback format. Since its publication, Thompson has continued to explore new subjects. For example, in *Simon Pure* (Scholastic, 1987, $12.95), he pokes fun at academe by way of a wacky plot to turn a small liberal arts college into a highly profitable business school. His novels are read by both junior and senior high school students.

Plot Summary

The faculty members of the Coldbrook Country School certainly have a way with words. For instance, if they say a student is "grounded," they really mean it. It seems that some parents send their teenagers to this expensive, discreet, and "different" boarding school because they're "lemons"; they just don't conform, don't fit in. And so, for a fee, the school will "ground" them. At Coldbrook that means dropping their bodies into one of the limestone faults near the school. It works like a charm; not one of the bodies has ever been discovered.

The five sixteen year olds who arrive at Coldbrook, and are assigned to Group 6, are aware only that for various reasons their parents have shipped them off to this remote, exclusive boarding school as some kind of test, as some way in which to prove themselves, although they're not sure what or how.

The group is made up of two boys and three girls. There is Coleman DeCoursey, called Coke, the kid whose hair wouldn't stay in place, whose shirttail wouldn't stay tucked in, who could never learn hockey or practically any other skill, who has been a loser from the word go, and whose parents, in disgust, finally have taken his name out of the school register so he won't embarrass them. Coke figures Coldbrook is kind of his last chance to shape up.

There is Sully, or more formally, Arthur Robey Sullivan, a smallish kid who people tend to regard as a nerd, although he isn't. What he has been is kind of a pain to his mother since he seems to get in the way of all the "uncles" or whatever who often come to stay at their house for periods of time. One day Sully was so surprised at his mother's admission of her faults that he has somehow agreed to give Coldbrook a try.

Sara Slayman Winfrey embarrassed her parents by being thrown out of school for plagiarism. Her surgeon father is not amused; hence, Coldbrook Country School.

Marigold grew up in a household where her parents (Roz and Toby) were very open about everything, including sex. Then one day she told her mother she was pregnant. Her mother most understandably arranged for an abortion, then thought to ask Marigold the name of the father. When Marigold mentioned her mother's lover—Coldbrook Country School.

Louisa Rebecca Locke (Ludi) sees things in a different way from most people. She used to tell her mother about that, and her mother would understand. But then Ludi's mother died and her stepmother came into the house, and when Ludi tried to talk to her father about how she saw things, could predict them sometimes, almost, her father shouted that she was out of step with everything. Ludi felt perhaps that she spoiled his perfect life, so here she is at Coldbrook.

The Group 6 leader is Nat Rittenhouse. The dean of the school told him to expect the dregs, "the ultimate bad seeds." All Nat has to do is lead the group off into a camping expedition in the woods and then poison them. The faculty members will take care of the grounding. Why is young Nat willing to take on such a ghastly assignment? It has to do with a father who refuses to pay any more of his son's gambling debts, and a son who has gotten himself in so deep that the only way out seems to be this "assignment," which, as repulsive as it is to him, will certainly get him out of his personal trouble.

But the misfits of Group 6 gradually became real to Nat as he leads them on a winding, hours-long trail to Spring Lake Lodge, where he tells the five that they will be spending some time in that rustic atmosphere.

Although the misfits somewhat question his youth and just what they are expected to accomplish in this remote outpost, they are willing to go along and follow Nat's lead. But when Nat decides that he cannot go through with the plan, he secretly returns to Coldbrook where he uncovers the faculty's full intentions—after Group 6 is grounded, so will be Nat Rittenhouse.

Nat returns to Spring Lake Lodge where he tells the incredulous group that their families are paying to have them killed! When the shock wears off, the teenagers try to decide what to do. Realizing that the faculty will soon be after them as soon as they figure out that Nat has not fulfilled his part of the plan, they leave the lodge and take up "part-time" residence in a house that is occupied only on weekends. During this period, the five teenagers and their youthful leader grow in friendship and responsibility as they make plans to deal with their future and with their families.

Eventually the group decides to return to the school in order to gain access to the papers that must prove the conspiracy between the school faculty and their parents. But before they do, Sara is nearly killed by one of the faculty who has been searching for them. Sully saves her life and shoots the man with a bow and arrow.

When Nat and Group 6 do gain access to the school files, they are unable at first to find the evidence they seek. But they finally do come upon the Group 6 folder, containing letters from their families, in of all places—the bottom of a bureau drawer.

"I've got them," cries Sara; but before they have time to congratulate themselves, the door opens and in walk the remaining four "teachers." They are armed.

Through the conversation and explanations that follow, Nat fixes the four a drink, which they accept, perhaps as a toast to their victory. The drinks are poisoned, just as the five members of Group 6 were to be poisoned.

The rest of it goes according to the Group 6 plan: remove any evidence, dispose of the bodies in the way Group 6 was supposed to be grounded, call their respective parents and let them know what they've discovered, then show up at the school as though they've been out in the wilderness all these weeks.

And that, according to the story, is just what they do.

Thematic Material

Julian Thompson has written an offbeat, suspenseful yet comic novel that pulls no punches in its depiction of the deceits to which humans can succumb. And yet the characters of the Group 6 members and of the young leader are sympathetically and interestingly drawn, as is their gradual blossoming into adulthood and responsibility under the most harrowing of circumstances.

Book Talk Material

An introduction to the members of Group 6 is a good orientation to this novel (see pp. 6–12). See also: how Nat gets involved (pp. 18–20, 52–60); Nat tells the five about their "grounding" (pp. 92–100); the Group decides on a plan for survival (pp. 114–122); Group 6 goes into training (pp. 137–141); and the Group discusses getting back at their parents (pp. 155–157).

Additional Selections

Five teenage orphans are subjected to experiments that could lead to their deaths in William Sleator's *House of Stairs* (Dutton, 1974, $12.95; pap., Scholastic, $1.95; condensed in *More Juniorplots*, Bowker, 1977, pp. 43–46). A fifteen-year-old boy faces a sadistic camp leader during his summer at an all-boys' riding camp in Steven Kroll's *Breaking Camp* (Macmillan, 1985, $11.95). A busload of children is hijacked by terrorists in Robert Cormier's *After the First Death* (Pantheon, 1979, $9.99; pap., Avon, $2.50). Members of a camping trip are terrorized by three motorcyclists in P. J. Petersen's *Nobody Else Can Walk It for You* (Delacorte, 1982, $13.95; pap., Dell, $2.50). Four students sent to colonize an Earth-like planet try to escape in Jean Karl's *But We Are Not of Earth* (Dutton, 1981, $10.95; pap., Dell, $2.50). In Patricia Lee Gauch's *Morelli's Game* (pap., Pocket Bks., 1982, $2.25), two teams of teenagers are sent on a 200-mile bike race. Three teenagers embark on a harrowing survival test and trip to self-discovery in *Going for the Big One* (Delacorte, 1986, $14.95) by P. J. Petersen. In Gary Paulsen's disturbing novel *Sentries* (Bradbury, 1986, $11.95), four young people face obliteration during a nuclear war.

About the Author

Commire, Anne, ed. *Something about the Author*. Detroit: Gale Research Co., 1985. Vol. 40, p. 210.

May, Hal, ed. *Contemporary Authors*. Detroit: Gale Research Co., 1984. Vol. 111, pp. 473–474.

Yep, Laurence. *Liar, Liar*
Morrow, 1983, $10.25; pap., Avon, $2.50 (same pagination)

Laurence Yep first made his mark in young adult literature in the late 1970s with several books like *Child of the Owl* (Harper, 1977, $12.89) and *Dragonwings* (Harper, 1975, $12.85), about Chinese Americans living in San Francisco's Chinatown where he was born. Subsequently he has written several successful science fiction novels, for example, *Dragon of the Lost Sea* (Harper, 1982, $11.89) and a Star Trek book *Shadow Lord* (Pocket Bks., 1985, $3.50). In *Liar, Liar* he has written a taut mystery adventure set in a small town in Silicon Valley. The fast action plus the final cat-and-mouse climactic chase will attract readers from grades seven through ten.

Plot Summary

In the eight months that Sean Pierce has lived in the town of Almaden, California, with his divorced father, the only true friend he has made is a fellow junior in high school and next-door neighbor Marsh Weiss, an unconforming practical joker. Marsh's rebellion against the pretentions and phoniness in life has made him many enemies but has also gained him the respect of others. One day the two boys are caught letting the air out of the tires of a gold Porsche by its owner and only narrowly make their escape in Marsh's beat-up Pinto. Through the back window, Sean sees the owner, a bald, middle-aged man with steely radarlike eyes, jotting down their license number. They expect to be contacted by the police, but amazingly nothing happens and life continues as usual.

Sean's parents separated five years ago when his mother, to whom he is still strongly attached, moved to Seattle with younger sister Caitlin. Mr. Pierce, a computer expert, failed in his bid to start his own business and has recently come with Sean, whom he calls Sport, to Almaden where he is a programmer with a large computer company.

Very early one Sunday morning, after a late movie, the two boys are driving home at about 60 miles per hour. Sean has his seat belt buckled, but Marsh, true to his nature, does not. When Marsh tries to stop for a traffic light, the rear brakes malfunction and the car overturns. Sean sees next to him the crumpled body of his friend and seconds later is barely able to jump free of the Pinto before a truck crashes into it, turning the car into a tower of flames.

Although Sean has suffered only a few cuts, and Lieutenant Silva of the police department has declared it an accident, he remains extremely upset and shaken by the incident. The indifference and callousness of everyone at school disturb him, as does the thought that he might have saved Marsh from the fire. Actually, the autopsy shows the boy had died of a broken neck. But, more seriously, Sean begins to wonder if it really was an accident or if someone had tampered with the brakes. He solicits the help of Marsh's younger sister, fifteen-year-old Nora, to help in the investigation. They make a list of all the victims of Marsh's practical jokes, but one by one each is eliminated. Suddenly Sean remembers the man with the radarlike eyes, and when Nora recalls a gold Porsche being parked by their house the night before the accident, the search takes a serious turn.

By checking automobile agencies they find that the owner is Russ Towers, a computer magnate who Sean recalls had dealings at one time with his father. Mr. Pierce describes him as a tenacious, ruthless man with a mean disposition who had suffered a terrible personal tragedy some years before. Further searching in public library files reveal that Mr. Towers's wife and daughter had been killed in an automobile accident caused by a drunken teenage driver.

Nora and Sean locate Mr. Towers's street address, and from talking with the local newspaper boy, they discover that another teenager who had run afoul of Mr. Towers also had had brake problems on his car. They are frightened away when Mr. Towers appears at his front door and glares at them with his radarlike eyes.

Sean and Nora visit Lieutenant Silva, who has been doing his own investigating and found that four years ago Sean had been involved in a series of breaking and entering escapades and that his psychiatrist had declared him a pathological liar. Sean protests that those were the actions of a mixed-up kid; but now even Nora questions Sean's truthfulness, and Sean finds himself in the position of the boy who cried wolf.

On the day of Marsh's funeral, Mr. Pierce brings home for coffee Russ Towers, whom he had encountered while jogging. Sean knows this is more than a coincidence, particularly when Russ offers to drive him to the funeral chapel. On the way, Mr. Towers confesses to the brake tampering and his sorrow at not anticipating the consequences, and attempts to bribe Sean to stop the investigation. When the boy refuses, Mr. Towers threatens him and Nora with another "accident." At the chapel, Sean tries to warn Nora, who now totally disbelieves him. A scene ensues and the boy is forcibly ejected.

Without anyone to turn to, Sean decides to break into Mr. Towers's house to collect evidence but is thwarted by tripping a burglar alarm that activates a television camera. Although he escapes, Sean realizes that he has left a photographic record for Mr. Towers.

That evening Mr. Pierce is suddenly called out of town on business. Sean is left alone. In the middle of the night he is awakened by noises in the house and he realizes that it is Towers, who has come to silence him. The telephone lines have been cut and Sean is trapped. He tries frantically to hide but without success. Finally he is trapped on the roof, but the rain gutter to which both he and Towers are clinging breaks. Sean's fall is broken by a large bottle tree and he escapes uninjured, but Towers lands on the driveway, where he lies immobile but alive. Soon neighbors aroused by the noise arrive, and Sean, safe at last, is reunited with Nora.

Thematic Material

This is essentially a suspenseful, fast-paced adventure novel that is a variation on the boy who cried wolf story. The helplessness that one who is not believed feels is interestingly explored. Other areas touched on are friendship, relations with divorced parents, life in a computer culture, and courage.

Book Talk Material

An explanation of the title and a brief introduction to Sean's predicament should interest readers. Some incidents of importance: the encounter with the gold Porsche (pp. 3–7); Sean and his father (pp. 17–21); the car crash (pp. 25–28); the visit to Russ Towers's neighborhood (pp. 77–83); and Lieutenant Silva reveals Sean's past (pp. 84–91).

Additional Selections

No one believes fifteen-year-old Andy when he reports hearing about a killing in Avi's *Wolf Rider: A Tale of Terror* (Bradbury, 1986, $12.95). LeRoy must decide if it is worthwhile risking his life to identify some known criminals in *LeRoy and the Old Man* (Macmillan, 1980, $8.95; pap., Scholastic, $2.25) by W. E. Butterworth. Eighteen-year-old Michael Thorn is suspected of a murder he didn't commit in Patricia Windsor's *The Sandman's Eyes* (Delacorte, 1985, $15.95). Twins, Sean and Erin, possess amazing psychic powers and use them to catch their parents' murderers in Chester Aaron's *Out of Sight, Out of Mind* (Lippincott, 1985, $10.89). Four boys fleeing from a murder are trailed by a policeman in Jim Murphy's *Death Run* (Clarion, 1982, $11.95). A courageous young man is hunted by a cynical business tycoon in Robb White's *Deathwatch* (pap., Dell, 1973, $2.50; condensed in *More Juniorplots*, Bowker, 1977, pp. 149–152). Good and evil clash in a summer camp in William Butler's *The Butterfly Revolution* (pap., Ballantine, 1986, $1.95). Two fine mysteries by Jay Bennett are *Say Hello to the Hit Man* (pap., Dell, 1977, $1.95) and *The Pigeon* (Methuen, 1980, $8.95; pap., Avon, $2.50).

About the Author

Commire, Anne, ed. *Something about the Author*. Detroit: Gale Research Co., 1975. Vol. 7, pp. 206–207.

Estes, Glenn E., ed. *American Writers for Children since 1960: Fiction (Dictionary of Literary Biography*, Vol. 52). Detroit: Gale Research Co., 1986, pp. 392–398.

Evory, Ann, ed. *Contemporary Authors* (New Revision Series). Detroit: Gale Research Co., 1980. Vol. 1, p. 728.

Holtze, Sally Holmes, ed. *Fifth Book of Junior Authors and Illustrators*. New York: Wilson, 1983, pp. 339–340.

Kinsman, Clare D., ed. *Contemporary Authors*. Detroit: Gale Research Co., 1975. Vols. 49–52, p. 597.

Kirkpatrick, D. L., ed. *Twentieth-Century Children's Writers* (2nd edition). New York: St. Martin's, 1983, pp. 850–851.

Senick, Gerard J., ed. *Children's Literature Review*. Detroit: Gale Research Co., 1978. Vol. 3, pp. 235–239. ·

Who's Who in America: 1986–1987 (44th edition). Chicago: Marquis Who's Who, Inc., 1985. Vol. 2, p. 3050.

3

Science Fiction and Fantasy

THIS is an area that within the last generation has consistently grown in popularity. Perhaps space exploration and our increasing feeling of the relativity of existence have produced this. Certainly the spate of television and films on science fiction subjects has helped. This section stresses the literature of the quest typical of fantasies and the adventures in future worlds found in science fiction.

Alexander, Lloyd. *Westmark*
Dutton, 1981, $11.95; pap., Dell, $2.50

Lloyd Alexander has long been considered a master writer of fantasies. He is perhaps best known for his five-volume Prydain cycle (for a slightly younger audience), which recounts the adventures of Taran, the Pigkeeper. Of *Westmark*, Alexander says, "It isn't a fantasy but it is, I hope, no less fantastic." However, the book does contain most of the elements of a first-class fantasy: mythical kingdoms, a hero's quest, and an epic struggle between good and evil. Missing is the use of magic or spells to either solve or thwart the plans of the central characters, but in the richness and singularity of its setting and plot, *Westmark* transports the reader to a never-never land where one experiences simultaneously both magic and reality. The Westmark trilogy is completed by *The Kestrel* (Dutton, 1982, $10.95; pap., Dell $2.75) and *The Beggar Queen* (Dutton, 1984, $11.95; pap., Dell, $2.95). Because events and themes cumulate in this series, they should be read in sequence to avoid confusion. Brief plot outlines of the two later volumes are given after the story of *Westmark*. These novels are suitable for readers in grades seven through ten.

Plot Summary

The novel takes place in the medieval-like kingdom Westmark (a map is in *The Kestrel*), where King Augustine and Queen Caroline are still so prostrate with grief at the disappearance of their only child, a daughter, some six years before, that they have allowed power to centralize in the hands of the wicked, tyrannical chief minister, Cabbarus. This villain uses every means possible to perpetuate his control and to stifle any criticism to the point of requiring prior government approval to printing any publications in Westmark.

The enormity and injustice of this edict soon become apparent to an idealistic young printer's devil, Theo, who is working for his master, Anton, in the town of Dorning. Thinking he will get official permission in the morning, Theo accepts an overnight printing commission from a dwarf named Musket on behalf of his master, a certain Dr. Absalam. During the night, however, the press is raided by militiamen. In the ensuing struggle, both Anton and Theo flee. Anton is shot dead in the street but Theo escapes by hiding in a high-wheeled coach. Inside he again encounters the dwarf Musket and meets Dr. Absalam, alias Count Las Bombas, an itinerant, genial mountebank and charlatan who lives off his wits and the gullibility of others. Without any viable alternative, Theo reluctantly joins this motley duo but soon learns, when Las Bombas is outfoxed by his nemesis, Skeit, that his new master is even inept at thievery. In the next town Las Bombas's efforts to sell his elixir (actually ditch water), are interrupted by the voice-throwing antics of a young street urchin named Mickle. Mickle knows little of her past except that she is without family, that her former protector, a thief named Hanno, has just been hanged, and that she is now completely alone. Seeing the possibilities of a good ventriloquist in the act, Las Bombas invites her to join them. Theo is attracted to this girl, her courage and forthrightness as well as her beauty. He is disturbed by her frequent nightmares that seem to be caused by trying to remember a terrifying experience in her past. Las Bombas devises a new presentation, the Oracle Priestess, in which a disembodied spirit—actually a few sheets manipulated by strings, together with the voice of Mickle—foretells the future. The act is immensely successful but, in time, Theo becomes increasingly sickened by its trickery and deception. Finally in desperation he secretly leaves his beloved Mickle and friends and sets out on his own.

At the inn of Master Jellinek in the university town of Freyborg, Theo meets a firebrand, the charismatic Florian, and the group of students he leads. He calls them his children and together they hope to topple the power of Cabbarus and establish democracy in Westmark. The group consists of the poet Stock; angelic but fiercely courageous Justin; an old man, Luther; and two high-spirited girls, Rina and Zara. Theo is happy to join this band of adventurers and help them clandestinely build a printing press.

Back at the palace, Cabbarus carries through a plot to rid himself of his enemy, the court physician, Dr. Torrens. The good doctor is against King Augustine's plans to communicate with his supposedly dead daughter through means of a spiritualist. Cabbarus stresses this difference of opinion until the King banishes Torrens, over Queen Caroline's objections. During his flight, the doctor is seriously wounded by a would-be assassin hired by Cabbarus. Unconscious, he falls into the river, is found by two scavenging "water rats," Sparrow and Weasel, and is nursed back to health by a refugee journalist named Keller, who is also escaping Cabbarus's fury. When Torrens recovers he and Keller leave to join their fellow revolutionary, Florian.

Theo learns that Count Las Bombas and Company have been discovered in their chicanery and are being held prisoners by the townspeople of Nierkeeping. Florian decides that he and his group should free the prisoners during their attack on Cabbarus's garrison. In a daring raid both are accomplished; Theo frees the Count, Mickle, and Musket, and all four flee the town.

In a neighboring inn, Las Bombas encounters the cheat Skeit. Realizing that their fraudulent act of clairvoyance might be of some value to Cabbarus's scheme to control the King through the search for his daughter, Skeit has all four brought to the palace where they are confronted by Cabbarus in a former torture chamber in the cellar. During the interrogation, filled with threats of imprisonment and instructions for a royal spiritualist performance, all notice that Mickle is transfixed with horror on the center of the floor where there is a narrow well, the shaft of which leads to water fathoms below.

Mickle continues to behave strangely during the evening's presentation and when she first speaks, the Queen screams out that she is listening to her own child's voice. Like one possessed, Mickle falls into a trance, and through this trauma regains her memory. She recalls an incident when years before as a young princess she had disobeyed her parents and wandered into the torture chamber, where she toppled into the well. Clinging to the rim, she screamed for help. Cabbarus heard her calls, but instead of helping, dislodged her fingers so that she fell, he thought, to her death below. But she had survived and, suffering from amnesia, wandered the streets scavenging for food, until years later she met Las Bombas.

In his attempt to escape, the now-unmasked villain, Cabbarus, is saved from falling to his death by Theo who, because he believes in the sanctity of human life, asks that banishment, not death, be Cabbarus's punishment. This is granted. Mickle, now Princess Augusta, is reunited with her parents, Dr. Torrens is reinstated, and Las Bombas and Musket once more take to the road. As for Theo, he is made adviser to the King and will, as a result, be close to Mickle. But, best of all, he is accepted by Florian as one of his children.

In *The Kestrel*, Theo and a group of guerrillas led by Florian join forces with the royal troops to repel an invasion from neighboring Regia. In this novel Theo changes from the peace-loving dove of *Westmark* to the predatory falconlike Kestrel of the title when he is forced to kill prisoners who might betray his cause. Mickle has become Queen Augusta in *The Beggar Queen* and Theo one of her consuls. Both, along with their friends, are forced into hiding when Cabbarus returns and seizes the government. In a dramatic confrontation, Mickle and Theo escape from Cabbarus through the same well that almost caused Mickle's death years before. Inevitably the forces of good triumph. Cabbarus is killed, but so is the gallant Justin. Mickle marries Theo, and both she and Florian—who has been revealed to be a member of the royal family—renounce their claims to the throne so that Westmark can at last become a democracy.

Thematic Material

Westmark is basically a tale of derring-do and hair-breadth escapes that could rival an Indiana Jones movie. It moves quickly with a challenging plot and memorable characters but also explores serious themes involving such political and ethical questions as who should rule and why; the nature of leadership; benevolent monarchy versus democracy; various forms of courage; loyalty to principles; and the nature of friendship. Most importantly, Lloyd Alexander explores the question of when, if ever, is one justified in taking another's life.

Book Talk Material

The covers of both the hardbound and the paperback editions introduce two views of Theo and his friends. Both Theo's story until the encounter with Las Bombas or palace conditions up to the attempt on

Torrens's life would interest readers. Specific episodes: Anton's shop is raided (pp. 9–14; pp. 14–19, pap.); Theo joins Las Bombas (pp. 24–28; pp. 30–33, pap.); Skeit tricks Las Bombas (pp. 38–42; pp. 44–48, pap.); the troupe meets Mickle (pp. 46–59; pp. 52–55, pap.); Torrens leaves the palace (pp. 60–65; pp. 65–69, pap.); and Theo meets Florian and his children (pp. 83–88; pp. 87–92, pap.).

Additional Selections

A young hunter reaches maturity in prehistoric Siberia in Chester G. Osborne's *The Memory String* (Atheneum, 1984, $11.95). Peace and war become the themes in Patricia McKillip's *The Forgotten Beasts of Eld* (Atheneum, 1974, $14.95; pap., Avon, $2.75), in which a wizard agrees to raise the heir of a country at war. In *The Sword and the Stone* (Putnam, 1958, $11.95; pap., Dell, $3.50; condensed in *Juniorplots,* Bowker, 1967, pp. 202–204) by T. H. White, a young boy, Wart, emerges as King Arthur through arduous training. The full story is told in *The Once and Future King* (Putnam, 1958, $16.95; pap., Berkley, $4.95). In a similar vein as Lloyd Alexander's adventure, but for a younger audience, is a series by Joan Aiken that begins with *The Wolves of Willoughby Chase* (pap., Dell, 1981, $2.50). Dido Twite, the central character of several of these novels, is also highlighted in *Dido and Pa* (Delacorte, 1986, $14.95). Nab's quest involves seeking the Faradawn through magic grains guarded by the Elflords in Richard Ford's *Quest for the Faradawn* (Delacorte, 1982, $14.90; pap., Dell, $3.95). A fourteen-year-old boy from the planet Gundra saves Earth from an alien invasion in Jim Slater's *The Boy Who Saved Earth* (pap., Dell, 1986, $1.75).

About the Author

Block, Ann, and Riley, Carolyn, eds. *Children's Literature Review.* Detroit: Gale Research Co., 1976. Vol. 2, pp. 11–18.

Commire, Anne, ed. *Something about the Author.* Detroit: Gale Research Co., 1972. Vol. 3, pp. 7–9.

de Montreville, Doris, and Hill, Donna, eds. *Third Book of Junior Authors.* New York: Wilson, 1972, pp. 6–7.

Ethridge, James M. *Contemporary Authors* (First Revision). Detroit: Gale Research Co., 1967. Vols. 1–4, p. 17.

Hamilton, Virginia. *Sweet Whispers, Brother Rush*
Philomel, 1982, $10.95; pap., Avon, $2.25 (same pagination)

Virginia Hamilton is one of the most honored and respected contemporary writers of juvenile fiction. For example, her 1974 novel *M. C. Higgins, the Great* (Macmillan, 1974, $10.95; pap., Dell, $2.50; condensed in *More Juniorplots*, Bowker, 1977, pp. 195–199) was awarded both the National Book Award and the Newbery Medal. Many of her works, like the book being analyzed, use black children as central characters in situations that effectively combine fantasy and realism. Another example is the Justice Cycle trilogy consisting of *Justice and Her Brothers* (Greenwillow, 1978, $12.88; pap., Avon, $1.95), *Dustland* (Greenwillow, 1980, $12.88; pap., Avon, $1.95), and *The Gathering* (Greenwillow, 1980, $11.75; pap., Avon, $1.95). In these books, eleven-year-old Justice, her twin brothers, and a friend discover that they have powers that allow them to mind-travel into the future. All of these books are enjoyed by better readers in grades six through nine.

Plot Summary

Considering the number of responsibilities that fourteen-year-old Teresa Pratt, nicknamed Tree, has had to assume, one would think that she is old for her years. But because she lives so much of her life only with her brother, isolated from the outside world, she is actually a fearful child, craving for the love, security, and possessions that other youngsters have. Tree's mother, Viola, or Vi, whom she adores, is a practical nurse who, because of her job—and sometimes perhaps partly for pleasure—is away from their apartment for days, occasionally weeks, at a time. She is careful to leave enough food and money to cover her absences and in addition has arranged for an old bag lady named Miss Pricherd to clean up once a week.

Tree's major responsibility is caring for her eighteen-year-old retarded brother, Dab, short for Dabney. Tree fiercely loves and protects this gentle, handsome youngster, whom she regards as only being a little slower and dreamier than other people his age. Both go to school. Tree is a good student, but Dab sits in his classroom always silent and withdrawn. Girls are often charmed by his looks and gentleness, and when Vi is away he will sometimes bring one of them to the apartment to spend the night with him.

One day on her way home from school, while trying to avoid the catcalls and suggestive remarks of the many young men she passes, Tree sees and is immediately attracted to a handsome young black man impeccably dressed from his pinstriped suit to patent leather shoes. On two other occasions she sees him staring at her in the street and her curiosity and infatuation increase.

Tree has her own special playroom in the apartment, a walk-in closet furnished with a little round table and chair, where she frequently goes to draw pictures and be alone. One Friday after school she enters the room, gazes at the table, and sees inside the table's surface the young man from the street. He is named Brother Rush. Suddenly she realizes that her newfound friend is really a ghost. In his hand Rush holds an oval, mirrorlike screen in which action is taking place. Tree enters the scene and finds herself in a house in the country. In the house are a two-year-old girl and her mother named Vi. They are soon visited by Vi's only surviving brother, Brother Rush, a numbers man. After he leaves, Vi and the child, Tree-sa, go upstairs to a bedroom where a young boy named Dabney is cruelly tied to a bed. The vision ends when someone arrives announcing that Brother Rush has been killed in an automobile accident.

Tree wants to return to the room but is distracted, first, because Dab develops severe stomach pains and needs care and, then, the following morning, Miss Pritcherd arrives. Unfortunately, Miss Pritcherd also sees Brother in the table, but after much thought, attributes it to lack of proper food. When she leaves, Tree brings Dab into the room. Both enter the mirror, but each witnesses a different scene. Tree sees Vi and her two children in an automobile with Brother Rush. The mother beats the boy with a switch for disobedience but finally Brother intervenes. Later, back home, the girl overhears Vi telling Brother that she will soon leave her husband, Ken, because of his wanton, spendthrift ways.

Dab's vision was more unpleasant—he had attended an uncle's funeral. He is so unhappy with this and so filled with pain from his strange illness that he wants no more visions. Instead, Tree reads him a passage from his favorite book, *The Cool World* by Warren Miller.

That night Vi comes home. Under questioning, she tells Tree that for some time she has had a boyfriend with whom she wants to start a catering business. His name is Sylvester Smith, nicknamed Silversmith, and with his help, Vi, for the first time, has been able to buy a car.

Tree tells Vi about the table and Brother Rush. Vi believes her daughter but is unable to see the vision. In the mirror Tree joins Brother Rush again. This time she sees him having a picnic with the two children and later she witnesses a fearful automobile accident in which a now middle-aged Brother jumps from a speeding car driven by the father, Ken.

Vi becomes so alarmed at Dab's condition, particularly after finding hidden barbiturates in his room, that she phones Silversmith and together the three take Dab to the hospital where his condition worsens. Vi explains that Dab has a hereditary ailment called porphyria, a disease that surfaces when the victim takes drugs or alcohol. This is what killed her other brother and, because he drank excessively, would have killed her Brother Rush had he not died in an automobile accident. Tree now realizes that through the mirror she was reliving experiences from her own life and that she is the little girl in these visions. After further questioning, she learns that somewhere she has a real father who survived the crash but disappeared after Vi left him. She also knows that Vi's cruel behavior toward Dab as a child shows that she never really accepted him or his condition.

Feelings of hostility and rejection against her mother well up inside Tree. Silversmith proves to be a kindly, understanding man who tries to help Tree forgive and forget. Tree tells him about the table and he says that perhaps such visions are intended for only the guiltless.

Dab dies, and Tree, in a dramatic confrontation, blames Vi for his death and decides to leave home after the funeral. In one last encounter with Brother Rush she sees him together with Dab. Her brother looks beautiful. The two are laughing and enjoying themselves with their faces full of sunlight and without pain. Perhaps Brother Rush's visit was to take Dab to a better place.

Before the funeral Miss Pricherd moves in to relieve Tree of all the housework. She is also thankful for this new home and tells the girl about the horrors of the street life Tree would face should she run away.

By funeral time, Tree has become more reconciled to her brother's death. After the funeral she talks to Silversmith's eighteen-year-old son Don, who shamelessly flirts with her and invites her to a movie. Vi announces that sometime in the future when their business is established she and Silversmith will marry and be able to establish a proper home for Tree. The young girl is torn about her future, but finally decides to stay. Working things out will be difficult but at least possible.

Thematic Material

Although the supernatural elements in this story supply fascination and suspense for the reader, this is basically a novel of human relationships that involve a comingling of present and past. It deals with the power of love, of family ties and devotion, as well as guilt and acceptance. The sister-brother interdependence and later the mother-daughter situation are brilliantly portrayed in their complexity. The reader learns to know and understand all of the characters and their individual struggles and conflicts.

Book Talk Material

Telling about Tree's first encounters with Brother Rush should interest readers, as well as perhaps a discussion of ghosts and ghost stories. Some important passages: an introduction to the main characters, including Brother Rush (pp. 9–13); Tree discovers that Brother Rush is a ghost (pp. 18–23); Tree's first journey into the past (pp. 27–34); Miss Pritcherd sees Brother Rush (pp. 58–61); Tree reads to Dab (pp. 81–84); and Vi comes home (pp. 90–98).

Additional Selections

The power of love to transcend time and space is one of the themes in Madeleine L'Engle's *A Wrinkle in Time* (Farrar, 1962, $10.95; pap., Dell, $2.95; condensed in *Juniorplots*, Bowker, 1967, pp. 188–190). Braddy befriends a mentally retarded girl in Robert Newton Peck's *Clunie* (Knopf, 1979, $6.95). A young boy is terrified by three scarecrows that symbolize three people who had died decades ago in Robert Westall's *The Scarecrows* (Greenwillow, 1981, $11.75). Three friends and two ghosts solve a mystery and save an old mansion in *Who Knew There'd Be Ghosts?* (Harper, 1985, $11.50) by Bill Brittain. A fable filled with romance, horror, and voodoo set on a Caribbean island is Rosa Guy's *My Love, My Love, or, the Peasant Girl* (Holt, 1985, $12.95). A blind thirteen-year-old boy helps save his older brother and grandfather from a haunted place in *Annerton Pit* (Little, 1977, $11.45) by Peter Dickinson. When his mother mysteriously escapes a drowning accident, her son believes she is now possessed by a creature from space in Gail Freeman's *Alien Thunder* (Bradbury, 1982, $10.95). Three people brought together by visiting a garden find their lives and minds becoming intertwined in Joan Phipson's *The Watcher in the Garden* (Atheneum, 1982, $10.95).

About the Author

Block, Ann, and Riley, Carolyn, eds. *Children's Literature Review.* Detroit: Gale Research Co., 1976. Vol. 2, pp. 103–107.

Commire, Anne, ed. *Something about the Author.* Detroit: Gale Research Co., 1973. Vol. 4, pp. 97–99.

de Montreville, Doris, and Crawford, Elizabeth D., eds. *Fourth Book of Junior Authors and Illustrators.* New York: Wilson, 1978, pp. 162–164.

Estes, Glenn E., ed. *American Writers for Children since 1960: Fiction* (*Dictionary of Literary Biography,* Vol. 52). Detroit: Gale Research Co., 1986, pp. 174–184.

Kirkpatrick, D. L., ed. *Twentieth-Century Children's Writers* (2nd edition). New York: St. Martin's, 1983, pp. 353–354.

Nasso, Christine, ed. *Contemporary Authors* (First Revision Series). Detroit: Gale Research Co., 1977. Vols. 25–28, p. 299.

Senick, Gerard J., ed. *Children's Literature Review.* Detroit: Gale Research Co., 1986. Vol. 11, pp. 54–95.

Who's Who in America: 1986–1987 (44th edition). Chicago: Marquis Who's Who, Inc., 1986. Vol. 1, p. 1169.

Who's Who of American Women: 1987–1988 (15th edition). Chicago: Marquis Who's Who, Inc., 1986, p. 330.

Jones, Diana Wynne. *Howl's Moving Castle*
Greenwillow, 1986, lib. bdg., $10.25

This is a lighthearted fantasy complete with battling sorcerers, demons, and a heroine who refuses to be nonplussed by the events around her. Jones's novels often contain elements of mythology and science fiction as well as fantasy. This English writer's best-known series is the Chrestomanci Cycle, which contains such titles as *The Magicians of Caprona* (Greenwillow, 1980, $11.75; pap., Ace, $2.25) and *Charmed Life* (Greenwillow, 1984, $13). In this series, Chestomanci is appointed as chief enchanter by the government to prevent magic from being badly used. These books are suitable for both junior and senior high school readers.

Plot Summary

Sophie Hatter and her two younger sisters live in the land of Ingary, where cloaks of invisibility and seven-league boots are not at all uncommon. The town of Market Chipping is pleasant enough, and life is good for the Hatter girls since their father is rather well off and keeps a hat shop.

Life really would not be half bad, except that Sophie, who is quite a studious girl, is hoping for something a little more exciting in the way of a future than the sort of run-of-the-mill life generally allotted to eldest daughters.

Of course, Ingary does have something a little out of the ordinary— two things actually. There is the Witch of the Waste, who goes about the countryside terrorizing people and things now and again. The witch has been quiet for a while. She had threatened the king's daughter and had even killed off the Wizard Suliman, who had been sent to reason with her.

The other out-of-the-ordinary thing is the black castle. Suddenly, there it is, moving about the countryside and blowing dark smoke out of its four turrets, hovering here and hovering there, and generally scaring the townsfolk half to death. People are sure it is the witch about to take off on a tear again. But the castle actually belongs to the Wizard Howl. He is apparently no prize either, for it is said that he enjoys sucking the souls of young girls, and so the Hatter sisters, along with all the other young ladies of the town, are warned never, never to venture out alone.

Then one day changes come into Sophie's dull life. Her father dies and her stepmother takes over the hat shop, apprenticing Sophie in her employ and her two sisters elsewhere in town. Sophie is a very good hatter, but she is more bored than ever. One day a lady comes into the shop when she is in a bad mood. Unfortunately for Sophie, the customer turns out to be the Witch of the Waste, who is not at all pleased with Sophie's attitude. She casts a spell that turns Sophie into a very old woman.

But at least it is different, and so Sophie leaves the shop and sets out into the world. Before long she see's Howl's moving castle in front of her, and because she is tired and grumpy and in need of a rest, she calls for the castle to stop—and it does.

Once inside, Sophie discovers Michael, the wizard's apprentice, and Calcifer, the fire demon, who is under an enchantment by the wizard. At the moment, the wizard himself is off in town, probably after the soul of some young girl, thinks Sophie. However, it turns out that the wizard does not really suck out souls. He does, however, have the rather bad habit of wooing young maidens until they fall in love with him, and the moment they do, he drops them completely.

Calcifer and Sophie strike a bargain. If she can break his contract with the wizard, then the fire demon will break her enchantment. But Sophie has to hang around the castle to find out what the bargain is because the fire demon isn't allowed to tell her.

When the wizard returns, Sophie finds him to be a bit of a dandy and she passes herself off as a castle cleaning woman, which doesn't please the wizard much, although he does allow her to stay.

One day the king calls the wizard to his castle and reports that his brother Prince Justin is missing. Since he thinks the wizard can do anything, he asks him to find the prince. Instead, the wizard asks Sophie to go see the king disguised as his mother and tell his majesty how unfit this wizard is for such a job. Because Wizard Howl himself has been caught up in the spell of the Witch of the Waste, he needs all his energies to devote to himself and not the king.

Through some rather involved happenings that involve Sophie's two sisters, the wizard's former teacher, a dog-man who is under a spell, and the Witch of the Waste, Sophie discovers that the fire demon was once a falling star that was caught by Wizard Howl. Because the fire demon was terrified of dying, the wizard offered to keep him alive as humans stay alive, and so the contract was struck.

And Sophie discovers that the witch has been trying to combine parts of the missing Prince Justin and the supposedly dead Wizard Suliman in order to make a new person who would be the new king of Ingary, and the witch would rule as the queen. In fact, she was only waiting to get Wizard Howl's head in order to have the perfect person.

Sophie is having none of this. With her help and a good deal of wizardry, the Witch of the Waste is dispatched, Prince Justin and Wizard Suliman are restored, Sophie's spell is broken, and she and Wizard Howl hold hands and smile at each other. The contract is broken for Calcifer, too, and the wizard and Sophie are surprised to find him still flickering among the logs in the fireplace. But Calcifer says he doesn't mind being there now, just as long as he is free to come and go.

Thematic Material

The author takes the young reader on a delightful romp through a fantasy world of fire demons and moving castles and a slightly offbeat wizard who dresses in tunics of silver and blue or scarlet and gold. There is much excitement, adventure, and whimsy in this tale of wicked witches and various characters under all kinds of enchantments. Sophie is a plucky heroine who takes her spell in her stride and doesn't let it get her down until she finds a solution.

Book Talk Material

Enchantment abounds in this delightful tale. Readers should especially enjoy the following: Sophie discovers that she has suddenly become old (pp. 18–22); Sophie confronts Calcifer in the fireplace (pp. 28–31); Sophie cleans the castle (pp. 45–47); Wizard Howl and the slime (pp. 59–61); the scarecrow and the speeding castle (pp. 64–67); and Michael and Sophie take the seven-league boots (pp. 75–82).

Additional Selections

Patricia Wrightson writes excellent fantasies like *The Dark Bright Water* (Atheneum, 1979, $7.95; pap., Ballantine, $2.95) in which an Australian aborigine ventures on a journey to encounter evil spirits. Other titles by this author include *A Little Fear* (Atheneum, 1983, $12.95) and *The Ice Is Coming* (pap., Ballantine, 1986, $2.95). Two young people separately engage on quests through time and space in Susan Cooper's *Seaward* (Macmillan, 1983, $10.95; pap., Collier, $3.95). Kenneth Lillington has created a lighthearted romp by pitting a woman of the twenty-second century against the ignorant peasants of Urstwile, an eighteenth-century village in *An Ash-Blonde Witch* (Faber, 1987, $10.95). In Paula Danziger's humorous *This Place Has No Atmosphere* (Delacorte, 1986, $14.95), it is 2057 and a teenager adjusts to life on the moon. Robin McKinley has compiled a collection of nine short fantasies, each taking place in different *Imaginary Lands* (Greenwillow, 1986, $11.75) and written by such luminaries as Jane Yolen and Peter Dickinson. When Paul turns eighteen he and his friends enter the land of Xhandarre in the thought-provoking fantasy by Christopher Carpenter, *The Twilight Realm* (Putnam, 1986, $14.95).

About the Author

Commire, Anne, ed. *Something about the Author*. Detroit: Gale Research Co., 1976. Vol. 9, pp. 116–118.

Evory, Ann, ed. *Contemporary Authors* (New Revision Series). Detroit: Gale Research Co., 1981. Vol. 4, pp. 336–337.

Holtze, Sally Holmes, ed. *Fifth Book of Junior Authors and Illustrators*. New York: Wilson, 1983, pp. 166–167.

Kinsman, Clare D., ed. *Contemporary Authors*. Detroit: Gale Research Co., 1975. Vols. 49–52, pp. 286–287.

Kirkpatrick, D. L., ed. *Twentieth-Century Children's Writers* (2nd edition). New York: St. Martin's, 1983, pp. 412–413.

Le Guin, Ursula K. *A Wizard of Earthsea*
Parnassus, 1968, $12.95; pap., Bantam, $3.50

Ursula K. Le Guin has written many science fiction novels and fantasies and is the winner of both the Hugo and Nebula awards. This is the first book of the Earthsea trilogy, all of whose books take place on Earthsea, an imaginary archipelago that consists of hundreds of islands of various sizes. The land is governed by the rules and powers of sorcery and, in addition to humans, is inhabited by such exotic beasts as fire-breathing dragons. In Earthsea every object—inanimate and living—has two names. The first is the regular name, known and spoken by all, but the second is the secret, sacred name that represents the soul or essence of each thing. To ascertain and use the real name is to gain control of its inner power. The trilogy tells the story of Sparrowhawk, a wizard whose holy name is Ged. Book One tells of the boy's first nineteen years. In the second, *The Tombs of Atuan* (Macmillan, 1971, $15.95; pap., Bantam, $2.95), he searches for the missing half of an enchanted ring and, in a labyrinth of tombs on the island of Atuan, encounters a high priestess in bondage to the powers of evil. In Book Three, *The Farthest Shore* (Macmillan, 1972, $16.95; pap., Bantam, $2.25), Ged, now the Archmage, or most powerful wizard, travels with a young prince, Arren, on a perilous final mission. Ruth Robbins has contributed excellent maps to help readers follow Ged's many voyages. These books are enjoyed by youngsters in grades six through nine.

Plot Summary
When he was born in the town of Ten Alders on the island of Gont, he was first named Duny. After his mother's death he was reared by an aunt, a witch who soon realized the boy's extraordinary powers and began teaching him some magic spells and secret words. At only age seven he was able, through rhymes, to control the movements of the herd of goats he tended. Because of his age and powers he became known as Sparrowhawk, although his holy, real name was still unknown

to him. Now Duny is almost thirteen and the pirate Kargs are attacking his island. By using a trick called fogweaving he is able to engulf them in a cloud of mist so thick that in their confusion they fall easy victims to the residents of Ten Alders. This spell making weakens the boy so much that he falls into a coma, from which he is awakened by a stranger who arrives in the village. He is a wizard, or mage, named Ogion. Sensing Sparrow-hawk's unusual potential, he asks permission from the boy's father to take him away for special tutelage. He also whispers to the boy his real name, Ged.

Although Ged loves his new teacher, he finds it difficult to adjust to Ogion's silent ways. After several months both agree that Ged would learn more at the school of wizardry on Roke, the Isle of the Wise. Here he makes many acquaintances, including the school's sagacious leader, the Archmage Nemmerle, and two older students: friendly, outgoing Vetch and Jasper, a haughty, conceited young man who shows distain for Ged and his naivete.

During his first two years at the school, Ged learns from the Nine Masters of Roke control over wind and weather, the power to change himself and objects into other forms, the true names of many things, and other basics of sorcery that can be practiced without disturbing the divine Equilibrium. His dislike for Jasper grows; and one night, in response to his nemesis's goadings, he uses his powers recklessly and calls up the spirit of a dead heroine. Instead, the earth opens and a terrible black shadow emerges with four taloned paws and attacks Ged savagely. He is saved by the intervention of Archmage Nemmerle, whose physical powers are so drained by the struggle that he dies.

It is months before a badly scarred and guilt-ridden Ged recovers sufficiently to resume his studies. Both Jasper and Vetch graduate as sorcerers. Vetch, as a sign of trust and friendship, reveals to Ged that his real name is Estarriol.

When he is eighteen, Ged is also ready for his first assignment. He is sent to Low Torning whose residents need help in ridding the neighboring island of Pendor of a family of voracious dragons.

Once away from the safety of the wizards' powers at Roke, Ged again feels the ominous presence of the evil shadow he has unleashed and knows that he is being stalked for a final, fatal encounter. Utilizing the spell of changing states and the power of real names, he is able to subdue the chief dragon at Pendor and receives assurances of Low Torning's future safety. To relieve his omnipresent foreboding of doom he leaves the island to confront the evil shadow. During his journey he meets a man who suggests that he travel to the island of Osskill where at the Court of the Terrenon he will receive proper weapons to fight his enemy. On the way to the Court, he is again attacked by the shadow, who mysteriously knows Ged's real name, making the boy powerless to fight back. Ged narrowly escapes death but manages to reach the Court and safety. Here he finds that he is the pawn in another power struggle. Assuming the form of a hawk, he flies from the island to Ogion's hut on Gont.

After he recovers from this ordeal, Ged sets out again by boat armed only with a yew staff that Ogion has shaped. On the isle of Iffish he encounters Vetch, who is now a well-respected and loved mage. Vetch insists that he accompany Ged on his quest, and the two sail to the outmost reaches of Earthsea and enter into the unknown area of the open sea. Here Ged once more confronts the shadow, but this time he is well prepared because he knows its real name. In gaining wisdom he also realizes that the shadow is also Ged, the dark side of his own nature. He calls out his own name and his body absorbs the shadow. Ged now becomes a whole man in control of his own nature and strong enough never again to be possessed by any power other than his own. The two friends return to Earthsea.

Thematic Material

This allegory is really a coming-of-age story in which a young man reaches maturity through confronting and accepting his own weaknesses. The story shows the consequences of actions motivated by hatred, envy, and pride. This is also a tale of courage and adventure and, like all fantasies, one that uses the quest motif. The author has created a totally believable fantasy world and fascinating descriptions of the curriculum and instruction in a school of wizards. The author's style and poetic use of language are other hallmarks of this exciting story.

Book Talk Material

After a description of the land of Earthsea and the power of the name, one of the following passages might be used: Ged's childhood (pp. 12–15; pp. 2–5, pap.); the attack of the Kargs (pp. 17–23; pp. 6–12, pap.); Ged arrives at school (pp. 46–49; pp. 34–36, pap.); the loosing of the shadow (pp. 73–77; pp. 57–62, pap.); and the fight with the dragon (pp. 102–109; pp. 87–93, pap.).

Additional Selections

Our hero Stile tries to end his serfdom and perfect his gift of magic in Piers Anthony's lightweight, often humorous trilogy *Split Infinity* (Ballantine, 1981, $9.95; pap., $2.50), *Blue Adept* (Ballantine, 1981, $10.95; pap., $2.95), and *Juxtaposition* (Ballantine, 1982, $13.50; pap., $2.95). Thirteen-year-old Nita and friend Kit battle forces of evil in Diane Duane's *So You Want to Be a Wizard* (Delacorte, 1983, $14.95; pap., Dell, $2.75) and they are caught by an evil force in *Deep Wizardry* (Delacorte, 1985, $15.95), also by Diane Duane. A space setting and magic combine in a land inhabited by humans and such exotic beasts as gargoyles in Meredith Ann Pierce's trilogy that begins with *The Darkangel* (Little, 1982, $14.95; pap., Tor, $2.95). For younger readers, Mary A. Whitely's *A Circle of Light* (Walker, 1983, $11.95) is set in a mythical time and tells of a boy's love of horses. An alien invader threatens the lives of Anra and her people in Pamela Sargent's *Homesmind* (Harper, 1984, $10.89; pap., $7.95). Shimmering ghosts and dark woods are ingredients in Elizabeth Marie Pope's *The Perilous Gard* (Houghton, 1974, $12.95; pap., Ace, $2.25). Also use Pope's *The Sherwood Ring* (pap., Ace, 1985, $2.25).

About the Author

Commire, Anne, ed. *Something about the Author*. Detroit: Gale Research Co., 1973. Vol. 4, pp. 142–144.

de Montreville, Doris, and Crawford, Elizabeth D., eds. *Fourth Book of Junior Authors and Illustrators*. New York: Wilson, 1978, pp. 221–223.

Estes, Glenn E., ed. *American Writers for Children since 1960: Fiction (Dictionary of Literary Biography*, Vol. 52). Detroit: Gale Research Co., 1986, pp. 233–241.

Evory, Ann, ed. *Contemporary Authors* (New Revision Series). Detroit: Gale Research Co., 1983. Vol. 9, pp. 332–336.

Harte, Barbara, ed. *Contemporary Authors*. Detroit: Gale Research Co., 1969. Vols. 21–22, p. 315.

Kirkpatrick, D. L., ed. *Twentieth-Century Children's Writers* (2nd edition). New York: St. Martin's, 1983, pp. 466–467.

Nasso, Christine, ed. *Contemporary Authors* (First Revision Series). Detroit: Gale Research Co., 1977. Vols. 21–24, p. 526.

Senick, Gerard J., ed. *Children's Literature Review*. Detroit: Gale Research Co., 1978. Vol. 3, pp. 117–125.

Who's Who in America: 1986–1987 (44th edition). Chicago: Marquis Who's Who, Inc., 1986. Vol. 2, p. 1659.

Who's Who of American Women: 1987–1988 (15th edition). Chicago: Marquis Who's Who, Inc., 1986, p. 474.

McCaffrey, Anne. *Dragonsong*
Atheneum, 1976, $14.95; pap., Bantam, $2.95

Anne McCaffrey's world is a planet named Pern that circles about the star Rukbat. Readers first read about this astral system in a trilogy, *The Dragonriders of Pern*, that consists of *Dragonflight* (Ballantine, 1981, $8.95; pap., $2.50), *Dragonquest* (Ballantine, 1979, $8.95; pap., $2.50), and *The White Dragon* (Ultramarine, 1981, $12.50; pap., Ballantine, $2.50). *Dragonsong* is the fourth book about Pern and the first one in the Harperhall trilogy. It is not necessary to have read the preceding books to understand this one, although toward the end of the novel, when Menolly, the heroine, is in Benden, there are references to previous happenings. These have been omitted from this summary. The author also supplies a helpful foreword, a list of characters, and a map of Pern.

Life on Pern is conducted largely underground because a neighboring malevolent rogue planet named Red Star periodically emits silvery spore strands that eat anything organic in their way. This rain of ravenous Threads can be destroyed only by the flaming breath of the giant dragons that have been trained by their riders from birth through a system known as "impressing" to comb the skies of Pern destroying the Threads. The dragonriders and their entourage live in five larger communities known as Weyrs, but the general population inhabits many smaller subterranean communities called Holds.

Time is measured on Pern by "turns," corresponding to our years, but dragons and their much smaller distant relatives, fire lizards, can move through time by a process called "between."

These fantasies are popular with readers in junior and senior high school as well as with adults.

Plot Summary

Menolly, a young girl of almost fifteen turns, lives in the large family community of Half Circle Sea Hold on the remote eastern coast of Pern. Half Circle is a gigantic partially man-made cave. With its many rooms, carved staircases, and great meeting hall, it resembles an underground medieval castle. As in the Middle Ages, life is very primitive. The community relies on fish, other marine life, and wild plants and berries for food. Their leader, the Sea Holder, is Menolly's father, Yanus, a harsh, inflexible man whose wife is the equally severe Mavi. Menolly is the youngest in the large family. Her next oldest sister is Sella, a grumpy, ill-tempered girl. Menolly's favorite brother is Alemi, who unfortunately is often absent from the Hold. In each of the communities on Pern, a place of honor is always given the Harper, the minstrel who keeps legends and history alive by his singing ancient ballads, composing new ones, and teaching both to the children. In the Sea Hold, this man is Petiron, beloved by all but particularly by his best pupil, Menolly, whose original works have so impressed the old man that he has sent some to the Masterharper of Pern, Robinton, at Harperhall.

Petiron dies and, because women are never Harpers, Yanus grudgingly allows Menolly to teach the youngsters until the new Harper arrives, provided that she doesn't sing or compose her own songs. One day she forgets, and in the midst of her song Yanus intervenes, forbids her to sing again, and beats her so violently for her disobedience that she has large, painful welts on her back.

One day, while out seafood gathering at Dragon Stones, her pain is momentarily forgotten when she sees the mating flight of a group of fire lizards. These are highly intelligent beasts about a foot in length. They are much sought after because they are almost extinct in Pern.

The new Harper arrives. He is tall, handsome Elgion. Unfortunately, Menolly does not meet him because on the night of his welcoming reception she must take care of her great-grandfather named Old Uncle.

Menolly revisits the secret haunt of the fire lizards and is able to gain their confidence sufficiently to move the queen's clutch of eggs into a cave to escape destruction from unusually high tides.

While she is gutting packtail fish one day, Menolly's knife slips and cuts a deep wound in her hand. She is now convinced that even playing her music will be denied her, and, completely discouraged, she runs away from the Hold one night and hides in the cave with the fire lizards. The night their eggs hatch, the deadly Thread begins dropping. The only way she can keep the hatchlings safe in the cave is by feeding them, thus producing the impressing or bonding phenomenon that makes them her faithful helpers for life. Thus, she inadvertently becomes mother to nine fire lizards. In the next weeks she continues to nourish them. She names them—her favorite is the one female, Beauty—and is gratified that they accompany her singing with humming sounds.

At the Hold the family thinks that Menolly died during the Thread attack and doesn't mount a search for her. Elgion is curious about the person who wrote the songs that have impressed Robinton, but Yanus, ashamed that it was a girl, tells him they were composed by a young man who has left the Hold and swears the inhabitants to secrecy.

One day, while looking for food on a distant beach, Menolly sees another clutch of fire lizard eggs. She is intent on ensuring their safety when, in the near distance, she sees Thread approaching. Frantically she runs until her feet are raw and bleeding, but the terrible pestilence continues to gain on her. Fortunately, T'gran, a dragonrider scoops her up in time and transports her via between to Benden Weyr and safety.

Here she is cared for by several women in the lower caverns, including Mirrim, Felena, and the Headwoman Manora. She has never experienced such kindness and friendliness before and she begs not to be sent back to the Sea Hold. Under her direction, the fire lizard eggs are brought to the Weyr where she helps incubate them. As well, by the marvel of between she is often visited by her nine loving pets, including the most attractive, Beauty. In time, she also returns to her music playing and singing.

At dragon hatching time there is a great gathering of people at Benden, many of the young men hoping to impress a hatchling and become a future dragonrider. By accident, Menolly meets the Masterharper Robinton and Elgion. Slowly they discover her true identity as the talented balladeer from the Sea Hold. Robinton insists she accompany him back to Harperhall, the great music conservatory of Pern. Menolly accepts ecstatically.

Her adventures at Harperhall are told in *Dragonsinger* (Atheneum, 1977, $14.95; pap., Bantam, $2.95). It is followed by *Dragondrums* (Macmillan, 1979, $8.95; pap., Bantam, $2.95), the story of a young music student and his adventures on a secret mission for Robinton.

Thematic Material

Pern is a fully conceived, believable fantasy world and Menolly's journey from outcast to secure womanhood is convincingly portrayed. Her courage and resoluteness make her particularly appealing. The oppression and unfairness of a male-dominated society and the close relationship between humans and animals are well portrayed. The power and importance of music, even in this primitive society, are an interesting subtheme.

Book Talk Material

A description of Pern, the Sea Hold, the Thread, and the between phenomenon should intrigue readers. Some important passages are: Menolly gets instruction about teaching from Yanus (pp. 11–15; pp. 8–11, pap.); her disobedience (pp. 24–26; pp. 19–21, pap.); she sees her first fire lizards (pp. 27–30; pp. 22–24, pap.); taking care of Old Uncle (pp. 37–43; pp. 31–36, pap.); saving the queen's eggs (59–70; pp. 50–59, pap.); and the Thread attack (pp. 123–126; pp. 107–109, pap.).

Additional Selections

Anne McCaffrey's *Crystal Singer* (pap., Ballantine, 1986, $3.95)—one of the Pern books—tells how a girl travels to a distant planet. Her adventures are continued in *Killashandra* (Ballantine, 1986, $16.95). Darkover is a distant planet where mental powers have taken the place of machines. It is also the setting of more than a dozen science fiction novels like *Hawkmistress!* (pap., DAW, 1982, $3.95) by Marion Zimmer Bradley. Theo, a scientist on an earthlike planet, forms a friendship with an orphan girl while battling a mysterious death-dealing presence in H. M. Hoover's *Rains of Eridan* (Viking, 1977, $9.95; pap., Avon, $1.50). Also use Hoover's *The Delikon* (Viking, 1977, $9.95; pap., Avon, $1.50) and *The Lost Star* (Viking, 1979, $11.50; pap., Avon, $1.50). From the pen of C. S. Lewis suggest the Narnia Chronicles series and the trilogy that begins with *Out of the Silent Planet* (Macmillan, 1943, $10.95). Philip, an older cousin, and a feral child called "No Name" must survive off the land in the science fiction thriller *Earthquake 2099* (Lodestar, 1982, $9.95) by Mary W. Sullivan.

About the Author

Commire, Anne, ed. *Something about the Author.* Detroit: Gale Research Co., 1976. Vol. 8, p. 127.

Holtze, Sally Holmes, ed. *Fifth Book of Junior Authors and Illustrators.* New York: Wilson, 1983, pp. 206–207.

Metzger, Linda, ed. *Contemporary Authors* (New Revision Series). Detroit: Gale Research Co., 1985. Vol. 15, p. 309.

Nasso, Christine, ed. *Contemporary Authors* (First Revision Series). Detroit: Gale Research Co., 1977. Vols. 25–28, pp. 470–471.

Riley, Carolyn, ed. *Contemporary Authors.* Detroit: Gale Research Co., 1971. Vols. 25–28, pp. 489–490.

Who's Who in America: 1986–1987 (44th edition). Chicago: Marquis Who's Who, Inc., 1986. Vol. 2, p. 1845.

McKinley, Robin. *The Hero and the Crown*
Greenwillow, 1984, $11.25; pap., Berkley, $2.95

Readers were introduced to the fantastic land of Damar in Robin McKinley's *The Blue Sword* (Greenwillow, 1982, $13; pap., Berkley, $2.95), a Newbery Honor book. In this novel, a young heroine, Harry (short for Anghared) Crewe, is spirited off to the land of the Damarians by King Corlach, who believes that she has the mysterious power, kelar, to lead his people against the invading Northerners. In preparing for and fulfilling this quest, Harry is encouraged and guided by the spirit of a dead female warrior, Aerin, who centuries before had also saved Damar. Harry learns to use Aerin's magical blue sword, Gonturan, and is given advice from an immortal soothsayer, Luthe, who also guided Aerin. However, it is only in *The Hero and the Crown* that Aerin's full story is finally told. It received the 1985 Newbery Medal and is recommended for lovers of fantasy and romance in grades seven through ten.

The Hero and the Crown is divided into two parts. In the first, the reader is introduced to the court of King Arlbeth in the mystical kingdom of Damar and learns of the apprenticeship of his daughter, Aerin, who longs to be a warrior knight like her male cousins. In the second, Aerin sets out on a mission to save her beloved kingdom.

Plot Summary
Aerin is the only child of widowed King Arlbeth, whose wife, an enchanting witch woman from the North country, died shortly after Aerin's birth. Because of the mystery involved in her ancestery, Aerin is not fully accepted at the court, although her father and her older cousin, Tor, who has assumed the role of the king's future successor, love her dearly. Her chief enemies are two other cousins, Galanna and her husband, Perlith.

Aerin is a high-spirited, brave, young girl who, in spite of admonitions from her loyal and caring maidservant, Teka, tries to emulate the ways of the warrior knights around her.

When she is fifteen, Aerin succumbs to the goading of the jealously wicked Galanna and eats of the hallucinogenic surka plant, which is supposed to give superhuman strength and visions to royalty. To Aerin, it brings only convulsions and nightmares. During her long period of convalescence and while Teka ministers to her needs, Aerin begins creeping out of the castle to the pasture where the king's gallant but now very lame white stallion, Talat, is kept. The horse suffered a crippling wound while saving his master in battle. Aerin begins secretly riding this magnificent beast and bringing him back into shape. She also learns the rudiments of swordplay from Tor, who is beginning to view his redheaded, attractive cousin with more than a platonic interest.

In an old book on the history of Damar, Aerin discovers a recipe for kenet, an ointment that protects one from dragon fire. She begins collecting the herbs that are its ingredients and experimenting for long painstaking months to discover their correct proportions. When she thinks she is successful, she smears her body and clothes with the salve. She gallantly enters a bonfire and emerges unharmed.

About the time of her eighteenth birthday, Aerin learns that a nearby village is being troubled by a small dragon that has been killing chickens and frightening farmers. Without telling anyone, she gathers together a supply of kenet, and on her trusting steed, Talat, successfully vanquishes her first dragon. Soon she has gained a reputation within the kingdom of dragon slayer and Aerin now feels that her days of squiring are over and that she is ready to fulfill her destiny.

She hasn't long to wait. Troubles begin to break out within the kingdom, and King Arlbeth blames it on the disappearance from the earth many years ago of the Hero's Crown, a magical talisman the possession of which brings power to its owner. As the king, Tor, and the army prepare to leave to quell an uprising in the North, news arrives that in another part of the kingdom the fearful giant Black Dragon, Maur, has reappeared and is on a rampage destroying villages.

After the army leaves, Aerin decides to do battle single-handedly with this savage monster, and she leaves accompanied by the loyal Talat and armed only with a supply of kenet and a sword her father has given her. But Maur is unlike the small dragons Aerin has encountered in the past—it is as big as a mountain and its teeth alone are as long as Talat's legs. In the ensuing battle, Aerin's face and body are severely burned when part of her clothing and helmet fall off, her mouth and lungs are scorched raw from breathing in dragon fire, and after Talat accidently falls, her ankle is crushed. However, as the dragon leans toward her for the kill, she is able to free a dagger from her boot top, and before she faints, she stabs it through the right eye into its brain. When she awakes, she finds Maur dead and on the ground a glowing red stone—the solidified last drop of its heart's blood.

Aerin spends days at the death site trying to gain sufficient strength for the journey home. In her feverish dreams, a tall, blond man appears to her and promises her aid. Still suffering great pain, she begins her journey back to the castle, but even there, under the tender care of Teka, Aerin fails to respond. As a trophy, Maur's head has been mounted in the great hall and the girl senses that the power of evil it represents is slowly destroying her.

Once again the man in her dreams appears promising help, and so, in desperation, she once more mounts Talat and leaves the castle. After many days she arrives at a stone building where the tall, blond man greets her. He is Luthe, a soothsayer equipped with superhuman power. Through the enchanted magical waters of the nearby Lake of Dreams, he cures Aerin, but when she is well, Luthe informs her that she has one more mission to fulfill. He tells her that the evil power that controls the Hero's Crown and that has unleashed forces like Maur on the world is actually Aerin's uncle, the wizard Agsded. According to an ancient prophecy only one of his own blood can destroy him. Fearful of Aerin's mother, Agsded had destroyed her. It is only Aerin who can kill him. Before she leaves, Luthe gives Aerin a magical blue sword, Gonturan.

On her journey she recruits a strange army of followers: a group of folstza, catlike creatures, and a pack of wild dogs called yerig. Together with Talat they are able to clear a passageway into the tower where Agsded lives. There, equipped with only a wreath of surka gathered outside the castle, the dragon's stone, and Gonturan, she confronts her wicked uncle. In the ensuing battle, good triumphs over evil and Aerin emerges victorious and with possession of the Hero's Crown.

Luthe once more appears to her. Although she loves him dearly and would like to stay with him, she tearfully says good-bye and returns to Damar. At the death of her father, Aerin marries Tor and together they reign over a now peaceful and prosperous land.

Thematic Material

While being entranced by this enthralling story, readers learn much about the elements of fantasy, such as the quest, the struggle of good versus evil, unusual beasts, and the use of magical powers. It is a story of great heroism and, in spite of its exotic trappings, a moral tale in which justice triumphs. The use of sometimes complex symbolism enriches the story and will deepen the rewards for the better, more perceptive, readers. The character of Aerin is interesting, particularly for girls, as she represents a model of both physical and moral courage.

Book Talk Material

A brief introduction to the land of Damar, its troubles, and the king's daughter should intrigue young readers. Specific passages of interest: Aerin eats the surka plant (pp. 23–25; pp. 22–24, pap.); she first visits Talat in his pasture (pp. 27–29; pp. 26–27, pap.); Aerin finds the right recipe for kenet (pp. 60–62; pp. 57–59, pap.) and tries it out (pp. 80–82; pp. 75–77, pap.); Aerin's first encounter with dragons (pp. 86–91; pp. 80–85, pap.); and the fight with Maur (pp. 112–118; pp. 104–110, pap.).

Additional Selections

Sisters from the ruling family of Sherath find that the special gift they possess is both a blessing and a curse in Ardath Mayhar's *Makra Choria* (Atheneum, 1987, $13.95). A fourteen-year-old girl is pulled into another world on a magical horse in Marilyn Singer's *The Horsemaster* (Atheneum, 1985, $13.95). Olwen and her guardian welcome settlers to their planet Isis in *The Keeper of the Isis Light* (Atheneum, 1981, $11.95), the beginning of the Isis trilogy by Monica Hughes. Time shifts back and forth from the seventh to the eleventh centuries in an adult novel of reincarnation, Katharine Kerr's *Daggerspell* (Doubleday, 1986, $16.95). Caribou, a South Arctic orphan, takes care of a magical baby who later helps her tribe escape earthquakes in Meredith Ann Pierce's *The Woman Who Loved Reindeer* (Atlantic Monthly Pr., 1985, $13.95). Fourteen-year-old Zan Ford is transported to the Stone Age in the unusual fantasy *Saturday the Twelfth of October* (pap., Dell, $2.95) by Norma Fox Mazer. Also use Susan Cooper's Dark Is Rising series of fine Arthurian fantasies, including the 1976 Newbery Medal winner *The Grey King* (Atheneum, 1975, $12.95; pap., Aladdin, $3.95), and Diana Wynne Jones's *Power of Three* (pap., Ace, $2.25), about little people whose existence is threatened when humans plan to flood their moor.

About the Author

Commire, Anne, ed. *Something about the Author*. Detroit: Gale Research Co., 1983. Vol. 32, p. 136.

Estes, Glenn E., ed. *American Writers for Children since 1960: Fiction* (*Dictionary of Literary Biography*, Vol. 52). Detroit: Gale Research Co., 1986, pp. 262–266.

Holtze, Sally Holmes, ed. *Fifth Book of Junior Authors and Illustrators*. New York: Wilson, 1983, pp. 212–213.

May, Hal, ed. *Contemporary Authors*. Detroit: Gale Research Co., 1983. Vol. 107, pp. 328–329.

Senick, Gerard J., ed. *Children's Literature Review*. Detroit: Gale Research Co., 1986. Vol. 10, pp. 121–126.

Park, Ruth.   *Playing Beatie Bow*
Macmillan, 1980, $9.95; pap., Puffin, $3.50 (same pagination)

Since the success of such movies as *Back to the Future*, Hollywood has increased its output of time warp stories. This device has been a mainstay in the field of children's and young adult literature for many years (see Additional Selections), whose authors perhaps took their original inspiration from the H. G. Wells science fiction classic, *The Time Machine* (a dozen paperback editions are available, including Bantam, $2.50; New Amer. Lib., $3.50; Airmont, $1.50). Ruth Park, a "down under" author, is a prolific writer of quality children's books. *Playing Beatie Bow* won the Australian best children's book award in 1981 and is suitable for readers from ages eleven through sixteen.

Plot Summary

Abigail Kirk is a most unhappy girl growing up with her mother, Kathy, in a high-rise apartment building in the heart of Sydney, Australia. Her unhappiness stems from the fact that her adored and adoring father, Wayland Kirk, left her and her mother four years before for another woman. The sense of betrayal and worthlessness that resulted has transformed the girl into a withdrawn, hurt being reluctant to give or receive love and affection. Her sense of loss and disillusionment and desire to lose her former identity were so great that she even changed her given name from Lynette to Abigail. Her mother, Kathy, is much more resilient. She spends her time in the curio shop she owns, Magpies, and has recently been seeing her estranged husband, who has been thoroughly chastised after his affair has collapsed.

In her loneliness, Abigail often visits her neighbors, Bill and Justine Crown, to take care of their two children: the high-rise monster, six-year-old Vincent, and four-year-old Natalie, a silent, fearful girl. She frequently takes them to the playground to watch them play a game called Beatie Bow in which a child dressed as a ghost chases the other children. In the distance they sometimes notice a strange waiflike girl watching the game. Abigail also spends her time sewing; she has just completed a long dress from an Edwardian curtain her mother had found and, as a yoke for it, Justine has given her a piece of yellowed crochet that had been in her family for years.

One day Kathy announces to Abby that she wants to reconcile with her husband, who would like his wife and daughter to accompany him for a three-year assignment in Norway. "No way," announces Abigail, and she storms out of the apartment dressed in her new finery. Once again she sees the strange girl watching the game of Beatie Bow. As the Town Hall clock begins chiming the half hour, she follows the urchin down a steep alley and finds herself in an unknown world that seems of a bygone era. While chasing after the waif, she is knocked down in the street by a sword-wielding man and loses consciousness. She awakens with a painfully sprained ankle in a comfortable old-fashioned bedroom where she is being nursed by three women: elderly Granny Tallisker, the frightened little girl whose name is Beatie Bow, and Dorey, short for Doreus, Beatie's orphan cousin. Gradually Abby realizes that she has been miraculously transported to the year 1873 and that she is in the home of Scottish immigrants from the Orkney Islands. In time she meets the rest of the family. First, her assailant, Beatie's father, Samuel Bow, an ex-soldier in the Crimean War, and an ordinarily gentle man who is prone to violent rampages when given a whiff of alcohol; then Beatie's older brother, an eighteen-year-old, attractive sailor named Judah; and another brother, whiny eight-year-old Gibbie. Three other children and Mrs. Bow, Mrs. Tallisker's daughter, have recently died of typhoid fever, and Gibbie, who is recovering from a bout, proudly and continually announces that he, too, will shortly join this angelic band. While recovering, Abby gradually adjusts to her hosts and their ways. She learns to use the chamber pot and drink Granny's possets, to understand their quaint expressions, and to wear the unfamiliar garb of these poor folk. In turn, they shower their guest with love and attention. They believe her to be an immigrant girl with no family but of good education. Granny often speaks of the family's Gift and of the role a Stranger will play in their fates.

Abby knows that in spite of how she is growing to love this family, she must leave when the opportunity arrives. She tries to escape, but in her flight she is taken prisoner by a group of white slavers who hold her captive in a warehouse in the slums of Sydney. Judah and his friends rescue her and for the first time in her life, Abby feels an attraction to a boy and the first pangs of love.

Granny and Dorey now explain the family secret to Abby. From the Orkney elves, the Talliskers, and now the Bows as well, have inherited the Gift, which gives some members of the family great wisdom and the powers to heal and see into the future. In this generation a Stranger is to appear to help the family preserve the Gift. Because the faded crochet that Abby wore when she arrived bore a Tallisker design, Granny believes that Abby is indeed that Stranger and that soon this act of salvation will occur. When it does, Granny explains, Abby will be given back her dress and magical crocheted yoke, the passport to her return into the twentieth century. The family prophesy has also decreed that Beatie will not marry and that another young member of the family—Judah, Dorey, or Gibbie—will die young. Abby is convinced that this will be Gibbie because of his frequent pronouncements of his imminent demise.

Abby wonders if she can bear to part with Judah when her time comes to leave, with whom she is now completely infatuated. Beatie senses her feelings and angrily tells her that Judah has for years been promised to the loving, gentle Dorey. On a picnic with Judah, Abby senses his strong attraction toward her but realizes that he must fulfill his obligations to Dorey. When she returns, Abby finds the neighborhood in an uproar. Run amuck, Mr. Bow has set fire to his own home. In an amazing act of courage, Abby saves both Dorey and Gibbie, who have been trapped in the building after the others escaped.

The mission of the Stranger has now been completed and Abby knows she must leave. When she reenters her neighborhood the familiar clock is still chiming—though she has been away for months, not a second has elapsed. Through her experiences of having loved and lost, she is now able to accept her parents' situation, and after a tender reunion with her father, she agrees to go to Norway.

Before leaving, Abby checks old newspapers in the library seeking news of the Bow family. To her horror she finds that in 1874, Judah's ship, *The Brothers,* is reported sunk with all hands lost. Frantically, she retrieves the crochet in order to warn him but its power is waning. In spite of her trancelike concentration, Abby is only able to conjure up the joyous wedding of Dorey and Judah. At the end of this vision the crochet is only threads, its power ended.

Years later, Abby, now eighteen, returns to Sydney, and on visiting the Crowns meets Justine's younger brother, twenty-year-old Robert. For an uncanny moment Abby thinks she is staring into the eyes of Judah, the resemblance is so great. Robert's middle name is Judah, and his last name is Bow. He is the great-grandson of Gilbert "Gibbie" Bow who, in spite of assurances otherwise, had lived to be seventy. After several encounters Abby tells Robert her story and together they look at the Bow family Bible. They learn that Beatie had become the headmistress of a famous high school, and thus her name had been perpetuated in a children's game. Judah had indeed drowned at age nineteen. As Abby quietly sobs at the news of this terrible injustice, Robert gently kisses away her tears. Perhaps she has found her Judah after all.

Thematic Material

This is a fantasy that not only explores the concept of a fourth dimension, but also probes the many meanings of love and the various commitments it can require. An important theme in this novel is the power of love to transcend the barriers of time and space. Life in Sydney in two different centuries is portrayed realistically and the reader gets a fascinating picture of how the poor lived in Victorian times. Families and the necessity of family ties form important subplots, as do the emergence of women and the need for universal public education.

Book Talk Material

A brief description of the plot to the point where Abby enters Beatie's nineteenth-century life should attract readers. Some specific episodes: playing Beatie Bow (pp. 19–21); Abby learns about going to Norway (pp. 17–21); Abby follows Beatie into the past (pp. 29–32); Abby realizes her predicament (pp. 43–48). Abby's attempted escape and a description of the slums of Sydney are given on pages 83 to 96.

Additional Selections

Fifteen-year-old Jack is transported in time to the Cape Cod of 1902 in Jan Adkins's *A Storm without Rain* (Little, 1983, $14.45). In Annabal Johnson and Edgar Johnson's *The Danger Quotient* (Harper, 1984, $13.89; pap., $2.95), Casey goes back in time after a nuclear holocaust. Candy's pony carries her into past times in a story of friendship that transcends time in Jean Slaughter Doty's *Can I Get There by Candlelight?* (Macmillan, 1980, $9.95). Kevin understands his father better when he time travels to the time of his father's boyhood in Cynthia Voigt's *Building Blocks* (Atheneum, 1984, $10.95; pap., Fawcett, $2.25). A girl and boy are transported to Arthurian England in Andre Norton's *Here Abide Monsters* (Atheneum, 1973, $6.95; pap., Tor, $2.95). Also use these excellent fantasies that involve contact with the past: Nancy Bond's *A String in the Harp* (Atheneum, 1976, $12.95) and Alan Garner's *The Owl Service* (pap., Ballantine, 1981, $1.95; condensed in *More Juniorplots,* Bowker, 1977, pp. 88–91). Mayhem results when a time machine takes Max, as a knight, and Steve, as a horse, to the Middle Ages in Gery Greer and Bob Ruddick's *Max and Me and the Time Machine* (Harcourt, 1983, $11.95).

About the Author
Commire, Anne, ed. *Something about the Author.* Detroit: Gale Research Co., 1981. Vol. 25, pp. 190–191.
Kirkpatrick, D. L., ed. *Twentieth-Century Children's Writers* (2nd edition). New York: St. Martin's, 1983, pp. 598–599.
Locher, Frances C., ed. *Contemporary Authors.* Detroit: Gale Research Co., 1982. Vol. 105, pp. 376–377.

Pascal, Francine.   *Hangin' Out with Cici*
    Viking, 1977, $12.95; pap., Archway, $2.25; pap., Dell, $2.50

This is a witty, often uproarious, comedy that utilizes zingy remarks, slang, exaggeration, understatement, and often pure slapstick to produce a laugh-aloud farce with somewhat serious undertones. Victoria's story is continued in *My First Love and Other Disasters* (Viking, 1979, $11.95; pap., Dell, $2.50), in which she falls hopelessly in love with Jim and spends a summer on Fire Island, and in *Love and Betrayal and Hold the Mayo* (Viking, 1985, $11.95; pap., Dell, $2.95), which tells of Victoria, now a sixteen year old, and her crush on a handsome camp counselor. These novels are popular with girls in grades six through eight.

Plot Summary
Eighth-grader Victoria Martin thought that when she turned thirteen things would be different and she would be treated as an adult. No way. Life is still a bummer with the same old hassles and naggings from her mother about cleaning up her room, stopping the endless arguments with her pain-in-the-neck younger sister, eleven-year-old Nina, walking the dog, etc., etc. Actually, Victoria has many things going for her. She lives in a very comfortable apartment building on Central Park West in New York City, has caring (too much?) parents—mother is a well-known

sculptor, her father, a successful real estate lawyer—and she attends a posh private school named Brendon.

Unfortunately for her, however, Victoria's inventive, mischievous mind often thinks up seemingly innocent pranks and practical jokes that invariably misfire and get her into trouble. Her latest is the worst. She has been accused (not without cause) by her gross English teacher, Mrs. "Fatso" Serrada, of totally disrupting a Friday afternoon special showing of *Richard II*. That evening, the new principal, Mr. Davis, phones and informs Felicia, Victoria's mother, that her daughter is not only suspended but faces expulsion. A Monday morning conference is hastily arranged, but her mother's punishment is swift and terrible. Not only is Victoria completely grounded, but worst of all, no telephone calls for a week! Victoria wonders if this well-meaning ogress had herself ever been a teenager. Luckily, intervention by her kindly grandmother reinstates her weekend trip to Philadelphia to attend Cousin Elizabeth's fourteenth birthday bash.

The party is another downer. Midway through this disaster, Victoria is on the back porch with Liz and a couple of boys who begin passing around a joint. When it's Victoria's turn, Aunt Hildy happens on the scene and suddenly hysteria reigns. Everyone is sent home. New York is called about Victoria's shameful behavior, and the following morning the girl is unceremoniously dumped on a train bound for the Big Apple.

Victoria is sitting at a window seat staring miserably into space when the train gives a sudden lurch and she bumps her head violently against the windowpane. There is a momentary blackout, and when she wakes the train has reached Penn Station. Everything there seems different, including the building, and people seem to be dressed in a very old-fashioned way. Furthermore, her mother is not there to meet her as promised and she is unable to contact her by phone. Victoria is becoming increasingly alarmed and disoriented when she meets a girl her age named Cici who looks very familiar. Cici stays with her and, when Victoria is still not able to get in touch with her mother, invites her home to Queens.

Victoria is amazed at how similar Cici is to herself, but Cici is much more daring and active at general hell-raising. For example, they stop at a Woolworth's, where, to Victoria, everything appears to be on sale and Cici engages in some petty shoplifting. When caught by the manager, she extricates herself by pretending to be an immigrant who "no-speak-de-English." Later, at the local movie theater, which seems to Victoria to show only revivals, Cici creates such a riot when a dirty old man touches her that both have to escape into the street.

Although Victoria likes her new friend, she is somewhat disconcerted by her antiquated attitudes and the slang expressions she uses like "TS" and "hubba hubba." Cici also seems unable to comprehend references to such subjects as television and frozen food. When they stop at a candy store to make another unsuccessful telephone call, part of the puzzle is solved. The newspapers for sale bear the date May 19, 1944, and at Cici's home another piece falls into place. Victoria recognizes Cici's mother as her own grandmother and, therefore, Cici, short for Felicia, is really her mother!

Victoria is made very welcome, but when she hears her grandmother and mother bickering and Cici's arguments with her older brother, later to be known as Uncle Steve, she experiences a feeling of déjà vu. Cici explains that she is in serious trouble. If she flunks her science test on Monday she will not graduate from eighth grade. Because she lacks the class notes to study from, she has arranged to buy that evening a copy of the test from Ted Davis, the son of her science teacher.

That night, when everyone is asleep, they precariously climb down from Cici's second-floor bedroom via a dead tree to meet Ted the Creep. His price has gone up from two dollars to ten dollars and they are forced to reenter the house for more money. The tree snaps at the time that the police, alerted by a neighbor, arrive. Ted escapes, and, faced with having to give an explanation to her parents, Cici blurts out the truth. She is so upset that later she almost runs away but is dissuaded when the two girls talk about the need to be mature and face responsibilities.

Later there is an air raid alarm, and in the dark Cici falls and loses consciousness. She awakens with a bad bump on her forehead on the train to New York. Never had she ever been more pleased and happy than when she is greeted at the station by her mother and Nina. The next day, when they appear for the conference at school, Felicia and Victoria recognize the new principal as Ted Davis, the nerd who had deceived them years before. Using a combination of nostalgia and black-mail, Felicia has Victoria reinstated after the young girl promises faith-fully to mend her ways. Felicia tells Victoria about the test paper incident and how she had later negotiated and reached an agreement with her science teacher, Mrs. Davis, that allowed her to graduate. Mother and daughter seem to have reached a new understanding and peace reigns in the Martin household. Well, at least temporarily.

Thematic Material

This is basically a wonderfully comic novel with an appealing, self-deprecating gamine as heroine. The elements of fantasy are well integrated into the plot. Conflicts even within happy families and the agonies of adolescence are well portrayed, as are problems involving the generation gap, reaching maturity, and accepting responsibility. Life in 1944 New York City is nicely re-created, and the contrast between that relatively safe, secure, more simple life and that of the present day is both amusing and revealing.

Book Talk Material

A discussion on the question "Did you ever wonder what your parents were like at your age?" could introduce Victoria and her unique situation. Some amusing passages are: the incident during the school movie (pp. 2–5; pp. 3–8, Archway, pap.; pp. 11–14, Dell, pap.); the quarrels with Nina at the train station (pp. 23–27; pp. 35–40, Archway, pap.; pp. 31–35, Dell, pap.); pot smoking at the party (pp. 28–29; pp. 42–44, Archway, pap.; pp. 37–38, Dell, pap.); shoplifting at Woolworth's (pp. 49–51; pp. 74–77, Archway, pap.; pp. 62–65, Dell, pap.); and the riot at the movie theater (pp. 52–58; pp. 78–87, Archway, pap.; pp. 66–73, Dell, pap.).

Additional Selections

Mother and daughter switch places in Mary Rodgers's now classic *Freaky Friday* (Harper, 1972, $10.89; pap., $2.95; condensed in *More Juniorplots*, Bowker, 1977, pp. 19–21) and Ben and his father do the same in *Summer Switch* (Harper, 1982, $10.89; pap., $2.95), also by Rodgers. Using her sixth sense, Blossom helps recover stolen treasures for the ghost of an Egyptian princess in Richard Peck's *Blossom Culp and the Sleep of Death* (Delacorte, 1986, $14.95), one of many books about this irrepressible heroine. Steppie's mother becomes a pool shark when she converts their basement into a pool hall for problem teenagers in Judith St. George's *What's Happening to My Junior Year?* (Putnam, 1986, $13.95). Time travel is also featured in William Sleator's *The Green Future of Tycho* (Dutton, 1981, $11.95) in which a boy discovers an egg-shaped object that takes him back and forth in time; and in Diana Wynne Jones's *The*

Homeward Bounders (Greenwillow, 1981, $11.75; pap., Ace, $2.95) a group of hooded figures sends Jamie Hamilton into adventures in time and space. Time and time travel are the themes of Jack Finney's *About Time: Twelve Stories* (pap., Simon & Schuster, 1986, $7.95) and of John Rowe Townsend's *The Visitors* (Lippincott, 1977, $12.25).

About the Author

Commire, Anne, ed. *Something about the Author*. Detroit: Gale Research Co., 1985. Vol. 37, p. 150.
Holtze, Sally Holmes, ed. *Fifth Book of Junior Authors and Illustrators*. New York: Wilson, 1983, pp. 235–236.
May, Hal, ed. *Contemporary Authors*. Detroit: Gale Research Co., 1985. Vol. 115, pp. 348–349.

Sargent, Pamela. *Earthseed*
Harper, 1983, lib. bdg., $11.89; pap., $6.95 (same pagination)

Pamela Sargent's science fiction novels are noted for their provocative concepts and challenging stories. *Earthseed* deals with the concept of interplanetary colonies and how to inhabit them with a type of human who no longer has destructive instincts. In the *Eye of the Comet* (Harper, 1984, $11.89; pap., $8.95) a young girl discovers her origins are on the planet Earth and she returns there to help the primitive peoples. Sargent has also edited several collections of science fiction stories by women such as *Women of Wonder* (pap., Random, 1975, $4.95). Her novels are enjoyed by readers in grades seven through ten.

Plot Summary

As Ship reckons time, Zoheret is fifteen years old. To her and to the other young people, Ship has been mother, father, family, educator, comforter, and disciplinarian. Ship has been traveling through space for all of Zoheret's life, and for some time before that. Launched by humans from the dying planet Earth, it seeks a habitable planet where it will deposit its living cargo and begin a new civilization. Zoheret and the others have been "created" from the genetic material that was placed on board Ship at the time of launch.

Zoheret, however, does know her real "parents" because Ship has often shown them to her on the screen: Her mother, Geula, was a chemical engineer and her father, Hussein, a medical researcher and poet. They are her parents at least in the sense that she was created from their genetic material. They had both been part of what Zoheret has learned was the great Project that sent Ship into space from a fading civilization to give life to Zoheret and the others. Ship has been traveling for more than a century.

Although Zoheret is intelligent and learns well, she often does not apply herself to her lessons as diligently as she should, a fact noted by Ship, and her self-doubts cast her in the role of follower rather than leader. Often, for instance, she becomes disgusted with herself when she allows someone like bold Manual to take over as group leader in such events as the Competition, which Ship organizes periodically to test their skills. And often she does not stand up strongly enough against the others who contend that crippled Anoki and simple Willem are a couple of Ship's "mistakes" and should not have been allowed to survive.

For the upcoming Competition, Ship divides all the youngsters into groups and challenges them to see which group will be the first to cross the Hollow. Large enough to take at least two days to traverse, the Hollow is the most extensive part of Ship and is made to resemble Earth, humankind's natural environment.

Zoheret's team loses the Competition to Ho's group, but he wins only by cheating and causing serious injury to others. When Zoheret complains to Ship in the manner in which the Competition was won, Ship tells her: "He broke no rules. You may not like what he did, but it worked—he won. Life involves trading one thing for another . . . setting priorities. You have to decide whether or not your goal justifies the means used to achieve it."

Zoheret senses that the time is nearing for Ship to deposit its cargo to begin a new civilization because Ship now tells her that the next part of the Project will be for the youngsters to be sent into the Hollow to live for a time in order to prepare them for life on their new planet. Ship will shut off its own sensors so that they cannot contact it, and so must rely on themselves for life and survival.

Out in the Hollow with the others, Zoheret once again allows herself to be led, even taking up a relationship with Dmitri, whom she does not love. But at least she does not have to put up with the troublemaking Ho, who with his group has made a settlement by the lake, away from Zoheret and Dmitri and their associates. But when some of their supplies are stolen, Zoheret suspects Ho and his followers and along with others sets out to find them. When they can't be found at the lake, over Zoheret's protests some of her group burn the cabins of Ho's group. Soon after, the fields of Zoheret's group are burned, and she decides that in order to settle this problem, she must go back and talk to Ship.

But back at Ship, Zoheret learns a startling fact—she and the others, born of genetic material carried on Ship, are not alone! Others before them had also been born and sent to live in the Hollow to prepare for life on another planet. But something went wrong with the new planet worlds that Ship had discovered for them. Without a future, ten of them were placed in suspension by Ship, and now seven have awakened. Aleksandr meets Zoheret and tells his story.

When Zoheret tries to return to her group, undecided whether to tell the others what she has discovered, she and her friends are captured by Ho's followers. She learns that a second group of Earthpeople have also been in suspension, and this group is trying to take over the running of the entire settlement. And most devastating of all, Zoheret learns that the great Project Ship had told her of, the effort to save civilization from a dying planet, the Project that had caused her and the others to be born out in space, was actually only the wishes of a tiny group back on Earth who hated what was happening to their planet and wanted to preserve their own ways.

Am I to live and die on some unknown planet, thinks Zoheret, just because some people want their own way? She realizes that the Earthpeople do not care about preserving her civilization or about her.

Now filled with determination and a new strength as she realizes that she and the others must stand up for themselves, that neither Ship nor anything or anyone else will protect them, Zoheret escapes from Ho, returns to Ship, and persuades Aleksandr's people to join them.

During the battle that follows, Zoheret is shot at by a woman who looks strangely familiar to her. It is her own mother who attacks her!

Zoheret loses her left arm but is assured that Ship can fashion a new one for her. Ship also tells her that the time has come for them all to begin life in a new world, where Ship will leave them. Does she want to begin this new life, keeping the bitter rift between herself and her group and those from Earth? It is truly something for her to ponder as Zoheret, now the leader of her group, bids farewell to Ship and begins her new life.

Thematic Material

This is a serious study of human instincts and aggressions, somewhat reminiscent of *The Lord of the Rings* in an interstellar setting. The author asks some questions that have validity for young people today. Can these young people, in a new and hostile world, conquer the feelings of competition and aggression that so plagued their ancestors on Earth? Can they, as Ship urges them to, be responsible for what they are, for what they will become? Can they survive?

Book Talk Material

Earthseed tackles many serious issues of human instincts and aggressive tendencies. Some important episodes are: Ship talks to Zoheret about the ends justifying the means (pp. 77–78); Zoheret ponders her relationship with Dmitri (pp. 87–90); Zoheret stands up to Ho (pp. 168–170); Zoheret talks to Ship for the last time (pp. 259–261).

Additional Selections

A young girl saves a mysterious man from drowning and thus makes many enemies in the science fiction novel *Angel with the Sword* (DAW, 1985, $15.95) by C. J. Cherryh. John Christopher has written several science fiction novels, including *The Lotus Caves* (pap., Macmillan, 1971, $4.95; condensed in *More Juniorplots,* Bowker, 1977, pp. 25–28) and the famous Tripods trilogy that begins with *The White Mountains* (pap., Macmillan, 1970, $3.95). After the nuclear holocaust, a young girl realizes she is not the sole survivor in Robert C. O'Brien's *Z for Zachariah* (Atheneum, 1975, $13.95; pap., Macmillan, $3.50; condensed in *More Juniorplots,* Bowker, 1977, pp. 37–40). Andre Norton is a name synonymous with fine science fiction. Try some of her Witch World series like *The Crystal Gryphon* (Atheneum, 1972, $5.50; pap., DAW, $2.25; pap., Tor, $2.95). John Forrester began his Bestiary series with *Bestiary Mountain* (Bradbury, 1985, $11.95), the story of four teenagers, including twins, who are forced to leave the Moon and flee to Earth. In its sequel, *The Secret of the Round Beast* (Bradbury, 1986, $12.95), they battle a mad geneticist and half-beast, half-human creatures that he has created. After a nuclear war a pack of wolves and two humans struggle for survival in Whitley Streiber's *Wolf of Shadows* (Knopf, 1985, $9.95).

About the Author
Commire, Anne, ed. *Something about the Author*. Detroit: Gale Research Co., 1982.
Vol. 29, pp. 169–170.
Evory, Ann, ed. *Contemporary Authors* (New Revision Series). Detroit: Gale Research Co., 1983. Vol. 8, pp. 442–443.
Fadool, Cynthia, ed. *Contemporary Authors*. Detroit: Gale Research Co., 1976.
Vols. 61–64, p. 482.

Sleator, William.   *Interstellar Pig*
Dutton, 1984, $11.95; pap., Bantam, $2.95 (same pagination)

William Sleator is noted for exploring original and daring themes in his science fiction/horror stories. In *House of Stairs* (Dutton, 1974, $12.95; pap., Scholastic, $1.95; condensed in *More Juniorplots*, Bowker 1977, pp. 43–46), he examines the levels to which human behavior can be changed to ensure survival; in *The Green Futures of Tycho* (Dutton, 1981, $11.95), through time travel a young boy experiences several possible versions of his own future life; and in *Singularity* (Dutton, 1985, $12.95; pap., Bantam, $2.95), twin brothers enter a different universe. The author has said, "I can't seem to keep outer space, time travel and aliens out of my work." In this ultimate novel about aliens from space, at the end the author piles climax upon climax—each more horrifying than the last—so that the astute reader might detect a tongue-in-cheek approach to the subject. At any level of appreciation, however, this is a good read for students in grades seven through ten.

Plot Summary
Ted Martin, the caretaker, tells the narrator, sixteen-year-old Barney, and his mother and father that the house they are presently renting in Indian Neck on Cape Cod is believed by some to be haunted. Over a hundred years before, a sea captain named Latham had imprisoned his crazed younger brother for twenty years in the front bedroom as punishment for the seemingly irrational murder of an unknown survivor they had fished out of the water on one of their voyages. Barney is using the front bedroom, which has a wonderful view of an island in the bay, and he has noticed strange claw marks on the walls, obviously made by the madman during his confinement.

Their conversation is interrupted by the arrival next door of three

extremely attractive college-age young people—two boys and a girl—
who, though they vehemently demanded to rent the house Barney and
family are in, have settled for the neighboring cottage when their first
choice was unavailable.

That evening, Barney, at their request, takes them some kindling for
their fireplace and meets all three: Zena, Joe, and Manny. They are an
unusual trio: charming in their flashy, flamboyant speech, flattering in
their interest in Barney and his summer home, but mysteriously reticent
about revealing anything about their own pasts. They show Barney a
board game they enjoy playing, a futuristic science fiction adventure
called Interstellar Pig.

The next day while Barney's parents are away, the three ask to tour
the house. Barney is mystified by the thoroughness of their examination
and their abnormal fascination with the markings on his bedroom walls.
After lunch Barney accepts their invitation for a return visit and, finding
no one home, does his own exploring. In Zena's room he finds a photo-
copy of Captain Latham's diary describing the murder. When he hears
footsteps on the patio Barney hides the papers in his pocket and rushes
downstairs to be greeted by the supposedly unsuspecting threesome.
While the two men go to pick up windsurfers, Zena gives Barney an
introduction to Interstellar Pig. They play outdoors after Zena assures
Barney that the special sun cream she gives him will thoroughly protect
his super-sensitive skin from sunburn. The game is a very complex one
in which, through choosing or being dealt various cards, each player
becomes a different creature from outer space, vulnerable to certain
misfortunes but equipped with weapons and disguises to avoid others as
they travel from one hostile planet to another. The object is to gain and
keep possession of The Piggy, a card depicting an ugly creature with one
eye, before the timer signals the end of the game when all are destroyed
except the owner of The Piggy. In the trial game Barney is a carnivorous
lichen from planet Mbridlengile, and Zena is Zulma, an arachnoid
nymph from Vavoosh.

Later at home, Barney reads the section of the captain's diary describing how the survivor had been placed in the cabin with his younger
brother. That night, the captain had discovered his brother clutching a
small trinket and babbling deliriously about the devil over the dead
man's body. The captain looks at the corpse and momentarily sees an
ugly, misshapen creature certainly not of this world. An instant later, it
once more assumes a human form. Barney is shaken by this account and

begins to examine carefully the scratch marks on the wall. He discovers a pattern of lines that converge on the window pane in line with a large boulder at the tip of the neighboring island.

The next day, even though Barney is in agony because of a terrible sunburn, he asks to accompany his three friends who are going to visit the island by windsurfers, and is reluctantly given permission. On the island he manages to elude the others for a few moments. Under the boulder he finds a rotting lean-to and under its floorboards is a trunk containing a small box, which he hides in his pocket just before the others arrive.

Back on the mainland, his neighbors challenge Barney to another game of Interstellar Pig. Zena once again draws Zulma (only a coincidence?), Manny becomes Moyna, a female octopuslike creature from Flacioub, Joe is Jrlb, a grill-man from Thrilb, and Barney draws Luap, a sapient reptile whose description uncomfortably fits that of the vision Captain Latham had seen years before. Barney becomes totally absorbed in the moves as though he is actually living this galactic adventure. At the end of the game (Moyna possesses The Piggy and wins), Barney returns home, opens the box, and finds a repellent, carved figure—the real Piggy—obviously the object of his neighbors' search. By cutting parts of pages out of an old school yearbook and placing the carving inside, he finds a perfect hiding place for The Piggy.

The next night, because of the violence of an unpredicted storm, Barney's parents are detained on a visit and the boy accepts a dinner invitation from his neighbors. Each of his hosts contrives to spend a few moments alone with Barney in order to bribe him with a supernatural gift—eternal life, an intelligence booster, hyperspace travel—to possess The Piggy. Barney knows he is in the hands of aliens, each of whom will stop at nothing to gain the security of owning The Piggy. After dinner, the three suggest one final game at Barney's house. Powerless to oppose them, he reluctantly agrees. There in the shadowy light of candles—both the electrical and telephone lines are down—they draw cards. The neighbors pull the same identity cards as before and Barney realizes these are actually their true identities. Likewise, his identity card reads: "Barney, Homo sapiens of the planet Earth." It is suddenly no longer a game but a life or death struggle for possession of the magical talisman. Armed with only the few defenses dealt him at the start of the game, he is miraculously able to escape the attacks of the three monsters. At one time he uses his only change-of-identity card to become part of the man-eating lichen who have also arrived to claim The Piggy. The lichen prevails and escapes into space with the figurine, followed closely by the three other aliens. During the ordeal Barney has communicated with The Piggy in light of its responses, and believes that its possession of magical powers is really a cosmic hoax. But as they travel in space, his three former companions maintain that at the end of the game, Barney and the planet Earth are doomed because of the loss of The Piggy. We will have to wait and see who is right.

Thematic Material

This book reminds one of a surreal Nibelung Saga with The Piggy taking the place of the Rhine Gold. It is, nevertheless, a solid, thrilling science fiction adventure whose ending is farcical enough to verge on a parody of the genre. Barney is a most likable, courageous hero.

Book Talk Material

The cover of the paperback edition shows Moyna and Jrlb in the foreground of a gameboard, Zulma at the back, and a dazed Barney in the center. There are many passages that could be used to interest readers: Ted talks about the haunted house (pp. 1–4); the neighbors explain the game (pp. 15–20); the three explore Barney's house (pp. 26–31); Barney explores their house (pp. 34–39); and Barney examines the scratches on the walls (pp. 61–64).

Additional Selections

Spawned by a BBC radio series, Douglas Adams's *Hitchhiker's Trilogy: Omnibus Edition* (Crown, 1984, $15.95) is a humorous satire involving a modern-day Englishman's travels through time and space. The first volume is *The Hitchhiker's Guide to the Universe* (Crown, 1980, $9.95; pap., Pocket Bks., $3.95) and, like the other parts, is available separately. The trilogy is continued in *So Long and Thanks for All the Fish* (Crown, 1985, $12.95; pap., Pocket Bks., $3.95). A dead actress turns two children invisible to find a necklace in E. L. Konigsburg's *Up from Jericho* (Atheneum, 1986, $13.95). Beginning with *Exiles of ColSec* (Atheneum, 1984, $9.95) and continuing with *The Caves of Klydor* (Atheneum, 1985, $9.95) and *ColSec Rebellion* (Macmillan, 1985, $9.95; pap., Bantam, 1986, $2.75), Douglas Hill has written an engrossing science fiction trilogy about a group of teenagers banished from Earth because of their rebellious ways. Three young people discover that their friend is actually an interplanetary alien in Margaret Mahy's *Aliens in the Family* (Scholastic, 1986, $12.95). A boy uses karate to defeat an evil emperor in Donald Wismer's *Starluck* (pap., Dell, 1986, $2.75). Keill Randor is the hero of a series of books by Douglas Hill including *Deathwing over Veynaa* (Macmillan, 1981, $7.95) and *Galactic Warlord* (Macmillan, 1980, $8.95; pap., $3.95).

About the Author

Commire, Anne, ed. *Something about the Author.* Detroit: Gale Research Co., 1972. Vol. 3, p. 207–208.

Evory, Ann, ed. *Contemporary Authors* (First Revision Series). Detroit: Gale Research Co., 1978. Vols. 29–32, p. 645.

Holtze, Sally Holmes, ed. *Fifth Book of Junior Authors and Illustrators.* New York: Wilson, 1983, pp. 295–296.

Kinsman, Clare D., ed. *Contemporary Authors.* Detroit: Gale Research Co., 1972. Vols. 29–32, p. 585.

Vinge, Joan D. *Psion*
Delacorte, 1982, $12.95; pap., Dell, $2.95 (same pagination)

Joan D. Vinge has written novelizations of some films—for example, *Return to Oz* (pap., Ballantine, 1985, $2.95)—but is best known for her adult Hugo Award–winning novel *The Snow Queen* (pap., Dell, $3.95). *Psion* is her first book for young adults, but she promises more installments in the history of our hero, Cat, the narrator of this novel. This is a complex, challenging science fiction story that is enjoyed by science fiction buffs in grades seven through ten.

Plot Summary

It is the twenty-fifth century in Quarro, the principal city of Ardattee, the hub of the Federated Galaxy. Cat, a young boy of sixteen or seventeen who has been alone as long as he can remember, lives through his wits and thievery in Oldcity, the slimy bottom of this vertical city. One night he resists capture by a press-gang seeking slave labor for the ruling cartel, the Federation Transport Authority, and is arrested. During routine testing, the security officers discover that Cat has the potential for becoming a psion, or person capable of using extrasensory powers. There are three powers with which psions can be endowed: teleportation, the ability to move oneself instantly to another place; telekinesis, the ability to move objects; and telepathy, the ability to enter another's mind. Cat appears to have potential in the latter area.

Because ordinary people fear and distrust their amazing power, psions are considered outcasts of society. Psions are a rarity, and although some are human beings, an entire race called Hydrans possessed the gift. However, there are few Hydrans remaining because they have been persecuted almost into extinction by humans. It is believed by his appearance—grass-green eyes and yellow hair—that one of Cat's parents was a Hydran.

Cat is taken to the Sakaffe Research Institute where, under the oppressive tutelage of Dr. Ardan Siebeling, he and some other unfortunate psions are having their psychic abilities heightened. Cat is particularly attracted to fellow student Jule ta Ming, a sad, wispy girl in her twenties who has been ostracized by her very wealthy family because of her freakish powers. He also likes one of his teachers, an understanding and kindly psion named Dere Cortelyou.

Soon the purpose of the project is made clear. An evil psion, Rubiy, using the code name Quicksilver, is organizing other psions on behalf of an interstellar conglomerate to take over the galaxy. When the course is finished it will be their responsibility to infiltrate Rubiy's ranks and thwart his plans. Rubiy's first target will probably be the telhassiun (an element essential in starship fuel) mines found on the star fragment Cinder in the Crab Nebula. One evening Rubiy, through teleportation, visits Jule and Cat and, after reminding them of the miserable lot meted out to psions in their society, questions the wisdom of their participation in the project. He promises to visit again; but before he can, Cat is thrown out of the program because he has taken from Siebeling's office a glass bauble that had belonged to the doctor's long-lost son, the only child of his marriage to a now-deceased Hydran woman.

Cat is once more found by the press-gang and is shipped thousands of light-years away to the mines at Cinder. He unfortunately alienates one of the chief authorities, Kielhosa, and is relegated to the pits where, like slaves, men work until death comes from telhassiun poisoning.

One day, while Cat is traveling on an ice field delivering supplies with a fellow bondsman and an overseer, Joraleman, their snowtrack goes out of control and crashes. When Cat awakens he is underground in the presence of fugitive Hydrans. The other two are released, but Cat undergoes with these creatures a mystical mind-sharing experience so shattering that his brain almost explodes and he collapses.

He awakes in a hospital bed and finds to his amazement Dr. Siebeling, Jule, and Dere visiting him. They have come to foil Rubiy's plans and to infiltrate his ranks as Dere already has. Through telepathy and teleportation, Siebeling has saved Cat from the Hydrans who have misguidedly become allies of Rubiy. Cat and Siebeling distrust one another and Cat has further reason to dislike and be jealous of him when he learns that Jule is in love with the scientist.

Rubiy appears to Cat and explains his scheme to send the boy back to the mines where he will join him by teleportation and with the help of the Hydrans take over the central controls. When Rubiy discovers that Dere is an informer, he murders him while Cat watches, helpless and horrified. The boy now realizes that this force of evil must be stopped.

When the mine takeover plan is set in motion, Cat telepathically informs the Hydrans of Rubiy's true nature and convinces them not to cooperate. With Jule as ransom, Rubiy flees and takes possession of the planetary shield headquarters where deadly radiation is filtered from entering the star's atmosphere. Cat follows and in mortal mind-to-mind combat kills Rubiy.

Back on Ardattee, Jule and Siebeling announce their impending marriage and Cat receives both his freedom and generous gifts of money from the Federation. In a gesture of reconciliation, the doctor gives Cat the glass toy. The boy is uncertain of his future—but then a cat has many lives.

Thematic Material

The question of how much loyalty and allegiance is owed to a culture by individuals who have been debased and brutalized by it is well introduced. Both the salutary and destructive aspects of psychic powers are explored in a fascinating way, and the world of the future is believably portrayed. Cat is a courageous, principled young man filled with bitterness about the injustice in his past but hopeful for the future. This novel also traces his coming to terms with his part-alien, part-human nature and assimilating the strengths of both cultures.

Book Talk Material

An introduction to the world of the psion should interest readers. Some passages of importance: Cat is caught by the authorities (pp. 3–7); Quicksilver (Rubiy) explained (pp. 56–61); Rubiy visits (pp. 77–84); Cat is processed for his trip to Cinder (pp. 100–109); and life in the mines (pp. 123–129).

Additional Selections

After a disease wipes out most of the adult population, some of the children begin to disappear mysteriously in Mary Haynes's *Raider's Sky* (Lothrop, 1987, $11.75). A fourteen-year-old girl's unusual psychic powers cause her trouble in the science fiction novel *The Dream Catcher* by Monica Hughes (Atheneum, 1987, $11.95), which was preceded by *Devil on My Back* (Atheneum, 1985, $9.95; pap., Bantam, $1.75). Thirteen-year-old Carson has a telekinetic sister Caryl and together they flee an earthquake-devastated West Coast in Wilanne Scheider Belden's *Mind-Hold* (Houghton, 1987, $14.95). A young slave is bought by a cripple at the beginning of *Citizen of the Galaxy* (Scribner, 1957, $15; pap., Ballantine, $2.25; condensed in *Juniorplots,* Bowker, 1967, pp. 160–162) by Robert Heinlein. Paul uses ESP for a sinister purpose in a novel set at the present time in Mary Towne's *Paul's Game* (Delacorte, 1983, $13.95; pap., Dell, $2.50). A terrifying trip into the fourth dimension occurs in William Sleator's *The Boy Who Reversed Himself* (Dutton, 1986, $12.95). An attempt to colonize the planet Astra produces unforeseen problems in Timothy Zahn's *Spinneret* (Bluejay, 1985, $15.95). In Barbara Peritz's *Hitchcock's Sightseeing: A Space Panorama* (Knopf, 1985, $24.85), the reader is treated to eighty photographs from NASA spaceflights.

About the Author

Commire, Anne, ed. *Something about the Author.* Detroit: Gale Research Co., 1984. Vol. 36, pp. 194–196.
Locher, Frances C., ed. *Contemporary Authors.* Detroit: Gale Research Co., 1980. Vols. 93–94, p. 524.

Yolen, Jane.   *Dragon's Blood*
Delacorte, 1982, $14.95; pap., Dell, $2.75 (same pagination)

Jane Yolen is a writer of many and varied talents. Her output extends from alphabet and counting books for the very youngest readers to sophisticated science fiction for adults. In between are such books as the wacky Commander Toad series on the spaceship *Star Warts,* also for younger readers. Her historical novel about Shaker life, *The Gift of Sarah*

Barker (Viking, 1980, $12.50; pap., Scholastic, $1.95), like *Dragon's Blood,* is suitable for junior high school readers. This later novel is Volume One of the Pit Dragon trilogy.

Plot Summary

The principal recreation and tourist attraction for both free men, named Masters, and the Bonders, or slaves, on the planet Austar IV of the Erato Galaxy is visiting the gaming pits in the large cities where fights are staged between the giant thirteen-foot-long dragons that are native to this planet. There are in fact many nurseries on this two-mooned planet where dragons are bred and raised for this purpose.

A fifteen-year-old bond boy named Jakkin works on such a dragon farm owned by Master Sarkkhan. Under the cruel supervision of the blisterweed-smoking (a mind-affecting drug) overseer Likkarn, Jakkin, together with his friends Slakk and Errikkin, clean the stud stables of fewments (dragon droppings) and bathe the male dragons. Jakkin was born into the Master caste, but after his father was killed while trying to train a feral dragon and his mother's equally sudden death, he was sold into bondage.

Now he and his fellow workers each wear a leather bond bag around their necks, hoping by some miracle to collect enough coins to buy their freedom. Most, however, waste their meager earnings on dragon betting or on the loose women that live in the Baggeries. Jakkin has his own plan to buy his freedom. He has found a small oasis five kilometers from the nursery where he has planted patches of burnwort and blisterweed, the staple food of dragons. Soon he hopes to steal a fertile egg from the incubarn and raise his own fighting dragon.

Unfortunately, at hatching time, because of an incident involving Likkarn's vindictiveness, he is attacked by an enraged dragon, Blood Brother, and spends a week in the farm's hospice under the special care of a fifteen-year-old attractive nurse named Akki. When he emerges he finds that the eggs have hatched and the hatchlings counted.

One night he steals out of the bondhouse to visit the hen dragons' room in the incubarn. Jakkin sees momentarily silhouetted against the moon Akkas, a drakk, the fierce pterodactyl-like bird that lives on the eggs and the young of dragons. Inside the hens' room he notices that the hatchlings of Heart O'Mine have been miscounted. There are ten, not nine, as the stall label reads. Marveling at his good fortune, he takes the strongest of the brood and hides it in the shelter he has constructed at the oasis. He gets back to the bondhouse only moments before the nightly near-killing frost called Dark-after strikes. His return is detected, but the other boys and men think Jakkin has been out with Akki and tease him unmercifully about it.

When Jakkin reports seeing the deadly drakk, a hunting party with himself included is organized by Likkarn in Master Sarkkhan's absence. Due in part to Jakkin's courage and fast action, a female drakk and her seven young are spotted and killed. Jakkin becomes a hero but there is worry that perhaps the male has survived.

Every free moment he has, the boy spends with his hatchling dragon. Painstakingly he feeds it and protects it, but one day he discovers a stranger's footprints at the oasis and realizes that someone else shares his secret. One day the surviving drakk attacks Jakkin and his dragon at the oasis. With exceptional bravery, the boy kills the predator just before passing out from the wounds he has received. When he awakens he is being cared for by Akki. It is she who had discovered his hiding place.

Back at the nursery both are feted for killing the drakk, but Akki, in a rare display of bitterness and petulance, mysteriously refuses her share of the reward money given by Master Sarkkhan.

Jakkin now begins the many months of training his dragon to become a fighter. Akki obtains manuals for him on the subject and every spare moment the boy spends at the oasis teaching his pet maneuvers and fighting tactics. Jakkin's Red, as the animal is known because of its amazing color, responds willingly with almost telepathic insight. A close bond of trust and affection grows between them. After one year the dragon is ready for the first fight. Again Akki helps and this time displays a background knowledge of the world of dragon tournaments that amazes Jakkin. She obtains the necessary registration papers, makes a fight booking at the Minor Pits fifteen kilometers from the nursery, and arranges truck transportation for Jakkin and his Red.

At the pits, Jakkin learns two pieces of disconcerting news: one, his master, Sarkkhan, is present, and the other, Red is matched against a veteran named Bottle O'Rum. At first the savage fight goes decidedly in favor of Red's adversary, but when all seems lost, Red, utilizing a clever ploy learned at the oasis, emerges victorious. However, Jakkin believes his triumph is short-lived when he is spotted by Likkarn and is confronted by Sarkkhan.

A series of revelations from his master restores his well-being. Because Sarkkhan realized Jakkin's potential, he had deliberately falsified the hatchlings' count, hoping that the boy would steal the young dragon to obtain his freedom in the same way Sarkkhan had years before. Actually, Jakkin's frequent trips to the oasis and the training period had been closely monitored. Furthermore, Sarkkhan reveals that, although Akki refuses to acknowledge it, she is his daughter. Her mother was a casual contact from the Baggeries.

Jakkin's dragon is renamed Heart's Blood and, as a result of his victory, the boy now has enough coins to buy his freedom and the hope of taking Akki as his bride. But the girl has other plans. Believing that she can be of no further use to Jakkin, she leaves the nursery. Jakkin swears he will wait for her return.

In the second volume of the Pit Dragon trilogy, *Heart's Blood* (Delacorte, 1984, $14.95; pap., Dell, $2.95), Jakkin and Akki are reunited but not until after our hero encounters a treacherous underground gang on the planet and has many further adventures in the gaming pits of Austar IV.

Thematic Material

The galaxy that the author has created may be exotically futuristic, but such eternal verities as courage, resourcefulness, and justice are still present. The necessity of freedom to lead a dignified life is stressed, as is the binding relationship of human beings and nature as seen through the interdependence of the boy and his dragon. The details of dragon lore given by the author are fascinating and believable, as is the society she has created. Jakkin's growing maturity and his tender feelings toward Akki are interesting subthemes.

Book Talk Material

A description of Austar IV and Sarkkhan's dragon nursery should fascinate readers. A mock encyclopedia article and a map appear as frontispieces. Some exciting passages are: Jakkin takes Blood Brother into its bath (pp. 21–30); he is injured because of Likkarn's rage (pp. 34–39); he steals a hatchling (pp. 69–72); the drakk hunt (pp. 94–103); Jakkin begins working with the dragon (pp. 109–114); and the male drakk attacks (pp. 140–145).

Additional Selections

Humans become slaves when beings from another planet take over Earth in John Rowe Townsend's *The Creatures* (Lippincott, 1980, $11.50).

In her Dragonbards series, Shirley Rousseau Murphy recounts the adventures of sixteen-year-old Tebriel and his battle against the Dark. *Nightpool* (Harper, 1985, $11.89; pap., $2.95) tells how Tebriel finds the dragon to whom he is bonded, and in *The Ivory Lyre* (Harper, 1987, $12.89) he and his dragon join forces to combat the evil forces that control the land of Tirror. A thirteen-year-old girl and her grandmother try to solve the mystery of a space alien in H. M. Hoover's *The Shepherd Moon* (Viking, 1985, $11.95). Laurence Yep writes exciting stories about dragons, for example, *The Dragon of the Lost Sea* (Harper, 1982, $11.89) and its sequel, *Dragon Steel* (Harper, 1985, $12.89), in which a dragon princess is imprisoned when she returns home from years of exile. Jane Yolen and others have edited a collection of stories, *Dragons and Dreams* (Harper, 1986, $12.50), that is aimed at young fantasy readers. In *Tulku* (pap., Ace, 1984, $2.25), by Peter Dickinson, a young boy high in the Himalaya, holds the key to the birth of the all powerful one.

About the Author

Commire, Anne, ed. *Something about the Author*. Detroit: Gale Research Co., 1973. Vol. 4, pp. 237–239; updated 1985. Vol. 40, pp. 217–230.

de Montreville, Doris, and Crawford, Elizabeth D., eds. *Fourth Book of Junior Authors and Illustrators*. New York: Wilson, 1978, pp. 356–358.

Estes, Glenn E., ed. *American Writers for Children since 1960: Fiction* (*Dictionary of Literary Biography*, Vol. 52). Detroit: Gale Research Co., 1986, pp. 398–405.

Evory, Ann, ed. *Contemporary Authors* (New Revision Series). Detroit: Gale Research Co., 1984. Vol. 11, pp. 542–545.

Kinsman, Clare D., ed. *Contemporary Authors* (First Revision Series). Detroit: Gale Research Co., 1975. Vols. 13–16, p. 888.

Kirkpatrick, D. L., ed. *Twentieth-Century Children's Writers* (2nd edition). New York: St. Martin's, 1983, pp. 850–853.

Sarkissian, Adele, ed. *Something about the Author: Autobiography Series*. Detroit: Gale Research Co., 1986. Vol. 1, pp. 327–346.

Senick, Gerard J., ed. *Children's Literature Review*. Detroit: Gale Research Co., 1982. Vol. 4, pp. 255–269.

Who's Who in America: 1986–1987 (44th edition). Chicago: Marquis Who's Who, Inc., 1986. Vol. 2, p. 3052.

4

Historical Fiction

MANY writers have tried to replicate the triumphs and sorrows that have brought us to our present culture. In young adult fiction there are several excellent examples, some dealing with our own history, others with other times in Western Civilization.

Collier, James Lincoln, and Collier, Christopher. *The Winter Hero*
  Macmillan, 1978, $9.95; pap., Scholastic, $2.25 (same pagination)

These authors first gained recognition for their touching novel about tragic events during the American Revolution, *My Brother Sam Is Dead* (Four Winds, 1974, $12.95; pap., Scholastic, $2.25; condensed in *More Juniorplots,* Bowker, 1977, pp. 79–82). Since then they have produced an impressive number of novels about American history. In *The Bloody Country* (Four Winds, 1985, $12.95; pap., Scholastic, $2.25), for example, a family tries to eke out a living in spite of floods, a massacre, and legal battles in the area that was later to be Wilkes-Barre, Pennsylvania. Most of their novels contain "afterwords," outlining the factual bases for their stories. These novels are suitable for junior high school readers.

Plot Summary
During 1786–1787, Daniel Shays, who had fought in the American Revolution, led an armed revolt in western Massachusetts when economically depressed farmers attacked the Springfield arsenal and tried to prevent the courts from sitting. The rebellion was broken up by state troops; Shays escaped and was pardoned in 1788.

With the true story of Shays' Rebellion as background, the authors recount the fictional tale of fourteen-year-old Justin Conkey, too young to fight in the Revolution and anxious to prove himself in what looks like an upcoming battle between Massachusetts farmers and the government.

Justin, who makes his home on the farm of his sister, Molly, and her hot-tempered, headstrong husband, Peter McColloch, hears much talk in the small community of Pelham, Massachusetts, about how the General Court has unfairly levied tax after tax on the struggling farmers to help pay the rising costs of bringing a new country into existence. Then, one day, a collector comes to take away Peter's oxen because he can't pay back his loan in time to the wealthy Major Mattoon. Peter protests that without his oxen, he cannot work the farm to repay the money. In despair, Peter talks the matter over with Daniel Shays, who had fought as a captain in the Revolution and is considered a leader by the village people. Shays suggests that young Justin be sent into the Mattoon household to work off the debt for the oxen, instead of surrendering them, and in that way might be in a position to do a little spy work for the farmers' cause.

Justin is given a job in the Mattoon home, where, with a little ingenuity on his part, he is able to get a look at some papers listing those who are suspected of helping to foment trouble against the government; Shays' name and Peter's are on the list.

More and more Massachusetts farmers begin to back Shays, who is calling for changes in the laws, for fair tax levies, and an end to debtors' prison. And when Shays bands together his own militia to march to Springfield to prevent the courts from sitting, Justin demands to join them. At last, here is a war in which he has a chance to become a hero!

Reluctantly, Molly allows her young brother to march off along with Peter to join the rebellion. With only his father's old sword as a weapon, Justin is proud to be part of such a glorious adventure. He is certain that when the time comes, he will prove himself a stalwart fighting man.

Instead, after marching through bitter cold and heavy snow, the first time Shays' men are bombarded with fire from the state militia, most of them, Justin included, turn and run. For Justin, his chance to be a hero has turned into cowardice.

Even though Shays' forces are routed, the rebellion continues. In February 1787, Justin and Peter are among the rebels attacked by government troops at the town of Sheffield. Desperate to prove his bravery, Justin is nonetheless terrified when he sees the forest of bayonets coming toward him, and once again he attempts to flee—until he sees Peter, lying on his back with a government soldier about to bayonet him. Without thinking, Justin swings his musket like a club at the man's head. The soldier is stunned, and both Peter and Justin escape.

Shays' Rebellion has been stopped. When Justin finally returns to the farm, he learns from Molly that Peter, who had returned home earlier, has been put in jail along with other members of the uprising. Seventeen are declared guilty of treason—Peter among them. When sentences are passed, it is declared that six of the seventeen will be hanged, including Peter.

But Molly devises a plan to free Peter. With the help of others, she draws up a petition to the State Council begging clemency for the condemned men. The petition buys a few days' time. The men are to be hanged on June twenty-first. This time Molly writes a letter for Peter to sign—which he does with reluctance—humbling himself and begging for mercy.

On June nineteenth, the answer comes back from Boston. The men will be hanged on schedule.

Justin and Molly travel to the town of Northampton, where Peter is to be hanged. With heavy hearts, they watch as Peter climbs the steps of the gallows, the townspeople gathered as though witnessing a splendid drama. The noose is slipped over Peter's head, and Justin can almost feel the rope himself. . . .

But as Peter stares ahead and Justin awaits the awful moment of his brother-in-law's death, the drums stop and the sheriff steps to the corner of the gallows platform. He pulls a paper from his coat pocket and reads: By the order of the Governor . . . the man Peter McColloch is to be reprieved. . . .

Young Justin Conkey, hero of Shays' Rebellion, unashamedly lets the tears stream down his face.

Thematic Material

Here is history made alive and dramatic as the authors bring to life a critical period in the history of the young United States. For Shays' Rebellion, although a failure in that it did not accomplish what it set out to do, was successful in that it had great consequences on the future of the nation. Whereas many citizens believed it important for the states to retain most of the power and for the federal government to be relatively weak, Shays' Rebellion and the circumstances surrounding it showed them that a strong federal government was necessary in order to prevent grievances such as the farmers' protest against overtaxation and debtors' prison from flaring up continually and hindering the country's growth.

Book Talk Material

The grim reality of battle seen through the eyes of a young boy is a good introduction to this period of American history (see pp. 69–71, 76–83, 97–99). For an understanding of the injustices felt by the farmers who rebelled: Shays explains the situation to Justin (pp. 14–18); the proclamation of the Governor's Council (pp. 49–51); and the young soldiers discuss why they are fighting (pp. 89–93).

Additional Selections

There are many fine historical novels that deal with America's past. Elizabeth George Speare gives a fascinating account of colonial life in *The Witch of Blackbird Pond* (Houghton, 1958, $11.85; pap., Dell, $2.50), as does Ann Petry in *Tituba of Salem Village* (Crowell, 1964, $14.38; condensed in *Juniorplots*, Bowker, 1967, pp. 23–26). One eventful day in the life of a thirteen year old during the Revolutionary War is recounted in *The Fighting Ground* (Lippincott, 1984, $11.89; pap., Harper, $2.95) by Avi. Some other novels set in the Revolutionary War are Patricia Clapp's *I'm Deborah Sampson* (Lothrup, 1977, $11.88), about a girl who disguises herself as a man to fight for her country; Wayne Dyre Doughty's story of a white boy raised as an Indian chief's son in *Crimson Mocassins* (pap., Harper, $2.95); and Esther Forbes's award-winning *Johnny Tremain* (Houghton, 1943, $11.95; pap., Dell, $3.25). David Kherdian has fictionalized the account of Jim Bridger's adventurous exploration of the Missouri River and the discovery of Great Salt Lake in *Bridger* (Greenwillow, 1987, $11.75); and in Lou Kassem's *Listen for Rachel* (McElderry, 1986, $11.95), set during Civil War times, orphaned fifteen-year-old Rachel moves to the mountains of Tennessee and finds romance. A pioneer father's advertisement for a bride is answered in Patricia MacLachlan's *Sarah, Plain and Tall* (Harper, 1985, $8.89). Turn-of-the century Texas is the locale in Patricia Beatty's story of a traveling preacher's daughter in *Behave Yourself, Bethany Brant* (Morrow, 1986, $11.75). The story of the westward movement and its pioneers is well told in Trudy J. Hammer's nonfictional *The Advancing Frontier* (Watts, 1986, $10.90).

About the Author (Collier, Christopher)
Commire, Anne, ed. *Something about the Author.* Detroit: Gale Research Co., 1979.
Vol. 16, pp. 66–67.
Evory, Ann, ed. *Contemporary Authors* (First Revision Series). Detroit: Gale Research Co., 1978. Vols. 33–36, pp. 201–202.
Holtze, Sally Holmes, ed. *Fifth Book of Junior Authors and Illustrators.* New York: Wilson, 1983, pp. 80–81.
Metzger, Linda, ed. *Contemporary Authors* (New Revision Series). Detroit: Gale Research Co., 1984. Vol. 13, pp. 116–117.

About the Author (Collier, James Lincoln)
Commire, Anne, ed. *Something about the Author.* Detroit: Gale Research Co., 1977.
Vol. 8, pp. 33–34.
Evory, Ann, ed. *Contemporary Authors* (New Revision Series). Detroit: Gale Research Co., 1981. Vol. 4, pp. 149–150.
Holtze, Sally Holmes, ed. *Fifth Book of Junior Authors and Illustrators.* New York: Wilson, 1983, pp. 78–80.
Kinsman, Clare D., ed. *Contemporary Authors* (First Revision Series). Detroit: Gale Research Co., 1974. Vols. 9–12, p. 179.
Senick, Gerard J., ed. *Children's Literature Review.* Detroit: Gale Research Co., 1978. Vol. 3, pp. 44–49.

Fox, Paula. *One-Eyed Cat*
Bradbury, 1984, $11.95; pap., Dell, $3.25 (same pagination)

Paula Fox was awarded the 1974 Newbery Medal for *The Slave Dancer* (Bradbury, 1973, $10.95; pap., Dell, $2.25; condensed in *More Juniorplots,* Bowker, 1977, pp. 82–86), a powerful novel about the slave trade in America and its effects on a young boy kidnapped and forced to work on a slave ship. *One-Eyed Cat,* a Newbery Honor Book in 1985, takes place in upstate New York in the mid-1930s. Its action spans an autumn, winter, and spring. It is highly recommended for readers in grades six through eight.

Plot Summary

It is September 1935, and the country is in the midst of a terrible economic depression but buoyed up somewhat by the reforms being instituted by President Roosevelt. For young Ned Wallis, these events are remote but he is becoming aware that in a few days he will be eleven. Ned is the only child of James Wallis, the Congregational minister of the town of Tyler, New York, and his wife, Martha. When one speaks of a *good* man, someone like Reverend Wallis must come to mind. He is understanding, kind, dedicated to his parishioners and family, and never speaks ill of anyone. His wife, now frequently confined to a wheelchair by crippling rheumatoid arthritis, is somewhat less devout than her husband and more poetic and imaginative but is also a fine wife and mother. The fourth member of the household is their new housekeeper, Mrs. Scallop. She is peevish, eratic, moody, and continually craving attention and gratitude. Even Papa admits that employing her was a mistake.

They live modestly fifteen miles out of town in an old farmhouse built by Ned's grandfather overlooking the Hudson River. Often the view is spectacular, and on clear days one can see as far as West Point. There are a few neighbors nearby: the prolific Kimballs, one of whose many children, Evelyn, goes to school with Ned, and Mr. Scully, a kindly eighty-year-old man who lives alone and pays Ned thirty-five cents a week to do chores and visit with him. Basically, Ned is a homebody, quiet and introspective, who loves to read, talk to his papa, and spend time with his mother when she is well enough to have visitors.

On the eve of Ned's birthday, Mama's brother, Uncle Hilary, arrives for a few days. He is an ebullient, globe-trotting writer who loves his nephew dearly and brings him as a birthday gift a Daisy air rifle. Much to Ned's disappointment, Papa, though not wishing to appear unappreciative or rude, puts the gun in the attic. He is a nonviolent person who dislikes guns, but he tells Ned that when he is older he may, if he wishes, use it.

That night, Ned creeps to the attic and takes the gun outdoors. He shoots at a gray shadow by the barn and the shadow disappears. He looks up at the attic and thinks he sees a face staring down at him.

During the hot Indian summer, Ned spends many hours with Mr. Scully, who talks about the past and his dead wife and daughter, Doris, who lives in Seattle. He shows Ned a scrapbook of family pictures, including some of Mr. Scully's father who died in the Civil War. They notice a gray feral cat in the backyard. There is dried blood on its face because it has lost one eye. They begin leaving food for it by an outdoor icebox. Ned is convinced that the cat is the victim of his disobedience, and his guilt and disquiet grow.

He becomes preoccupied with caring for the cat, which is too wild to be enticed into Mr. Scully's house. He is also fearful for his dear old friend, who is becoming more forgetful and less capable of caring for himself.

Uncle Hilary writes inviting Ned to accompany him on a trip to Charleston at Christmas. Though he feels ungrateful, Ned secretly wants to stay home with his family, Mr. Scully, and the cat.

Heavy snows come and a period of extreme cold. The cat develops an illness so severe that he lies for several days without eating on an old quilt Mr. Scully has placed on the icebox. Miraculously, he recovers and once again escapes into the woods.

Mrs. Scallop's behavior is becoming increasingly difficult, and Reverend Wallis, not wishing her ill, arranges for a position for her in the Waterville Nursing Home. Mrs. Kimball, a practical nurse, will help out in her absence.

One day, Ned finds Mr. Scully unconscious lying on his bathroom floor. He has suffered a stroke and is rushed to the hospital. Ned knows he cannot leave his old friend and responsibilities behind, and thus asks his parents to be excused from Uncle Hilary's trip. They agree. Mr. Scully's daughter, Doris, arrives. She is an unfeeling woman who leaves after admitting her father to the nursing home where Mrs. Scallop works and arranging to sell the house. Using his few savings, Ned secretly buys milk and collects scraps to feed the cat. He often visits the nursing home. Mr. Scully is partially paralyzed, unable to speak and sinking gradually. During his last visit to his friend, Ned confesses that it was he who shot the cat. The old man tenderly encloses the boy's hand in his own as a gesture of forgiveness and understanding. A few days later Mr. Scully dies.

In the spring, Mr. Scully's house is sold and Ned must stop feeding the cat, but one night, while exploring the deserted Makepeace mansion, he sees the cat in the distance with prey in its mouth.

Mama responds well to a new treatment called chrysotherapy involving the use of gold salt. Soon she is once more able to walk and move without the agonizing pain.

One night, unable to sleep, Ned walks to the Makepeace mansion. His mother joins him; and in a tender moment under what she calls a cat's moon, they see the one-eyed cat, his mate, and two kittens. As they begin to walk home he confesses to the rifle incident. Mama says it was she who witnessed it from the attic. In her wisdom she had remained silent. She also makes a confession. Years before, when Ned was only three, she left her husband for three months because she felt unworthy of him and unable to live up to his goodness. At home, they are greeted by Papa in the doorway. He was worried about them and welcomes them back.

Thematic Material

Though set in a period more than fifty years ago, this is a mood piece that deals with timeless values and conflicts. It is a story of the goodness of one man and the obligations and guilt that this produces in others. It also deals with a friendship gained and lost that transcends age, with the strength of the family unit, and with gentleness and kindness. Ned's acceptance of the consequences of his action and the eventual expiation of his guilt are powerful themes. This novel also masterfully re-creates a quiet more temperate time when poverty was commonplace but neighborliness and trust more prevalent.

Book Talk Material

The significance of the title could be explained. Some interesting passages are: Ned visits his mother (pp. 28–32); he receives Uncle Hilary's present (pp. 36–40) and retrieves it from the attic (pp. 43–46); Mr. Scully reminisces and they spot the cat (pp. 49–68); an electric storm (pp. 77–80); and the cat's illness (pp. 135–136, pp. 139–140).

Additional Selections

In *Nelda* (Houghton, 1987, $12.95) by Pat Edwards, a young girl, daughter of migrant workers, hopes for money and a home during the dark days of the depression; and in Candice F. Ransom's *Nicole* (Scholastic, 1986, $2.25), a sixteen year old and her mother book passage on the *Titanic*. World War I is evoked in Margaret I. Rostkowski's *After the Dancing Days* (Harper, 1986, $13.95), the story of Annie, who visits a veterans hospital to help her father. The depression is also explored in Clayton Bess's *Tracks* (Houghton, 1986, $12.95), about a boy and his brother who ride the rails and face death at the hands of Klan members. In Pennsylvania of the 1920s, a fifteen-year-old boy grows up and accepts responsibility after his brother is killed in Jay Parini's *The Patch Boys* (Holt, 1986, $14.95). In Walter D. Edmonds's *The South African Quirt* (Little, 1985, $14.95), a novel set in upstate New York, a boy rebels against his father's inhumanity. Growing up in Appalachia is recalled in Cynthia Rylant's *Waiting to Waltz: A Childhood* (Bradbury, 1984, $10.95). A history of the 1929 stock market crash and the Great Depression is given in Bruce Glassman's *The Crash of '29 and the New Deal* (Silver Burdett, 1986, $10.47; pap., $5.75). Another fine novel of the depression is Chester Aaron's *Lackawanna* (Lippincott, 1986, $11.95).

About the Author

Block, Ann, and Riley, Carolyn, eds. *Children's Literature Review*. Detroit: Gale Research Co., 1976. Vol. 1, pp. 59–60.
Commire, Anne, ed. *Something about the Author*. Detroit: Gale Research Co., 1979. Vol. 17, pp. 59–60.
de Montreville, Doris, and Crawford, Elizabeth D., eds. *Fourth Book of Junior Authors and Illustrators*. New York: Wilson, 1978, pp. 135–136.
Estes, Glenn E., ed. *American Writers for Children since 1960: Fiction* (*Dictionary of Literary Biography*, Vol. 52). Detroit: Gale Research Co., 1986, pp. 143–156.
Locher, Frances C., ed. *Contemporary Authors*. Detroit: Gale Research Co., 1978. Vols. 73–76, pp. 214–215.

Highwater, Jamake. *The Ceremony of Innocence*
Harper, 1985, $11.25; lib. bdg., $10.89

In the three novels that comprise the Ghost Horse Cycle, Jamake Highwater has written a powerful social history of the American Indian that covers almost ninety years from the 1860s into the 1950s. Through the tragic experiences of a single family, the reader witnesses the gradual erosion of the Indians' family structure, culture, and traditions. Each volume has a distinct unity but the trilogy, *Legend Days* (Harper, 1984, $11.70; lib. bdg., $11.89), *The Ceremony of Innocence*, and *I Wear the Morning Star* (Harper, 1986, $17.25; lib. bdg., $11.89), is best read in sequence. It is suitable for mature junior high and senior high school readers.

In the first book, *Legend Days*, we meet Amana from the Blood tribe of Plains Indians. When she is only eleven years old a smallpox epidemic destroys most of her tribe and she escapes into the wilderness where she is rescued and cared for by Grandfather Fox. While in his care she has a mystical experience where she gains the courage and powers of any male warrior or hunter. When she is reunited with the remnants of her tribe she marries Far Away Son, the husband of her invalid sister, Sooda Wa. Through many years of hardship and humiliation when she assumes male responsibilities, she cares for her family, but first her sister dies and then her husband is killed in a buffalo hunt. At the beginning of *The Ceremony of Innocence*, Amana, now twenty-eight, is wandering the Northwest Territory aimlessly because her people have abandoned her, blaming her for the death of her husband.

Plot Summary

It is three years since the death of Far Away Son and Amana, bitter and disheartened, is begging for food from the white men at Fort Benton, Montana, when she encounters the high-spirited, uninhibited Amalia, a French Cree half-breed. Amalia lives in a sod house and makes a living by selling bones and skulls scavenged from the plains or, in tough times, by selling herself to white men. Since her French husband's death, Amalia has also been alone. All this she explains in a patois consisting of some French and a little, very ungrammatical, English. The two instantly become close friends and Amana begins sharing Amalia's home. When the two attend a dance at the Fort, Amana meets a handsome young French trapper, Jean-Pierre Bonneville, whom she had met years before at the trading post. She also recalls meeting his partner, Hugh Monroe, an enigmatic, usually taciturn man who had once tried to rape her, but for whom she later feels pity. Jean-Pierre and Amana are attracted to one another and, in spite of Amalia's disapproval, a courtship is begun and Amana secretly moves out to live with the Frenchman. For many months the romance is idyllic. Amana even tries for a reconciliation with Amalia but finds the sod house deserted. After a move to winter quarters to buy furs, Amana has many encounters with other Indian tribes. She longs for some contact with her own people but these are the days of Little Big Horn and, later, Wounded Knee, and because she has deserted her people and adopted the ways of the white man, she is regarded with suspicion and often shunned. The two are equally unacceptable to the white community. Amana, now pregnant, is fearful that her days with Jean-Pierre are numbered. As predicted, the Frenchman soon deserts her to return to Montreal where, Amana learns, he has a wife and children.

Amana's child is born, a girl she names Jemina, and together they rejoin the Indian settlement at Fort Benton. It is the dead of winter, and they find their lodges have been destroyed by the U.S. Army. They are forced to march to a wasteland reservation where there is neither food nor game. Amana is near starvation and has even resorted to feeding her child with her own vomit, when miraculously Amalia finds her. She has become the most successful madam in Fort Benton, running a house called Chez Amalia. Amana and her baby move in and Amana finds a job washing dishes in Mr. Fuller's Fine Restaurant.

The years pass happily and Jemina becomes the darling of the whores.

When she is thirteen, however, the upright townspeople force Amana to send her to school. She does, and for two years Jemina attends the very proper Miss Wells Girl's School. At age fifteen she returns totally Anglicized and without a shred of empathy with her native roots.

When the circus visits Fort Benton all are entranced with the feats of a daring horseman, Jamie Ghost Horse, who brags that he contains the best mixture of both the Negro and Indian races. Through the efforts of Mr. Fuller, Jemina meets this swaggering but highly personable young man. There is a mutual attraction and, at the age of sixteen, much to Amana's delight, Jemina becomes Mrs. Jamie Ghost Horse.

They leave to rejoin the circus and, coincidentally with the end of World War I, a son named Reno is born. Jemina finds it impossible to travel with a baby and so Reno, like his mother, spends his first seven years under the care of Amana and the establishment ladies. Gradually things change. Mr. Fuller and Amalia die in the same year. Once again homeless, Amana and Reno join Jemina and Jamie on the road. Jamie's behavior is changing. It is the Depression and jobs are scarce. Gradually Jamie turns to alcohol for escape and frequently disappears for days.

In Utah they meet Jamie's former boss, Alexander Milas from The Great Milas Family Troupe of Aerialists. Milas has become Alex Miller the successful Hollywood producer of westerns. He offers Jamie a job as a stuntman and the whole family moves to the guest house on Miller's estate in the San Francisco Valley where a second son, Sitko, is born. Jamie's drinking bouts continue and his marriage seems finished when he decides that his sons should not be brought up in this atmosphere and sends Amana and the boys back to the reservation in Montana. Amana is once more happy. Although Reno is too old to change to the old ways, Sitko readily accepts the lore and traditions of his people and spends a happy few years absorbing and listening to his grandmother's stories of his native culture. But again Amana's life is disrupted. Jemina suddenly reappears to take the boys from their grandmother. In Jamie's absence, she has become Mr. Miller's mistress and has now persuaded him to pay for a boarding school for Reno and Sitko. The boys leave and once more Amana is alone.

In the third volume, *I Wear the Morning Star*, events reach a shattering climax. The story is now narrated by Sitko. First we learn of the heartless, cruel boarding school where he is persecuted and physically abused because of his Indian ways, while his brother, by denying his background, prospers. After this ordeal the boys move back to Mr. Miller's guest house where Amana, now an old woman approaching death, also lives. Reno is now a young man and joins his foster father in the movie business but, like Jamie, soon sinks into alcoholism and mental illness. In high school, Sitko, still proud and defiant, finds an outlet for his loneliness in art. One night, through a misunderstanding, Mr. Miller orders both boys off his property even though Reno is dangerously ill. Somehow Jamie hears of this; he finds an apartment for them, gives them money and then, gun in hand, visits the Miller house where he fatally shoots Jemina and seriously wounds Alex. The saga of Jamie Ghost Horse is over and now Sitko is left to pick up the pieces.

Thematic Material

On page 66 of *I Wear the Morning Star,* Amana tells Sitko, "One day there were many animals and many good things of the earth for all to eat. . . . These were the good days but the grass began to die and the animals no longer spoke to us. The land was filled with strangers and there were no more days for us." These books not only tell of the irreparable harm that has come to the Indians through assimilation into the white man's culture, but it also shows how many have been able to withstand this brutal condescension through their innate dignity, courage, and belief in tradition. The results of the denial of one's heritage is well depicted in this series, as is the spiritual richness of the Indian people. This series gives a realistic picture of frontier life, but readers will probably best remember the character of Amana—courageous, indomitable, and inspiring.

Book Talk Material

An introduction to Amalia and her plight should interest readers as should a discussion of the white man's treatment of the Indians during the opening up of the West. Mr. Highwater writes about his people in poetic rhythmic prose and a clean, forthright style. Some examples: Amana meets Amalia (pp. 3–6); Amana settles in and describes her past (pp. 8–11); Amana at a dance with Jean-Pierre (pp. 22–26); Indians visit Amana (pp. 47–51); a foreshadowing of Amana's fate (pp. 56–59); and her relocation to a reservation where she feeds a starving Jemina (pp. 73–78).

Additional Selections

The Battle of Little Big Horn is re-created in the story of a young Indian brave, Dark Elk, in *Only Earth and Sky Last Forever* (pap., Harper, 1972, $2.95) by Nathaniel Benchley. John Raincrow, a sixteen-year-old Miccosukee Indian, is torn between old and new cultures in Luke Wallin's *Ceremony of the Panther* (Bradbury, 1987, $11.95). In Russell Freedman's nonfiction *Indian Chiefs* (Holiday, 1987, $15.95), there are profiles of six Indian chiefs who led their people during the mid and late 1800s. In the contemporary novel, *Winners* (Dial, 1986, $10.95) by Mary-Ellen Lang Collura, orphaned Jordy Threebears gets to know his grandfather who lives on a reservation. American Indians are the central figures in several of Scott O'Dell's books including *Sing Down the Moon* (Houghton, 1970, $11.95; pap., $2.75) and *Zia* (Houghton, 1978, $11.95; pap., Dell, $2.50). *American Indians Today* (Watts, 1986, $11.90) by Judith Harlan explores the conditions and issues involved in lives of contemporary Native Americans. Also use Arlene Hirsch Felder's *Happily May I Walk: American Indians and Alaskan Natives Today* (Scribner, 1986, $13.95).

About the Author

Bowden, Jane A., ed. *Contemporary Authors.* Detroit: Gale Research Co., 1977. Vols. 65–68, pp. 293–294.

Commire, Anne, ed. *Something about the Author.* Detroit: Gale Research Co., 1983. Vol. 30, p. 128; updated 1983. Vol. 32, pp. 92–96.

Estes, Glenn E., ed. *American Writers for Children since 1960: Fiction (Dictionary of Literary Biography,* Vol. 52). Detroit: Gale Research Co., 1986, pp. 185–192.

Evory, Ann, ed. *Contemporary Authors* (New Revision Series). Detroit: Gale Research Co., 1983. Vol. 10, pp. 227–228.

Holtze, Sally Holmes, ed. *Fifth Book of Junior Authors and Illustrators.* New York: Wilson, 1983, pp. 149–150.

Kirkpatrick, D. L., ed. *Twentieth-Century Children's Writers* (2nd edition). New York: St. Martin's, 1983, pp. 373–374.

Who's Who in America: 1986–1987 (44th edition). Chicago: Marquis Who's Who, Inc., 1986. Vol. 1, p. 1282.

O'Dell, Scott. *The Road to Damietta*
Houghton, 1985, lib. bdg., $14.95

Scott O'Dell can truthfully be considered to be one of the fathers of the young adult novel. In his many years of writing quality novels he has been awarded every prestigious prize in the field including the Newbery Medal for *Island of the Blue Dolphins* (Houghton, 1960, $9.95; pap., Dell, $2.95; condensed in *Juniorplots,* Bowker, 1967, pp. 47–50). Although he is no stranger to the historical novel, this is one of the few he has written with settings outside North America. Like his other novels, it is suitable for junior high school readers.

Plot Summary

In Italy of the thirteenth century, it will soon be time for Cecila Graziella Beatrice Angelica Rosanna di Montanaro, known as Ricca, to marry. Although not yet fourteen, she is well aware that Count Giuseppe di Luzzaro of Monte Verde has spoken for her hand to her father, the leading member of the commune that governs the town of Assisi. Ricca, a willful lass with a sharp wit, has decided that if her father decrees she should marry the count, she will take herself off to a nunnery.

Young Ricca has a strong reason for avoiding such a marriage. She is already in love, and not with Count di Luzzaro. The object of her adoration is the handsome playboy and son of one of the richest of the city's merchants, Francis Bernardone. All the young ladies of Assisi speak highly of Francis, although Ricca's brother, Rinaldo, declares that the youth "has a fly in his head."

Nonetheless, Ricca follows Bernardone about town, adoring him from afar as he cavorts in the town square, although Francis acknowledges nothing of her passion. And, indeed, Raul de los Santos, who is her father's librarian and Ricca's tutor in astronomy, numbers, and world languages, chides her on being "the possessor of an immense conceit" if she thinks Bernardone will ever cast an adoring eye in her direction.

As Ricca's love grows stronger during the following months, strange tales begin to circulate about Francis. It is said that the youth has stolen expensive cloth and some money from his own father. The cloth he gave to a beggar and the money he spent on a wild party. Ricca is one of those who watch Francis's trial as he is asked to repent for his actions before his father, and she is astonished as he declares his respect for his father and his love for the Lord, stripping himself naked before all. Some time later, reacting to a vision, Ricca herself sheds her clothes in the square, to her father's most angry reaction when he hears of it.

Even Ricca, however, cannot deny the changes in Francis when they chance to meet and he coaxes her into releasing the pet falcon she usually carries. When her father hears of this, he decides that she needs more to occupy her mind and he sets Raul de los Santos to the task of teaching his daughter the arts of copying letters.

To her surprise, Ricca enjoys copying the Scriptures, but Francis never leaves her mind. She hears that, having been instructed by the bishop to give back the stolen money to his father and thus be forgiven, instead he strips himself naked and returns the clothes, saying, "Until this day I have called you my father. But now and in the days to come I can only say, 'Our Father who art in Heaven.' "

When next Ricca meets Francis Bernardone, he has taken a vow of chastity. Attired in a ragged gown, he heads a band of followers who walk barefoot through the countryside proclaiming that poverty is a virtue while begging for his supper. Already people are beginning derisively to call him a saint—Saint Francis of Assisi.

Ricca is at first stunned by the news that Francis has taken such a vow. But she remains steadfast in her belief that her own love for him will eventually bring him to see that his life is with her. She begins an act of painstaking devotion, the first of many letters, copied in her beautiful hand, to be sent to Francis in an effort to tell him of her adoration. But Francis acknowledges only her friendship and goes about his journeys. But soon Ricca embarks on her own journey. Her father, not convinced that she has settled down as a proper young lady should, sends her off to the carnival city of Venice to spend some time with an aunt. From there, she eventually learns that Francis is to travel to Damietta on the Nile River. There in that city long besieged by the crusading wars, he seeks an end to the strife between Moslems and Christians. Defying all others, and even Francis himself, Ricca embarks on a journey to Damietta, where she is witness to the confrontation between Francis and the all-powerful sultan of Syria and Egypt.

It is after this historic meeting between these two determined men, and the destruction of Damietta, that Ricca comes to realize the true depth and meaning of her devotion to this playboy become saint.

Thematic Material

Through the eyes of a young girl, the author brilliantly re-creates the world of thirteenth-century Italy and the maturing of Francis Bernardone from a reckless playboy to the saint who protected animals and shunned all wealth. The strong character of Ricca and her own maturation add depth and sensitivity to this story.

Book Talk Material

Some descriptions of Ricca's life in the city of Assisi and in Italy can be used to introduce the medieval period and the wars of the Crusades. See: Ricca thinks about when she fell in love (pp. 4–5); Ricca watches Francis in the square (pp. 12–13); Ricca watches the trial (pp. 34–35); reacting to what seems a vision, Ricca sheds her clothes in the square and angers her father (pp. 38–41).

Additional Selections

Mollie Hunter tells the story of Mary Queen of Scots in her historical novel *You Never Knew Her As I Did!* (Harper, 1981, $11.49). A girl is transported in time to Ancient Egypt in a novel that mixes reality and fantasy, Mary Stolz's *Cat in the Mirror* (pap., Dell, 1978, $2.95). Fifth-century Greece in the time of the battle of Marathon is the setting for Margaret Hodges's exciting *The Avenger* (Scribner, 1982, $11.95). A slapstick satire on knights and knighthood is contained in *Henry's Quest* (Atheneum, 1986, $12.95) by Graham Oakley in which Henry, astride his donkey, sets out on a quest for gasoline. Zoe Coralnik Kaplan writes about one of the strongest women in the twelfth century who was also a queen of England and France in *Eleanor of Aquitaine* (Chelsea, 1986, $16.96) and E. L. Konigsburg has written an excellent novel on the same subject, *A Proud Taste for Scarlet and Miniver* (Atheneum, 1973, $12.95; pap., Aladdin, $1.95; pap., Dell, $2.50). The Oedipus story is retold in Norma Johnston's *The Days of the Dragon's Seed* (Atheneum, 1982, $10.95). Among Scott O'Dell's other historical novels are *The Black Pearl* (Houghton, 1967, $11.95; pap., Dell, $2.25), about the enemies Ramon makes when he possesses the fabulous Pearl of Heaven, and *The 290* (Houghton, 1976, $7.95), a Civil War story about a Confederate navy ship.

About the Author

Block, Ann, and Riley, Carolyn, eds. *Children's Literature Review*. Detroit: Gale Research Co., 1976. Vol. 2, pp. 145–149.

Commire, Anne, ed. *Something about the Author*. Detroit: Gale Research Co., 1977. Vol. 12, pp. 161–164.

Estes, Glenn E., ed. *American Writers for Children since 1960: Fiction* (*Dictionary of Literary Biography*, Vol. 52). Detroit: Gale Research Co., 1986, pp. 278–295.

Fadool, Cynthia, ed. *Contemporary Authors*. Detroit: Gale Research Co., 1976. Vols. 61–64, p. 402.

Fuller, Muriel, ed. *More Junior Authors*. New York: Wilson, 1963, pp. 161–162.

Kirkpatrick, D. L., ed. *Twentieth-Century Children's Writers* (2nd edition). New York: St. Martin's, 1983, pp. 588–589.

Metzger, Linda, ed. *Contemporary Authors* (New Revision Series). Detroit: Gale Research Co., 1984. Vol. 12, pp. 346--347.

Who's Who in America: 1986–1987 (44th edition). Chicago: Marquis Who's Who, Inc., 1986. Vol. 2, p. 2095.

Taylor, Mildred D.   *Let the Circle Be Unbroken*
Dial, 1981, $14.95; pap., Bantam, $2.95

The story of the Logan family, first begun in *Song of the Trees* (Dial, 1975, $7.95), for a younger audience, is continued in *Roll of Thunder, Hear My Cry* (Dial, 1976, $12.95; pap., Bantam, $2.50; condensed in *More Juniorplots*, Bowker, 1977, pp. 72–74), a Newbery Medal winner in which many of plot threads are introduced that are later tied together in this, the third volume in the series.

The Logan family members are Mama and Papa, grandmother Big Ma, and four children: Stacey, the beloved oldest brother now fourteen, the narrator, ten-year-old Cassie, and two young boys, Christopher-John and Big Boy. Their hired hand is a giant of a man, Mr. Morrison, who has become like one of this loving family. It is depression time in rural Mississippi, but the Logans are fortunate and own their own land. Most of their friends and neighbors are sharecroppers whose land and livelihood are controlled by such heartless landowners as Harlan Granger. Some of the Logans' friends are Mrs. Lee Annie, a feisty sixty-three-year-old woman who lives with her grandson, a strong, uncommunicative boy of fourteen named Wardell. Another grandson, Russell Thomas, has just joined the army. The Averys are also good friends. They have a son named T. J. who became involved with two trashy white boys, R. W. and Melvin Simms, and was caught after a robbery attempt of a local store during which the owner was killed by one of the Simms boys. The brothers have escaped undetected, but T. J. is in jail awaiting trial for murder. The Logan kids have many other friends, including the Wiggins and Ellis families and Dubé Cross, a sixteen-year-old boy with a severe stutter who is still in the fifth grade like Cassie. Though they are all dirt poor and are completely at the mercy of their white overseers, they live dignified, moral lives filled with feelings of caring and sharing.

This novel begins a few months after *Role of Thunder, Hear My Cry* ended and spans time from late 1935 through the beginning of 1937. It is a long novel, full of a large cast of characters and crowded with incidents, many of which cannot be reported on in this brief summary. The novel's title is also the title of a song of family love that the Logans sing at Christmastime. This book, though intended for upper elementary and junior high students, is also enjoyed by an older audience.

Plot Summary

Son Boy and Don Lee Ellis have been given a present of some marbles, including a beautiful blue and emerald-green glass one. Cassie, a crack marble shot, challenges them to a game and is about to triumph when Papa interrupts. He tells Cassie that it is a form of gambling, and he not only makes her return her winnings but also forbids her to play again or face a licking. However, Son Boy's taunts become too much. She borrows marbles and in a suspenseful match skunks Son Boy. This flush of victory fades and punishment is swift when Papa once more intervenes.

News arrives that T. J.'s trial is scheduled shortly in Strawberry, their local town center. T. J.'s lawyer is Mr. Wade Jamison, a liberal white man whose office had been burned and dog poisoned for previous legal aid he has given to Negro families. Although he is a fine lawyer, everyone holds out little hope for the outcome of a trial in which there is an all-white jury and a redneck judge. On the day of the trial several of the local youngsters, including the Logans, skip school, borrow a horse and wagon, and head for town.

In the branches of a tree that overlooks the courthouse, Cassie literally has a bird's-eye view of the trial. Mr. Jamison produces a brilliant defense and shows with witness after witness that there is much more than a shadow of a doubt concerning T. J.'s guilt. But the dire predictions come true and he is sentenced to death—another victim of white "justice." Stacey calls out to T. J. as he is led from the courthouse. He looks up and smiles wanly. They never see their friend again.

There is trouble in the land. President Roosevelt's farm policies involving the AAA (Agricultural Adjustment Administration) and crop reduction policies are being misapplied with the result that the sharecroppers are becoming poorer and the landowners richer. Two union leaders, Morris Wheeler and John Moses—one Negro and one white—come to town to organize the farmers, but landowners like Harlen Granger warn them not to cooperate.

Uncle Hammer, from Chicago, comes to visit in his Ford car. He is a rough but kindly bachelor who, through bitter experience, mistrusts and hates all whites. The Logans are soon joined by another visitor, Mama's cousin, Bud Rankin, an outgoing, cheerful man who has married a white woman and has a fifteen-year-old daughter, Suzella. Hammer's beliefs and Bud's marriage cause differences within the family, but Bud gets permission to bring his daughter to spend some time with the Logans.

Labor troubles continue. The government's county agent, Mr. Farnsworth, who is opposed to the misapplication of federal farm laws, is found beaten up by Cassie and friends and taken for treatment with the help of a white boy, Jeremy Simms, the young brother of R. W. and Melvin.

As summer approaches, times are so difficult for the Logans that, after planting, Papa, reluctantly, is forced to take a job on the railroad far from home, but filling the void somewhat, Suzella arrives. She is completely charming and soon captures everyone's hearts and attention, except Cassie's. No longer the only young female in the family, she is jealous and resents the presence of this pretty girl who is so fair she could pass for white.

One day some white boys try to date her and when Mama finds out, in a rare display of anger she tells Suzella that like it or not, she is and always will be colored.

As winter approaches, Stacey feels he must do more to help the family. One night, he and friend Moe Turner steal away, leaving only a short note of explanation. The family is devastated and Mama sends for her husband to return home and search for their son. Uncle Hammer also arrives and the two men, thinking that Stacey might have gone to Louisiana to work on plantations cutting sugarcane, set out to find the boy.

Shortly after Christmas, Bud revisits. His marriage is ending in divorce and he has come to take Suzella back to New York. When Bud, Suzella, and the Logan children go by car to the neighbors for farewells, they are accosted by the same white teenagers who many months before believed Suzella to be white. They hurl insults at Bud because of his marriage and humiliate him by forcing him to strip before his daughter and the children. When he is down to his briefs, luckily big Mr. Morrison happens along and frightens the boys into leaving. When the time of parting comes, even Cassie admits she will miss Suzella.

Mrs. Lee Annie, though now almost sixty-five, decides that more than anything in this world, she wants to vote. All her friends try to deter her because even trying to register might lead to a lynching. She is adamant, however, and with Mrs. Logan's help, begins to study the Constitution to pass the qualifying test.

The day Lee Annie enters the courthouse for registration, other events reach a climax. Through the efforts of Mr. Jamison, the Logans think they have a lead on Stacey and so Mama, Papa, Uncle Hammer, and Cassie also come to Strawberry, as does a group of white and black farmers, their worldly goods now on trucks and wagons because they have been dispossessed for cooperating with union men. Not only is Lee Annie made to fail the test but, also, when the landlord Granger is told what she has attempted, he orders her and Mrs. Ellis, who had simply accompanied her to town, off their property within twenty-four hours. As well, the rally is broken up by appeals to bigotry and threats of calling in the National Guards. The union leaders and young Dubé Cross, who had been helping them, are handcuffed and taken to prison. Only the Logans receive encouraging news. Two Negro boys who fled from a sugar plantation are being held in jail in a town called Shokesville. In Uncle Hammer's Ford they drive through the night and into the next day. Their prayers are answered. Though more dead than alive, Stacey and Moe emerge from the darkness into their arms. The Logans are together again.

Thematic Material

This is a bleak, unremitting picture of poverty among people who are denied basic human rights. The novel brilliantly depicts the injustice, oppression, and humiliation forced on people solely because of skin color and also gives indications of the civil rights movement to follow. Though filled with bitterness and disillusionment, Cassie's family and friends have the dignity and sense of values that never allow their souls to be enslaved. This is also a portrait of a loving family and the strong ties that keep them together. Cassie is a resourceful, courageous girl who could serve as a role model for children of any race.

Book Talk Material

Both *Thunder* and *Circle* could be introduced by describing social conditions of the 1930s and by introducing the Logan family. Some specific passages: the first marble game (pp. 11–16; pp. 9–14, pap.) and the second (pp. 16–23; pp. 14–20, pap.); in the courthouse Cassie learns about segregated washrooms (pp. 54–59; pp. 47–51, pap.); T. J.'s trial (pp. 60–86; pp. 52–74, pap.); a typical day for Cassie at school (pp. 107–

109; pp. 92–94, pap.); saving Mr. Farnsworth (pp. 168–172; pp. 144–148, pap.); and Suzella arrives (pp. 211–215; pp. 181–185, pap.).

Additional Selections

Blacks' roles in the American Revolution and its aftermath are portrayed in three books by James Lincoln Collier and Christopher Collier: *Jump Ship to Freedom* (Delacorte, 1981, $12.95; pap., Dell, $3.25), *War Comes to Willy Freeman* (Delacorte, 1983, $13.95; pap., Dell, $5.25), and *Who Is Carrie?* (Delacorte, 1984, $14.95; pap., Dell, $3.25). Three escaped slaves journey north to join the Union side during the Civil War in Joyce Hansen's exciting *Which Way Freedom?* (Walker, 1986, $12.95). Though set in modern times, the history of the abolition movement and the Underground Railway come alive in Virginia Hamilton's *The House of Dies Drear* (Macmillan, 1968, $12.95; pap., Collier, $3.50) and its sequel, *The Mystery of Drear House* (Greenwillow, 1987, $11.75). Another of Hamilton's novels, *Willie Bea and the Time the Martians Landed* (Greenwillow, 1983, $13), is a warm family story set in Ohio on the fateful Sunday in 1938 when Orson Welles's radio broadcast supposedly reported an invasion from outer space. The moving tragedy of a black sharecropper and his dog is told in William H. Armstrong's *Sounder* (Harper, 1969, $10.89; pap., $3.95; condensed in *More Juniorplots,* Bowker, 1977, pp. 1–4). Belinda Hurmence's *Tancy* (Clarion, 1984, $11.95) is the story of a young slave girl who is freed during the Civil War.

About the Author

Commire, Anne, ed. *Something about the Author*. Detroit: Gale Research Co., 1979. Vol. 15, pp. 275–277.

Estes, Glenn E., ed. *American Writers for Children since 1960: Fiction (Dictionary of Literary Biography,* Vol. 52). Detroit: Gale Research Co., 1986, pp. 364–368.

Holtze, Sally Holmes, ed. *Fifth Book of Junior Authors and Illustrators*. New York: Wilson, 1983, pp. 307–309.

Kirkpatrick, D. L., ed. *Twentieth-Century Children's Writers* (2nd edition). New York: St. Martin's, 1983, pp. 754–755.

Locher, Frances C., ed. *Contemporary Authors*. Detroit: Gale Research Co., 1980. Vols. 85–88, p. 579.

Senick, Gerard J., ed. *Children's Literature Review*. Detroit: Gale Research Co., 1985. Vol. 9, pp. 223–229.

Westall, Robert. *The Cats of Seroster*
Greenwillow, 1984, lib. bdg., $13

Robert Westall's novels cover both the real world and the supernatural. This novel spans both, and in *The Devil on the Road* (Greenwillow, 1979, $11.88; pap., Ace, $2.95) past and present fuse when a university student, John Webster, begins traveling back and forth in time. However, the novelist is perhaps best known for his realistic novel *The Machine Gunners* (Greenwillow, 1976, $11.88), for which he won the Carnegie Medal. It is about a group of youngsters who capture a German soldier during World War II and is followed by a sequel, *Fathom Five* (Greenwillow, 1980, $13). These novels are all suitable for junior high students.

Plot Summary

It is a time of superstition and heretics and diabolical happenings. It is France of the sixteenth century, when cities war against each other and heretics are burned at the stake. It is the time when the ruling duke, seated at dinner with his young son, is knifed to death by one of his servants. The young duke would have been killed, too, were it not for Sehtek, the golden cat, who not only saves the boy but leads him to safety in the mausoleum in the depths of the city. There the brightest of all the cats in the city were drawn, the golden Miw, twice the size of ordinary cats and friends of the now dead duke, who had been friend to them. There were also the Brethren—huge, and with a reputation for dirty fighting. They mourned the passing of the duke and feared for their own safety, recalling times when cats were blamed for the evil that befalls men and women and were driven from the city, and much, much worse. They decide to keep the young duke safe and send out messengers to inform Horse of the news, for, according to the old custom, Horse is a catfriend, too.

In the meantime, a young itinerant jack-of-all-trades called Cam is wandering about the countryside. He goes from place to place fixing things, for that is what he does best. There is almost nothing he cannot fix. But, alas, his talent keeps him on the move, for people often declare that he is a wizard, that his eye for fixing is really magic, and so it is best that he stay on the go.

One night in an inn Cam meets a blacksmith. A powerful man, the blacksmith insists that Cam deliver a note for him to a neighboring city that is now under siege. The note is to a man called Seroster. Cam is most reluctant to do so, but in the end he agrees. The blacksmith also presents Cam with a knife, which Cam does not want but which seems to have a will all its own. Cam soon discovers that he cannot get rid of it.

But the knife leads our reluctant hero on many adventures. When he comes upon an old man and his daughter who are being accosted, the knife fairly jumps from Cam's hand and attacks the thugs. Cam is aghast at the killing, but he soon learns that if he attempts to leave the knife somewhere, he will only end up walking in circles or somehow returning to where he left it.

In time Cam asks a landlord how to find someone named Seroster. The man denies there is such a person. It is said, the landlord tells him, that the Seroster built the city by magic and that he will return one day if the city is in danger. And since the city is, indeed, in danger, perhaps the tale is just a legend after all.

Reluctantly Cam is drawn into the battle for the city. Suddenly he is befriended and aided by a golden cat that saves his life. The cat leads Cam to a strange hidden place in the city where he sees a richly decorated room containing three beds in a shadowed alcove. On two of the beds are bodies of men, dead but not fearful to look at. On the body of each a golden cat is curled. The third bed is empty. On its foot is carved the word Seroster. The bed is waiting. Somehow Cam knows it is waiting for him. Someday he will lie in this bed, honored and mourned by all, for he is becoming the Seroster.

It is definitely something Cam does not want to become. But why, then, does he know things he cannot possibly know? Why does he understand things he should not understand?

And now a terrible massacre begins, for it is said that a cat was seen killing a man, so the hunt for all cats goes on.

A great battle rages for the life of the city, with ever-reluctant Cam as the leader against the evil forces. With the aid of the cats and their magic, and with his magical knife, Cam saves the city, and the young duke, the rightful heir and catfriend, is restored to the throne.

The morning after the terror has ended, the young duke tells Cam that the Miw are gone but hundreds of white horses stand outside the city gates. Cam tells the young ruler that the horses want the entire valley cleansed of evil so they can live in peace.

"If I cleanse the entire valley of evil, will the horses be mine, too?" asks the duke.

Cam realizes that dukes have an instinct for acquiring things.

But indeed the duke's forces do clean up the valley. And when it is time for Cam to leave, he learns that the blacksmith who tricked him into carrying the note and the knife was the Seroster, and he, too, always wanted to get away, but the knife would never let him. Then he tricked Cam into carrying the knife and so he was free. But Cam . . . reluctantly once again, Cam picks up the knife. With a golden cat under his arm, he prepares to leave. He waves good-bye and runs down the cobbled streets. But those he leaves behind just smile . . . they'll wait until he returns.

Thematic Material

This is fantasy created partly of myth and of history and mostly of imagination. It has all the elements of historical adventure, with knights and battles and cities under siege, enhanced by the magical lure of mystical cats and spiced with humor as well.

Book Talk Material

Readers will enjoy many scenes of adventure with the magical knife and the magic of the cats. See the first meeting in the mausoleum (pp. 6–17); Cam tries to leave the knife (pp. 31–36); the knife kills the robbers (pp. 41–47); Cam meets a cat in the ruins (pp. 60–63); and Cam learns of the Seroster (pp. 120–122).

Additional Selections

A shipwrecked girl and an outcast boy live with ospreys on the sea cliffs in *The Hawks of Chelney* (Harper, 1978, $7.95) by Adrienne Jones. The Middle Ages come to life in a novel about a boy accused of being a werewolf in Gloria Skurzynski's *Manwolf* (Clarion, 1981, $9.95). In Erik Christian Haugaard's *A Messenger for Parliament* (Houghton, 1976, $6.95), a young boy is engulfed in intrigue at the time of Oliver Cromwell and the English Civil War. In mid-eighteenth-century England, a young girl hides a mysterious stranger in Rosemary Sutcliff's *Flame-Colored Taffeta* (Farrar, 1986, $11.95). Life in eighteenth-century England is brilliantly re-created in Jenny Overton's *The Ship from Simnel Street* (Greenwillow, 1986, $10.25). Elizabeth Borton de Trevino tells in novel form about the artist Velazquez and his slave in *I, Juan de Pareja* (Farrar, 1965, $10.95; pap., $3.45; condensed in *Juniorplots*, Bowker, 1967, pp. 170–172). In Astrid Lindgren's *Ronia, the Robber's Daughter* (Viking, 1983, $12.95; pap., Penguin, $3.50), set in the Middle Ages, a young girl forms a friendship with the son of her father's archenemy.

About the Author

Bowden, Jane A., ed. *Contemporary Authors*. Detroit: Gale Research Co., 1978. Vols. 69–72, p. 601.

Commire, Anne, ed. *Something about the Author*. Detroit: Gale Research Co., 1981. Vol. 23, pp. 235–236.

Holtze, Sally Holmes, ed. *Fifth Book of Junior Authors and Illustrators*. New York: Wilson, 1983, pp. 322–324.

Kirkpatrick, D. L., ed. *Twentieth-Century Children's Writers* (2nd edition). New York: St. Martin's 1983, pp. 812–813.

Metzger, Linda, ed. *Contemporary Authors* (New Revision Series). Detroit: Gale Research Co., 1986. Vol. 18, pp. 480–482.

Sarkissian, Adele, ed. *Something about the Author: Autobiography Series*. Detroit: Gale Research Co., 1986. Vol. 2, pp. 305–323.

5

Sports Fiction

ONE of the principal interests of adolescents is sports, both as spectators and as participants. Most of the sports stories in this section not only contain good sports action and a feeling of the excitement of the game, but also probe the deeper moral issues in sportsmanship and its relation to lasting values.

Brooks, Bruce. *The Moves Make the Man*
Harper, 1984, $13.70; lib. bdg., $13.89; pap. $2.75 (same pagination)

This, Bruce Brooks's first novel for young adults, received great critical acclaim when it was published in 1984. It was hailed for its humor, spirited characters, and the electric tensions it portrays. These are also the characteristics of his second novel, *Midnight Hour Encores* (Harper, 1986, $13.95), in which a musically talented but bossy girl travels across the country to attend an audition and also to meet the mother who deserted her after her birth. Both novels make excellent reading for junior high school students.

Plot Summary
Jerome Foxworthy—the Jayfox, cheeky, hip, irreverent—is about to get himself integrated. And Chestnut Junior High School, the biggest white school in all of Wilmington, North Carolina, is getting itself its first black student. Well, that's okay with the Jayfox. He doesn't much like the idea of leaving his friends and the teachers and surroundings he knows, but, as his momma says, Jerome knows who he is and he'll be fine anywhere. And, actually, Chestnut Junior High turns out to be no big deal for the Jayfox, whose test scores have made him the second highest seventh grader in the whole city.

Jerome also has something else going for him; he's got the moves.

There is just about nothing he cannot do with a basketball—the reverse spin, the stutter step, the triple pump, the blind pass—Jerome has them all.

Then, one day, while watching a baseball game in town, Jerome sees someone else who has the moves. His name is Braxton Rivers the Third, Bix, and this young white dude plays shortstop like no one the Jayfox has ever seen before. Jerome can't take his eyes off Bix; he also notices a beautiful woman all gussied up in a black dress watching Bix, too. And Jerome can't help noticing how weird she's acting—jumping up and waving her arms every time Bix does anything at all at shortstop and shouting his name over and over in a birdlike voice. Turns out to be Bix's momma.

Sometime after that, Jerome's momma notices that everytime *he* practices his great moves with his basketball, he's talking to himself. The moves make the man, he tells himself, like he's trying to beat some mystery opponent. Then Jerome realizes that his mystery opponent is really that natural shortstop. He stops making his moves for a while after that.

Jerome doesn't actually get to meet his mystery opponent until later in the year, in of all things, home economics class. Right away, Jerome knows that he has found a friend; they hit it off from the beginning. Yet there's this strange thing about Bix. He wants only truth in his life—no faking, no fooling, no little white lies, just the truth. So, okay, thinks Jerome, but Bix carries this to extreme. After a cooking class in which they learn to make mock apple pie, which tastes and looks much like real apple pie but isn't, Bix truly throws a fit when all the students pretend it's real.

Bix stays out of school for a while after that and Jerome is busy anyway because his momma has an accident and has to go to the hospital for an operation, which means that Jerome becomes cook and the whole family has to pitch in at home. After his mother returns and is on the road to recovery, she tells Jerome to take his basketball and get out of the house for a while each day again.

Jerome has found an old, abandoned court, where with the aid of "Spin Light," a lantern he has won, he practices his moves each evening. One night, Bix appears, and gradually the two boys become friends. Over the weeks that follow, Jerome teaches Bix all the moves he knows, and just as he figured, Bix is a natural athlete. But there is only one thing missing; no matter how good Bix gets, he will not "fake." Jerome tries to tell his friend that in order to be really tops in this sport, you have to learn to fake out your opponent, to fool him into thinking you're going somewhere else with the ball. Bix refuses even to listen to Jerome, finally throwing one of his "fits" again and stalking off.

Time passes, and once more Bix turns up at the court. This time he tells his friend what has been happening to him. His mother has tried to commit suicide and for months has been in a mental institution where she is receiving shock treatments. His stepfather refuses to let Bix see her. Finally, Bix has goaded his stepfather, a former basketball athlete, into a bet. If he can beat the older man one-on-one on the basketball court, Bix can go see his mother.

Jerome referees the strange game in which the stepfather pulls far ahead, once again because Bix will use no fake moves to win. But, finally, faced with losing his chance to see his mother, Bix gives in—and fakes his stepfather right off the court. Jerome is delighted, at first. He also learns the reason that the stepfather has been preventing Bix from visiting his mother. Some time before her suicide attempt she walked into Bix's room, naked and carrying a knife. Obviously not in control of herself, she asks her son if he loves her. Because he will not fake the truth, and because at that moment he truly does not love her, Bix merely tells her no. His mother attempts suicide, and the stepfather does not want the boy to see her.

But Bix has won the bet, and the stepfather agrees to take him to the mental hospital. Bix asks Jerome to accompany them that weekend. On the way, the three stop for gas and lunch at a place run by someone Bix has long considered a friend of his. He is in for another shock when he finds that the friend is a bigot and will not serve Jerome.

The scene at the hospital turns into a total disaster. When Bix finally sees his mother, she does not recognize him and asks whose boy he is. In desperation, Bix flings himself at a woman in the next bed, calling, "Mother, Mother!" Then he runs from the hospital before his mother begins to scream his name.

That is the last time Jerome sees Braxton Rivers the Third because Bix runs away, and no one is able to trace him. Months later, Jerome receives a postcard from Washington, D.C.; no message, just Jerome's name and address. But he knows.

Jerome hasn't played ball since Bix ran away. But he doesn't think his moves are gone. In fact, maybe he'll just take Spin Light out tonight, and we'll see.

Thematic Material

Friendship, mental illness, obsession, sport, humor are intertwined in this fast-paced entertaining novel. Against a sports background that is vivid and exciting, readers are introduced to a most likable young hero and a satisfying look at family life for a black family in a southern town after the Supreme Court decision on integrating the schools. The picture of mental deterioration is presented matter of factly but with compassion.

Book Talk Material

Some of the most fascinating scenes in the book depict the growing friendship of the two boys and Bix's obsession with the "truth"; see Jerome and Bix in home economics class (pp. 90–91, 93–97, 99–105); Bix and the Spin Light (pp. 136–146); Jerome teaches basketball to Bix (pp. 149–154, 157–162); Jerome referees the basketball game (pp. 185–202).

Additional Selections

A new twenty-three-year-old coach takes his small school's team to victory in Thomas J. Dygard's *Tournament Upstart* (Morrow, 1984, $9.50). Also use his *Rebound Caper* (Morrow, 1983, $10.25). In Robert Lehrman's mature novel, *Juggling* (Harper, 1982, $11.25; pap., Putnam, $2.25), a star soccer ace has two aims in life: to get to college and have a sex life. In the adult mystery *Fadeaway* (Harper, 1986, $15.45), by Richard Rosen, the star forward of the Boston Celtics suddenly disappears. Ice skating forms an important plot element in Gary Paulsen's *Dancing Girl* (Bradbury, 1983, $9.95). Some novels in which boys face difficult situations are Larry Bograd's *The Kolokol Papers* (Farrar, 1981, $9.95; pap., Dell, $2.25), in which a boy must speak out to help his father, who is a Russian civil rights leader; Nat Hentoff's *Does This School Have Capital Punishment?* (Delacorte, 1981, $13.95; pap., Dell, $2.50); and Arthur Roth's *The Caretaker* (pap., Fawcett, 1981, $1.95).

Crutcher, Chris. *Stotan!*
Greenwood, 1986, $10.25

Like *Stotan!*, Chris Crutcher's first novel for young adults, *Running Loose* (Greenwillow, 1982, $10.25; pap., Dell, $2.75), is on the surface a sports novel, this time about football, but actually it deals more basically with concepts of honor and values as well as the problems a likable young senior in high school faces in upholding them. *Stotan!* has as its setting the author's hometown of Spokane, Washington, and proceeds in chronological order through a series of journallike entries from November 3, when Stotan week is announced, to March 10 of the following year. These are written by eighteen-year-old Walker Dupree. Both of these novels are enjoyed by readers, mainly boys, in grades seven through ten.

Plot Summary

It is more than just the love of swimming that has kept Walker, Lion, Jeff, Nortie, and the "den mother" Elaine together since grade school. Bonds of friendship and loyalty have forged the five almost into a family unit even though each is very different in personality. Walker Dupree, a senior, as are the others, is the captain of the Frost High School swimming team of which his three buddies are the only other members. Walker is a popular, very honest young man who at present is troubled with four major concerns: the team winning at the Washington State swim meet, getting along with elderly parents with whom he has little in common, coping with his diminishing ardor toward his steady girlfriend, pretty Devnee, and caring for his drugged-out brother, Long John, a Vietnam veteran who has dropped out of life and lives a skid row existence.

Lion, or Lionel Serbousek, was orphaned at fourteen, and on the proceeds of his legacy lives alone in two cluttered rooms. He is the joker of the group, extravagant in gesture, outrageous and unpredictable, but has a strong sense of justice and is a lover of beauty which is exhibited in his many drawings. Jeff Hawkins is the gorilla of the group—big, blustering, good-natured, and a born trickster and con artist. The most pathetic, and ironically the best swimmer, is Nortie Wheeler, whose father is a mean, ornery truck driver who regularly beats up Nortie and his pathetically docile mother. The boy tries to please and love his father but his life is one of brutality and terror. He is, however, very successful working with young children at his part-time job in a day-care center. Swimming, helping kids, and his friendship with a black girl, Milika, who also works at the center, serve as the glue that holds Nortie together. Elaine Ferrel is the fifth member of the gang. Though not on the team, she is an excellent swimmer and interested in its welfare. She is an independent freethinking girl, wise beyond her years, whom all respect.

Their coach and often surrogate father is a teacher at Frost named Max Il Song, a Korean American who has spent some time in his parents' homeland. His sagacity, Eastern wisdom, and strength in body and character have produced a feeling of respect verging on adoration in the boys.

Early in November, Max announced that during the holidays prior to Christmas there will be a Stotan week for five mornings, 8 to 12, and asks the boys to volunteer. They do and decide to stay at Lion's rats' nest during that period. None knows what Stotan means until Jeff, always wanting to be on top of things, finds the answer, but not before Elaine can beat him to the revelation. It is an Australian sporting term from the late 1950s and refers to the perfect athlete who must be part stoic and part Spartan. Evidently Max has great hopes and plans for them.

When someone begins distributing copies of a filthy racist rag called *Aryan Press* in the school, Lion seizes a bundle and burns it on the school sidewalk. Marty O'Brian, another senior who is known to be both a bully and a bigot, protests this action in vain and Walker wonders if Marty is not involved in this hate sheet.

Meantime, Nortie's troubles increase. One day, a destructive child in a temper tantrum causes so much havoc at the care center that, to stop him, Nortie slaps his face. Horrified at what he has done, he quits his job convinced that as the statistics show he, too, will be a child abuser. Walker tries in vain to lessen the crisis and Nortie's fears.

Stotan week arrives but no one is prepared for the backbreaking exertion and deadening fatigue it involves. Each morning consists of push-ups, drills, sit-ups, endless laps in the pool, and, at the point of complete exhaustion, trips to the Torture Lane, a series of special gut-busting exercises. More dead than alive, the four drag themselves back to Lion's pigsty each day and collapse. One night they tell Stotan stories involving their own experiences. Jeff recounts happenings in the marine reserves of which he is a member, and in an almost confessional way Nortie tells about his older brother, who, when only thirteen, driven by his intolerable home life, committed suicide and left a note of apology for his six-year-old brother. Even though tears are streaming down his face, Lion changes the mood by telling of his battle with a gigantic zit that appeared on his forehead before a heavy date. The next day, united in the trust and truth of the previous evening, the boys outperform themselves in memory of Nortie's lost brother. At the end of the week, Max presents each with a gold ring engraved with their names and the word Stotan.

At the gala Christmas dance at the Sheraton, Nortie arrives late with Milika. The boy has been beaten badly by his father, who was told by Marty O'Brian that his son is dating a black girl. To relieve the pain, the boy has taken drugs given him by Walker's brother Long John. Some take Nortie to the hospital, but Walker seeks out his brother and, in a fit of temper, punches him in the face for his irresponsible action. While Nortie is recovering, the boys visit the Wheeler household to collect Nortie's things. In an amazing show of courage and resourcefulness, Jeff, along with Lion and Walker, challenge Mr. Wheeler's gun-toting bravado and move the boy's possessions to Walker's home, where he will stay.

Walker's love life continues to trouble him. He wants to call it off with Devnee but lacks both the courage and conviction to tell her. In the meantime, he believes he loves old friend Elaine, who, against the rules, is dating a practice teacher from their school.

The boys travel to Billings and Havre, Montana, for swim meets. On the way they stop at a farmhouse, where Max plays for a few moments with a little girl. He later tells the boys it is his daughter from a failed marriage.

The meets are going well when, in Havre, Jeff suddenly collapses and is taken to the hospital. An overheard conversation between Max and the doctor indicates that the situation is serious. When back in a Spokane hospital, the boy is given chemotherapy. One day he calls the group together, including his girlfriend Colleen, and tells them he has a form of blood cancer. Though it is not spoken, they realize it is terminal. The news is devastating, particularly for Nortie, whose tears seem never to stop.

A few weeks later, Nortie and Milika are in a pizza parlor where they are taunted with racial insults by Marty O'Brian and two others, including Marty's sidekick, John Dolan. When they make snide remarks about Jeff's condition, Nortie attacks them, but they drag him outside and the three beat and kick him almost into unconsciousness. Lion and Walker know that Marty, whose connection with the newspaper has been proven, must be stopped. They visit Jeff for advice. As usual, he has a plan and insists on leaving the hospital if only for a few hours to carry it out. They locate Marty's and John's cars by the school's field house close to a riverbank and, using Lion's Jeep, push them into the river. When the owners come to collect their cars, insult is added to injury by charging them towing expenses to get them out. Marty threatens revenge, but when Max hears the story he confronts the boy and threatens him with real trouble if this harassment doesn't stop.

The three remaining team members score well at the state swimming meet in Seattle chiefly because they know their victory is really a victory for Jeff. As their senior year ends, Walker muses that it has produced more questions than answers but it has also taught him a greater spirit of acceptance. Perhaps that is part of being a Stotan and the concept of testing physical endurance.

Thematic Material

In addition to sports and sportsmanship, this novel is about friendship, loyalty, compassion, the development of values, and the meaning of courage. The boys learn that life is not always fair and that its elements are rarely as simplistic as fairy tales suggest. Good and evil don't exist separately in a person, nor do attitudes of love and hate. Max helps them to accept those conditions they cannot change (the stoic element) and also to sacrifice and fight for those principles that can be upheld (the Spartan). The novel also portrays the devastating results of racial prejudice and the uncertainty of adolescent love relationships. In an unsentimental fashion the author also explores the effects of illness and death on teenagers.

Book Talk Material

An introduction to Elaine, the members of the swimming team, and Stotan week will entice readers. Some of the important passages are: the first announcement of Stotan week (pp. 1–3); the *Aryan Press* and Lion's bonfire (pp. 24–27); what a Stotan is (p. 27); the first encounter with Marty O'Brian (pp. 36–39); Nortie and the day-care incident (pp. 41–48); and the first day of Stotan week (pp. 52–56). The three stories told during Stotan week are Jeff's (pp. 63–66), Nortie's (pp. 66–70), and Lion's (pp. 70–73).

Additional Selections

A star athlete, handicapped in an accident, runs away and gets help at One More Last Chance High in Chris Crutcher's novel *The Crazy Horse Electric Game* (Greenwillow, 1987, $10.25). Gary must learn new rules when he is paralyzed in a football accident in *Winning* (pap., Bantam, 1978, $2.50) by Robin F. Brancato. A friendship leads to a homosexual affair and death in *Dance on My Grave* (Harper, 1983, $13.89; pap.,

$5.95) by Aidan Chambers. Two fine baseball novels are Robert Lipsyte's *Jock and Jill* (Harper, 1982, $9.25; pap., Scholastic, $1.95), also about a boy's awakening to inner-city problems; and the classic adult story, Mark Harris's *Bang the Drum Slowly* (Buccaneer Bks., 1981, $16.95; pap., Univ. of Nebraska Pr., $6.50), about a team player who has Hodgkin's disease. The Cunnigan brothers have taken great abuse from their father until eighteen-year-old Shawn decides to stop it in *Center Line* (Delacorte, 1984, $14.95; pap., Dell, $2.75) by Joyce Sweeney. Sixteen young adults give first-person accounts of their battles with cancer in *Teenagers Face to Face with Cancer* (Messner, 1986, $9.79) by Karen Gravelle and Bertram A. John; and another interesting title is Anne Allen's *Sports for the Handicapped* (Walker, 1981, $10.85).

Knudson, R. R.   *Zan Hagen's Marathon*
Farrar, 1984, lib. bdg., $10.95; pap., New Amer. Lib., $2.25

In the author's first story about Suzann, or Zan, Hagen, *Zanballer* (pap., Penguin, 1986, $3.95), this feisty but likable girl persuades the coach of the football team of which she was a star to play the boys. In the second, *Zanbanger* (Harper, 1978, $11.89; pap., Dell, $1.95), she tries her hand at baseball. In *Zan Hagen's Marathon* she is training for track. Her zany friend and sometimes coach Rinehart is also the subject of some books for a slightly younger audience. The Zan books are enjoyed by a junior high school audience.

Plot Summary

At first, Zan Hagen thinks that Arthur Rinehart, her best friend, irrepressible coach, and fellow student at Robert E. Lee Junior-Senior High, is a "madman." Zan is a runner, and Arthur is a scientific nut, fascinated with numbers, currently with the numbers 26 and 300. Zan can do it, he says, she can race 26 miles and 300 yards—385 yards to be precise—her official marathon distance. And what is madman Rinehart leading up to, Zan asks? To the summer Olympic Games in Los Angeles—a long way across the country from Arlington, Virginia—where for the first time women will be allowed to run in an Olympic marathon. All Zan has to do, according to ever-confident Rinehart, is gain one of the three spots on the U.S. Olympic marathon team. And all she has to do to qualify for the team is to win at least third place in the trial marathon.

"Never, madman!" declares Zen. But Arthur's enthusiasm and endless statistics that prove how talented she is, how wonderful his training methods are, and how she will probably end up in glory, perhaps even beating the great Grete Waitz of Norway, finally wear Zan down. And in a moment of heady fantasy, she blurts out to teachers and school friends that she intends to win a gold medal!

The enthusiastic reaction created by her announcement causes an outbreak of Olympic fever in Zan, so much so that she imagines herself to be strong enough, and certainly talented enough, to qualify for a marathon right at the moment. But coach Rinehart says no; it will require a good three months, according to his calculations, of training until Zan is ready for the trial.

But the fever is too strong. Caught up fully now in her dream, Zan dumps her coach and takes off on her own. She enters a marathon in Durham, North Carolina, where after finishing in six hours, she is totally exhausted, barely able to cross the finish line, and in complete disgrace.

Yet Zan remains determined and Rinehart is still irrepressible, so they· team up once more. This time, Zan follows his instructions to the letter and in the designated period she is in top running form and ready for the trial. All she has to do is come in third to qualify for Los Angeles.

At the trial, Zan faces the two top American women marathon runners. This time, however, she is prepared. This time she knows she can do it. She may not overcome the first two—Rinehart doesn't even want her to try—but the third spot is hers. However, in this race it's not a physical mistake that brings Zan Hagen in just behind the third-place finisher. It doesn't matter; she hasn't qualified.

For Zan, life has reached the lowest rung. She has let down her teachers and friends, and Rinehart, and has greatly disappointed herself. Then comes the phone call from the U.S. marathon coach for the Olympic Games; there may be a "hamstring" problem with the third-place runner on the team. Zan is an alternate!

And now Zan's training truly begins in earnest, even though this time she isn't even sure she will get into the race.

By late July, Zan has a complimentary airline ticket to Los Angeles and a plane reservation, plus a room assignment in the Olympic Village, a U.S.A. warm-up suit and uniform, and all the credentials needed to prove she is a bona fide alternate on the U.S. Olympic marathon team.

Once in Los Angeles, Zan discovers that she will be running the practice sessions with none other than Song Mai, who Zan soon learns is the "Nadia Comaneci of China." During the next training sessions, Zan and Song Mai learn much about each other and their methods of training. And still Zan has no reason to think that she will actually get on the course to test herself against this athlete from China.

But come marathon race day, Zan cannot believe what has happened! The third-place runner for the United States has been pretending for weeks that her hamstring problem was not serious, and the pills she has been taking for the pain have finally taken her down. So, on this beautiful fifth of August at 8:00 A.M. California time, Zan is swinging out with all the other marathoners for the twenty-six-mile run through the City of the Angels.

For the first few miles, she and Song Mai run together. About halfway through the marathon, Zan begins to wonder if she should start making her moves to psych out Song Mai and take over the race. Mile by mile, the two runners overtake the others—Great Britain, Belgium. Winning the gold is what matters.

By the last miles, Zan is ready to drop from exhaustion, but she will not give in. As her knees turn to jelly on a turn, she dimly feels Song Mai nudge her and keep her upright. Some moments later when the leaders reenter the Coliseum, Zan looks back to see that Song Mai has fallen.

A moment's hesitation. Zan runs back and grabs the hand of her friend. Together, China and the United States, their hands joined, cross the finish line together. Let them cry for disqualification if they want to, Zan thinks; this just feels great!

Thematic Material

R. R. Knudson tells this story with wit, warmth, and a good interspersing of the statistics and nitty-gritty details that encompass the hard work of doing well in any sport. The relationship between Zan and Rinehart is especially well drawn, as is the growing friendship between Zan and Song Mai; and the young American runner's determination is nicely presented.

Book Talk Material

Some of the marathon running statistics and details are especially interesting and might initiate conversation on what it takes—both mentally and physically—to try to become one of the world's best at anything;

see a discussion of steroids and other drugs (pp. 53–55; pap., pp. 48–52); some running techniques (pp. 67–69; pap., 58–61); and Zan "hits the wall" (pp. 103–107; pap., pp. 89–92).

Additional Selections

Cynthia Voigt has produced a fascinating portrait of a fiercely independent marathon champion in her novel *The Runner* (Atheneum, 1985, $11.95), and volleyball brings three girls together in their first college year in the same author's *Tell Me if the Lovers Are Losers* (Atheneum, 1982, $11.95). An East Berlin high-jump champion, Erika, faces threats to her future when her family's past in Nazi Germany is exposed in Peter Carter's *Bury the Dead* (Farrar, 1987, $14.95). Three very different types compete in the Boston Marathon in Mark Kram's novel *Miles to Go* (Morrow, 1982, $11.50). Otto R. Salassi's lighthearted novel, *On the Ropes* (Greenwillow, 1981, $11.25), is about efforts to save a farm by opening a wrestling college. Also use Robert McKay's *The Girl Who Wanted to Run the Boston Marathon* (pap., Ace, 1982, $2.25). Judie faces problems when she qualifies for her school's boys' basketball team in Lori Boatright's *Out of Bounds* (pap., Fawcett, 1982, $1.95); and in Bonnie Butler's *Olympic Hopeful* (pap., Fawcett, 1983, $1.95), skiing brings a shy teenager out of her shell.

About the Author

Commire, Anne, ed. *Something about the Author.* Detroit: Gale Research Co., 1975. Vol. 7, pp. 145–155.

Evory, Ann, ed. *Contemporary Authors* (First Revision Series). Detroit: Gale Research Co., 1978. Vols. 33–36, pp. 476–477.

Metzger, Linda, ed. *Contemporary Authors* (New Revision Series). Detroit: Gale Research Co., 1985. Vol. 15, p. 251.

McKay, Robert. *The Running Back*
Harcourt, 1979, $7.95

Although he is not a prolific author, Robert McKay has written several excellent novels for young adults. Two of his earlier novels, now both out of print, *Red Canary* and *Dave's Song* (condensed in *More Juniorplots,* Bowker, 1977, pp. 162–166), use plots that deal with raising birds, a subject the author learned while serving a prison sentence many years ago. *The Running Back*, however, is a pure sports novel with fast sports action and interesting moral themes. It is read by students in grades six through nine.

Plot Summary

How do you act when you're eighteen years old and you've got a record? For Jack Delaney the question was very real, and his record is not one of which he is proud. Before he came to live with his Aunt Frieda and Uncle Fred, he was a city kid, a street-smart city kid, with a mother who didn't care for him and shows no interest in him now. The friends he had were in his gang, and if they did things for the older kids, even if those things involved theft, at least he belonged somewhere.

Jack Delaney wants nothing more than to put all that behind him and make a fresh start. But can he? Can he begin to trust what he senses is real devotion from his aunt and uncle, simple, good people who trust him and believe in doing what is right? Will the other kids at Holbrook School shun him when they learn he has spent two years in reform school?

Naturally shy, Jack's worries about his past and future make him even more of a loner. But even though he enters his senior year at Holbrook with much anxiety, little by little, ever so slowly, it begins to look, even to wary Jack, that things really are happening for the better. Unsure of himself in his new situation, despite his street-smart city background, he starts to relax at home in the quiet but loving attention of his aunt and uncle. Never at ease with girls, he meets a very special one—Cindy Farr—and even begins to think that perhaps he won't make such a fool of himself with her on the dance floor.

Another great change occurs for Jack when, at the urging of the Holbrook coach, he tries out for the lackluster football team. To the coach's amazement and delight—and to the instant jealousy of some of the "old-time" players—Jack turns out to be that rare discovery, a truly talented running back. He is simply a natural. After a couple of standout games, Jack hears his uncle begin to talk of a "football college scholarship in the future."

However, Jack soon learns that as fast as things can get good, they can get bad. Soon after he begins to find confidence in his role as football hero, his success causes some of the team members to quit. This in turn causes an ever-widening rift among the Holbrook students. Then, to add to his troubles, inadvertently Jack hurts Cindy's feelings by being seen with another girl. He is given no chance to explain.

Yet even these things are not the end of Jack's troubles. Shortly after he loses his favorite cap, the principal's office is burglarized. Jack is somehow not surprised to learn that his cap has been found at the scene.

Although Jack realizes that he has been framed and although he thinks he knows just the guy who did it—his enemy and leader of the team walkout, Peanuts Gilliam—who is going to believe a loser? Who is going to believe a reform school kid?

With his newfound confidence shattered and his growing newfound love for Cindy rebuffed, Jack's hard-won but shaky self-confidence hits bottom. Should he quit the team? Should he withdraw into himself once more and let people think what they will?

But Jack Delaney finally decides not to retreat into his shell and to confront his problem head-on, and this turns an otherwise predictable tale of a football hero into a heartwarming story for today. Jack stands up to Peanuts Gilliam and is surprised to learn that, as dishonest as Peanuts's actions and intentions may have been, Peanuts has problems with his confidence, too. And improbable as it seems, Jack senses that the two of them might even become friends. Jack learns that standing up to your enemies and your problems is often the best way to change them. And as he grows more secure in the way his family and friends stand up for him during this crisis, he also summons the courage to approach the reluctant Cindy. And in that way he learns a most enjoyable lesson: that sometimes even a brand new love can survive a misunderstanding. The future for Jack Delaney, star running back, looks very good indeed.

Thematic Material

This is basically a story of relationships with football as a backdrop: a growing relationship of trust and love between a young man and his aunt and uncle, a growing young love between a shy boy and a more secure young girl, and the beginning of friendship between two young men who act far more secure on the outside than they feel on the inside.

Book Talk Material

Conversations between Jack and various people can be used to introduce the book and to discuss how Jack slowly matures and grows more confident in his life and his dealings with people. See Jack's talk with Uncle Fred and Aunt Frieda (pp. 23–27); Jack's meeting with Cindy and his mistaken assumption over what school she attends (pp. 29–32; 66–70); and Jack and team member Jake talk about small-town life (pp. 39–42).

Additional Selections

A high school senior loses his position on the football team when he won't harm a black opposition player in Chris Crutcher's *Running Loose* (Greenwillow, 1982, $10.25; pap., Dell, $2.75). Joe Atkins tries to outrun his past and the football team in Thomas J. Dygard's *Halfback Tough* (Morrow, 1986, $11.75), and in the same author's *Quarterback Walk-On* (Morrow, 1982, $11.75) a fourth-stringer is suddenly thrust into a crucial game. Also use his *Winning Kicker* (Morrow, 1978, $11.88). The screenplay for the TV movie about football star Gale Sayers and his dying friend Brian Piccolo is given in William Blinn's *Brian's Song* (pap., Bantam, 1972, $2.50). Dan Keith thinks he will gain acceptance at school through football in David Guy's *Football Dreams* (pap., New Amer. Lib., 1982, $3.50). Phyllis Hollander and Zander Hollander tell eighty fascinating stories in *Amazing but True Sports Stories* (pap., Scholastic, 1986, $2.75); also, Dave Anderson's *The Story of Football* (Morrow, 1985, $13; pap., $8.95) gives an excellent history of the sport's beginnings in the late 1800s to the present.

About the Author

Commire, Anne, ed. *Something about the Author*. Detroit: Gale Research Co., 1979. Vol. 15, p. 192.

Evory, Ann, ed. *Contemporary Authors* (New Revision Series). Detroit: Gale Research Co., 1983. Vol. 10, p. 319.

Kinsman, Clare D., ed. *Contemporary Authors* (First Revision Series). Detroit: Gale Research Co., 1975. Vols. 13–16, p. 544.

Myers, Walter Dean. *Hoops*
Delacorte, 1981, $13.95; pap., Dell, $2.50 (same pagination)

Though born in West Virginia, Walter Dean Myers grew up in Harlem, an experience and setting he uses in this novel and such other young adult novels as *The Young Landlords* (Viking, 1979, $11.50) and *It Ain't All for Nothin'* (pap., Avon, 1979, $1.75). The dialogue in these books uses street jive expressions amply but without vulgarity or profanity. As well the one sex scene in *Hoops* is handled with taste and without explicit details. The novel is read and enjoyed principally by sports-loving boys in both junior and senior high grades.

Plot Summary

Ever since he can remember, basketball has been part of the life of seventeen-year-old Lonnie Jackson, the narrator of this story. He is an excellent player; and for him, the game is not only a release from all the tensions and frustrations that have accompanied his growing up, but also he hopes it will be a passport that might lead him out of Harlem via a college scholarship or even a chance with the big leagues. Lonnie, who soon will graduate from high school, is an only child who lives with a nagging mother. His father split some years ago, and from that experience, Lonnie still harbors feelings of hurt and betrayal. His part-time job as general cleanup man at Grant's Hotel, managed by unscrupulous Jimmy Harrison, at least allows him the privilege of using one of the rooms on nights when home life becomes intolerable. He has a best friend, Paul, who also plays a good game of ball and a devoted girlfriend, Paul's sixteen-year-old sister, Mary-Ann, whose part-time job is working for a shady character named Tyrone in an after-hours bar.

Lonnie and some of his ball-playing friends, including Paul, Breeze, JoJo, and Ox, an Alley Oop look-alike, have organized themselves loosely into a team. When they hear about the forthcoming citywide Tournament of Champions and the fact that scouts from all over the country will attend, they report to their gym and are assigned Cal Jones as their coach. Lonnie recognizes him as the drunk he had tripped over the previous night on the playground and is so disappointed at the assignment that at first he refuses to play for this man he calls a wino. Gradually he is won over, however, partly because of Cal's excellent playing and knowledge of the game and partly because of his tough training tactics and the particular interest he shows in Lonnie's future career in basketball. Lonnie realizes that Cal is a troubled man, often erratic in behavior and definitely saddled with a drinking problem.

After losing one of the preliminary games, Cal takes Lonnie back to his room and, over a glass of whiskey, he talks about his past. He tells Lonnie that he is separated from his wife, Allie, whom he still loves, and then shows him his scrapbook of clippings. Cal's career in basketball had been an illustrious one, reaching pro status with an NBA team. Unfortunately, he became involved with gamblers and eventually sold his game in point-shaving intrigues. He was caught and received a suspended sentence, heavy fine, and expulsion from basketball. Later, Lonnie meets Allie, and another unfortunate part of Cal's life is uncovered. After the scandal, he had also been indirectly responsible for the death of their three-year-old child. His subsequent drunkenness and despondency led to separation, even though Allie obviously still cares for this tragic figure.

Both Mary-Ann and Lonnie notice that Paul is behaving strangely. In an effort to impress some rich black girls he has met, he has been spending money way beyond his means, and when questioned about it becomes so hostile that at one point he strikes his own sister. When Mary-Ann sees an envelope on Tyrone's desk with her brother's name on it she becomes suspicious. One evening, Mary-Ann and Lonnie break into Tyrone's office and find that the envelope contains cashed welfare checks. Paul later confesses that he has stolen the checks from mailboxes and cashed them through a fence. Tyrone has secured them and is now blackmailing Paul. They realize they must stop Tyrone but seem powerless to do so.

Tournament preparations begin and preliminary games are held. Cal's team shows increased strength, but one day the tournament sponsor, Mr. O'Donnel, contacts Cal and suggests that because of his unsavory past Cal should stop coaching. O'Donnel had been given the background information from one of Tyrone's henchmen, Juno Brown. Lonnie begins to suspect a game-fixing racket at work.

After a particularly hard-won victory in the initial round robin, Lonnie retreats to his room in Grant's Hotel to rest. There he is visited by Mary-Ann, who asks for a demonstration of his affections for her. Tenderly they make love for the first time.

Suddenly and without explanation, Cal disappears, and the team's morale sinks, even though a major league player and friend of Cal's, Sweet Man Johnson, helps with the coaching. Lonnie's sense of frustration and betrayal results in an alarming record of fouls.

Cal is finally located in jail where he has been booked for being in a fight. Actually, he had been beaten up by Tyrone's men as a warning that his team must lose the tournament. Mary-Ann steals money from Tyrone to make Cal's bail; when he finds out, Tyrone injects her with enough drugs for it to be assumed that she overdosed. Fortunately she is found in time and rushed to a hospital. Realizing now how dangerous Tyrone really is, Lonnie is fearful that, under the pressure of the situation and a possible offer of money, Cal might have agreed to sell the game. Also, O'Donnel once again confronts Cal and orders him to bench

Lonnie because of his record of fouls. Could he also be part of the racket?

On the night of the big tournament, Lonnie is convinced that Cal has succumbed. First, Lonnie has not been allowed to play, and secondly, Cal is giving signals to Tyrone and his two thugs in the audience. But at halftime when all the bets have been finalized, Cal shows his true colors. He orders Lonnie into the game and through his efforts the team emerges victorious. When Lonnie finally is able to tear himself away from the crowd and TV cameras and get to the locker room, he finds Cal being attacked by Tyrone and his men. The police arrive and arrest them but not before Cal is fatally stabbed. Lonnie has been given a bright future but has lost a dear friend.

Thematic Material

This is a tough, realistic portrait of ghetto life, complete with racial oppression, injustice, and crime. It is also a story of heroism, retrieved honor, and trust and friendship. Lonnie's growing affection for Cal until he becomes almost a substitute father is tenderly portrayed, as is the honest, sensitive depiction of first love. Though specifically about Harlem life-styles, it deals with universal emotions and ambitions. These powerful themes are supplemented by many descriptions of fast sports action.

Book Talk Material

A description of Lonnie's situation and his hopes for the tournament should stimulate readers. Some interesting passages are: Lonnie steals a case of Scotch (pp. 4–6); Lonnie meets a drunken Cal (pp. 7–9) and sees him again at the gym (pp. 14–20); Cal challenges Lonnie to a game (pp. 40–43); and Cal shows Lonnie his scrapbook (pp. 57–61).

Additional Selections

In the sequel to *Hoops, The Outside Shot* (Delacorte, 1984, $14.95), Lonnie deals with corruption in college sports when he enters a small midwestern college. The early days of baseball when all-black teams existed are explored in the novel *The Original Colored House of David* (Houghton, 1981, $8.95), by Martin Quigley. Nelson's father hopes to be a big-time wrestler even though it is causing a family breakup in Bruce

Stone's *Half Nelson, Full Nelson* (Harper, 1985, $12.25; pap., $2.95). Track and running become the bond of two students—one white from the affluent white neighborhood and the other a part black, Talley, in Virginia Hamilton's *A White Romance* (Putnam, 1986, $13.95). Mike wants to become a famous hockey player but learns about important principles in life instead in Alice Bach's *The Meat in the Sandwich* (pap., Dell, 1986, $2.25). In Michael French's *The Throwing Season* (Delacorte, 1980, $8.95; pap., Dell, $2.50), Henry refuses a bribe to throw a shot-put title. John Craig Stewart's *The Last to Know* (pap., Ace, 1982, $1.95) is about sailing and problems between a boy and his uncle. Monty Davis feels the pressure to excel as a high school track star in Kin Platt's *Brogg's Brain* (Lippincott, 1981, $11.89). Another sports novel by this writer is *Run for Your Life* (pap., Dell, 1979, $1.95).

About the Author
Commire, Anne, ed. *Something about the Author*. Detroit: Gale Research Co., 1982. Vol. 27, p. 153; updated 1985. Vol. 41, pp. 152–155.
Evory, Ann, ed. *Contemporary Authors* (First Revision Series). Detroit: Gale Research Co., 1978. Vols. 33–36, pp. 592–593.
Holtze, Sally Holmes, ed. *Fifth Book of Junior Authors and Illustrators*. New York: Wilson, 1983, pp. 225–226.
Kinsman, Clare D., ed. *Contemporary Authors*. Detroit: Gale Research Co., 1973. Vols. 33–36, p. 638.
Sarkissian, Adele, ed. *Something about the Author: Autobiography Series*. Detroit: Gale Research Co., 1986. Vol. 2, pp. 143–156.
Senick, Gerard J., ed. *Children's Literature Review*. Detroit: Gale Research Co., 1982. Vol. 4, pp. 155–160.

Wells, Rosemary.   *When No One Was Looking*
Dial, 1980, $14.95; pap., Fawcett, $1.95

Rosemary Wells is not only a prolific but also a versatile artist. In the children's book field she is perhaps known best as the author-illustrator of such mainstays as *Noisy Nora* (Dial, 1973, $9.95; pap., $3.95), but in the young adult field she has written a number of well-paced exciting stories. For example, in *Through the Hidden Door* (Dial, 1987, $12.95) she has written a gripping psychological adventure about a young boy in a posh private school who, in trouble for informing on star athletes, discovers an archaeological ruin that indicates an ancient lilliputian culture. These novels are enjoyed by junior high students.

Plot Summary

"Someday," her best friend, Julia, said, "you're going to start believing in yourself."

But for fourteen-year-old Kathy Bardy, that isn't always easy. Two years before, someone discovered that she could play tennis—really play tennis. And now her present and possibly her future are changed forever. Her parents, never comfortably off, seem to be scraping together every penny they have for Kathy's lessons and tournament fees. But even more than that, it is as though their entire lives have begun to revolve around tennis—Kathy's tournaments, Kathy's lessons, Kathy's schoolwork in relation to her tennis (and which is the more important in the long run), Kathy's attitude toward her next match—on and on.

Although she has many inward doubts, Kathy says nothing for the most part as she watches her sister, Jody—the smart one—grow more and more antagonistic and jealous over the attention and concern that their parents pay to her older sister. And Kathy says nothing as she watches her own grandmother being transferred to a "less expensive" nursing home because her parents can't afford anything better, not as long as Kathy's tennis future is on the line. All the money and energies of the Bardys are going into their daughter's future, into all of their futures in a way. But whether she talks about it or not, Kathy often feels the weight of such responsibility.

As if all this isn't enough to live with, in her heart of hearts Kathy isn't precisely sure that she wants to play tennis "as her life's work." What she really wants—as she has informed Julia a thousand times, and as she tells her new friend, Oliver—is to become the first woman shortstop for the Boston Red Sox. But since that seems somewhat unlikely (although Oliver is very impressed with her throwing arm), she dutifully practices her tennis and tries very hard to do what she feels her family and her friends expect of her.

There is one other major problem, however. Kathy has a temper, and when she becomes upset on the court she blows the match. No matter how her coach, Marty, tries to calm her down, her temper eventually gets the better of her.

Kathy confides all of her problems to Julia, and she feels that her best friend really understands, even though Julia's world is really miles apart from Kathy's. Julia, who has known nothing but money all her life and whose mother is glamorous and understanding and fun to be with. Where would Kathy be without the comfort of Julia?

This summer Kathy has a shot—a long shot to be sure—to get in the New England championship. She could be on her way from there. But an obstacle appears in the ungainly form of Ruth Gumm, who suddenly appears in town. Ruth Gumm is such an unlikely tennis prospect that Kathy hardly notices her, until she faces her in a match. Ruth so annoys Kathy with her boorish actions that Kathy is well on the way to losing when Ruth is disqualified because she hasn't paid the tournament entrance fee. Ruth hasn't the money on her to pay, and Kathy, who has, does not offer. So Ruth Gumm must forfeit. However, when the two girls meet sometime later, Kathy can't beat her either. Ruth Gumm seems to have Kathy Bardy's number. And if Kathy can't control her temper and beat a mediocre player like Ruth, how can she ever hope to reach the top?

Then, tragically, Ruth drowns in what appears to be a swimming pool accident. Not long after, Kathy gets a chance to enter an important tournament in Florida; this could be another step closer to the coveted New England championship. Kathy does reach the finals in Florida, and although she loses that match, she is beginning to make a name for herself in the tennis world.

When Kathy returns home, she learns that the police are looking into the death of Ruth Gumm on the chance that it was not, after all, an accident. Too much chlorine in the pool—dumped there on purpose, they now say—caused Ruth to choke and drown. Someone probably just meant to give the girl a scare, the police reason, perhaps to get Ruth out of Kathy's way to the top. Perhaps even Kathy is responsible.

Sick with the thought that anyone could possibly think her capable of such an act, for whatever reason, Kathy contemplates giving up tennis forever. And now she must come face to face with herself and her true feelings. How does she truly feel about playing tennis? How does she truly feel about carrying the hopes of her parents on her shoulders? Can she face up to and understand the jealousy of her younger sister? Can she face up to her own self-defeating temper?

As Kathy Bardy takes on her first challenge in the New England championship, she learns to deal with her own shortcomings and those of others. She faces her temper and controls it in a crucial match. Now she knows that tennis does hold the future for her. This is what she wants to do and the sacrifices are worth it.

But in gaining at last an understanding of what she is and where she stands, Kathy loses something very precious. To her great horror, she learns the truth of Ruth Gumm's death; with great sorrow, she begins to understand the mistakes that people make in the name of love and of friendship. Julia, her best friend, only wanted to help Kathy on her way to the top. . . .

Thematic Material

When No One Was Looking is not just a novel of sport or a young girl's growing up. It deals realistically with the emphasis that today's society often places on winning and how parents often try to live out their own dreams through the lives of their children. It shows the pressures placed on young shoulders when they are forced into the position of winning, not just for themselves but for the fulfillment of others. It is an honest portrayal of a talented, likable young girl trying to do what is expected of her as she tries to overcome a crippling temper and find her own niche in life.

Book Talk Material

The various reactions and needs of different characters in this book might make excellent material for discussions: Kathy loses her temper with Ruth Gumm (pp. 33–39; pap., 32–37); Jody's reaction to Kathy's outburst (pp. 40–42; pap., 38–40); Kathy's parents discuss the importance of algebra versus tennis (pp. 74–78; pap., 77–82); Oliver breaks the news (pp. 79–80; pap., 83–85).

Additional Selections

Beth, a young swimmer, has sacrificed her social life to become an Olympic hopeful in Janice Stevens's *Circles in the Water* (pap., New Amer. Lib., 1984, $1.95). Jason's father is dying, his girlfriend is straying, and the pitcher on his baseball team is sensitive to heckling in Robert Montgomery's *Rabbit Ears* (pap., New Amer. Lib., 1985, $2.50). Baseball and romance are combined in Nancy Willard's *Things Invisible to See* (Knopf, 1984, $14.95; pap., Bantam, $3.50). Lisa finds a new interest after the loss of her boyfriend in Dorothy Bastien's *The Night Skiers* (pap., Scholastic, 1982, $1.95). Uncle Richard helps Marsha become a skating champion in Carol Fenner's novel for young readers, *The Skates of Uncle Richard* (Random, 1978, $6.99; pap., Scholastic, $1.95, under title *Ice Skates*). Stephie becomes a track star in her first year at high school in *Footfalls* (Macmillan, 1982, $11.95; pap., Fawcett, $1.95) by Elizabeth Harlan; and a young American Indian girl trains for the Olympics in R. R. Knudson's *Fox Running* (pap., Avon, 1977, $2.50). Two novels in which girls face difficult moral problems are Susan Beth Pfeffer's *A Matter of Principle* (Delacorte, 1982, $13.95) and Jean Van Leeuwen's *Seems Like This Road Goes on Forever* (Dial, 1979, $8.95; pap., Dell, $1.75).

About the Author

Commire, Anne, ed. *Something about the Author*. Detroit: Gale Research Co., 1980. Vol. 18, pp. 296–298.

de Montreville, Doris, and Crawford, Elizabeth D., eds. *Fourth Book of Junior Authors and Illustrators*. New York: Wilson, 1978, pp. 343–345.

Kirkpatrick, D. L., ed. *Twentieth-Century Children's Writers* (2nd edition). New York: St. Martin's, 1983, pp. 810–811.

Locher, Frances C., ed. *Contemporary Authors*. Detroit: Gale Research Co., 1980. Vols. 85–88, pp. 624–625.

Sarkissian, Adele, ed. *Something about the Author: Autobiography Series*. Detroit: Gale Research Co., 1986. Vol. 1, pp. 279–291.

6

Biography and True Adventure

TEENAGERS are interested in people and personalities and enjoy reading about their heroes and their villains. There is particular interest in the formative years of those people and how they felt and acted when they were adolescents. In this section there is a wide variation of subjects from writers and artists to sports figures and civil rights activists, but all have had lives of accomplishment.

Foster, Rory C. *Dr. Wildlife: The Crusade of a Northwoods Veterinarian*
   Watts, 1985, $14.95

"Dr. Wildlife" is Rory C. Foster, who, with his wife, Linda, and colleagues, has given time, energy, and healing skills to the care of injured and diseased wildlife in northern Wisconsin. His story is one of courage, dedication, joy, and sometimes heartbreak. In a postscript to the book, Foster states that shortly after submitting the manuscript for the book to his publisher, he was diagnosed as having amyotrophic lateral sclerosis (ALS), also known as Lou Gehrig's disease. Since the book's publication, he has had to stop working in the wildlife clinic he founded. However, this enforced retirement has given him time to write a sequel, *I Never Met an Animal I Didn't Like* (Watts, 1987, $14.95). Both books are nicely illustrated with photos and make excellent reading for junior and senior high school students.

Plot Summary
In *Dr. Wildlife,* there are two plot threads—one involves humans and Dr. Foster's crusade to found the Northwoods Wildlife Hospital in Wisconsin; the other is the story, told in anecdotal form, of many of the animals he has treated.

It is the night of June 18, 1982, the eve of the opening of Rory Foster's dream project, a separate clinic adjacent to his own well-established animal hospital that will be devoted entirely to the treatment and care of injured wildlife. As he and his wife, Linda, sit outdoors while she tries to bottle-feed a fawn that has been brought to them with a broken leg, he thinks back to the beginnings of this huge undertaking.

After his four-year postgraduate work in veterinary medicine at Michigan State University, Foster became a resident in the Department of Small Animal Medicine at Iowa State. There, early in 1976, he married Linda, who had worked in the college admissions office. Together they decide to leave academia and start a practice in Minocqua, in Wisconsin's north woods. Later they are joined by a former student, Marty Smith, who stays for two years and helps found the Foster-Smith Animal Hospital, and also by Rory's brother, Race, who, as a veterinary student at Rory's alma mater, is able to spend summers at the clinic.

In May 1977, they admit their first wildlife patient, a two-day-old fawn they later name Faline (after Bambi's cousin). The deer has been struck by an automobile and has head wounds and a broken leg. Because of differences in anatomy and living habits, treating wildlife is often different than working with domestic pets, but an operation is performed and steel pins inserted to hold the broken segments of bone together. They bring the animal into their house during the nursing period and soon a special bond of love grows between Linda and the deer. During the summer Faline grows in strength and health, and inevitably the sad day comes when she must be returned to the wild. She is released in a wooded area miles from their compound, and Linda and Rory return home too filled with emotion to speak.

More and more injured wild patients are brought in for treatment. No fees are charged and most of the work helping these animals and birds is done during hours when the regular clinic is closed.

One day a college student brings in a seagull she has named Orville that is unable to fly. Foster detects a massive cancerous growth on the bird that he removes by a delicate operation. However, the growth soon reappears, and Rory agonizes about destroying Orville, but, as the bird is not suffering and a miracle of remission might occur, he decides against it. The hoped-for miracle does not happen though and Orville dies.

Other stories have happier endings. Mrs. Mosely, a lively, very sharp octogenarian, brings in a barred owl she has struck with her automobile. She is very disturbed and insists on calling regularly and visiting the clinic to check on the bird's progress. The owl, which she named Stanfield, responds slowly to treatment, but everyday Mrs. Mosely brings encouragement for both the bird and the staff. Soon Race, who has taken on the case, is giving the bird flight lessons and Mrs. Mosely insists that she be present when it is released from captivity. Before this can take place, the bird, which is now stronger than expected, escapes. Fortuitously, another barred owl is brought in that day. A switch is made, and a few days later Mrs. Mosely witnesses the release of a bird she doesn't realize is actually Stanfield II.

As more and more wildlife patients are brought in (usually victims of human behavior—for example, beaks torn by fishhooks, paws and wings mutilated by steel traps, bodies violated by shotgun pellets), Rory's clinic is unable to house and care for both these refugees and his regular domestic pets. One evening in 1979 he and his wife decide to mount a campaign to found a nonprofit foundation and eventually build a wildlife hospital. Although he gains support from many agencies and individuals, two areas of opposition emerge. The first is, surprisingly enough, the State Department of Natural Resources (DNR), which, from its top leaders down to game wardens, believes it is a waste of time and money to give first aid or treatment to animals other than those on the endangered lists. Foster fights angrily and effectively at all levels to combat this inhumane, brutal policy. The second comes from some owners of private roadside wildlife exhibits with their abysmal animal quarters and flagrant abuse of their captives. Foster has tried to expose these conditions but often to deaf ears.

The opposition underestimates Rory Foster's tenacity and dedication. Through using the press, letters, telephone, and any other method of communication available, Foster gradually overcomes government opposition and collects the necessary funds.

As the dawn of the opening day approaches, Rory explores the new facilities, and then Linda gives him yesterday's unopened mail. One letter is from a vet in Oregon who would like to start a similar project and asks what problems he could anticipate. While caressing the fawn, Linda says, "I don't remember any problems, do you?" Rory replies, "Can't say as I do."

Thematic Material

In a foreword to the book, the director of the Humane Society of the United States compares Dr. Foster's attitudes to those of St. Francis of Assisi, because with their common values and virtues, Foster helps people "to regard each animal as an individual, with its own intrinsic worth, interests, rights, and in so doing he brings us all a little closer to appreciating the divinity within each living creature." This is an inspiring, heartwarming story in which we share the author's triumphs and tragedies, his joy and anger, and his uncompromising devotion to a cause. It is a reaffirmation of the sanctity of life and an indictment of those who use wild animals for profit and of those government officials who, given public trust, are often indifferent and insensitive to the real nature of their responsibilities. This is also a story of a loving family and a happy marriage.

Book Talk Material

The book is filled with incidents that could be retold. Some examples: the story of Faline (pp. 11–20); Orville the seagull (pp. 22–29); Mrs. Mosely and Stanfield (pp. 32–40); Rory's struggles with a DNR warden over an otter named Little Joe (pp. 43–48); the idea of the wildlife hospital and the opposition emerges (pp. 49–52); Rory visits a roadside wildlife exhibit (pp. 52–55); and another run-in with a warden (pp. 69–73).

Additional Selections

The name James Herriot comes to mind when thinking of a veterinarian who writes. Herriot's series, which begins with *All Creatures Great and Small* (St. Martin's, 1972, $14.95) and ends with *The Lord God Made Them All* (St. Martin's, 1981, $14.95; pap., Bantam, $4.50), could be used. The story of America's counterpart to James Herriot is told in *Creature Comforts* (pap., Berkley, 1984, $3.50) by Stephen Kritsick and Patti Goldstein. A family's relationship with Clem, a raven rescued when blown from its nest, is told in Jennifer Owings Dewey's *Clem—The Story of a Raven* (Dodd, 1986, $11.95). Jim Arnosky shares his love of nature in general and trout fishing in particular in *Flies in the Water, Fish in the Air* (Lothrop, 1986, $11.75). David Taylor has written many books about his life as a vet. One is *My Animal Kingdom* (Stein & Day, 1984, $14.95). Two books on careers involving animal care are Edward R. Ricciuti's *They Work with Wildlife: Jobs for People Who Want to Work with Animals* (Harper, 1983, $11.89) and Charlotte Lobb's *Exploring Careers in Animal Care* (Rosen, 1981, $9.95). Twelve short stories about people whose lives are changed by their relationship with animals are included in Cynthia Rylant's *Every Living Thing* (Bradbury, 1985, $9.95); and Barbara Brenner's novel, *A*

Killing Season (Four Winds, 1981, $8.95; pap., Dell, $2.50), reveals a great deal about bear habitats and habits.

Gooden, Dwight, with Woodley, Richard. *Rookie: The Story of My First Year in the Major Leagues*
   Doubleday, 1985, lib. bdg., $13.95

Dwight Gooden's career in the major leagues has been a combination of triumph and controversy. During his third year he admitted to a drug problem which at that time placed his promising future in doubt. This book, however, tells about happier times and is enjoyed by baseball fans in both junior and senior high schools.

Summary
   Dwight Gooden is the ace right-hander of the New York Mets, a member of the 1986 World Series Mets, a quiet, unpretentious young man in his early twenties whose skyrocket ride to the top of the baseball world nose-dived at the start of the 1987 season with his admission of drug abuse. After spending some time in a rehabilitation center, young Dwight began the long, hard road back. *Rookie* is the story of the first major league season for the young player, the dizzying excitement, the fan frenzy, the pressures, the expectations—the victory after victory, the strikeout after strikeout.

At the end of his rookie season, in 1984, Dwight Gooden's record was 31 starts and 7 complete games, 17 wins and 9 losses, an earned run average of 2.60, 73 walks given up, and 276 strikeouts. He was 1984's National League Rookie of the Year; he led the majors with most strikeouts in a single game (16, tied with Mike Witt); he set the major league strikeout record; he was the youngest player ever chosen to play in the All-Star Game—and he was nineteen years old.

In early April 1984, Gooden is watching the Mets' last spring training game in St. Petersburg, Florida. The next day the Mets are flying north to begin the season and Dwight figures he is flying to Virginia to join the Mets' Triple-A farm team in Tidewater. Then Davey Johnson, new manager of the Mets, walks up to him and gives him the news: "You made the team."

Without a chance to say good-bye to his friends, Dwight is on the plane for the opener in Cincinnati. But he isn't due to pitch until the Mets' fourth game of the season, in Houston. By the time he walks out to the mound in the Astrodome in Houston, he is a nervous wreck. He lasts five innings, which is what the manager had wanted, and he has his first win. It would prove to be some season.

Dwight Gooden has been playing baseball for as long as he can remember. He was a Little Leaguer at seven, which he quit because the team was terrible and he couldn't stand the idea of losing all the time. He joined again at ten, was a starting third baseman, and went to the Little League World Series, but couldn't play because he wasn't eleven years old. His team lost to Taiwan.

Dwight was born in Tampa, Florida, and attended Hillsborough High School, where he played third base and the outfield and was learning to pitch. In his senior year his earned run average was 0.75, with 135 strikeouts in 74 innings. He figured he might get drafted by the major leagues, and his first choice was the Cincinnati Reds because he was a fan. And although his mother wanted him to go to college, and the University of Miami said it was interested, Dwight hoped for a draft because that's what he really wanted.

When Gooden found out he had been drafted (fifth in the entire country!) by the New York Mets, he couldn't believe it. He didn't even know the Mets held their spring training in St. Petersburg, that's how little he had kept up with the Mets. Now, suddenly, he was a part of them.

Gooden's starting salary was $600 a month (which is what all first signers get), plus an $85,000 signing bonus (which is not what all first signers get).

His first few months as a Met were spent mostly traveling around the country in the rookie league to gain experience. As Gooden recalls, he also had to gain experience in being on his own, in being away from his family. By 1983, he had moved up the ladder into what is called Class A ball. The next step for some of the players would be the majors. But Dwight thought Tidewater was in his future—until the okay from manager Davey Johnson.

By the mid-1984 season, Dwight Gooden is gaining the confidence in his own vast ability that a true superstar major league pitcher needs in order to survive. As he says, "If you don't get me by the third or fourth inning, I find my rhythm and get everything flowing my way."

Dwight also talks about what goes on in the clubhouse of a big league baseball team, about the joking and camaraderie during the long season. But most of the time, he says, he pays attention to the game and to the hitters, because the more he knows about individual hitters, the better pitcher he will be.

At the end of the long season, Gooden earns Rookie of the Year and is glad to be going back home to Tampa to see his family. He picks up a new Mercedes and buys a new house for his parents, and he tries to adjust to all the fan attention that goes on constantly, even in his hometown.

A phenomenal rookie, Dwight Gooden learned a lot about pitching in the major leagues and about growing up in general during his rookie year—and he was not yet twenty years old. But as his friend Darryl Strawberry, Mets' star outfielder, told him at the end of the 1984 season, things would be a lot tougher next season for Dwight because people were going to expect him to do more than he did in his first year. Strawberry was right. . . .

Thematic Material

For the sports-minded young reader, this is an excellent inside look at the world of the rookie in major league ball, at what goes on inside the dugout and off the mound for a star. It is also a close look at a quiet young man trying to keep his equilibrium in the frenzied atmosphere of fan adoration and superstar status, a story made all the more poignant because of Gooden's troubles that culminated in his admission of drug use at the start of the 1987 season.

Book Talk Material

Young baseball fans will probably be familiar with many of the statistics of Dwight Gooden's rookie year. A good introduction to this book might be the experiences of a young pitcher in the interval between signing a contract and actually getting called up to the big leagues. See waiting for the draft (pp. 29–32); leaving home for the first time and the flight to Kingsport (pp. 33–35); moving up to Class A ball (pp. 39–43); the turning point and pitching against the Yankees (pp. 46–48).

Additional Selections

A few other baseball biographies are *Thurman Munson* (pap., Ace, 1980, $2.50) by Thurman Munson and Martin Appel, an autobiography in the form of a series of interviews with the late New York Yankee; *Mike Schmidt: The Human Vacuum Cleaner* (Childrens Pr., 1983, $9.95; pap.,

$2.95) by Mike Herbert, about one of modern baseball's home-run kings; and an autobiography popular with Yankee fans, Ron Guidry and Peter Golenbock's *Guidry* (pap., Avon, 1981, $2.50). Maury Allen writes accurately and affectionately about one of baseball's greats in *Jackie Robinson* (Watts, 1987, $16.95). Also use, by Tom Seaver, *Tom Seaver's All-Time Baseball Greats* (Wanderer, 1984, $8.95). In Abbot Neil Soloman's *Secrets of the Super Athletes—Baseball* (pap., Dell, 1982, $1.95) the reader goes behind the scenes with top athletes in baseball. One of the fine historians of baseball, Lawrence S. Ritter, has written a fascinating, fact-filled book, *The Story of Baseball* (Morrow, 1983, $13; pap., $8.95); and for the scorekeeper, suggest Eric Compton and Jeff Shermack's *Baseball Stats* (pap., Scholastic, $1.95), subtitled "What Are They? How to Figure Them, Who's Got the Best?" *Mary Lou: Creating an Olympic Champion* (McGraw-Hill, 1985, $16.95) by Mary Lou Retton and Bela Karolyi is the story of a gold medal gymnast and her coach.

Hamilton, Virginia. *W. E. B. Du Bois: A Biography*
Crowell, 1972, $11.49

Virginia Hamilton is known almost exclusively for her imaginative novels of black youngsters and their problems in growing up. In many of these stories she draws on the history and traditions of her black race, but in this book she enters directly into the world of nonfiction by retelling the life story of this great teacher, writer, and political activist. This biography is read by students in grades six through nine.

Summary
William Edward Burghardt Du Bois was a black scholar and teacher of unusual depth and talent. He was a poet, a prophet, an intellect, and American. Had he so chosen, he probably could have lived his life in comfortable, upper-class surroundings. But Dr. Du Bois did not so choose. Instead, although he was largely ignored by Americans for many years, he was perhaps the single most important leader for black civil rights during the twentieth century. He died thousands of miles from his native land, on the coast of West Africa, in Ghana, August 27, 1963. Ironically, on that evening, back home in his native land's capital city, thousands of blacks and whites were preparing for tomorrow's monu-

mental march on Washington, D.C., the largest civil rights (or any other) protest demonstration in the United States.

William was born in 1868 in the small southwestern Massachusetts town of Great Barrington on the shores of the Housatonic River. The infant's ancestors, with a mixture of West African, Dutch-African, and French blood, were rebels long before his birth. His paternal grandfather, for one, was an outspoken critic of race prejudice. But his mother's family, the clannish Burghardts, did not care much for William's father, whom they regarded as having few prospects and was too good-looking and "too white." His father left Great Barrington some time after William was born, promising that his wife and baby would soon join him. But they never did, and William never saw his father again.

But his family was large and loving, and William had a happy childhood. There had been a long tradition of education in his family, unusual for blacks at that time, and in high school, his fine intellect, having been recognized by the school principal, William found himself in the most unusual position for a black boy (and most whites) of the late 1800s—he was going to college.

William wanted to go to Harvard; instead, he was given and accepted a scholarship to Fisk University, a black school (today a prominent, mainly black college) in Nashville, Tennessee. It was at school that this largely sheltered boy learned the ugly truth about racial prejudice and discrimination.

Although William graduated from Fisk in 1888, he still yearned to go to Harvard. He realized by now that the world was divided into whites and blacks and he had, therefore, no great affection for "white" Harvard, but he did want the best education. So when Harvard offered a scholarship to students from the South and the West, he applied and was accepted.

Young Du Bois now believed in voluntary racial segregation and kept himself apart from whites as much as possible. He received his degree cum laude in 1890, majoring in philosophy. One of five students selected to speak at commencement, his speech on Jefferson Davis and slavery caused a sensation and was noted in the *Boston Herald*.

Already more educated than most whites of the day, Du Bois now went abroad to Germany, on a grant from the Slater Fund, which promoted the education of blacks. From 1892 to 1894, this experience changed his outlook forever. He began to see that it might be possible to live in a world without color prejudice.

When Du Bois returned home, he began teaching at Wilberforce University in Ohio. His Harvard doctoral thesis, *The Suppression of the African Slave Trade, 1638–1870,* became the first book published in the Harvard Historical Series (1896) and it got him a job offer from the University of Pennsylvania, where he went in 1896. By now a doctor of philosophy, Du Bois married Nina Gomer, who he had met at Wilberforce.

In 1897, Dr. Du Bois became a professor of economics and history at Atlanta University, a black school in Georgia. By now he knew what his life's work would be—to work toward a theory of sociology that would prepare the way for future social reform for his people.

Although Du Bois worked incessantly to bring his theories and ideas to the attention of the American people—he even won an award at the Paris World's Fair in 1900 for his study of black Americans and their problems—he gained little attention and little financial support. Now he became violently outspoken against white injustice to blacks.

Over the next few years, Dr. Du Bois came into increasing conflict with the person acknowledged at the time as the leader of black people in America—Booker T. Washington. Born a slave, Washington went on to build Tuskegee Institute. Washington firmly believed that blacks must go along with white opinion in order to gain jobs and wealth. Du Bois firmly believed that white public opinion must be forced to change. In 1905, Du Bois called together a group known as the Niagara Movement, because it met in Niagara Falls on the Canadian side. Their platform demanded reforms and opposed the appeasement policies of Booker T. Washington. The movement brought a storm of protest and a cry that Du Bois was ashamed of being black!

Although the Niagara Movement never gathered the strength Du Bois wished, it did give way to a new group that eventually became the National Association for the Advancement of Colored People (NAACP). Du Bois became the only black administrator on its list of officers.

Dr. Du Bois joined the Socialist party in 1911, distrusting white ownership of industry. From that time until 1934, he considered his life's work to be mainly tied up in *The Crisis* magazine, which he founded and which became the NAACP's official publication. In it, Du Bois discussed all aspects of black life in America.

Throughout the years, Du Bois worked and wrote and lectured on his country's social problems, trying to bring about a truly interracial culture in the United States. His disappointment in the social climate of America turned him more and more toward socialism.

He returned to Atlanta University in 1934, hoping to build the institution into the best in Georgia. But there was never enough money to bring his programs to fruition. Then World War II gripped the country, and in 1943 the doctor wrote of the problems he feared black Americans would face upon their return. Unfortunately, his words proved true.

Then, suddenly, at the age of seventy-six, he was retired from the university, for reasons never made clear. He returned to the NAACP, although many felt his life's work was done. Instead, he lectured and was involved with many organizations, such as the Peace Information Center, whose object was to inform the American public of the work of other nations to promote peace. The U.S. government later declared the center to register as an "agent of a foreign principal." In this time of America's zealous concern with being overrun by communism, Dr. Du Bois was indicted as a criminal. His trial was held in 1951, the defense cost more than $35,000; although his innocence was established, the country marked him a criminal.

After the death of his wife, Du Bois met and married Shirley Graham, a minister's daughter and a writer. They were denied passports to travel outside the country and were closely watched because of their communist sympathies. Finally, in 1958, the ban on traveling was lifted.

In 1961, Dr. Du Bois formally joined the Communist party of the United States. In 1963 he became a citizen of Ghana, where he died. Whether he turned away from America because of his treatment or because he was thoroughly committed to communism is not as important as the fact that all his life W. E. B. Du Bois urged black Americans to fight for their complete rights as free citizens.

Thematic Material
This is a powerful, clearly written story of an important American leader not generally well known or understood by the American public. All his life he stood for and fought for a principle of equality. His steadfastness, courage, and dedication are qualities that all Americans, of whatever age, have reason to admire.

Book Talk Material
Turning points in Du Bois's career can serve as good introductions to this fine biography. See the young Du Bois goes to Fisk (pp. 20–24); he founds the college newspaper (pp. 29–30); William Du Bois at Harvard

(pp. 37–43); his stay in Germany (pp. 48–53); he realizes his life's work (pp. 57–62); and his opposition to Booker T. Washington (pp. 75–88).

Additional Selections

There are several fine biographies of Martin Luther King, Jr. Four are Doris Faber and Harold Faber's *Martin Luther King, Jr.* (Messner, 1986, $9.79), James Haskins's *The Life and Death of Martin Luther King, Jr.* (Lothrop, 1977, $11.88), Ira Peck's *The Life and Words of Martin Luther King, Jr.* (pap., Scholastic, 1986, $2.25), and Jacqueline Harris's *Martin Luther King, Jr.* (Watts, 1983, $10.90). Justice Louis Brandeis fought both for the underdog and for a homeland for the Jewish people. His story is told in David C. Gross's *A Justice for All the People* (Dutton, 1987, $13.54). Two important present-day fighters for racial freedom and equality are the subjects of Dorothy Hoobler and Thomas Hoobler's *Nelson and Winnie Mandela* (Watts, 1986, $11.90). Also use Doris Faber and Harold Faber's *Mahatma Gandhi* (Messner, 1986, $9.79). The story of a twentieth-century activist is told in *The Autobiography of Malcolm X* (pap., Ballantine, 1977, $2.75). Books about female black activists include *Sojourner Truth* (Lippincott, 1974, $10.89) by Victoria Ortiz and *Harriet Tubman: Conductor on the Underground Railroad* (Crowell, 1955, $14.70; pap., Pocket Bks., $2.25) by Ann Petry. Julius Lester has collected a fascinating but shocking set of original documents in *To Be a Slave* (Dial, 1968, $11.95; pap., Scholastic, $2.25).

About the Author

Block, Ann, and Riley, Carolyn, eds. *Children's Literature Review*. Detroit: Gale Research Co., 1976. Vol. 2, pp. 103–107.

Commire, Anne, ed. *Something about the Author*. Detroit: Gale Research Co., 1973. Vol. 4, pp. 97–99.

de Montreville, Doris, and Crawford, Elizabeth D., eds. *Fourth Book of Junior Authors and Illustrators*. New York: Wilson, 1978, pp. 162–164.

Estes, Glenn E., ed. *American Writers for Children since 1960: Fiction* (*Dictionary of Literary Biography*, Vol. 52). Detroit: Gale Research Co., 1986, pp. 174–184.

Kirkpatrick, D. L., ed. *Twentieth-Century Children's Writers* (2nd edition). New York: St. Martin's, 1983, pp. 353–354.

Nasso, Christine, ed. *Contemporary Authors* (First Revision Series). Detroit: Gale Research Co., 1977. Vols. 25–28, p. 299.

Senick, Gerard J., ed. *Children's Literature Review*. Detroit: Gale Research Co., 1986. Vol. 11, pp. 54–95.

Who's Who in America: 1986–1987 (44th edition). Chicago: Marquis Who's Who, Inc., 1986. Vol. 1, p. 1169.

Who's Who of American Women: 1987–1988 (15th edition). Chicago: Marquis Who's Who, Inc., 1986, p. 330.

Kerr, M. E.   *Me Me Me Me Me*
Harper, 1983, $11.70; lib. bdg., $10.89; pap., New Amer. Lib., $2.50
(same pagination)

Occasionally, in the past, M. E. Kerr has drawn from her own experiences as Marijane Meaker to provide incidents for her novels. This is particularly true in *Is That You, Miss Blue?* (Harper, 1975, $11.89; pap., Dell, $1.75; condensed in *More Juniorplots*, Bowker, 1977, pp. 35–37), where she uses several of her own school experiences as plot material to the point of including a disguised self-portrait in the rebellious Carol Cardmaker. Now the real truth is revealed in her hilarious autobiography. It is popular with junior high school readers.

Summary

In this "not a novel," which is dedicated to all the kids who wrote to M. E. Kerr and all the teachers and librarians who urged them to read her, the author writes about things that really happened in her teenage years. From diaries and journals and old letters and stories she wrote years ago, she re-creates, with great warmth and wit, the salad days of the 1940s.

There was . . . Donald Dare, the sixteen-year-old undertaker's son, who was her "steady," and who swore that the last thing in the world he would ever be was an undertaker. And there was best friend Ella Gwen, who marked all the good parts in racy novels and whose father was a dentist who perpetually harangued about "niggers, wops, kikes, polacks, hunkies, and spics," and who was not particularly thrilled when (with the aid of the author and Donald Dare) his daughter ran off and married Hyman Ginzburg. The author lost track of Ella, but she did meet Donald again . . . and, yes, he had become an undertaker.

And there was . . . the fight with Dorothy Spencer over Ronald Reagan, who both saw in the movie *Brother Rat* and both loved instantly; and the author's "first real" boyfriend, William Shakespeare, with whom she discussed the fact that they would not name their first son William, but

Ellis. Both Dorothy Spencer and William Shakespeare (without Ellis) have faded away into memory.

And there was . . . the spy period when Millicent came to their small upstate town from New York City and the author couldn't rest until she found out why the new girl was so secretive until her digging produced the fact that the girl's father was in prison there, and it made our author feel very ashamed. . . . And there was the not to be forgotten "talk" with her mother, who was not very thrilled to hear that her daughter was known as the class clown and warned that "there isn't a female comedian alive who's happy."

Then, after all the fussing about getting out of that small town, began the period of boarding school in Staunton, Virginia, where the author met Jan Fox, whom she considered positively the most sophisticated girl she had ever encountered. Jan smoked Old Gold cigarettes on the train going down to Stuart Hall, wore white heels with sling backs, and knew practically everything there was to know about anything. Some time later Jan came to visit the small upstate New York town and the author was mortified because her parents didn't have a cocktail hour for someone as sophisticated as Jan Fox. It was somewhat disillusioning to discover that Jan's actual knowledge of social drinking was to down martinis *after* dinner and then throw up.

While all this growing up was going on, there were the constant attempts by the author to become a writer, with scant encouragement from family and friends. Her first pseudonym was Eric Ranthram McKay, chosen because it had a nice ring to it. All of McKay's stories were rejected, but a few of them did say "try again" and the author took that as at least some kind of encouragement.

The war was going on during all this, of course, and the author's older brother was in it, but she was not allowed to date the sailors from the nearby base—father's orders.

And then there was . . . college. After a number of years of fooling around and being class clown and troublemaker, the author's grades were not so hot; so the best she could do was Vermont Junior College. For her, it turned out to be wonderful. She also published her first article there, in the campus paper, of which she was the editor . . . but still.

There was also Justine Matso, who drove the curious author crazy because she was so secretive, until finally Justine blurted out that movie star Lizabeth Scott was her sister. Naturally, the author and all her friends pooh-poohed that silly idea. But Justine just went about her business as though she didn't care whether they believed her or not. It drove them crazy. In desperation they sent a letter to Lizabeth Scott explaining the deception that was going on there in Vermont. When they finally got an answer—well, Justine was no liar.

Success at Vermont Junior College paved the way to the school of journalism at the University of Missouri. That was her first encounter with sororoties and Rush Week. Although she could never quite figure out how, she was actually pledged, something the sorority might well have regretted since she was always coming up with suggestions like inviting blacks to join or some such other unthinkable propositions. Other interesting things happened in Missouri; she joined the Communist party for a spell and had her first poem published.

And then it was 1949 and graduation and off to find a job in publishing in New York City—just until she could get published herself and become a full-time writer. The job at Dutton lasted a year and was punctuated with rejection slips. Fawcett Publications wasn't any more lucky. Finally, she had an idea. She sold some shares of stock her father had given her to pay the rent for a time, told her roommates she'd do the cooking if they'd buy the food, and settled down to write in earnest.

The big day finally came, April 20, 1951, and a letter from the *Ladies' Home Journal* to Marijane Meaker. It bought her story for $750! When the story was published, her name was right in the contents page alongside those of John P. Marquand and Dorothy Thompson!

Another stepping-stone on the way to discovering one writer's full-blown talent.

Thematic Material

Because, as the author says, she knew she could interest today's kids in yesterday's kids, because they're the same kids, young readers today can indeed share the smiles and tears of a girl struggling to find herself and her niche in a world of parental rules and discipline, bewildering boys, and overdemanding teachers. This is also a "nonnovel" about families and the often rocky relationships between mother and daughter and father and daughter on that perilous road to growing up. Readers will especially enjoy the wit and compassion that compose the background of all these vignettes.

Book Talk Material

Readers might enjoy comparing some of the mores of the 1940s as they concerned teenagers contrasted with those of today. See her father's ritual before every date (pp. 8–9,); the "high school lovers" (pp. 17–21); mother and daughter discuss "filth" (pp. 21–24); the dancing class ritual (pp. 61–65); and the disasterous date during Jan's visit (pp. 129–133).

Additional Selections

Author Roald Dahl entertainingly writes about his life growing up in Britain and Norway in *Boy* (Farrar, 1984, $10.95; pap., Penguin, $4.95). Also use its sequel, *Going Solo* (Farrar, 1986, $12.95). Jean Fritz is noted for her amusing re-creation of American history in several books. She has also written two autobiographical works: *Homesick: My Own Story* (Putnam, 1982, $10.95; pap., Dell, $2.95), her account of growing up in China in the mid-1920s; and *China Homecoming* (Putnam, 1985, $9.95; pap., $4.95), about her return to China as an adult. The famous mystery story writer Lois Duncan has also written her story in *Chapters: My Growth as a Writer* (Little, 1982, $12.45); and Newbery Award winner Elizabeth Yates has written three books about her writing experiences: *My Diary— My World* (Westminster, 1981, $12.95), *My Widening World* (Westminster, 1983, $12.95), and *One Writer's Way* (Westminster, 1984, $14.95). Laura Ingalls Wilder's diary, edited by her daughter, is *On the Way Home* (Harper, 1982, $10.89; pap., $1.95). Also use Betsy Lee's *Judy Blume's Story* (Dillon, 1981, $8.95; pap., Scholastic, $1.95). Poets speak about themselves in Paul B. Janeczko's *Poetspeak: In Their Work, About Their Work* (Bradbury, 1983, $12.95). Budding authors might like to read Susan Tchudi and Stephen Tchudi's *The Young Writer's Handbook* (Scribner, 1984, $11.95).

About the Author

Commire, Anne, ed. *Something about the Author.* Detroit: Gale Research Co., 1980. Vol. 20, pp. 124–126 (under Marijane Meaker).

de Montreville, Doris, and Crawford, Elizabeth D., eds. *Fourth Book of Junior Authors and Illustrators.* New York: Wilson, 1978, pp. 210–212.

Kirkpatrick, D. L., ed. *Twentieth-Century Children's Writers* (2nd edition). New York: St. Martin's, 1983, pp. 428–429.

May, Hal, ed. *Contemporary Authors.* Detroit: Gale Research Co., 1983. Vol. 107, pp. 332–336 (under Marijane Meaker).

Sarkissian, Adele, ed. *Something about the Author: Autobiography Series.* Detroit: Gale Research Co., 1986. Vol. 1, pp. 141–154.

Who's Who in America: 1986–1987 (44th edition). Chicago: Marquis Who's Who, Inc., 1986. Vol. 2, p. 1902 (under Marijane Meaker).

Sufrin, Mark. *Focus on America: Profiles of Nine Photographers*
Scribner, 1987, lib. bdg., $13.95

Although many teenagers are interested in photography and pursue it as a hobby, few are aware of the great artists in photography that America has produced. In this book, Sufrin, an accomplished writer of fact books for younger children, has nicely filled the gap with thumbnail sketches of some of our greats. This book is intended for readers in grades seven through ten.

Summary

Although there is not an American alive today who can remember a world without photography, it is, nonetheless, a relatively modern science. Many individuals contributed to its processes and materials, but the beginnings of photography are generally said to be 1839, when Jacques Daguerre announced a way of making a positive image on a silver plate. Since that time, photography has become not only a recorder of our pleasures and pastimes, but a vivid recorder of our history as well.

Focus on America focuses on the lives and works of nine photographers, among the greatest ever to record life in the United States. Besides chronicling the social history of this nation, they all share a need and a talent to capture the sweep of historical events of a vast, ever-growing, ever-changing land. These nine men and women are Mathew Brady, William Henry Jackson, Edward Curtis, Lewis Hine, Dorothea Lange, Berenice Abbott, Walker Evans, Margaret Bourke-White, and W. Eugene Smith. Photographs that show the magnificent scope of their talents are also included.

Mathew Brady: He photographed the Civil War.
Born: 1823, New York
Died: January 20, 1896; buried in Arlington National Cemetery

Mathew Brady, who would become the most famous photographer of his time and the chronicler of the tragic Civil War, was born before his life's occupation was invented. It is to Brady that Americans owe much of their knowledge of nineteenth-century prominent figures, for Brady photographed presidents and inventors and actresses and lawyers and scientists and musicians and soldiers, and on and on. But his greatest work would begin in 1861, when—his eyesight poor, his reputation already made, his wealth established, and his white linen duster immaculate—he left Washington with the Union army and would stay in the field for the most part until April 1865. Brady spent more than $100,000 to capture his record of the war. Sunk in debt, he put his priceless collection up for sale. It went to the War Department for $2,840.

William Henry Jackson: He captured the West.
Born: April 4, 1843, Keeseville, New York
Died: 1942; buried Arlington, Virginia, at a National Park Service selected site

During his ninety-nine years, Jackson produced thousands of negatives. The son of a Quaker couple, he traveled west in the 1860s looking for adventure. Instead, he bounced from job to job until he hit the frontier town of Omaha and became a photographer. He would go on to become the "Picture-Maker of the West." Of all his magnificent photographs of such places as the Rockies, the Grand Canyon, Fort Bridger, the Oregon Trail, and other fabled places in western history, his photographs of Yellowstone are probably his greatest legacy, for they influenced the government's decision to name it the first national park.

Edward Curtis: He recorded the American Indian.
Born: February 16, 1868, Whitewater, Wisconsin
Died: October 19, 1952 in Los Angeles

Despite a hard farm childhood and little schooling, Curtis early became fascinated with photography. After traveling west in the late 1800s, he won a first-place medal for his pictures of three Indians in their native environment. From then on, his interest in and recording of the lives of the Indians of America grew until he would eventually produce twenty volumes of *The North American Indian.*

Lewis Hine: Spokesman for the worker.
Born: September 26, 1874, Oshkosh, Wisconsin
Died: November 4, 1940

Perhaps it was his first job in an upholstery factory for four dollars a week that started Hine on his fascination with the American worker. In

1904, now in New York City, he started a project to photograph Ellis Island, the landing place for some many thousands of immigrants to American shores. His pictures with their "unposed" quality made a historical record of the lives of the working class of the early country. Eventually he would be recognized as the best chronicler of social conditions in the land. As one of his last great works, he photographed the step-by-step construction of the Empire State Building in New York City.

Dorothea Lange: She recorded the Great Depression.
Born: May 26, 1895, Hoboken, New Jersey
Died: October 11, 1965

Called "Limpy" from childhood polio, this plain-looking woman would produce one of the most famous of all American photos—"Migrant Mother" (1936). Renowned photographer Ansel Adams would say of her: "She is an extraordinary phenomenon in photography." During World War II, she photographed the Japanese-American internment camps, and many think these photographs are even greater than her documents of the Great Depression.

Berenice Abbott: An instinctive social historian.
Born: July 17, 1898, Springfield, Ohio

After an education at Ohio State and Columbia universities, Abbott became bored with life and America and spent eight years in Paris. When she returned to New York, now a success in her field, she began to photograph the dynamic, ever-changing city. And perhaps more than any other photographer, all during her career she has fought for the acceptance of photography as an art in itself.

Walker Evans: He captured the ordinary and the native in America.
Born: November 3, 1903, St. Louis, Missouri
Died: 1975

Evans glorified the commonplace of the American nation. Educated mainly in the East, he was determined to be an artist, and in 1930 he took photographs of the Brooklyn Bridge for a publication of *The Bridge* by Hart Crane. The photos were exhibited at the New York Museum of Modern Art in 1933. Evans photographed many areas of the country, from tenant farmers to the New York subway and gained worldwide fame. Toward the end of his life he taught at Yale and lectured at Dartmouth, Harvard, and the University of Michigan.

Margaret Bourke-White: A twentieth-century compelling image-maker.
Born: June 14, 1904, New York City
Died: August 27, 1971, Stamford, Connecticut

Margaret Bourke-White is probably best remembered as a war correspondent during World War II. She took more risks than most of the male correspondents and once was in a Mediterranean convoy when it was torpedoed. While waiting for rescue from a lifeboat, she never stopped taking pictures. She photographed the clearing of Naples harbor in Italy and was with Patton's Third Army at the Buchenwald concentration camp, the first to photograph the horrors that were found. By the war's end, she was one of the most famous women in the world, but by 1957 she was forced to give up her life's work due to Parkinson's disease.

W. Eugene Smith: The romantic of American photography.
Born: December 30, 1918, Wichita, Kansas
Died: December 23, 1977

Dark, moody, and paranoid, Smith created powerful images of life with his camera. Wounded by enemy mortars during World War II, he became a photographer for *Life* magazine in 1948. His first great photo essay, called "Country Doctor," brought him the beginning of the fame that would grow throughout his troubled life.

Thematic Material
Mark Sufrin has brought to life the creativeness and humanness that characterize the nine remarkable individuals covered in this book. Photography becomes a true art form as the young reader senses the passion and skill that must combine to become a master of this science. Even in these brief biographical sketches, the depth of commitment and dedication of these artists is manifest.

Book Talk Material
The photographic insert is a good introduction to the individuals in this book and to the science of photography itself (see between pp. 98

and 99). Other discussions might concern: why Mathew Brady's photographs of the Civil War are regarded as a great pictorial essay (pp. 12–19); how Hine photographed the construction of the Empire State Building (pp. 69–71); and why Dorothea Lange's "Migrant Mother" became such a famous photograph (pp. 81–82).

Additional Selections

A full history of photography is given in text and more than 125 illustrations in Giovanni Chiaramonte's *The Story of Photography* (Aperture, 1983, $17.30), and Jerry La Plante interviews thirteen famous photographers and gives examples of their work in *Photographers on Photography* (pap., Sterling, $5.95). Some guides for good picture taking are Tom Grimm and Michele Grimm's *A Good Guide for Bad Photographers* (pap., New Amer. Lib., 1982, $7.95), Ralph Hattersley's *Beginner's Guide to Photography* (pap., Doubleday, $7.95), and George Laycock's *The Complete Beginner's Guide to Photography* (Doubleday, 1979, $7.95). Interesting biographies of such movie directors as Griffith, Ford, and Hitchcock are given in Dian G. Smith's *Great American Film Directors* (Messner, 1987, $9.79). Two books about a thrilling part of moviemaking are Gloria D. Miklowitz's *Movie Stunts and the People Who Do Them* (pap., Harcourt, 1980, $3.95) and Daniel Cohen's *Horror in the Movies* (Clarion, 1982, $10.50; pap., Pocket Bks., $2.25). Teens interested in music will enjoy Pete Fornatale's *The Story of Rock and Roll* (Morrow, 1987, $11.75), from Chuck Berry to the "Boss" himself.

7

Guidance and Health

ADOLESCENCE is a time of change—social, physical, intellectual, and emotional. For teenagers, every day seems to require a new set of responses and adjustments. This section covers a wide spectrum of topics, from personal appearance to family problems and sex education.

Getzoff, Ann, and McClenahan, Carolyn. *Stepkids: A Survival Guide for Teenagers in Stepfamilies (. . . and for stepparents doubtful of their own survival)*
Walker, 1984, lib. bdg., $13.95

This is a clear, well-researched account that offers sound advice to young adults on tackling problems involved in second-family relationships. It is interesting to note that the authors are not only qualified therapists, but also members of stepfamilies. This is a useful book for both junior and senior high school students.

Summary
Stepfamilies have been getting bad press since before Cinderella. Of the more than twenty-five million stepfamilies in the United States today, probably about one million include a teenager. The point is, say the authors, that even if there are problems in these stepfamilies, teenagers can do something about them in a way that younger kids cannot. And that's what this book is about.

Authors Getzoff and McClenahan are child, family, and marriage therapists; they are also mothers and stepmothers. They begin by discussing the number of and different kinds of stepfamilies in the 1980s, the high divorce rate that often creates a new stepfamily, the single parent families, and parents in others kinds of relationships. Many times the teenage children have witnessed the pain and heartache of a marriage falling apart and the subsequent divorce and rejection that follow. But the teenager has the power to make some changes, say the authors, to make the stepfamily a better place for all to be.

Divided into fifteen chapters, the book covers all aspects of step-families and their problems for the teenager. Chapter 1 goes into "normal" teenager behavior—the rebellion that is often part of the growing-up process, the need for privacy, the moodiness, and the anger. Add a stepparent into this atmosphere, someone the teenager probably doesn't know very well, and the problems multiply. So Chapter 2 discusses "negotiations"—how to talk to that new stepparent, the messages teen-agers send without realizing it, how to say what you actually feel and mean, how to listen, and how to communicate.

Chapters 3 and 4 tackle divorce and remarriage, the actions that cre-ated the stepfamily in the first place. The authors ask the teenage reader to take a look at his or her parents' reasons for divorce: How does the teenager really feel about it? How did he or she really feel when a parent remarried to create this new family? The authors help readers to see that, even if they are feeling somewhat unloved and left out of things at this juncture, they might reflect that since their parents were not happy in the family as it was, this is a chance for all of them, including the teenager, to find a family unit that is close and loving for everyone. It just needs help from all family members.

Chapters 5 through 9 cover the stepparents themselves. Who are these people? Is it okay to love them? To not love them? What do you call them anyway? The authors remind young readers that in most stepfamilies, it takes three to five years to get used to living with one another, so obvi-ously there are adjustments to be made.

A discussion follows of stepmothers and stepfathers insofar as what they may generally have in common, how many women must cope with the "cruel stepmother" myth of Cinderella and other tales. Most step-mothers, say the authors, do care about their "new" children and want very much to please them. However, stepmothers have problems, too. They think they should be perfect parents instantly; they think they should love their new children instantly. Sometimes they are jealous of their new husband's children. The young reader gets some practical tips on coping with whatever the situation in his or her particular setup. There are ways of meeting head-on "Mrs. Clean" or "Mrs. Hung-up-on-Responsibility" or "Mrs. Smother," as well as the stepmother who has no children of her own or the stepmother who shows obvious favoritism toward her own children.

Stepfathers get their share of attention, too. Is your stepfather in competition with your real father? Sometimes this can be a difficult situation for a "new" father. Perhaps he isn't sure that you want him in your family (and perhaps at the moment you're not sure either). The reader is shown hints for coping with the "dictator" stepfather, the grouch, the invisible or indifferent stepfather, the one who tries to be too "sexy" with his new daughter, the physically abusive, and the "invisible" man.

In any family where step relations are involved, life can be complicated for the teenager (or any child), especially when the matter of seeing or sharing time with the other parent is involved. The child may visit the other parent regularly, but it isn't his or her home. How does the teenager cope with this? How do you deal with feelings of disloyalty when, for instance, you want to be with your friends instead of visiting your father or mother? Chapter 10 deals with these visiting problems; and Chapter 11 is concerned with the other end of the scale—when the teenager doesn't see the other parent at all. Many reasons account for this; one parent may simply disappear, one parent may forbid visitation rights for some reason; there may simply be too much pain involved for one or both of the parents to have contact; mental illness or alcoholism or other drug dependencies may be involved; or, of course, one of the parents may have died. The authors point out ways in which the teenager can cope with any of these situations to make his or her own life smoother and to ease tensions within the new family.

Chapter 12 deals with the mixed feelings and mixed problems between and among stepbrothers and stepsisters; and Chapter 13 delves into "sex in the stepfamily," including the fact that living with a single parent, or with a new parent, forces the teenager to recognize the sexuality of a parent. Sometimes the teenager may be sexually attracted to the new stepmother or stepfather. How do you deal with that reaction? What about sexual assault? In Chapter 14, the authors deal with the teenager who discovers that a parent is gay. The last chapter turns away from the problems of stepfamilies and talks about what is good about them.

The book ends with many helpful appendixes, including advice on how to hold a family council to discuss problems, ways for children and stepparents to become friends, where to get professional help if it is needed, books that will be of interest to both children and parents in stepfamilies, and details on the organization known as the Stepfamily Association of America.

Thematic Material

In a society where the divorce rate is climbing and new families often, therefore, include "step" members, this straightforward, factual guide to getting along in a stepfamily can be a practical help to teenage readers who must deal with these problems at a vulnerable period in their lives. The authors deal matter-of-factly with all sides of the issues that may crop up in a newly structured family that includes teenage children.

Book Talk Material

Each reader will find his or her main concerns discussed in this guide to better life within a stepfamily. The "how to cope with" aspects may be of especial interest; see coping with rudeness from a new stepparent or relative (p. 42); coping with "types" of stepmothers (pp. 51, 53, 54, 56, 57, 59) and stepfathers (pp. 69, 72, 73, 74, 77, 78–79); coping with feelings of disloyalty to the "other" parent (pp. 86–87); and coping with sexual attraction toward a new stepbrother or stepsister (p. 113).

Additional Selections

Richard Gardner has written extensively for young people about families and family problems. One of his titles is *The Boys and Girls Book about Stepfamilies* (pap., Creative Therapeutics, 1985, $3.50). Two others by Gardner are *The Boys and Girls Book about Divorce* (Aronson, 1983, $15.00; pap., Bantam, $3.50) and *The Boys and Girls Book about One-Parent Families* (pap., Bantam, $2.95). A book that helps youngsters cope when a parent remarries is Janet Sinberg Stenson's *Now I Have a Stepparent, and It's Kind of Confusing* (pap., Avon, 1979, $2.95). In nine brief chapters, each with a case study, Linda Craven explores *Stepfamilies: New Patterns in Harmony* (Messner, 1982, $9.79; pap., $4.95). Sara Gilbert has produced a sensible, helpful book on *How to Live with a Single Parent* (Lothrop, 1982, $9.94). Two fine books for teens caught in the trauma of a family divorce are Dianna Daniels Booher's *Coping . . . When Your Family Falls Apart* (Messner, 1979, $9.29; pap., $4.95), and the product of twenty students ages eleven to fourteen at the Fayerweather Street School in Cambridge, Massachusetts, *The Kids' Book of Divorce: By, for and about Kids* (Greene, 1981, $9.95). A guide that explores questions and issues involved in adoption is Laurie Wishard and William R. Wishard's *Adoption: The Grafted Tree* (pap., Avon, 1981, $3.50).

Hellmuth, Jerome. *Coping with Parents*
Rosen, 1985, $9.97

This useful guide is slight in size but filled with practical tips to help young people get along with their parents. The problem of parental conflict often increases during adolescence as youngsters wish to become independent decision makers and assume responsibilities denied them in childhood. This is a useful book in junior high collections.

Summary

Says the author, a teacher, psychotherapist, and director of a residential school for mentally handicapped adolescents, "Whether you like it or not, you become pretty much what your parents did or did not do for or to you during all those years you lived with them." Therefore, to find out "what kind of a person you might become, what kind of a youngster you are now," young readers are encouraged to try to find out more about their parents, real or surrogate.

Each chapter in *Coping with Parents* deals with a different aspect of parenting, and each is followed by questions for discussion. Ideally, the reader is encouraged to hold a discussion of these topics with his or her parents.

Early chapters discuss love between parents—the concept of romantic love and the desire to live together; why many parents are so concerned about family differences in a young couple, why they generally wish their son or daughter to marry someone with a similar family background and beliefs. But living together, even with love, is not always easy, warns the author, and many children have been mentally damaged because their parents were unable to live in any kind of harmony throughout their lives.

Chapter 5 discusses the all-important "How does a parent learn to be a parent?" Where are the diplomas and medals given out for good work in such a role? How do you learn to "raise kids"? If the young reader begins to understand how his or her own parents feel about raising children, or whether they have any set policy or rules, these future parents may be able to follow such examples or keep as far away from such examples as possible!

Other high-risk areas of friction between children and parents are up for discussion, too, such as different expectations concerning schooling. Parents want their children to be excellent in all their studies; children don't always want to be or can't always fulfill that expectation. How can that gap be bridged? Do parents play favorites? What does that do to the favored child? To the unfavored one?

The most difficult time in any family is probably when the children reach adolescence. It is difficult for parents to let go of the authority they have held over their children for so many years, even while they realize that this is the time for young people to start letting go and start thinking for themselves.

Basic issues are discussed: Are mothers and fathers different? What about parents' personalities? What kinds of personalities between two people aid their success as a couple or as parents? Do children have any rights if the personalities of their parents endanger their welfare? Do parents make good friends? Should they be?

Young readers are encouraged to view their parents, at least for the reading of this book, simply as individuals. What kind of citizens are they? Do they vote or otherwise participate in the political processes of this country? Do they set a good example? Can the children understand that their parents are people who, just as sons and daughters do, grow and change, are growing and changing even as their children are growing up. Sometimes that growth and change will result in dire consequences for the family, such as divorce.

Even young children are at least dimly aware that people grow up and grow old, although often they can't ascribe that to their own parents. But parents do grow old, unless tragedy strikes the family early and results in their premature death. How does a child cope with aging parents? How does a child face the eventual death of parents?

Young readers are encouraged to think of the legacy their own parents leave them—their teachings, their influence, their love, or even their lack of it.

At the end of the book, readers are asked to rate their own parents, to see if there is "room for improvement." And if, after discussion, the family realizes that their unit could benefit from outside counseling, the book lists social service organizations; mental health services, marriage, family, child, and individual counselors; and social workers as places to start.

Thematic Material

Young readers may be turned on by the idea of "reversing roles" with their parents and judging them on performance rather than the other way around. The author touches on all aspects of parenting, all areas of conflict between parents and children. It also offers insight for young readers into why and how they grow and develop as they do, and lists services available to those families in need of outside help.

Book Talk Material

Children are asked to discuss the questions at the end of each chapter with their parents, if possible, but these areas are also suitable for discussion among themselves. See, for example, questions on: how parents learn to be parents (Did your parents know how to take care of you when you were a baby? p. 19); Do you think your parents know what goes on in your school? (on schooling, pp. 30–31); Is your personality more like your mother's or father's? (on parent personalities, pp. 49–50); Do your parents abuse you? (on parents who are bad for you, pp. 53–54); and Have any great sorrows seriously hurt your family? (from when tragedy strikes a family, p. 75).

Additional Selections

The age-old struggle between teenagers and parents is given an unbiased treatment that explores the concept that parents are also people in Joyce L. Vedral's *My Parents Are Driving Me Crazy* (pap., Ballantine, 1986, $2.50). In Jane Rinzier's *Teens Speak Out* (Fine, 1986, $7.95), the results of a questionnaire on subjects like careers, sex, and drugs are detailed. Allied in subject matter is Claudine G. Wirths and Mary Bowman-Kruhm's *I Hate School: How to Hang In and When to Drop Out* (Crowell, 1986, $11.95; pap., Harper, $7.95). The celebrated author Judy Blume answers questions posed to her by her fans in *Letters to Judy: What Your Kids Wish They Could Tell You* (Putnam, 1986, $17.95). Fred Powledge's book *You'll Survive* (Scribner, 1986, $11.95) is subtitled "Early Blooming, Loneliness, Klutziness and Other Problems of Adolescence and How to Live through Them." Conflicts and tensions in the family are discussed in Sara Gilbert's *Trouble at Home* (Lothrop, 1981, $11.88). A book that will help teens reach their potential is Judy Zerafa's *Go for It!* (pap., Workman, 1982, $3.95). Three other books that deal with problems of adolescents are Ellen Rosenberg's *Growing Up Feeling Good* (Beaufort, 1984, $19.95; pap., $12.95), Hiley H. Ward's *Feeling Good about Myself* (Westminster, 1983, $11.95), and Sol Gordon's *The Teenage Survival Book* (pap., Times Bks., 1981, $9.95), an updated revised edition of *You.*

Madaras, Lynda, with Saavedra, Dane. *The What's Happening to My Body? Book for Boys: A Growing Up Guide for Parents and Sons*
   Newmarket, 1984, $14.95; pap., $8.95 (same pagination)

Lynda Madaras is a noted sex educator who has worked in schools with young people of all ages. She also lectures widely on puberty and related health subjects. In 1983, with the assistance of her teenage daughter, Area, she wrote the much acclaimed *What's Happening to My Body? Book for Girls: A Growing Up Guide for Parents and Daughters* (Newmarket, 1983, $14.95; pap., $8.95). As she states in the introduction addresssed to parents in this, its companion volume, there is probably greater need for accurate sex education for boys than girls because at least girls are made aware of basic facts about puberty, usually by their mothers, during their first menstrual period. Boys do not have such an opportunity and, therefore, often pick up half-truths from washroom walls, lurid novels, or ill-informed peers. She quotes such sobering statistics as the fact that more than one million babies are born to teenage mothers each year to remind us that some action in this area must be taken. Like the first book, this volume is based roughly on courses she has taught. The text was prepared with the help of Dane Saavedra, the teenage son of a friend, and through interviews with several adult males. The book is straightforward, truthful, and well written. It does not mince words, nor does it hedge on any particular topic. Although the emphasis is on the changes that occur during puberty, there is a section on sexuality. Controversial subjects like abortion, birth control, and masturbation are treated objectively. Various points of view and opinions on these subjects are stated. Sometimes the author will give her position, usually a moderate one that could be characterized as liberal. She suggests that ideally this book should be read together by boys and their parents (or parent); however, it also could be read alone. The recommended age range is from upper elementary grades through at least junior high school. The book is divided into eight chapters plus a brief but excellent list of further readings and an index.

Summary

In Chapter 1, the young reader is introduced to the term "puberty" and in general the changes that occur during this period. The male and female sex organs are described in text and illustrations, slang words for those body parts are listed, and sexual intercourse, pregnancy, and the birth process are briefly explained.

In Chapter 2, the author identifies the five stages of puberty and describes the characteristics of each with emphasis on genital development. The author tries to allay fears concerning normalcy by emphasizing that, although there are average ages for entering these stages and usual lengths of time spent in each, there are wide variations and each individual's development pattern is different. A chart for tracing each stage is given.

Chapter 3 is called Changing Size and Shape. It deals with growth patterns related to body size and points out that, although certain elements in body shapes are considered more desirable in our society, these preferences have varied considerably from one culture to another. The important thing is to learn to like and respect your own body. At the end of this chapter is a section on penis size that effectively explodes nine perpetually held myths on the subject (e.g., men with big penises are more masculine).

The fourth chapter deals with other changes that occur during puberty, problems associated with them, and adjustments that can be made. Topics covered are body hair, facial hair and shaving, underarm hair and perspiration, skin changes that can cause pimples and acne, breast changes, stretch marks, and voice changes. Again the author emphasizes that these changes are natural and healthy.

In Chapter 5, through diagrams and text, the organs and processes utilized to produce sperm and cause ejaculation are described. There are also sections on orgasm, erections, wet dreams, and masturbation. In the latter section, a question-and-answer approach is used based on the queries she most often receives in her classes (e.g., "Do most boys masturbate?" "Is masturbation bad for you?").

Chapter 6 shifts the focus of the book to girls, and in concise form gives descriptions of the changes girls experience during puberty with particular emphasis on the process of ovulation and the menstrual period.

Questions about sexuality are answered in Chapter 7. The topics covered with sample questions are homosexuality (Is homosexuality wrong?); sexual decisions (Should you wait until you are married for sex?); pregnancy (Are there certain times of the month when a girl can get pregnant?); birth control (What are the methods and which work best?); and sexually transmitted diseases (Can VD be cured?). There is no material on AIDS in the book. This chapter ends with a brief section of sexual crimes like child molestation and incest.

The last chapter is a brief summary and pep talk that tells youngsters that the changes described in this book will bring problems, involve making many difficult decisions, and produce new conflicts. As the author states, "Growing up is indeed a mixed bag of experiences."

Thematic Material

This is a well-written book on sex education. It is thorough in its coverage, not condescending or patronizing toward its audience, and honest and straightforward in handling difficult subjects.

Book Talk Material

The situation in which this book could be book-talked could probably be before sex education classes or parent groups. In such cases a description of the contents would be sufficient. In the "Introduction for Parents" section the author describes a consciousness-raising homework assignment she uses in her sex education classes. She gives each student an egg and for one week that egg is to be considered the student's baby and must be cared for accordingly. The fascinating results of the experiment and how, as a result, youngsters begin to understand the responsibilities of parenthood are given on pp. 1–3.

Additional Selections

Thirteen-year-old Jimmy and his two friends learn about their changing selves in Jeanne Betancourt's *Am I Normal?* (pap., Avon, 1983, $1.95). The companion volume, about a girl entering puberty, is *Dear Diary* (pap., Avon, 1983, $1.95) by the same author. Ruth Bell's *Changing Bodies, Changing Lives* (Random, 1981, $17.95; pap., $9.95) is subtitled "A Book for Teens on Sex and Relationships." For boys and girls about to enter puberty, an excellent guide to the physical and emotional changes that occur is *Growing and Changing: A Handbook for Preteens* (Putnam, 1987, $9.95) by Kathy McCoy and Charles Wibbelsman. Subtitled "A Teenager's Guide to Self-Health," Nissa Simon's *Don't Worry, You're Normal* (Harper, 1982, $10.89; pap., $4.95) is a guide to the changes that occur during adolescence. Wardell B. Pomeroy has written two of the classic sex education books: *Boys and Sex* (Delacorte, 1981, $10.95; pap., Dell, $2.50) and *Girls and Sex* (Delacorte, 1981, $10.95; pap., Dell, $2.50). Eric W. Johnston has also written a number of self-help books. Perhaps his most famous is *Love and Sex in Plain Language* (Lippincott, 1977, $11.25; pap., Bantam, $3.50). Young women's concerns are addressed in Andrea Boroff Eagan's *Why Am I So Miserable if These Are the Best Years of My Life?* (Lippincott, 1976, $11.70; pap., Avon, $2.25).

Parks-McKay, Jane.   *The Make-Over: A Teen's Guide to Looking and Feeling Beautiful*
   Morrow, 1985, $17.95; pap., $10.95 (same pagination)

The concept of the "make-over," where beauty specialists remodel and reshape a woman's looks, was made popular through television and mass market women's magazines. This is the first manual on the subject aimed at a relatively young audience. It is popular with girls in grades eight and up.

Summary
   Written by a beauty expert (who is head of her own modeling and image-consulting firm) on the assumption that most teenage girls feel themselves to be plain-looking, shy, and less popular than they'd like to be, here is a no-nonsense, fully illustrated, practical guide aimed at the special needs and concerns of young women. The author's philosophy is that there really is a beautiful person lurking behind every plain face, and that with a lot of hard work and determination the beautiful "you" inside can emerge and make a beautiful person "all over."
   The Make-Over is arranged in chapters, or steps, plus opening and closing commentaries. After an initial pep talk on the merits of self-improvement, the book deals with Your Inner Beauty. Here the author discusses how to determine a personal image instead of trying to copy someone else's in an effort to be more beautiful or more popular. There

are activities and exercises directed toward allowing the teenager to get to know herself better, an exercise that directs the reader to finding out how she spends her time each day and how she actually would like to spend it, hints on solving problems that might concern the young girl about her personal looks, and a guide to better manners, which also are part of the "make-over."

On the subject of dress, the author once again stresses how to find and develop personal styles instead of copying what may look good on someone else. There are hints on analyzing one's own figure, "optical-illusion" dressing to hide those negative points and enhance the positive ones, creative shopping, and how "to put the whole thing together." The next section deals with cosmetics, starting with the skin and its care, skin types and how to deal with them, complexions, and makeup and how to apply it.

Hair is a matter of concern for most young women. What is hair really all about and what's the best way to care for it? The author discusses shampoos and ways of combing hair, eating for healthy hair, and how to find the hairstyle that is just right for the individual.

Next, the book deals with what is probably the greatest personal interest for the teenager—her shape. The author first instructs the reader in putting together a picture of what she looks like now, and then talks about setting up goals to become "that great shape" of tomorrow. Once again, there is a discussion of nutrition and diet plans, eating for good health and for good looks. For those young readers who need to diet, the author lists hints that can help make dieting easier and more successful. She stresses the value and benefits of exercise to obtain a good-looking body. A number of exercises, fully illustrated, are included for trimming specific areas of the body, such as the waistline, bustline, stomach, and hips.

The next chapter takes shape a step further and deals with the young reader's body language, or the science of kinesics. As the author says, some teenagers may have to learn how to walk all over again! But posture, she contends, is vitally important to the way others look at a person and equally important to how that person views herself. And so there are instructions in ways of standing and walking up and down stairs, sitting, stooping, and even how to carry a handbag. There is also a section on putting on and taking off a coat and getting in and out of a car.

The last practical step in the book deals with the young reader's hands; as the author says, "Don't sit on them!" She gives a number of suggestions for making over one's hands into an attractive part of the overall you; even if you work hard and play hard, says the author, your hands can be beautiful.

At the end of each chapter, or step, the author asks and then answers what she feels young readers might ask her had they chance. Here are some examples:

"I'm black and I heard that blacks seem to have oilier skin than others. What should I do about my 'bumpy' skin?"
Answer: ". . . People with black skin are no more prone to oilier complexions than light-skinned people. Are you using the right kind of cleansing products?. . ."
"Sometimes I feel like I'm the shyest, most unconfident, and clumsiest person in the world. . . . Am I the only one who feels this way?"
Answer: "Not at all—you're feeling just what everyone else feels . . . make friends with some of the girls you admire. You might end up learning things from each other."
"What's the best way to carry a backpack?"
Answer: "Very similar to a shoulder bag, actually. . . . If you carry it on your side, take turns carrying it on either side for balance."

Thematic Material

An easy-to-read, basic guide for the young teenage girl who may be having problems with any aspect of how she looks and is sometimes unsure about how to act. The book is attractive, breezy, and fun to read.

Book Talk Material

Besides providing helpful hints in the basics of good grooming, the question-and-answer sections should give young girls a chance to "talk problems over among themselves"; see questions and answers on inner beauty (pp. 23–25); dressing for personal style (pp. 47–49); the right cosmetics (pp. 83–87); hair (pp. 105–107); shaping up (pp. 137–139); body language (pp. 154–156); and the hands (pp. 165–167).

Additional Selections

Bantam has produced a number of fine grooming guides for teenage girls. Three of these are *The Sweet Dreams Body Book*, *The Sweet Dreams Fashion Book* (pap., Bantam, $1.95 each), and *The Sweet Dreams Makeup Workbook* (pap., Bantam, $2.25). Also use *The Teen Girl's Beauty Guide to Total Color Success* (pap., New Amer. Lib., 1986, $2.50) by Marjabelle Young Stewart, and Rubie Saunders's *The Beauty Book* (Messner, 1984, $9.29). Sensible advice for overweight girls is given in Bonnie L. Lukes's

How to Be a Reasonably Thin Teenage Girl (Atheneum, 1986, $12.95). *Romance! Can You Survive It?* (pap., Dell, 1986, $2.25) by Meg Schneider is an interesting practical guide to dating, as are Marjabelle Young Stewart's *The Teen Dating Guide* (pap., New Amer. Lib., 1984, $2.25) and Jane Stine and Bob Stine's *Everything You Need to Survive First Dates* (pap., Random, 1983, $1.95).

Richards, Arlene Kramer, and Willis, Irene. *What to Do if You or Someone You Know Is under 18 and Pregnant*
   Lothrop, 1983, $10.88; pap., $7.00 (same pagination)

Teenage pregnancy is a growing problem in America. In this sensitive, simply written account, the authors try to help a pregnant young woman decide what is best for her without preaching or moralizing. Other books by this writing team include a guide to how to make friends, how to keep or break friendships, and how to handle rejection, *Boy Friends, Girl Friends, Just Friends* (Atheneum, 1979, $11.95), and a work that explores the problems of potential runaways, *Leaving Home* (Atheneum, 1980, $8.95). All of the above titles are useful in both junior and senior high school collections.

Summary
   More than one million teenagers become pregnant in the United States every year. Most of those young women did not plan on pregnancy, and for them there are three choices: have the baby and put the child up for adoption, have an abortion, or have the baby and raise it.

Without moralizing or passing judgment, the authors (a psychoanalyst and a teacher and counselor) discuss these three options as well as much other information a teenager should know about the facts of sex, about birth control, childbirth, what is involved in an abortion, what adoption means, and what faces a young woman who decides to raise a child herself. All the facts are here in clear, easy-to-understand terms.

Chapters 1 through 4 discuss conception and contraception, abortion, and the first three months of a pregnancy. Many young men and women have only the vaguest of ideas of how pregnancy comes about or how it can be avoided. Avoiding sexual intercourse is, of course, one way, but the authors also discuss the anatomy of the male and female bodies and what takes place during conception. The various methods of avoiding pregnancy through contraception are detailed—foam, condoms, the pill, diaphragm, IUD—along with the pros and cons of each method.

The authors touch on teenagers' legal rights concerning abortion and detail various abortion methods, including possible risks, where to go to find an abortion doctor, involvement of the girl's parents, financial help, the young father's role (or lack of it), danger signs in a postabortion period, and possible emotional trauma after the abortion is performed.

Included in the chapter on the first three months of pregnancy are the initial changes taking place in the young woman's body, the first visits to the doctor, caring for the baby's health before the child is born, the benefits of keeping healthy, sexual activity during pregnancy, and danger signals alerting the perspective mother to the fact that something is wrong with the growing fetus.

The "rest of the pregnancy" section is concerned with health care, danger signals, arranging for the hospital, and labor and delivery, as well as with feelings the young woman may experience, her schooling during this period, and the involvement of her own parents (and perhaps the father's) in her pregnancy.

Once the child is born, the all-important considerations of adoption or keeping and raising the baby are discussed in Chapters 6 through 9. The authors detail the different adoption methods and also discuss the finality of such a decision and the feelings the young mother may experience after making such a choice.

Equally as serious is the decision of a young teenager to raise her baby. What about returning to school? Who will care for the baby? The girl's own parents? What if they are not available? What if they do not want the responsibility? How does a young woman learn how to raise an infant, especially if she must do so on her own?

Chapter 9 treats a very serious concern, too. Should the young parents marry? Do they want to? Is it the right thing to do for the child? For them?

In Chapter 10, the authors provide the vital information that most all young pregnant teenagers desperately need upon first discovering their condition—where to get help. Whatever the outcome of the pregnancy, whether they opt for abortion or for adoption or raising the child, initially they will need advice and information on their choices and future prospects. The authors discuss general facts on where teenagers may go for help, and also give details on organizations that offer aid and counseling, such as Planned Parenthood and the Jewish Board of Family and Children's Services. Listed also are adolescent clinics set up to handle the health needs of young people. More help can come from such maternity service groups as the Florence Crittenton Services in a number of states, which run residential group homes for pregnant young women. Adoption agencies and women's support groups are listed, along with a bibliography of books and pamphlets on pregnancy and its consequences.

Thematic Material

In a simple, straightforward, easy-to-read manner, the authors present all aspects of pregnancy involving the teenage girl. With the high number of pregnancies occurring among young women in the United States today and the added fear brought on by the spread of disease through sexual contact, this book might well be on the reading list for every young teenage girl and boy. Readers should be advised that because this book was published in 1983, the addresses of some of the organizations listed may have changed. However, the organizations themselves remain viable, as are the instructions for locating them.

Book Talk Material

The book is so organized that each chapter can be discussed separately, depending on the ages and involvement of the readers—perhaps the chapter on conception and contraception for those who "hear things from friends" but are not yet involved in sexual activity (pp. 21–53), or the realities of abortion for those facing such a procedure (pp. 54–73).

Additional Selections

Questions asked by teenagers are answered by a renowned columnist in *Ann Landers Talks to Teenagers about Sex* (pap., Fawcett, 1981, $2.25). A comprehensive, well-written guide is Jacqueline Voss and Joy Gale's *A Young Woman's Guide to Sex* (Holt, 1986, $15.45). There are several excellent books about teenage pregnancy. Three of them are *Mom, I'm Pregnant* (pap., Stein & Day, 1982, $6.95) by Reni L. Witt and Jeannine Masterson Michael, *Kids Having Kids: The Unwed Teenage Parent* (Watts, 1980, $10.90) by Janet Bode, and *It Won't Happen to Me: Teenagers Talk about Pregnancy* (Delacorte, 1983, $14.95; pap., Dell, $7.95) by Paula McGuire. Helen Benedict's *Safe, Strong and Streetwise* (Little, 1987, $13.95; pap., $4.95) is a manual on how to cope with sexual assault and how to prevent sexual exploitation. Alan E. Nourse's First Book account *Men-*

struation: Just Plain Talk (Watts, 1987, $9.90) is a useful introduction with material on premenstrual and toxic shock syndrome. Sexually transmitted diseases are covered in a number of fine titles, including Elaine Landau's *Sexually Transmitted Diseases* (Enslow, 1986, $12.95), Sol Gordon's *Facts about STD—Sexually Transmitted Diseases* (Ed-U Pr., 1983, $6.95), and Bea Mandel and Byron Mandel's *Play Safe: How to Avoid Getting Sexually Transmitted Diseases* (Center for Health Education, pap., 1986, $4.95).

8

The World Around Us

Teenagers need increasingly to know and care about the world outside their immediate interests and concerns. In this section we glimpse two momentous events in twentieth-century history—World War II and the Vietnam War—view some scientific accomplishments, explore the insidious drug trade, and experience the world from the prospective of blind people.

Dolan, Edward F., Jr. *International Drug Traffic*
Watts, 1985, lib. bdg., $10.90

Youngsters are often aware of drug misuse and problems it involves. However, they probably do not know about the conspiracy of death and greed that brings the drugs and their accompanying misery to their many users. This book brings all of these horrifying details to light. This work will interest students in both junior and senior high schools.

Summary

Drug abuse has been a worldwide problem for centuries, increasing during some periods, decreasing during others. Since the 1960s, traffic in illegal drugs has been steadily increasing, as are the problems that abuse and misuse of drugs bring to any society. But where there is demand for a product, an enterprise will spring up to meet that demand, however illegal.

In nine chapters, Dolan deals mainly with three illegal drugs—cocaine, heroin, and marijuana. He also comments on less trafficked drugs such as opium and synthetics and points out that the routes by which drugs travel to various places are constantly being changed or reused as authorities seize shipments or come upon drug traffic lanes.

Illegal drug traffic in the United States alone takes in about $79 billion yearly, and it is a menace that is spreading. With legal use, drugs can cure illness, ease pain, and reduce suffering. Used illegally, they bring ruined lives, increased crime and mayhem, and death.

Cocaine has been called the drug of the 1980s. It is extracted from the leaves of the coca plant, grown principally in Bolivia and Peru. The leaves of the coca plant contain alkaloids, a poisonous substance found in certain plants, but used in small amounts it can be a powerful medicine. Cocaine is one of the alkaloids of the coca plant. When the leaves are burned, the sticky paste of cocaine is left behind. With the addition of hydrochloric acid, the paste turns into white flakes and rocks, which can be crushed into a white powder.

Although cocaine users say the drug gives them energy, confidence, and a feeling of euphoria, it also can cause a rise in blood pressure, quicken the heartbeat, curb the appetite, and turn the user into an addict.

The cocaine leaves the South American countries where it is grown and heads mainly for such European countries as Italy, Spain, Great Britain, and the Netherlands and for Canada and the United States. Smugglers use several routes to get cocaine into the United States and Canada. Most of it simply travels across the Caribbean Sea to the southern coast of the United States. Some of it travels by ship to Mexico City and then north, or up the Pacific Coast to the western United States and on to Canada. Large cocaine shipments may be stowed aboard small boats, cargo planes, or airliners. Small shipments are often brought in by individuals who "plant" cocaine on their bodies or in their belongings in various ways, risking, of course, discovery by government agents.

Once inside the country, the cocaine goes to a distribution network—the Mafia drug syndicate is said to be involved—then to dealers and ultimately to the individual users.

Heroin, unlike cocaine, is mainly a product of Asia, and it comes from the poppy plant. Opium can be extracted from the seedpods of the poppy plant, and as a medicinal drug, opium has long been used as a painkiller. (Morphine, for relieving severe pain, is extracted from opium.) But when abused, heroin, like cocaine, can cause overwhelming physical problems for the user and it is addictive. When an addicted user decides to quit, he or she suffers agonizing mental and physical withdrawal symptoms.

Heroin slows down the heart rate and can bring on drowsiness and a sense of euphoria. Severe addiction means fresh doses of heroin every few hours or else the user will experience the dreaded chills, sweats, pain, weakness, and unbearable agonies of withdrawal.

Turkey and Mexico used to be the big suppliers of heroin, but now most of it comes from southwestern and southeastern Asia. The countries of Iran, Pakistan, and Afghanistan are known as the "Golden Crescent" because of their rich harvest of opium crops. The Golden Crescent has been challenged by the "Golden Triangle"—the countries of Thailand, Burma, and Laos. Most heroin that enters the United States first goes to Europe; from there it travels to America by airfreight, by ship, and by individual couriers.

Once inside the United States, heroin, like cocaine, fans out through the illegal drug network to distributors and dealers and finally to the unfortunate user. Most of the heroin from Mexico makes its way into the United States across the border.

Marijuana is more used by people than any other illegal drug. It comes from the hemp plant and was grown in China for its fibers as early as 2800 B.C., and its abuse may extend that far back as well.

Although the United States does produce marijuana, the five main producing areas are southwestern and southeastern Asia, Mexico, Colombia, and the island of Jamaica in the Caribbean. From southwestern Asia comes the potent marijuana called hashish, with Lebanon probably the ranking grower. The hashish is smuggled to North America via sea or air. From southeastern Asia comes sinsemilla, which means "without seeds," a high-grade marijuana, but little of it seems to reach the United States. Most all marijuana that does enter the United States comes from Colombia, Mexico, and Jamaica (plus what is grown in the United States itself); about 75 percent comes from Colombia.

Marijuana acts on a user much like alcohol does. However, although alcohol can affect the user in various ways, marijuana usually brings on a feeling of restlessness, then well-being, and finally a state of relaxation. Like other drugs, marijuana causes physical changes in the body—faster heartbeat, rise in blood pressure, and feelings of hunger and thirst.

How are nations trying to reduce the traffic in illegal drugs? There are programs to attack it at its source, such as spraying the fields where the plants are grown; drug laws, in the United States, for instance, have been toughened; and a number of nations, including the United States, have banded together to try to stop the illegal flow of drug traffic throughout the world. But, as the author points out, these measures have had but limited success. In order for the world's population to beat the traffic in illegal drugs, the population of the world must talk out against it.

Thematic Material

The author feels that traffic in illegal drugs can be halted only by a massive effort. To engage young people in that effort, he feels they must be acquainted with the drug traffic so that they understand the evil it creates and how they can make some contribution to its end. Talking about the damage drugs can spread is a start, as is joining a local, regional, or national group that speaks out against drug use. The menace of international drug traffic must be acknowledged before it can be abolished.

Book Talk Material

The physical changes in the body caused by the three main drugs of cocaine, heroin, and marijuana are good introductions to this book. See the effects of cocaine (pp. 18–21); what happens with heroin (pp. 48–50); and the marijuana high (pp. 68–71).

Additional Selections

The shocking world of heroin addiction is introduced in Nigel Hawkes's *The Heroin Trail* (Watts, 1986, $10.90). Information about types of drugs and the dangers of addiction are given in such works as Arnold Madison's *Drugs and You* (Messner, 1982, $9.79), Margaret O. Hyde and Bruce G. Hyde's *Know about Drugs* (McGraw-Hill, 1979, $10.95), and Geraldine Woods's *Drug Use and Abuse* (Watts, 1986, $9.50). For teens who want to learn more about addiction and ways to get help there are several fine volumes in the Encyclopedia of Psychoactive Drugs series including *Getting Help: Treatments for Drug Abuse* by Sidney Schnoll and *Alcohol and Alcoholism* by Ross Fishman (both Chelsea, 1987, $14.95 each). The use and misuse of mind-altering drugs are explored in Margaret O. Hyde's *Mind Drugs* (Dodd, 1986, $10.95). Two recommended titles on alcohol are Alvin Silverstein and Virginia B. Silverstein's *Alcoholism* (Lippincott, 1975, $9.89; pap., $3.50) and Jane Claypool's *Alcohol and You* (Watts, 1981, $9.90). Some novels dealing with drug and alcohol abuse are Marilyn Halvorson's *Let It Go* (Delacorte, 1986, $14.95); S. E. Hinton's *That Was Then, This Is Now* (Viking, 1967, $10.95; pap., Dell, $2.50); W. G. Butterworth's *Under the Influence* (Four Winds, 1979, $9.95); C. W. Adler's

With Westie and the Tin Man (Macmillan, 1985, $10.95); and Anne Snyder's *My Name Is Davy—I'm an Alcoholic* (pap., New Amer. Lib., 1978, $2.25).

Fleisher, Paul. *Secrets of the Universe: Discovering the Universal Laws of Science*
    Atheneum, 1987, $17.95

Among other accomplishments, Paul Fleisher writes instructional computer software. Perhaps this ability to analyze material and divide it into cumulative steps has helped him in this book to explain simply and logically the scientific laws that govern our universe. Each explanation is accompanied by everyday analogies and simple, safe experiments using objects found in most homes. The book is well illustrated with black-and-white drawings by Patricia A. Keeler. Each important concept and experiment is explained both in text and illustration. The book is arranged roughly in chronological order and is geared to readers in the sixth through ninth grades.

Summary
The author begins by explaining what a natural law is, how natural laws are formulated and written, and what constitutes the science known as physics.

His first example is an explanation of Archimedes' principle, or the law of buoyancy, which states that a floating object displaces water equal to its weight. By using a scale on which is placed a plate and jar filled to the brim with water, the reader is able to discover that when a small block of wood is placed in the jar the weight of the water that spills into the plate equals the weight of the wood. From this, the concept of density is developed and explanations given on why certain objects float and others don't, and how submarines rise or sink by using their ballast tanks.

The steps taken by Kepler to develop his laws of planetary motion are next explained and, by using a piece of string, pushpins, and a pencil, the reader is shown how to draw various elliptical shapes and from this to determine the paths of the planets and the fact that planets move faster the closer they are to the sun.

By measuring the times of the swings of a pendulum of various lengths and weights, Galileo's law that states that the time of the swing varies only on the pendulum's length is demonstrated. By using a number of simple examples, the author also develops Galileo's laws on the speed and acceleration of falling bodies.

The famous trick in which a tablecloth is quickly pulled off a table leaving the dishes intact is one of several examples used to show the meaning of Newton's first law of motion involving the concept of inertia (the reader is warned not to try this trick at home!). Similarly, Newton's other two laws are explained and how their application has led to the development of rockets and space probes.

Following an explanation of Newton's law of universal gravitation, which calculates the force by which objects attract, there are again many examples of how this law has been applied, from the discovery of new planets to the development of the space shuttle.

Spinning tops, frisbees, and twirling ice skaters are only three of the examples used to explain the law of conservation of momentum. Following this is a chapter on optics in which concepts like refraction, the spectrum, temperature variation in colors, and light waves are discussed, again using many simple, safe experiments.

How liquids behave is explored in a section on Pascal's law that ends with citing such applications as hydraulic jacks and automobile brakes. In an accompanying chapter on the behavior of gases, Boyle's and Charles's laws are explained, and from these, the inner workings of such diverse objects as bicycle pumps and refrigerators are detailed. Bernoulli's principle is then used to show how the special shape of an airfoil gives airplane wings their lift.

There follows a chapter on the building blocks of substances, the elements, and how they combine to form compounds. Various past methods used to group elements (e.g., by atomic weight, chemical properties, valence) led to the development of Mendeleev's periodic law, the application of which led to the discovery of many new elements so that they now number 103.

Later chapters deal with laws involving thermodynamics and the conservation of energy, electromagnetism, and electric currents. There are also lucid explanations of Einstein's work on relativity and quantum mechanics and his thinking on matter and energy that produced the famous equation $E = mc^2$. The book ends appropriately with a question mark by discussing Heisenberg's uncertainty principle, which postulates that it is impossible for science to understand the universe completely.

Thematic Material

This is essentially a capsule history of the pure and applied sciences. The author has an amazing knack of making the most complex and difficult concepts understandable. The use of many examples, applications, experiments, and excellent illustrations helps immeasurably. A sense of wonder and the excitement of discovery are both well depicted, as is the awe with which one should regard our universe and the laws that govern it. The meaning of the scientific method and the cumulative nature of scientific knowledge are also interestingly explored.

Book Talk Material

Each chapter usually deals with a different law. Using an explanation of one of these and perhaps a simple accompanying experiment should interest readers in the entire book. Some samples: Archimedes' principle (pp. 5–11); Galileo's laws of motion (pp. 21–32); Newton's work in this area (pp. 33–43); optics (pp. 65–80); Pascal's law (pp. 86–96); and how gases behave (pp. 97–115).

Additional Selections

James Jesperson and Jane Fitz-Randolph give readers a tour of the universe, including an explanation of the theory of relativity in *From Quarks to Quasars* (Atheneum, 1987, $16.95). Tiny particles are the subject of Melvin Berger's *Atoms, Molecules and Quarks* (Putnam, 1986, $9.99). Modern developments in various branches of science are explored in a series from Watts that includes James A. Corrick's *Recent Revolutions in Biology* (Watts, 1987, $11.90) and his *Recent Revolutions in Chemistry* (Watts, 1986, $11.90). Roy A. Gallant introduces the stars of the universe in *Private Lives of the Stars* (Macmillan, 1986, $13.95), and Albert Stwertka and Eve Stwertka give an overview of modern physics in *Physics: From Newton to the Big Bang* (Watts, 1986, $9.90). With the subtitle "Tracing Its Origins and Development through Time," Michael Benton's *The Story of Life on Earth* (Watts, 1986, $13.90) covers the origin and evolution of life. Margaret O. Hyde faces the question of whether we will produce computers smarter than humans in *Artificial Intelligence* (Enslow, 1986, $12.95).

Hauptly, Denis J. *In Vietnam*
Macmillan, 1985, $12.95

The story of U.S. involvement in Vietnam is still a matter of conflict and controversy. The author tries to clarify this situation by using a straightforward, objective approach and sticking to the facts. The first part of the book gives historical background, including a section on French domination, and the second tells of America's involvement. This author's earlier, much praised *The Journey from the Past* (Atheneum, 1983, $12.95) traces the history of the Western world beginning in East Africa through the 1960s. Both books are recommended for readers in grades six through nine.

Summary
During the years 1954–1975, many thousands of Americans fought and many thousands died in a country now known officially as the Socialist Republic of Vietnam. It was a war that an increasing number of people in the United States and elsewhere protested, and far fewer ever understood. Denis Hauptly puts into focus the events, beginning centuries ago, that led to the formation of North and South Vietnam and to the eventual American involvement, with its dire consequences.

The Vietnam War was a complex of many events, says the author. And if it is impossible to understand fully the exact chain that led to the deaths of so many, at least we should be able to draw lessons from the stepping-stones.

Hauptly begins his story by tracing the troubled history of the Vietnamese people. This small country (approximately 128,401 square miles, or slightly larger than the state of New Mexico) in Southeast Asia is bordered by Cambodia, Laos, China, and the South China Sea. Its mostly mountainous terrain, including the northern Red River delta and the southern Mekong River delta, which are connected by a narrow strip, is primarily an agricultural area, where for centuries its people, basically of Mongoloid ancestry, have been mostly rice farmers when they were not fighting off the constant invasion of warring peoples. More than any other, the people of Vietnam long feared being overrun by the huge land of China to their north, although European traders began arriving in their land as early as the sixteenth century. The terrain and their system of communal village life bonded the Vietnamese people to fierce protection of their families and neighbors in their small communities, but did not bond them into a united nation. And the gentling influence of their Buddhist religion further left them open and exposed to exploitation by more industrial nations seeking whatever riches this land could offer.

Starting in the late 1700s, the French became deeply entangled in the history and future of Vietnam. Historically composed of the three regions of Tonkin, Annam, and Cochin China, Vietnam was merged with Cambodia in 1887 to form French Indochina. (The French took Saigon in 1859, organized the colony of Cochin China in 1867, and in 1884 declared themselves protectors of Tonkin and Annam.) With the idea of modernizing the rural country and taking its wealth, France set up a system of colonial rule that would last until 1954.

All was not peaceful for the French, however. The nationalist movement that sprung up in Vietnam in the early part of the twentieth century grew stronger during the Japanese occupation of the area during World War II. After Japan withdrew in 1945, communists and nationalists united to form the Viet Minh, headed by Ho Chi Minh. The battle between this group and the French became the French Indochina War (1946–1954) and ended with the defeat of the French at Dien Bien Phu. This French military base, near the border of Laos, became the scene of a weeks-long fight that saw the loss of thousands of French troops. It ended French power in the area and created a divided nation of Vietnam—north and south.

The Geneva Conference of 1954 declared that the divided country would hold free elections to determine the nation's eventual fate. But the south, fearing that the northern communists would win the election, declared itself an independent republic. So began the Vietnam War, and so began American involvement, with the United States aiding South Vietnam against the communists.

Hauptly now details, step by agonizing step, the increasing involvement of the United States in the affairs of the Vietnamese. He shows how, through several administrations, the growing U.S. fear of communist influence and takeover in the region led to more and more military commitments.

Probably the most crucial step toward such total involvement in the war was taken by the United States in 1964 with the Tonkin Gulf resolution. Then President Lyndon Johnson asked Congress for permission to retaliate against the communists after American destroyers were allegedly attacked in the Tonkin Gulf. This congressional resolution authorized American military force in the area, which was acted upon by Johnson and by his predecessor, Richard Nixon. By 1968, there were more than 500,000 U.S. troops fighting in that faraway land; nearly 50,000 would be wounded or die.

After a fierce communist offensive in 1968 and increasing opposition back home in the United States, the administration began a policy of withdrawing U.S. troops. The communists were victorious in 1975, the South Vietnamese army was routed, and the troubled land of Vietnam was reunited.

In one of the book's most significant chapters, the author details the growing uneasiness of the American people as more and more American fighting forces were sent to Southeast Asia. Mostly young, often black, unsure of their role, unskilled in jungle warfare, they fought and died or returned home to a nation immersed in such bitter turmoil and division over American presence in Southeast Asia that it often turned its back on or scorned those who had been sent off to defend it.

The wounds of the war in Vietnam have not fully healed in the United States today; perhaps they never will.

Thematic Material

With great clarity and little finger pointing, the author skillfully makes sense of the confusing, sometimes sketchy, and often perplexing events that combined to bring about the tragedy of the war in Vietnam and American involvement. If it holds true that to be ignorant of history is to be doomed to repeat its mistakes, every young American might be well advised to read this lucid account.

Book Talk Material

Discussions in three areas might serve to bring the conflict in Vietnam and American involvement into closer focus for young readers: the geography of the area and the culture of the people (pp. 3–10, 14–15); how and why France became involved and the lessons that might have been learned from its defeat (pp. 16–28, 60–64); and the youth and background of the American officers and enlisted men who found themselves embroiled in a tragic battle they could not win (pp. 115–123).

Additional Selections

Vietnam: The Valor and the Sorrow (Little, 1985, $27.50; pap., $14.95) by Thomas D. Boettcher is a well-illustrated history of the war in Vietnam on the battlefield, at home, and in politics. There are a number of other accounts for young people: E. B. Fincher's *The Vietnam War* (Watts, 1980, $10.90) deals succinctly with both the war and its aftermath; Don Lawson has two accounts: *The United States in the Vietnam War* (Crowell, 1981, $11.89), which gives good background information, and *The War in Vietnam* (Watts, 1981, $9.50), for a younger audience. In the Opposing Viewpoints series there is an interesting anthology of articles and editorials edited by David L. Bender and Gary E. McCuen called *The Indochina War: Why Our Policy Failed* (Greenhaven, 1975, $11.95; pap., $5.95). Another very useful volume is Margot C. J. Mabie's *Vietnam There and Here* (Holt, 1985, $11.95). A photographer's record of the war is *Tim Page's Nam* (Knopf, 1983, $22.50; pap., $14.95). The experiences of an army nurse in Vietnam are told by Lynda Van Devanter in *Home before Morning* (Beaufort, 1983, $16.95; pap., Warner, $3.95). In the novel *War Zone* (pap., Bantam, 1985, $2.25), by Larry Weinberg, a boy goes in the army to Vietnam to find his brother's murderer.

Hocken, Sheila. *Emma and I*
Dutton, 1978, $8.95

In *Emma and I*, Sheila Hocken introduces readers to a world that fortunately most will never have to experience firsthand—the world of the physically handicapped, in this case, the world of the sightless. The reader will also meet one of the most amazing and endearing of all literary characters, a dog named Emma. Although this autobiography was originally written for an adult audience, it is suitable reading in both junior and senior high schools.

Summary

Sheila was born in 1946 in Nottingham, England. She, her older brother, Graham, and her parents all suffer from various levels of impaired vision, although Sheila's problem, a type of cataract condition, is the most serious and is gradually becoming worse. Her parents, however, never treat her any differently than a normally sighted child, although some activities such as bicycle riding are forbidden. They also try every method possible and succeed in keeping her in regular schools and avoiding the segregation and isolation of attending those exclusively for the blind. Although this often causes many problems, like trying to play tennis with her friend Angela, she manages to muddle through without self-pity or demanding special attention. After graduation from secondary school she takes a job as a telephone operator. As the world of darkness gradually closes in upon her, she learns braille. At nineteen, Sheila is totally blind.

One night, after getting completely lost coming home from work and arriving three hours late, she is visited by Mr. Brown, her home teacher, who suggests that she should apply for a Seeing Eye dog. She is elated at the thought but fearful that she might be refused. However, she passes the necessary qualifying tests, and six months later, on July 1, 1966, Sheila is driven by a friend, Geoff, to the training center at Leamington Spa to get her dog. Under the guidance of a trainer she spends several days using a plastic dog to master the problems of the harness and directional commands. Finally she is assigned her own dog, a beautiful chocolate brown Labrador named Emma whom she instantly loves. There follows a further training period during which Emma displays such a rare level of intelligence, patience, and understanding that Sheila in time believes Emma is telepathically in tune to her wants and concerns.

Back home, Emma fits in nicely in the household, goes to work every day with Sheila, and in general basks in the attention and love showered on her. Her uncanny knowledge of direction and sixth sense in anticipating Sheila's needs continually astound everyone.

At her evening class in writing, Sheila becomes friendly with another nineteen-year-old girl, Anita, who even takes her on a horseback riding expedition. As their friendship grows, Anita suggests that they share an apartment and so Sheila moves out of her parents' home and experiences the thrill of almost total independence.

Through participation in a radio show aimed at blind people, Sheila meets the announcer's friend, a podiatrist named Don Hocken. She immediately likes this kindly man who shows rare understanding and sensitivity toward her but never signs of pity or condescension. After each meeting with him, Sheila is filled with a combination of anticipation concerning their next time together and dread that, because she is blind, he will not want to deepen their relationship. Love, however, does develop, but because Don is already married, he asks her to wait five years until his daughter is fourteen and old enough to weather a divorce.

When Anita is transferred to another city, Sheila finds another smaller apartment and with Emma manages living alone with only a minimum of mishaps. She helps organize and participates in several evening classes for the blind in such subjects as makeup application and sewing and, with the same group, tries her hand at amateur theatrics. With each success comes greater confidence. Sheila also accepts many speaking engagements on behalf of the Guide Dog Association and discovers that Emma is a professional scene stealer.

At the end of the five-year-period, Don and Sheila are married. Special permission is granted for Emma to attend.

One day Graham suggests to Sheila that she visit an eye specialist, Dr. Shearing, who has had amazing results with special eye surgery. After a thorough examination he tells Sheila that through an operation there is a slim hope that she might see again. It is nine months before the operation is scheduled, and after undergoing it she waits several days in agony of expectation before the bandages are removed. When they are, she experiences for the first time the miracle of complete sight.

Back home, the joy of seeing also causes many adjustments. She sees Don, Emma, her friends, and herself for the first time. As well, she must relearn the skill of reading and adapt to a world filled with color. In time these adjustments are made, and Emma, now eleven, can enjoy the benefit of retirement.

Soon another member joins the household. Sheila has a beautiful, completely sighted little girl whom they named Kerensa Emma Louise.

Thematic Material

This is an unforgettable book about a courageous young woman and the wonderful animal that becomes her eyes. The author is painfully honest in describing her inner feelings and self-doubts. Through everyday situations and details, she vividly projects the reader into the world of the blind and their concerns. It is a tale of patience, love, and endurance, as well as a plea for mainstreaming the handicapped into schools and the workplace. It also furnishes fascinating details on the training of guide dogs.

Book Talk Material

There are many excellent episodes that could be used. Some samples are: Sheila's experience at school (pp. 13–18); getting lost and hearing about applying for a guide dog (pp. 24–26); Sheila meets Emma (pp. 39–40); the training period (pp. 41–53); Emma and Sheila go to work (pp. 58–63); the horseback ride (pp. 66–68); the first apartment with Anita (pp. 73–78); and meeting Don and their first date (pp. 88–95).

Additional Selections

The true story of Jill Kinmont, Olympic skier, and her triumph over a paralyzing accident is told in E. G. Valens's *The Other Side of the Mountain* (pap., Warner, 1975, $3.50; Part II, pap., Warner, 1978, $3.50). *Joni* (pap., Zondervan, 1976, $3.95; pap., Bantam, $2.95), written with Joe Musser, is the inspiring autobiography of Joni Eareckson, who at seventeen was left a quadriplegic. It is continued in *A Step Further* (Zondervan, 1978, $6.95; pap., Zondervan, $3.95; pap., Bantam, $2.95), written with Steve Estes. A young blind man tells his triumphant story in *If You Could See What I Hear* (pap., New Amer. Lib., 1976, $2.95) by Tom Sullivan and Derek Gill. Also use Richard McPhee's *Tom and Bear: The Training of a Guide Dog Team* (Crowell, 1981, $11.70). Some novels that deal with people overcoming physical problems are Mildred Lee's *The People Therein* (Houghton, 1980, $10.95; pap., New Amer. Lib., $1.95), about a crippled girl in Appalachia; Susan Sallis's *Only Love* (Harper, 1980, $11.89) and *Secret Places of the Stairs* (Harper, 1980, $11.89); and Jean Ure's story of a girl's touching relationship with a blind music teacher in *See You Thursday* (Delacorte, 1981, $12.95; pap., Dell, $2.50). A blinded fifteen-year-old boy and a half-savage dog are caught in a forest fire in Maureen Crane Wartski's *The Lake Is on Fire* (Westminster, 1981, $9.95).

Koehn, Ilse. *Mischling, Second Degree: My Childhood in Nazi Germany*
Greenwillow, 1977, lib. bdg., $13.00

This is the moving autobiography of a girl growing up in Nazi Germany and of the cruel separation of her parents because her father had one Jewish parent. The same author's novel *Tilla* (Greenwillow, 1981, $11.75) tells about two teenagers and their growing love for one another set in Germany during the last days of World War II and immediately afterward. Both books are read by junior high school students.

Summary

Ilse Koehn was six years old in 1935 and she lived in Germany, a happy young girl in a happy family. By this time Adolf Hitler had been named German chancellor and he became known as "Der Führer," the leader of Germany. In September of that year he and his Nazi party enacted the so-called Nuremberg Laws, which had to do mainly with discrimination against the Jews. The degree of discrimination was based on one of three categories: a Jew was someone with at least three full Jewish grandparents; a Mischling, first degree, was someone with two Jewish grandparents; and a Mischling, second degree, was someone with one Jewish grandparent (provided any one of the three was not married to a Jew or was of the Jewish faith).

Not until the end of World War II would young Ilse Koehn find out that she was a "Mischling, second degree." She had a Jewish grandmother. But her family was anti-Nazi, and they did not tell Ilse of her heritage for her own protection.

Mischling, Second Degree is the true story of the Nazi nightmare lived by a young girl who becomes a member of the Hitler Youth and does not discover that she, too, is a Jew until after the defeat of the Nazis.

In 1939, the world edges ever nearer to war as Hitler and his troops invade Poland, and Britain and France declare war on Germany. Ilse is in school where Frau Katscher starts each day with a brisk "Heil Hitler." By the next year young Ilse is anxious to join the Hitler Youth, which she does despite the protestations of her father, who calls the organization "pigs." Her country is now at war and even the children are called on to be loyal to their Führer. When France falls to the Germans, the country rejoices, but not Ilse's family. However she is long used to this since she knows her family members are "freethinkers" and contemptuous of any political party.

The world is totally engrossed in war in 1941, and Ilse, nearing her teens, is evacuated with other schoolchildren to Czechoslovakia, where she spends dreary, bewildering months away from her family. She is allowed to return in late 1941, where for the first time she learns the terror of air raids and begins to recognize the fear of her family. She raises her arm in the Nazi salute and sings out the hymns of the Hitler

Youth, never realizing the terrible secret her parents and family are keeping from her to protect her life and theirs. . . .

Through the long despairing years of the war, Ilse acts and reacts like any other young girl growing up in a time of stress and upheaval. Perhaps because she does understand somewhat the political views of her father and mother, she learns to be silent for the most part, letting the Nazi propaganda swirl about her but never really becoming part of it. She has little emotional attachment to the Nazi cause as she and others of her age wait the end of the war.

Ilse and her family had many perilous times throughout the war, but in all she and they were lucky, for they survived. They came close to death in the bombing raids, and she and her mother had to hide behind a wall in her grandparents' house—much like Anne Frank—for four days when the Russian troops overran Germany. But they survived.

Here is a moving memoir told from the viewpoint of a young German girl who does not learn until Hitler has been toppled and the German nation is in ruins that, all along, she has been the object of her country's discrimination laws—a Mischling, second degree.

Thematic Material

Ilse Koehn has written an extraordinary human document of the horror of war seen through the eyes of a young girl who is unaware of how perilous her true situation really is. This book gives a vivid picture of how children existed in war-torn Germany, of the effects on them of the ever-increasing bombing raids of the Allies, and of the terror of the increasing likelihood of invasion. The author, born in Berlin, came to the United States in 1958. A former art director, she is a free-lance book illustrator and designer.

Book Talk Material

Many interesting episodes can be used to discuss the life of a child in Nazi Germany. See Ilse goes to school (pp. 32–35); the Hitler Youth meeting (pp. 40–43); evacuated to camp (pp. 44–49); Ilse returns to her family (pp. 60–65); the air raid (pp. 77–78); and camp again (pp. 84–95).

Additional Selections

Some histories of this period are Ronald D. Gray's *Hitler and the Germans* (Lerner, 1981, $6.95; pap., $3.95); William L. Shirer's *The Rise and*

Fall of Adolf Hitler (Random, 1961, $5.99); and Milton Meltzer's *Never to Forget: Jews of the Holocaust* (Harper, 1976, $13.89; pap., Dell, $3.25). Biographies of Hitler include Joshua Rubenstein's *Adolf Hitler* (Watts, 1982, $10.90) and Edward F. Dolan, Jr.'s *Adolf Hitler: A Portrait in Tyranny* (Dodd, 1981, $10.95). The moving story of how a Jewish woman helped some survivors in the post-World War II chaos is told in Lena Kuchler-Silberman's *My Hundred Children* (Dell, 1987, $3.50). The fictionalized story of the Nazi massacre of the Gypsies in World War II is told in Alexander Ramati's *And the Violins Stopped Playing* (Watts, 1986, $14.95). Anna and her family adjust to the imprisonment of their father for anti-Nazi activities during World War II in Barbara Gerhit's *Don't Say a Word* (Macmillan, 1986, $12.95). Other novels that deal with Europe during the Nazi period are Hans Peter Richter's *Friedrich* (pap., Penguin, 1987, $4.95; condensed in *More Juniorplots*, Bowker, 1977, pp. 40–43); T. Degens's *Transport 7-41-R* (Viking, 1974, $11.50; condensed in *More Juniorplots*, Bowker, 1977, pp. 32–35); Doris Orgel's *The Devil in Vienna* (Dial, 1978, $7.95); and *As the Waltz Was Ending* (Four Winds, 1982, $9.95; pap., Scholastic, $2.50) by Emma Macalik Butterworth. A look at the history of the American Nazi movement is given in Jerry Bornstein's *The Neo-Nazis: The Threat of the Nazi Cult* (Messner, 1986, $10.29).

AUTHOR INDEX

Author and titles fully discussed in *Juniorplots 3* and those listed as "Additional Selections" are cited in this index. An asterisk (*) precedes those titles for which full summaries and discussions appear.

313

TITLE INDEX

Titles fully discussed and summarized in *Juniorplots 3* as well as those listed as "Additional Selections" are cited in this index. An asterisk (*) precedes those titles for which full summaries and discussions appear.

SUBJECT INDEX

This brief listing includes only those titles fully summarized and discussed in the book. Additional titles relating to these subjects can be found in the "Additional Selections" that accompany the discussion of the books listed here. Unless otherwise noted with the label nonfiction, the subject headings refer to fictional treatment of the subject.